Sailing Warships of the US Navy

Sailing Warships of the US Navy

Donald L Canney

NAVAL INSTITUTE PRESS
Annapolis, Maryland

Frontispiece:
Watercolour by A Carlotta which purports to show the US
Mediterranean Squadron leaving Port Mahon, Menorca, 20
January 1825. Left to right, the ships are: *North Carolina*, 74;
the frigates *Brandywine* and *Constitution*; and the sloops of war
Erie and *Ontario*. [Naval Historical Foundation]

First published in Great Britain by Chatham Publishing,
99 High Street, Rochester, Kent ME1 1LX

Published and distributed in the United States of America
and Canada by the Naval Institute Press,
Beach Hall, 291 Wood Road,
Annapolis, Maryland 21402-5034

Library of Congress Catalog Card No. 2001091834

ISBN 1-55750-990-5

This edition is authorized for sale only in the United States of
America, its territories and possessions, and Canada.

Manufactured in Great Britain

Contents

Preface

THE AMERICAN navy in the age of sail is peopled with larger than life characters: John Paul Jones, Edward Preble, Isaac Hull–American equivalents of those in the Royal Navy's Trafalgar roll. And the heroic souls were matched by legendary ships: *Constitution, Enterprise, Constellation* . . . In consequence, the history of that era invokes heady and colourful images–a heritage fit for a world power.

And there has been no shortage of those who have chronicled that history: the field of titles ranges from the scholarly through the hagiographic, and published as far back as the era of onionskin and woodcuts. Of course, it is the action which has been the principal subject matter –at least judged by the sheer numbers of words produced. In comparison to the battle and operational books, little has been written on the more mundane subjects. For the ships themselves, the list of serious works on their design and development is short, with Howard I Chapelle's *The History of the American Sailing Navy*, originally published in 1949, being the standard work in the field. Certainly that is the only comprehensive history of the subject.

Works on individual ships have appeared, most notably on the frigates *Constitution, Constellation* and *Essex*. Other works have been published on other groups of ships: the subscription warships of the Quasi-War, for instance. And those who have written on these subjects have generally gone beyond Mr Chapelle and returned to the primary sources to accomplish their tasks.

However, Mr Chapelle remains the dominant figure in the arena.

Therefore, in writing a book on the same subject matter that Mr Chapelle covered, my task here is to justify my efforts. Certainly if his work could not be improved upon, there would be no need for another.

Before approaching the negative aspects, I must acknow-

ledge, as all maritime historians must, the debt we owe to Mr Chapelle. He created a magnificent body of work in a field which–then and now–is mined with enthusiastic amateurs long on sea-storytelling and short on scholarship. In his decades with the Smithsonian Institution he had ready access to what were then the 'raw' records of the Navy Department, before and after their transfer to the National Archives. It is apparent that he imbibed deeply in those dusty ledgers and rolled linens, as well as those in other repositories such as Mystic Seaport and the Pennsylvania Historical Society. Adding significantly to his sources were colleagues–both naval and civilian–who both loved naval history and in fact participated in it–men who still remembered holystones, quarter galleries, and kicking canvas. Dudley W Knox comes to mind, as well as David Taylor and George C Wales.

In addition to having been immersed in the records for decades, Chapelle added his own expertise to the mix which resulted in his published work. Certainly his knowledge of naval architecture and ship construction, plus his talent for impeccable draughtsmanship, was, when applied to the study of the sailing navy, his strongest contribution to the field. And, for over forty years, Mr Chapelle's works were the standards by which all other subsequent books were judged.

Unfortunately, there are obvious shortcomings in *The History of the American Sailing Navy*. The most blatant, from the professional historian's point of view, is the lack of footnotes and bibliography. Mr Chapelle was content to reference his sources within the text, though most of these 'citations' are certainly vague and oblique: 'correspondence of the period', 'letters of the commanding officers' and 'it was said that', are typical of the work. Certainly he is accurate in the basics: it appears that he was using primary 'official' sources as he worked through the era chronologically, delineating the particular vessels acquired and lost, etc, during each year. And, from the standpoint of naval architecture his comments are well founded.

However, one would be hard pressed to locate many actual quotations from a specific, named source in the book. The sole exception to this seems to be when he relayed information actually annotated on the original ship's draughts. On his own plans he assiduously reproduced this information.

Indeed, the ship plans themselves seem to have been the key to Mr Chapelle's approach to the subject. His goal seems to have been to reproduce accurately the ships of the sailing navy, from a museum curator's standpoint. His background in documenting the non-naval vessel as part of the Historic American Merchant Marine Survey of the 1930s certainly set a pattern for this. In order to do this, he set himself a long term project of studying the available plans and making sense of them, using other, more mundane, written records to supplement what he derived from the plans. And, as anyone who has seen these plans knows, the original plans leave very much information unsaid, and many questions unanswered.

Most typically, for instance, the dimensions on a particular plan may have differed from those in other sources, or even differed from the figures noted on other plans of the same vessel; or some feature of the vessel mentioned in correspondence did not appear on the plan. It then was necessary to explain the discrepancy and make some judgement call. In these instances, Mr Chapelle's judgements in the area of naval architecture were reliable, but he was at his weakest when he strayed far beyond the vessel plans. His speculations and opinions riffle through the book, many times with minimal indications that these are indeed his own commentaries. Not only are we given opinions on specific subjects, but entire sequences of events are presented without clear statements as to their basis in fact. My work in the archives and other depositories leads me to believe that it was not unusual for Mr Chapelle to create complicated scenarios of historical events based on very few existing documents. This lack of documentation leaves the reader and scholar in a state of uncertainty which I am attempting to dispel in this book.

Indeed, in most important instances Mr Chapelle was absolutely correct. His familiarity with the records was sufficient to make some things perfectly clear. Two specifics stand out. First was the matter of the 'administrative rebuilding' issue. Mr Chapelle's claim that the navy built new vessels to replace old ones and called it (for accounting purposes) 'rebuilding' was absolutely true. The most famous instance of this was that of the 1790s frigate *Constellation* vis-à-vis the 1850s sloop of war of the same name. It is only those who do not take time or care to 'read' the language of ship plans who fail to see the truth in this instance. Indeed, it was quite courageous for Chapelle to take what was an unpopular stand on a subject where historical accuracy and contemporary public policy were in conflict.

A second instance, though a less clear one, was in his final judgement on the designer of the *Constitution* and sister vessels. In his initial discussion of the subject in *The History of the American Sailing Navy* he left much room for speculation and seemed to lean towards Josiah Fox as the designer. Somewhat later in his book, however, he discounted Fox's influence on the vessels, based on the design philosophy of Fox as opposed to that of Joshua Humphreys. Indeed much of the complicated scenario Chapelle described in the design of these ships was obviously based on Fox's writing some thirty years after the fact—and not substantiated by more contemporary accounts.

In conclusion, I must reiterate my respect for Chapelle's work. At the same time I present a new work intended to complement the older, in the hope that both will continue to entice scholars and those interested in the sailing navy into further scholarship in the area.

Finally, on a personal note, it was *The History of the American Sailing Navy* which first drew my attention to naval history. I plainly remember writing an American history report on the subject of the original six frigates while in seventh grade—based for the most part on Chapelle's book. That certainly was unusual reading matter for a 13-year-old, but my fascination with the field began there and has remained, thanks in part to the work of Howard Chapelle.

Acknowledgements

I would like to express my appreciation to the individuals and institutions which supplied the raw materials from which this book was derived.

The three major institutions providing most of the resources were the National Archives, Library of Congress, and the US Navy. In the first instance, the personnel at Military Records, specifically Richard Peuser and John Van der Reedt, and those in the Cartographic and Architectural Branch – Ray Cotton and Keith Kerr. Thanks to those in the Early History, Ship's History, and Photographic Branches of the Naval Historical Center. As always, Charles Haberlein was extremely helpful in locating illustrations for the volume.

Among other institutions visited and utilised were: G W Blunt Library at Mystic Seaport, the Mariners' Museum, New-York Historical Society, Historical Society of Pennsylvania, US Coast Guard Historian's Office, Yale University Library, Peabody Essex Museum in Salem, Massachusetts, the Franklin D Roosevelt Library at Hyde Park, New York, and Nimitz Library at the US Naval Academy.

Thanks to C Kay Larson for her contribution regarding warships built in Connecticut up to 1815. Particular mention must be made of Dr Robert Browning for his continued support and advice, as well as Kevin Foster for his willingness to share his expertise and vast trove of information on this era.

Donald L Canney
21 June 2001

Introduction

THE PURPOSE of this book is to describe the sailing warships of the US Navy, concentrating on those specifically built as war vessels, whether built by the navy or by contract with the service. Because it is a design history, neither purchased nor converted ships are germane to the subject. On the other hand some captured warships are included, both for comparison purposes as well as to determine if the ships influenced American warship design. In one instance – the British frigate *Macedonian* – the ship is included because of the building of an American frigate of the same name and the controversy over the actual identity of the second *Macedonian*.

Because of the relative importance of the larger vessels, the narrative portion of this work includes only ship-rigged vessels, schooners and brigs. Smaller craft, such as the Jeffersonian gunboats and turn of the century galleys, are added as appendices in tabular form.

The navy of the American Revolution is another special subject. Unlike the balance of the book, in which each type of ship is dealt with chronologically, the portion on the Continental Navy is a self-contained chapter. This has been done for several reasons. First is the substantial chronological gap between the building of the Continental Navy and the re-birth of the US Navy under the Constitution, beginning in 1794. This interim brought significant changes in warship design, among them the advent of the 18pdr frigate in the British navy, the popularity of the carronade, and the demise of the beakhead bulkhead bow configuration. Second, the majority of the Continental naval construction was frigates, most of which were laid down in one year – 1776. Thus there was indeed little possibility of describing the development of these ships through time. Further, combining these vessels with the few of other types built during the war was more logical than attempting to integrate them into the appropriate chapters for each ship type in the Federal navy. Of course, any influence of the Revolutionary naval vessels on those of the 'new' navy is noted. I also must concede that the chapter on the Continental Navy is included somewhat pro forma – added for the most part in the interest of completeness – and certainly was not the subject of extensive original research.

My research has been an attempt to cast as wide a net as possible Of course, Howard Chapelle's work was consulted extensively, but, as far as possible, I have gone directly to the primary sources. Whether my conclusions and facts coincide with Mr Chapelle's was of much less import than whether they can be supported by the original documents. Conversely, my writing tends to be closely tied to the sources. Only where overwhelming evidence exists do I venture into my own opinions and speculations, particularly in the area of cause and effect.

I need also to address the subject of illustrations. As far as possible, only contemporary depictions are used to portray these ships. This applies both to plans and illustrations. With all due respect to Mr Chapelle, whose draughtsmanship was impeccable, I have purposely set out to reproduce only original plans, for the most part from the National Archives. Use of the originals has its drawbacks, of course. First, the age and condition of many of these plans made it impossible in many instances to get crisp, clear reproductions. Second is the fact that the majority of the plans are little more than hull lines with a minimum of deck and external appearance details. Original plans with the detail level of Mr Chapelle's work are nearly non-existent. Third, many plans differed from the vessel 'as built'. All these reasons were sufficient motivation for Mr Chapelle – who certainly had museum model builders in mind – to re-draw 'from scratch' the plans presented in his book.

My use of the originals, despite these problems, is based on the following considerations. First is the historian's penchant for, and love of, primary sources. Regardless of the skill and accuracy of any draughtsman, any re-drawn plan will be to some extent an interpretation. The researcher or student of the subject ought to be able to see the original document. My task is to present, in the text, where the plan might diverge from the vessel as built, or whether sister ships were indeed identical to the plans and each other, and other pertinent information. Presenting the originals also serves to form a base-line from which one can determine how much any modern draughtsman has added in the process of re-drawing or re-constructing the plan. Only in instances where the original is so poorly preserved as to be impossible to reproduce or where a modern version is demonstrably free of significant reconstruction have I used any plans but the originals. (Also modern plans are used where the original is no longer available.) A final reason for use of the old plans is to make the researcher aware of what sort of original plans actually exist for ships of this era. Though I was generally pleased with the percentage of originals which survive, I was disappointed in that there were rarely complete depictions of the ships. Deck and sail plans were uncommon and the minutiae of fittings were simply not there. Seeing the originals is truly an eye-opening experience.

The obvious ideal would have been to present the originals as well as accurate modern plans. However, limited space and exorbitant reproduction costs preclude that possibility here. To complement the plans I have included as many period illustrations and photographs as possible. Two problems occur with period photos. Of course, photography only goes back to around the 1840s, and the long exposure time for early photos was incompatible with moving or even rocking ships. Further, post Civil War photos are often misidentified, the vessels in question being very similar in many cases.

On the other hand, artwork and lithographs of these vessels was surprisingly abundant. Of particular interest were the works of Tomaso De Simone, Antonio Cammillieri, the Roux brothers, and J Baugean, all of whom painted portraits of vessels stationed in the Mediterranean, from around 1800 to the 1860s. It is obvious that all were interested in accuracy, a pursuit encouraged by the fact that their clients were often officers on the ships themselves. It was not unusual for De Simone to produce numerous versions of the same vessel. There are three, for instance, of the sloop of war *Constellation* in the 1850s and 1860s. Roux also pro-

duced three views of the frigate *President* around 1806. Again, though, misidentification is a problem, given the similarity of the vessels. When identification is a matter of counting the gunports, the results are often questionable, and it is quite possible some of these artists merely changed the ship's names on some of their portraits for a quick sale.

Two other illustrators were found who seemed to emphasise accuracy. First was Charles Ware, who was a draughtsman in the sailmaker's shop at Boston Navy Yard. His sail 'plans' are decorative and appear accurate. Second was William Alexander Kennedy Martin, who worked in Philadelphia from the 1840s to the 1860s. His views, most of which were watercolour or wash, included many ships which were at the navy yard during this era, and he went to the trouble of taking measurements of the vessels which he drew. Unfortunately for posterity, Martin rarely painted finished oil portraits. Also, his broadside views rarely showed the vessels fully rigged – merely with a sketchy diagram of the masting and spars. Martin's works are now scattered, but the largest number of originals is at Independence Seaport in Philadelphia. Some are published here for the first time.

I have used some contemporary commercial lithography. However, because I suspect the accuracy of these works, they were used only when other sources failed to produce an illustration of an important vessel.

Of special interest are the warships which were represented on some of the famous 'Liverpool jugs', made in England around the turn of the nineteenth century. I was excited to find designs showing the frigates *Merrimack* of 1799 and *Guerriere* of 1815. The excitement abated when the two were compared. The rigging of both was identical, and the basic profile of the hull was the same. Only details in quarter galleries and gunports were changed for each ship. A third instance was found where a merchant vessel was portrayed – using the same kinds of minor alterations of one basic ship illustration to show this vessel also. I have included *Merrimack* here for curiosity's sake.

With this variety of sources, I hope to present here a comprehensive 'view', both in words and pictures of the ships of the navy in the age of sail.

CHAPTER 1

Navy-built Ships of the American Revolution

THE FIRST formal Congressional action forming a naval component of the American revolutionary movement came as early as 5 October 1775. On that date George Washington was authorised to apply to Massachusetts, Connecticut and Rhode Island for armed vessels specifically to intercept two British ordnance brigs sailing for Quebec. Shortly thereafter, the Continental Congress called for two armed vessels to be fitted out to capture British troop transports en route to the rebelling colonies. With the latter action came the formation of a permanent committee to oversee naval affairs. This committee – the 'Naval Committee' – and the later 'Marine Committee' were responsible for the naval element of the American forces in rebellion against Britain. On 13 December 1775 the committee recommendation that thirteen frigates be built was passed into law by the Continental Congress. These thirteen ships would become the core of the Continental Navy.

The Continental Navy itself was, of course, more than these thirteen frigates. As noted above, it began with the fitting out of merchant vessels for war purposes. The thirteen colonies certainly had access to literally hundreds of sailing vessels, from smacks to ship-rigged merchantmen, as well as sailors to man them. By the end of the eight-year war, the navy had had over one hundred vessels under arms, mounting some thirteen hundred guns (and this figure does not include the various state navies or, or course, the privateers).

Of the various types of vessels, there were some seventeen schooners in the fleet. Only one, the *Mercury*, was built for the navy. Generally their speed made them appropriate for dispatch boats. By the same token, their light construction and small size made them useless in action. Even smaller were the sloops, of which there were around fourteen in the fleet. Again, their small size limited their use-

fulness in combat. About a dozen brigs and brigantines served in the Continental fleet, as well as ten ship-rigged vessels (smaller than frigates), most of which were converted merchant ships. In addition to the above, there was a variety of rigs and types, including cutters, gundalows, and galleys. Of the less common rigs, there was a ketch and two xebecs, the latter borrowed from the Pennsylvania State Navy. The majority of all these vessels were purchased or captured, and these types formed over three-fourths of the Continental Navy.[1]

To complete the picture, the subject of privateers can be injected here. These vessels, though of limited naval value, certainly contributed economically to the Revolutionary cause, striking at the British merchant class, who, in turn, ventilated their opposition in Parliament. Though an accurate count of these vessels is nearly impossible, a listing using appropriate sources was made by George F Emmons in his *Statistical History of the Navy of the United States* (1853). This list was actually a compilation of vessel captures, arranged alphabetically by the name of the 'private armed vessel'. As there were problems determining the identity of these ships (*Maria*, for instance, was listed as 'ship', 'brig', 'sloop' and 'schooner', ranging from five to twelve guns, from four different states and under five masters), Emmons simply listed all the captures, grouping them under the names of the capturing vessels. The number of privateers, arrived at simply by totalling the number of *ship names* on the list is over 676. Impressive as this number is, the total of enemy vessels captured is over 1600.[2] Thus privateering was certainly profitable to the rebels in search of plunder, as well as destructive to the British carrying trade. The negative aspect of privateering in the Revolution was that it made recruiting for naval vessels more difficult – as privateers were more likely to take lucrative prizes, and less likely to fall into pitched battles. And, of course, naval disci-

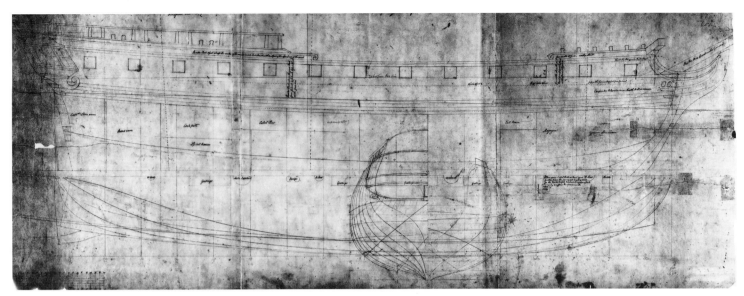

Continental Frigate *Randolph*, plan by Wharton and Humphreys. Note sparse detail-work on this draught. However, her basic dimensions show her a bit larger than her British counterparts, indicating the direction Joshua Humphreys' designs would take later. No doubt, like her contemporaries, she was given appropriate carved head and stern work. [National Archives NH 65618]

pline was much more severe than that aboard these privately financed and operated vessels.

At the opposite end of the naval spectrum from the free-and-easy privateering 'sea-rovers' were the sea-going naval vessels built at the behest and under the guidance of the Continental Navy. In addition to the original thirteen frigates authorised in 1775, two others were begun in 1777 and a sixteenth in 1779. (There were also four frigates authorised in 1777 but never built.) Additionally, two sloops of war were built, in 1777 and 1779 respectively. Finally, three 74-gun ships of the line were authorised, two of which were laid down, and one of which actually went to sea. (In a separate category were two frigates built in foreign yards: *L'Indien* and *Deane*, though the latter was properly in the navy of South Carolina.) The latter pair are beyond the scope of this work, as are the many purchased and captured ships. These included *Alfred*, the immortal *Bonhomme Richard*, and the latter's prize, *Serapis*.

The original thirteen frigates having been authorised by Congress in late 1775, the Marine Committee proceeded to let contracts for their construction and estimated a total cost of $866,666.67 for the project. They were to be built as fol-lows: one each in New Hampshire, Connecticut, and Maryland; two each in Massachusetts, Rhode Island and New York, and four in Pennsylvania. They were to be in three rates: 32-, 28- and 24-gun ships. Construction was begun on many of the ships as early as January 1776.[3]

The designer of these frigates is the subject of some disagreement. Joshua Humphreys of Philadelphia is certainly the one most often associated with these vessels, though Howard Chapelle, in *History of the American Sailing Navy*, did not believe his draughtsmanship matched that found in the few surviving original plans. It is certain that the firm of Wharton and Humphreys prepared the designs and Humphreys laid them before the committee on 13 January 1776. They were approved without demur and copies were made and sent to the appropriate cities and builders.

The 24-gun design was 'to be the same dimensions as the *Hero* privateer' built by the Penrose firm of Philadelphia during the French and Indian war. As Humphreys began his apprenticeship in that yard, no doubt the plans were still available to him. The source of the 32-gun design is said to have been that of the British 36-gun frigate *Pallas*.[4] However, Chapelle pointed out that the hull design of the 32s, as well as their dimensions, diverge significantly from any of the standard British designs. And the Americans had set a precedent as early as the 1740s by refusing to follow the official Admiralty draughts in building both the small frigate *Boston* and the 44-gun *America* for British service.[5]

However, the question of the design of these vessels is complicated by the circumstances and exigencies of the day. There was a significant delay in physically transporting the 'official' copies of the design to the northern shipyards, and, in the interim, some anxious builders took matters in hand on their own, resulting in vessels which deviated from the 'official' lines. Thus, as will be seen, these vessels are rather loosely arranged by rating rather than as strict 'classes'.

32-Gun Frigates, 1776-7

The four 32s were *Randolph, Hancock, Warren* and *Raleigh*. A fifth, *Washington*, was launched but was scuttled and destroyed before completion. *Randolph* was built by Wharton and Humphreys; *Washington* by Gehu and Benjamin Eyres, both in Philadelphia.[6] Three plans exist for these vessels: the first is the Wharton and Humphreys draught for *Randolph* – probably the 'official' plan for this class – and the second and third are British-drawn draughts of *Hancock* and *Raleigh* after their capture.

Randolph measured 132ft 9in on the berth deck, 34ft 6in

beam and 10ft 6in in the hold. A contemporary document indicates *Washington* was of the same dimensions.[7] In comparison, British 32s measured 125ft by 35ft 2in and 12ft hold; there was also a 36-gun type (of which only three were built) that were similar in dimensions but four feet longer. Thus the 'standard' Continental 32 was actually larger than the British 12pdr 36-gun class. In hull form, the American vessels exhibited more forward rake, deadrise and rounder bilges than their British contemporaries.[8] *Randolph* was launched 10 July 1776, and was the first of the new frigates to go to sea, on 3 February 1777. Her career was ended on 17 March 1778 when she blew up in action with the 64-gun HMS *Yarmouth* with the loss of most of her crew.

Hancock was a product of the Newburyport, Massachusetts yard of Jonathan Greenleaf and Stephen and Ralph Cross. Her dimensions were significantly different than the 'official' ones: she measured 136ft 7in on the lower deck, 35ft 6in beam and 11ft depth of hold. Thus, she was significantly larger than *Randolph* (about 80 tons in excess of that and the other Continental 32s) and therefore about 15 feet longer than a British 32. Her larger dimensions may

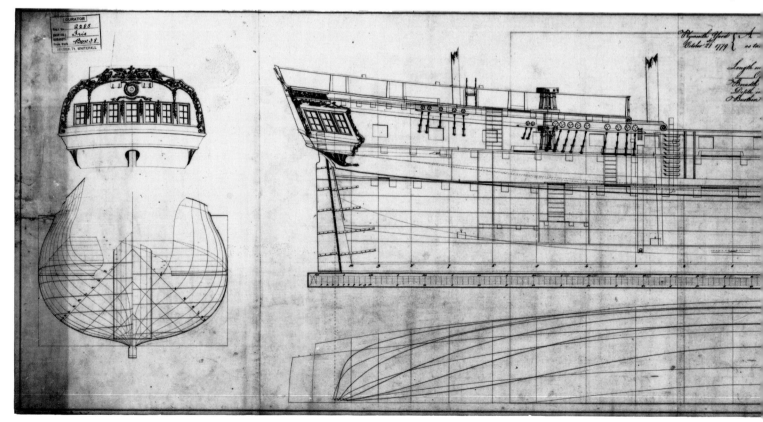

have resulted from her builders' having begun work before the plans arrived from Philadelphia.

Hancock was, by all accounts, a superior vessel – 'all accounts' included American, British and French naval officers, as she was captured by both the last two navies. A British officer called her the 'finest and fastest frigate in the world' and another wrote: 'she went (tho' foul) Thirteen knots, and could have carried much more Sail'. The French, after capturing her in 1781, were equally impressed with her qualities.[9]

Hancock was launched 10 July 1776, and went into service in May 1777.[10] Her appearance was described after capture as follows: [figurehead:] 'Man's head with yellow breeches, white stockings, blue coat with yellow button holes, small cocked hat, with a yellow lace, has a mast in lieu of an Ensign staff with a lateen sail on it, has a fore and aft driver boom, with another across . . . mounts 32 guns, has a rattle

Draught of the *Hancock*, as the British *Iris*, as taken off at Plymouth Yard, 21 October 1779. Re-named *Iris*, she was described as 'the finest frigate in the world' and a favourite command in Royal Navy service. [National Maritime Museum neg 2285]

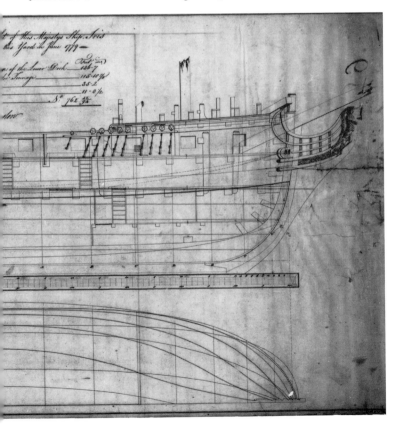

snake carved on the Stern . . .'[11] With the frigate *Boston*, she captured the British 28-gun *Fox*, then she in turn was captured by HMS *Rainbow*, 44 and a British squadron on 8 July 1777. She was re-named *Iris* in British service and captured the Continental frigate *Trumbull* in 1781. After her capture by the French in 1781 she eventually became a powder hulk at Toulon, where she was destroyed in 1793.

Raleigh was built at Portsmouth, New Hampshire by James K Hackett, James Hill and Stephen Paul. Plans for the ship did not arrive until late February 1776, but her keel was laid on the 21st of the following month. Given the fact that her moulding could not have begun before some plan was in hand, it is thought that a design had been obtained from William Hackett, a cousin of James K, and work had already begun before the official plans arrived. This would also account for differences in her design, as shown in the British draught, from that of *Randolph*. Among other things, there was less deadrise, much more tumblehome, and she had a lower forecastle than *Randolph*'s. Her dimensions were 131ft 5in on the berth (lower) deck, 34ft moulded beam and 11ft depth. She carried a full length figurehead of Sir Walter Raleigh. She was built quickly and launched 21 May, which was also an indicator that much work had been done before the plans arrived. Problems obtaining guns slowed her completion and she did not go to sea until August 1777.[12]

Raleigh was reportedly a fast sailer early on. Later, when her bottom was foul, her captain only expected (with cleaning) that she would sail 'tolerably well'. Other than that, he wrote: 'she is stiff, tight, strong & roomy, she works and steers well, and is a good ship in a sea, she carries and fights her Guns as well as any ship can do . . .'[13] She sailed to Europe in 1777 and returned to the West Indies, cruising with the ship *Alfred*, where she harassed British convoys. Her commanding officer was later cashiered for allowing the capture of her consort in March 1778. Her next commander was John Barry. *Raleigh* was captured in September 1778, after being driven ashore by HM vessels *Unicorn* (28 guns) and *Experiment* (50). She was sold out of the British navy in July 1783.

Warren was built at Providence by Benjamin Talman. Again, the delay in receiving plans induced the contractor

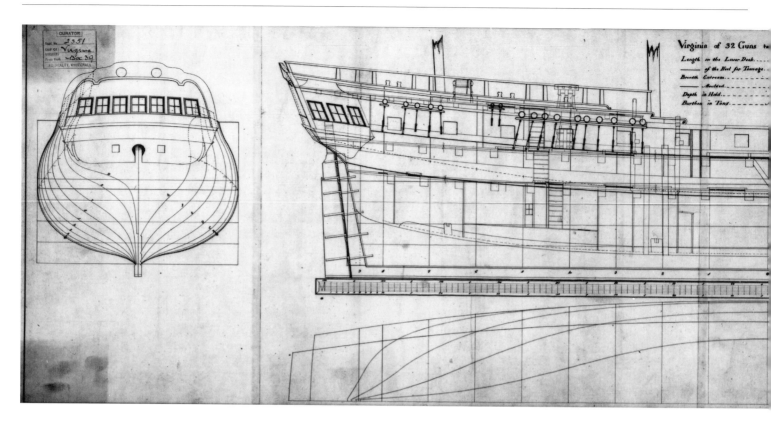

to have their own plans made locally, and these were done by master carpenter Sylvester Bowen. By the time the official draughts arrived the hull was too far along to be altered a great deal, though Bowers was directed by the local committee to make his plans agree with the official draught, if possible.[14] No plans of the ship survive, but her dimensions were said to be 132ft 1in on the lower deck, 34ft 5½in beam, and 11ft depth of hold. The *Warren* had the heaviest battery of this group. She was only one to carry 18pdrs, having twelve, in a mixed battery with fourteen 12s, as well as eight 9s. The remaining 32-gun frigates carried standard main batteries of twenty-six 12s, plus ten 6pdrs on all but *Raleigh*, which had six 6s.[15]

The ship was launched on 15 May 1776 and Esek Hopkins raised his pennant on her in December of that year. She remained blockaded in Narragansett Bay until March 1778. She made one short cruise and put in to Boston. A second cruise occurred in the fall of 1778 and she sailed with the ill-fated Penobscot expedition in July 1779. She was burned–as were the other vessels of the squadron –to prevent capture on 14 or 15 August 1779.

The frigate *Washington* was laid down in 1776 and launched on 6 August. She was still incomplete when Philadelphia fell into British hands and was towed up the Delaware to prevent her capture. She, along with *Effingham*, were scuttled in shallow water. The British found and burned them on 8 May 1778.

28-Gun Frigates, 1776-7

The number of 28- and 24-gun frigates built is uncertain, with some disagreement about which were to be of each rate, since the slight difference in dimensions makes it difficult to determine with exactness. It appears that five were contracted for, three of which–*Trumbull*, *Providence* and *Virginia*–were completed and went into service. Two, *Congress* and *Effingham*, were destroyed in 1777, the former by the Americans to prevent her capture, the latter as noted above, burned by the British.[16]

Virginia was built at Fells Point, Baltimore, Maryland, by George Welles. As there was no communication problem between Philadelphia and Baltimore, her design was probably faithful to Humphreys' plan. Her plan was preserved by the British after her capture. She measured 126ft 4in on the

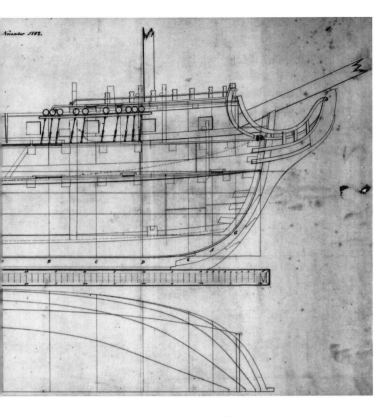

British draught of the *Virginia*, as taken off at Chatham Yard, November 1782. This probably represents the class design for these small frigates. [National Maritime Museum neg 2351]

gun deck, 34ft 10in beam and 10ft 6in depth of hold. There are interesting contrasts in the 32-gun and 28-gun designs. The latter, though shorter, was beamier, and had the old-style beakhead bulkhead. Her size, again, was larger than the comparable British frigates, as shown by the fact that the British rated her as a 32 after capture.[17] In Continental service she mounted twenty-four 12s and two 6pdrs.[18]

As with many of these vessels, the overwhelming British presence on the American coast effectively prevented any active service. Though she was launched 12 August 1776 and completed in 1777, she was trapped on the Chesapeake Bay. After five failed attempts to escape to sea, she finally set out from Annapolis on the night of 30 March 1778. The next morning she grounded and broke off her rudder. While repairing, two British frigates hove up and her commanding officer surrendered his ship. As HMS *Virginia* she served until the end of the Revolutionary War.

The 28-gun *Effingham*, built by Francis Grice in Philadelphia, again probably was built on the Humphreys official design. Her dimensions are not known and her fate has been noted above. She was named after Lord Effingham, a British supporter of the colonial cause.

Trumbull was built by John Cotton of Chatham, Connecticut. She was laid down in February 1776 and launched 5 September. No dimensions of the vessel are known and it is assumed that she followed the official design. Her completion was delayed by difficulties getting her across the bar of the Connecticut River, which was finally accomplished in 1779. She was commissioned by May 1780 and was captured by HMS *Iris* (ex-*Hancock*) on 9 August 1781.[19]

Providence was built by Sylvester Bowers at Providence, Rhode Island, and, like *Warren*, her design was Bowers', rather than Humphreys'. Her dimensions were: 126ft 7in on the gun deck, 33ft 10in beam, and 10ft 8in depth of hold. At 632 tons she was significantly smaller than others of the class. She was launched 18 May 1776, one of the first of the ships to go into the water.[20] She was captured at Charleston in 1780 and sold in 1783.

24-Gun Frigates, 1776-7

Two 24-gun ships were completed: *Delaware* and *Boston*. *Delaware* was built by Warwick Coates of Philadelphia and probably to the Humphreys plan. Dimensions mentioned after her capture by the British were 121ft on the gun deck, 96ft keel for tonnage, and 32ft 6in extreme breadth. Additional dimensions recorded were 119ft between perpendiculars, and 9ft 9in depth of hold, and 32ft 11in extreme beam.[21] As the former breadth dimension was taken in the field, the latter figure is probably more accurate.

Delaware was launched around 12 July 1776 and commissioned about March 1777. She was lost to the British on 17 September of that year and taken into the Royal Navy, retaining the name. She was reported as carrying twenty-four guns on the upper deck, all 12pdrs, except two 6s.[22]

Boston was built at Newburyport by the Crosses, and from her dimensions it appears she also differed from the Marine Committee's plans. She was 114ft 3in on the berth deck, 32ft beam and 10ft 3in depth of hold. She was described as having an 'Indian Head with a bow and arrow in the hand, painted white red and yellow, Two top gallant royal masts, pole mizen topmast on which she hoists a top-gallant sail . . . has a garf [gaff?] mast in room of an Ensign staff with a lateen sail on it and mounts 30 guns.'[23] Her battery was five 12pdrs, nineteen 9s, two 6s and four 4pdrs. Note that *Hancock* also had a lateen yard on a mast 'in room of an Ensign staff'.

Her commander wrote of her as being more weatherly than *Hancock*, but in 'fine weather, the *Hancock* bore the bill'. He also reported she was 'the most ticklish ship to keep in trim that ever I was acquainted with' but thought she might be a fast ship if 'her trim can be discovered'. Her need of ballast to keep her stiff resulted in her riding deep in the water and thus hampering her speed.[24] She was launched 3 June 1776, commissioned in 1777 and served until May 1780 when she was captured at Charleston, South Carolina. She was taken into the Royal Navy as a 20-gun vessel and sold out in 1783. Her small size is evident by the British down-rating her from 24 to 20 guns.

Montgomery was built at Poughkeepsie, New York by Lancaster Burling. No dimensions or plan has surfaced of this vessel. She was launched 4 November 1776 and was burned, still incomplete, on 7 October 1777, to prevent capture.

1776 Authorisation: Frigates *Alliance*, *Confederacy* and *Bourbon*

In November 1776, then in January 1777 the Continental Congress authorised additional construction, including sloops of war, frigates and ships of the line. Three 74s were authorised, with only one completed. Two sloops of war were built and seven frigates authorised, with only two of the latter completed. These were the 36-gun *Alliance* and *Confederacy*. The 28-gun *Bourbon* was still incomplete at war's end.

Alliance was built by William and James K Hackett at Salisbury, Massachusetts. No plans of the ship have been found, but her dimensions were 151ft between perpendiculars, 36ft beam and 12ft 6in depth of hold. She was rated for 36 guns and as such was very large for that rating–over 20 feet longer and slightly broader than the older British 36, and even 14 feet longer than the new 18pdr-armed 36-gun frigates that Britain began to build in 1778.

She became known as the fastest ship in the Continental Navy, and her reputation carried on to the time of the re-establishment of the navy in the 1790s. When builders were being asked to submit plans for the new frigates, Secretary

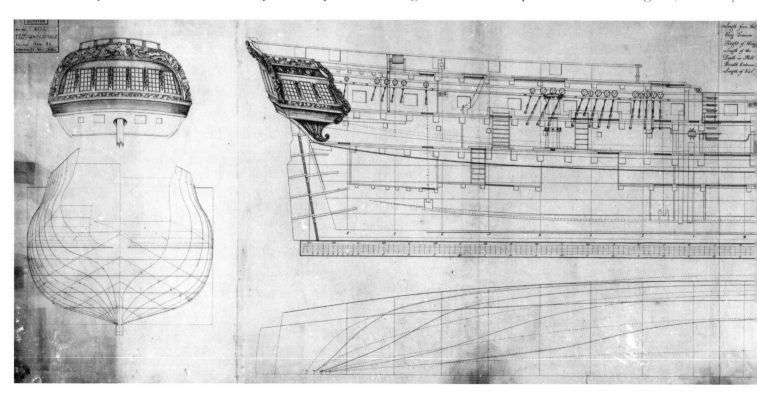

of War Henry Knox wrote James Hackett for his input, reminding him that as the builder of *Alliance* he had 'not been forgotten'.[25] Indeed, Hackett's tendency towards large dimensions fits well with the inclinations of the new navy's leadership. *Alliance*'s principal dimensions of 151ft by 36ft – up from the 136ft of the 32-gun *Hancock* – approach those finally settled on for the new navy's 36-gun frigates, *Constellation* and *Congress*: 163ft by 40ft , with main battery of 24pdrs or 18s – as compared to the 12pdr gun deck battery of *Alliance*.

The ship was launched 28 April 1778 and originally named *Hancock*. This was changed by Congressional action to *Alliance*. Appropriately, she was put under the command of Pierre Landais, a former officer of the French navy. She then sailed for France with Lafayette on board, on a mission to obtain additional support for the nation's struggle against Britain. Afterwards, she joined John Paul Jones in *Bonhomme Richard* cruising in European waters. Unfortunately, by this time Landais had become unruly and uncooperative, the culmination of which were his actions during

Draught of the *Confederacy*, as the British *Confederate*, as taken off. Note her unusual features: shallow draught, long hull, and sweep ports. [National Maritime Museum neg 6175]

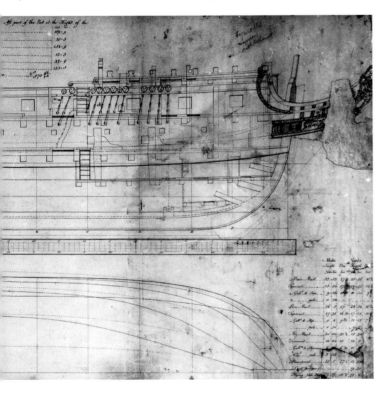

the fight with *Serapis* off Flamborough Head, firing indiscriminately into both vessels. After Landais was relieved of command, Jones took *Alliance*, but remained in France for some time, dealing with diplomatic and other issues. While Jones was occupied in Paris, Landais, bent on revenge, returned, re-claimed the ship and sailed her westward. His subsequent actions were of such an offensive nature that the crew relieved him of command before they arrived at Boston in August 1780. Landais was later court-martialled and ousted from the service.

Alliance was next sent to France with the American envoy, then cruised back to the United States, taking prizes as she went. She defeated two British sloops in a single pitched battle, then returned to Boston. After another voyage to France and prize-taking cruise under John Barry, *Alliance* returned to the US after the end of the war. She was sold on 1 August 1785, the last vessel of the Continental Navy. Little is known about her subsequent career beyond a merchant voyage to the East Indies in 1787 and 1788. It is said that her remains were finally dredged up and disposed of in 1901, near Philadelphia.[26]

Confederacy was authorised by Congress on 23 January 1777. She was built in Connecticut, on the Thames River, between Norwich and New London. Josiah Huntington was selected to superintend her construction in February 1777.[27] She was laid down later that year and launched 8 November 1778. A British plan of the ship was made after her capture, and her dimensions were 154ft 9in between perpendiculars, 37ft beam, and 12ft 3in depth of hold.[28] These represented rather peculiar ratios for a 36-gun frigate: not only was she very long for her rate, but she was narrower and shallower than comparable vessels. She was also set up for sweeps – one of the largest vessels of this type built. The necessity for operating the sweeps from the berth deck probably explains her shallow depth. No specific rationale comes to mind that might explain why she was given this feature, though they would have been useful in river and coastal operations, where close quarters limited the usefulness of sail. Her hull form was sharp for the period, and her lines aft were unusually fine and bordered on concave. This feature also may have been intended to create a fast hull for rowing. When completed she was particularly decorative, with a full length male figurehead, Neptune and allegorical figures on her stern.[29] She mounted twenty-eight 12pdrs and eight 6s. She crossed topgallants, but also carried royal poles, and had both spritsail and sprit topsail yards.[30]

Her career in the Continental Navy was short, with her going to sea delayed until February 1779 by problems with financing and recruiting crew members. She was dismasted in the West Indies, then captured without a fight by frigates HMS *Roebuck* (44 guns) and *Orpheus* (32) off the Virginia Capes (15 April 1781). She became HMS *Confederate* in the Royal Navy and was sold out in 1783.

The last frigate authorised was the *Bourbon*, by direction of Congress in January 1777 and begun in 1779.[31] Few specifics are known about her, other than her intended rate, which was 28 guns. She was superintended by Josiah Huntington and the builder was John Cotton of Portland, Connecticut. As with earlier large vessels built on the Connecticut River, she had difficulty passing over the bar, and this delayed her completion. At the end of hostilities she was sold unfinished (September1783).[32]

Sloops of War *Ranger* and *Saratoga*

Ranger was authorised by Congress in November 1776.[33] She was originally to have been a brig and was laid down in January 1777 at Portsmouth, New Hampshire.[34] She was built by James K Hackett and superintended by John

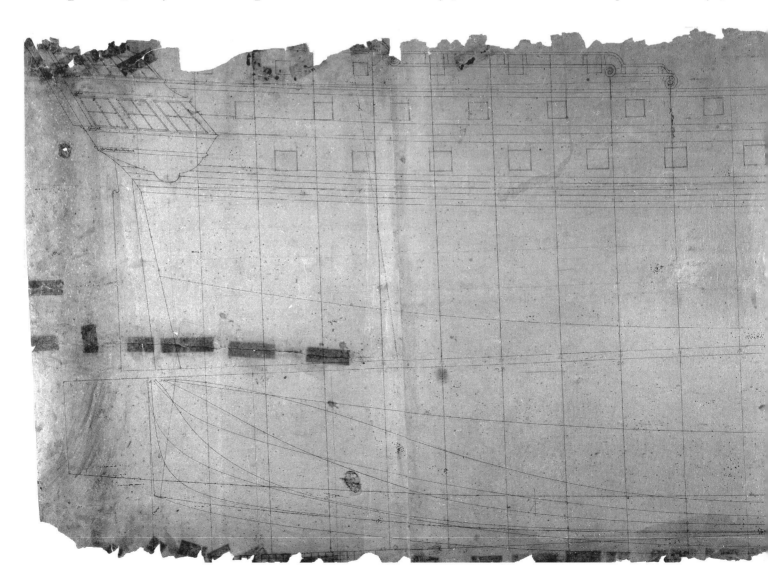

Roche. Shortly after her contract was let, the Continental agent for New Hampshire, John Langdon, recommended she be rigged as a three-masted ship, to decrease the 'unwealdy' size of her masts if built as a brig. He also noted that he had moulds on hand for a similar size vessel (300 tons) which had just been completed, and he intended to use those for the new ship.[35] As late as 24 December 1776, Langdon complained that the Marine Committee had not sent a plan for the vessel, so it is again quite possible that this ship was built to another design than that intended by 'headquarters'.[36]

She was launched 10 May 1777 and went to sea on 1 November, under the command of John Paul Jones. She mounted eighteen 6pdrs and had a crew of about 150 men.

According to British records, made after her capture, she was 116ft on the gun deck, 34ft beam and 13ft 6in depth of hold.[37] She was obviously under-armed for her size. *Ranger* was a notable ship, both under Jones' command and afterwards. She was not the perfect sailer, however. Jones wrote, after her initial passage to France, that she 'did not answer the general expectation, owing . . . to her being too deep, very foul, and overmasted, her ballast too high . . . with the extraordinaray weight of her lower masts occasioned her being very Crank . . .' Jones noted he would take steps to

Joshua Humphreys' 74-gun design of 1777. No vessel of this design was built: the 74-gun America was completed to very different dimensions. [National Archives 40-15-6H]

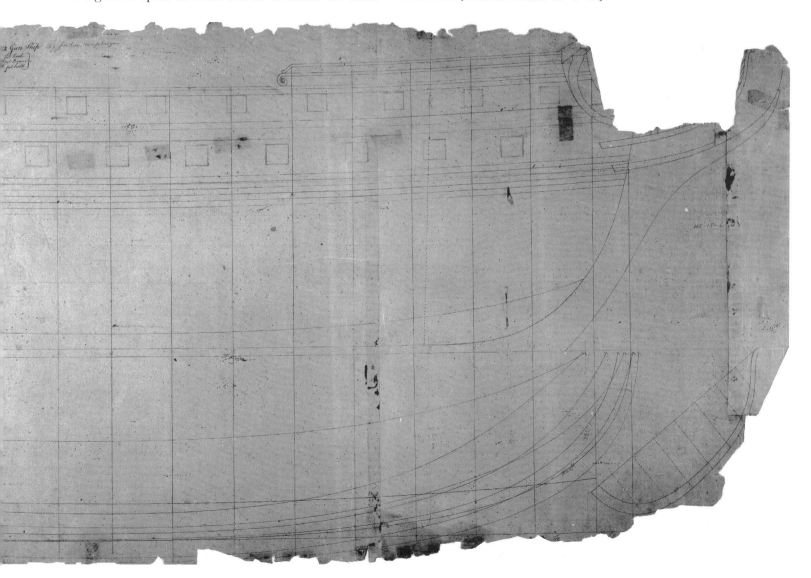

remedy these conditions, including shortening the masts, moving the main mast aft, etc.[38] She took many prizes while cruising in European waters, including the 20-gun HMS *Drake*, off Ireland. She was equally successful after Jones' departure, in a cruise in the North Atlantic and West Indies. She was captured on 11 May 1780 with the fall of Charleston, South Carolina. She was taken in to the British navy as HMS *Halifax*.

Saratoga was built by Humphreys at Philadelphia, and begun in December 1779. No plans for this vessel are known. She was ship rigged but rather small, with keel measurement of 68ft, beam of 25ft 4in and depth of 12ft. Her battery was sixteen 9pdrs and two 4s. She was launched 10 April 1780 and in service on 13 August.[39] Her career was short but eventful and she was particularly adept at convoy escort duties from the West Indies. She was lost at sea with all hands in March 1781.

The 74-gun Ships

Three 74-gun ships of the line were authorised by the Continental Congress on 20 November 1776. Two were begun and abandoned due to shortage of money; the third was the ship *America*, built at Portsmouth, New Hampshire.

Only one plan and a half-hull model of a 74-gun Revolutionary War vessel survive. The model is by Joshua Humphreys and possibly the draught also, though Chapelle notes some minor differences between the two. This design called for a ship 180ft between perpendiculars, 49ft beam and 19ft depth of hold. The three 74s were planned for Boston, Philadelphia, and Portsmouth, New Hampshire. As the first two were not completed, the question becomes whether the Portsmouth ship followed the official plan, which appears to have been the design described above. Unfortunately, the only dimensions of this vessel do not agree with the plan. They were: length 182ft 6in (upper deck), 150ft on the keel, beam 50ft 6in, and 23ft depth of hold. The differences in dimensions and other local sources tend to support a different designer for the *America*: William Hackett.

Her building was supervised by John Paul Jones, who made considerable changes in her upperworks. Also, at one point it was ordered that her rate be changed to a 56-gun frigate, though this was countermanded. Jones, despite his efforts, had little success in speeding up her construction, which was delayed by lack of carpenters and material shortages.[40] She was launched 5 November 1782, after the surrender at Yorktown. She was never part of the American navy as Congress voted on 3 September 1782 to give her to France as a replacement for a French 74 lost at Boston that year. It was said that her armament was too great for her size and thus her lower deck guns could not be used in a seaway. She remained in French service until 1786 when she was found to be rotten and was sold out.

* * * * *

This represents a survey of the major vessels built by the navy during the Revolutionary War. As can be seen, these ships seem to have been quite serviceable – and in some instances, such as *Hancock*, extraordinarily good – naval vessels. Some, however, suffered from poor construction materials. Nevertheless, it was not the vessels or their design which prevented the navy from effective service during the Revolutionary War. It was simply a matter of numbers: a miniscule force attempting to combat the massed hearts of oak of the world's largest navy.

This is evident in surveying the list of Continental vessels lost during the war, which represents a very large percentage of these ships. About half were lost in action to the British, and about a quarter of the total were lost while still incomplete – on the stocks or in the water fitting out. Both of these causes reflect the overwhelming naval superiority brought to bear by the Royal Navy, though of course poor leadership or incompetence on the American side contributed to the totals. The impotence of the Continental sea forces during the conflict is reflected in the fact that it took the appearance of a French battle-fleet to effectively stymie the Royal Navy's command of the sea, and finally allow the armies to deal the death blow to British hopes at Yorktown. Throughout the conflict, the Americans had neither the capacity nor resources to create a fleet like that which the French finally supplied, and which was, ultimately, the only arm which could defeat the British.

The Frigates Constitution, United States, President, Constellation, Congress, Chesapeake

The Original Concept

'I see trouble for Britain in those big frigates from across the sea' were the prophetic words attributed to Lord Nelson as early as 1803 – nearly a decade before one of the US Navy's 44-gun cruisers defeated one of Nelson's protégés in one-to-one combat.[1] From the defeat of HMS *Guerriere* to the advent of the navy's blue-water battleships, the medium-sized warship – frigate or sloop of war – was the mainstay of the American cruising fleet. And certainly the frigate carried the legacy of victory on the high seas, against Britain, France and the Barbary powers, throughout the pre-Civil War era. Even today, the iconic status of the USS *Constitution* reflects the significance of the sailing frigate in the history of the early republic.

The impulse for the construction of the six vessels which comprised the core of the new American navy was two-fold: the depredations of the Barbary powers committed on American commerce in the Mediterranean, and the outbreak of what became the Napoleonic Wars in Europe. In the first instance, relations with the North African states were based on annual payment of 'tribute' – protection money – for the privilege of safe passage near their coasts, with non-payment a pretext for seizure of ships and cargo, and enslavement of their passengers and crews. As early as 1790 some Congressional efforts were made to acquire armed vessels to combat these depredations, but these came to nothing. Then, in December 1793, the problem mushroomed when Algerine corsairs began seizing American merchant ships in the Atlantic.[2]

The subject of American military preparedness was also involved in discussions of the American position relative to revolutionary France. By February 1793, under the National Convention, America's former ally was at war with Austria, Prussia, Great Britain, Holland and Spain. These circumstances brought to the fore Secretary of War Henry Knox's plans for defence of the nation should American neutrality be compromised. Interestingly, the Algerine and European problems were thought by many to intersect, with the suspicion that the British had deliberately unleashed the corsairs.[3] In any event, the upshot was passage of the bill 'to provide a Naval Armament' of 24 March 1794.

Passage of this act may well have been predicated on the thought that the price of a few strong warships able to permanently end the problem was substantially less than the growing accumulation of moneys sent in barrels to buy off the grasping emirs of Tripoli, Algiers, Tunis and Morocco. Thus, the national government set a course to rectify the neglect which had led to the elimination of the old Continental Navy, of which the last vessel had been sold in 1785.

This path would lead to the establishment of the Department of the Navy in 1798, but at the outset the legislation simply called for acquiring, equipping and manning six warships specifically to deal with the Algerine crisis. The vessels were to be no larger than 44 guns, based on the largest ships reported in the corsair fleets. Four were to be 44s, and two 36-gun frigates, to be built or purchased. As the navy had no yards or construction facilities, contracts were to be let to private yards as follows: one 44-gun frigate

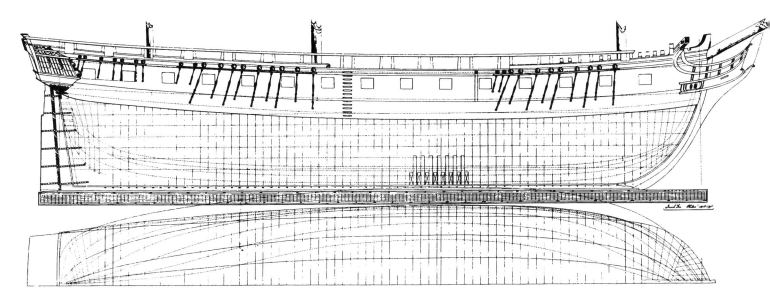

each to be built at Boston, New York, Philadelphia, and Norfolk, and one 36-gun vessel each at Portsmouth, New Hampshire and Baltimore. Finally, as a sop to a large Congressional minority opposed to any navy at all, a clause was inserted suspending vessel construction if peace was made with Algiers.

In the absence of a navy department as such, implementing the act fell to Henry Knox, Secretary of War, and former quartermaster general of the Continental army. To supplement his limited knowledge of naval affairs, he immediately began gathering expert opinion on how to proceed. Interestingly enough, the records show he had not been idle in navy matters before this. As early as 1790 he had solicited estimates on warship construction from John Foster Williams, former captain in the Continental Navy. Williams suggested a 40-gun frigate 140ft on the keel carrying thirty 24pdrs, six 9s and four howitzers. The next year Pierce Butler sent estimates for a 40-gun frigate and a 14-gun brigantine, and in January 1794 Samuel Hodgson submitted costs of a frigate of 800 to 1200 tons.[4] These estimates were in part for the benefit of the Naval Committee in Congress and such influential men as Robert Morris, the senator from Pennsylvania, who was probably the richest man in America.

Among the more significant letters to Robert Morris was one dated 6 January 1793 from Joshua Humphreys of Philadelphia, designer of many of the Continental frigates, and builder of the Continental frigate *Randolph*. In his proposal, Humphreys outlined his ideas for frigates which would 'in blowing weather as would be [*sic*] an overmatch for double deck ships and in light winds, to evade coming to action . . . or double deck ships that as would be [*sic*] an overmatch for common double deck ships and in blowing weather superior to ships of three decks, or in calm weather or light winds to outsail them.' Furthermore, he continued, these vessels would be 'no less than 150 feet [on the] keel to carry 28 32-pounders or 30 24-pounders on the main gun deck and 12 pounders on the quarter deck. These ships should have scantling equal to a 74 . . . .' They were to be constructed of red cedar or live oak, the latter in the lower futtocks, with North Carolina white pine deck beams.[5] His object was to create frigates larger than their European counterparts. Their greater armament would enable them to outfight enemy vessels of their nominal class; and their speed would make them capable of outrunning any larger opponents.

The strength of these ideas, as well as the recommendation of John Wharton, another prominent Philadelphia shipbuilder, appear to have impressed Secretary Knox, who appointed Humphreys naval constructor to design the six frigates. Humphreys' appointment was on 28 June 1794, with compensation retroactive to 1 May. These dates are somewhat irrelevant, however, as Humphreys had submitted a half-model incorporating his ideas sometime before 12 May, as well as detailed estimates of the quantity of timber required for a 44-gun ship.[6]

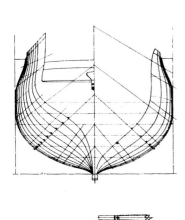

Humphreys' design for the *Constitution* class 44-gun frigates, incorporating his concept of larger dimensions and battery (in number and calibre of guns) than standard European frigates of the time. These hulls approximated 74-gun ship dimensions but without the upper deck – necessitating extraordinary means to prevent hogging. [National Archives 40-15-6A]

Also, by mid-May, a second plan for a 44-gun ship was in Knox's hands. This, by Josiah Fox, was in the form of a 'draft', rather than a model. Fox had come to the United States from England in late 1793. Influential friends, among them Andrew Ellicott, Surveyor General, and Captain John Barry had obtained for him an interview with Knox and, apparently, an invitation to submit a design for the new warships. Officially, he was hired in mid-1794 as a 'clerk' to assist Humphreys. Fox, like Humphreys, was a Quaker, and related to the founder of that sect, John Fox. When he arrived in the US he was thirty years old, with an apprenticeship at Plymouth dockyard behind him, completed in 1786. From that date to his arrival in Philadelphia he travelled to various European dockyards and studied his craft. He was a fine draughtsman but apparently up to that time had not built a major ship.[7]

At this point in the development of these vessels, the War Department had two proposed plans for the 44-gun frigates: one in the form of a model, by Joshua Humphreys; the other a plan drawn by Josiah Fox. It is also at this point that historians diverge on the relative influence Humphreys and Fox had on the final design. Chronologically, the actual controversy seems to have begun in 1827, when Fox learned that Samuel Humphreys, son of Joshua and a naval constructor in his own right, claimed his father was the designer. Fox, by then retired in Ohio, responded in a letter to *Niles Weekly Register*, touting his own primacy in the design process. He alleged that Humphreys'

plan was rejected by Knox and a committee of 'all the Master Ship Builders from the Swedes Church [of the] upper part of Kensington'. Fox also gave credit for the designs of the 36-gun ships to William Doughty, a draughtsman and shipwright in Humphreys' yard.[8] Unfortunately, history has not left us with the basic tools to answer the question: that is, neither Humphreys' half-model nor Fox's original draught survive. The model, and possibly the plan, were destroyed in the burning of Washington Navy Yard in 1814. However, we can deduce a great deal about the Humphreys model from the critiques made of it in 1794. We know little about the original Fox design.

It is logical to assume that Humphreys made the model in conformity to his ideas expressed in 1793 (quoted above) and we know the dimensions were 147ft on the keel, 43ft beam, and 14ft depth of hold.[9] Additionally, Fox himself is the source for its length on the gun deck, which was 175ft. It was pierced for thirty guns on the gun deck, had a roundhouse and relatively upright stem. Fox also mentioned some hollows in her fore body and waterlines of the hull.[10] As can be seen, many salient characteristics of the ships appear to have been present in Humphreys' model. The completed vessels were 145ft on the keel, 174ft 10½in on the gun deck, 43ft 6in moulded beam, 14ft 3in depth of hold, and were pierced for thirty guns on the gun deck (excluding bridle ports). It does appear that the upright stem was eliminated, some of the hollowness removed from the lines and adjustments made to the height of the wales.[11] However, the concept of a very large frigate for its day was very evident in Humphreys' model. Even the design for the 36-gun vessels was much larger than the contemporary British 36- or 38-gun frigate: 162ft 3in between perpendiculars and 40ft moulded beam.

However, some contend that those generous dimensions were not instigated by Humphreys, but were given him by Knox as the basis for the design and model, after the latter had consulted with various builders of the day.[12] Nevertheless, it should be remembered that Humphreys' 1793 proposal called for a *150ft* keel, and dimensions larger than European frigates.[13] Furthermore, in the original correspondence of 1793-5 these over-size characteristics were invariably credited to (or blamed on) Humphreys, and not on any pre-conceived dimensions imposed on the constructor by Knox or some anonymous committee. In fact, Fox himself roundly criticised the size of the vessels. Certainly, the final design benefited from advice of Josiah Fox and John Wharton, to whom it was presented for comment, but it appears to this writer that Humphreys set the general parameters for these frigates.[14]

Some final thoughts are in order regarding Fox's ideas on frigate design. As will be seen, in 1795 Fox was assigned to build the frigate at Norfolk. This vessel, the *Chesapeake*, was intended to be a 44-gun ship, and Fox referred to it as such throughout its construction. At some point Fox modified the design or replaced it with his own plan; but still referring to it as a 44-gun frigate. However, when completed its dimensions were so small that it was re-rated as a 36-gun vessel (measuring 153ft between perpendiculars – over 20ft shorter than the larger 44s). Furthermore, as it will be seen, the hull of *Chesapeake* was significantly different from that of the 1794 frigates. That Fox, when given his own 44-gun frigate to build, did not follow what he later claimed to have been his own design, significantly weakens the case for crediting him with designing the *Constitution* and class. In fact, Fox and others, notably Captain Thomas Truxtun, formed a vocal opposition to the 'unwieldy' large frigates of Humphreys' design even before they were launched. Howard Chapelle himself commented later in his *History of the American Sailing Navy* that the design of the *Philadelphia* – another Fox-designed 36-gun ship intended to be a 44 but which served as a 36 – 'by showing radical departures from both the model and dimensions of the *Constitution* and *Constellation* classes, obviously disposes of any claim . . . that Fox was solely responsible for the earlier designs.'[15]

It is worth noting here that Fox produced a sail plan for the 44s in 1794, in collaboration with Captain Truxtun. The plan was reproduced in a book on navigation written by Truxtun, and the plan itself showed the proposed frigates only carrying three sails on fore and main, with two on the mizzen.[16] This sail plan was superseded by the time of the War of 1812.

In any event, Humphreys' hull design seems to have been the starting point, with Fox's also considered. Both were critiqued by John Wharton, and possibly others,

including William Doughty. A final master building draught was the upshot, and this drawing is in the National Archives as 40-15-61, named 'Terrible', one of the names suggested by Humphreys, but not used.[17]

The design for the 44-gun ships was described in Humphreys' report later that year as 'similar with those adopted by France . . . they having cut down several of their seventy-fours to make heavy frigates; making them nearly the dimensions of those for the United States.'[18] Those vessels, he continued, would be a match for anything less than a 64-gun ship. Knox reported to Congress that these vessels would 'combine such qualities of strength, durability, swiftness of sailing, and force, as to render them equal, if not superior, to any frigates, belonging to any of the European powers.'[19] To be specific, the typical British or French frigate of this era was one of 38 guns, usually carrying twenty-eight 18pdrs on the gun deck, with a length between perpendiculars of around 150ft. The 24pdr gun was usually the main battery of small two-deckers, though there were a few 24pdr frigates in British service, notably *Endymion*. Even these were significantly smaller than the new American ships and were not considered satisfactory because the large weight of metal on the deck produced structural problems. Furthermore, handling the large 24s on the relatively lively deck of a frigate was troublesome.[20]

To deal with the potential structural problem, in his design concept Humphreys had specified 'the scantlings of a 74', use of live oak, and incorporation of 'diagonal riders' in the ships' hulls. To restate the problem: building vessels as long as a British 74, which ranged from 168ft to 180ft on the gun deck, was not in itself the problem.[21] However, a frigate had one less deck, so was deprived of one major longitudinal strength member, exacerbating the potential for hogging – and Humphreys' 44s, at 175ft on the gun deck, were prime candidates for this. Thus, extraordinary means were needed to overcome the problem.

In the first instance, Humphreys specified the use of live oak where possible for hull timbers. Secretary Knox concurred in this, recalling that live oak frames for the two 74s built during the Revolution were cut 'part at Sunbury and part at a place called Kilkenny, near the mouth of the Savannah River.'[22] On *Constitution*, for instance, the longi-

The earliest accurate representation of *Constitution*, about 1805, showing open forecastle and 'adam's apple' configuration of knee, supporting the original figurehead. Painting by Michel Felice Corné. [US Navy]

tudinal strength member, consisting of false keel, keel, keelson, keelson rider and transverse floor timbers, was nearly eight feet high, and composed of white oak and live oak (the latter in the floors). The keel and keelson were each sided (width) 18 inches. As a modern day engineer described it, this beam could support a two-lane highway bridge span.[23] The ship's sides, as shown in her plans, ranged from no less than 15 inches (at gun deck level) up to some two feet thick in the lower bilge area.

Live oak, a very heavy wood, unique to the southern coast of the United States, was specified because of its inherent density and was described as 'five times' stronger than white oak. Recent statistics show that live oak's expected life span when used for shipbuilding is about twelve years, four years longer than English oak. The only wood with longer usefulness is East Indian teak, rated at sixteen years.[24] However, the use of live oak was confined to shorter, curved timbers such as futtocks, knees and floors, whereas the straighter white oak timber was used for the keel and other straight pieces. It is noteworthy that specifying live oak inserted a great deal of uncertainty, delay, and additional expense into the building process.

Rather than easily accessible New England timber, this wood was native to the south-east coast, particularly South Carolina and Georgia, requiring the builders to send New England axe men, as well as the means of transporting the timbers, once cut, to the coast. Thus entire teams of oxen, as well as forage and 'timber wheels' were dispatched to Georgia for the purpose. Further delays were caused by the climate: the hot, humid 'sickly season' effectively delayed cutting until September of 1794 and heavy winter rains further hampered operations; all this in addition to the cost of actually shipping the timber to the six construction sites.[25]

Finally, to prevent 'hogging', the most prevalent problem in long wooden hulls, Humphreys prescribed a series of angled timbers running from the keelson upward to the lower deck beams. Six pairs of these 'diagonal riders' were to be fitted, each composed of three pieces, scarphed together and bolted through the bottom plank every two feet.[26] In the recent restoration of *Constitution*, these riders have been installed, with each made of single long, laminated timbers. Though the riders are included in the 'official' 'Dimensions and sizes of materials' for these vessels, there is mixed evidence as to their actual installation in the ships.[27] Written evidence points to both *Constitution* and *United States* having them put in, but *Constellation* and *President* did not. Thus far no positive evidence has been

unearthed regarding their use in the other ships. See the following sections on each vessel for specifics.

In addition to the extraordinary length of the ships, their battery was equally impressive. In addition to the thirty 24pdrs on the gun deck, original plans show open rails with stanchions forming ports for another thirty cannon on the upper deck running forward to the fore mast. This was at variance with the typical frigate of the day, which would carry guns on the quarterdeck and a few on the forecastle. Therefore, despite their later notoriety as 'double banked' frigates, the 44s never carried two complete batteries: in fact, the maximum number of guns ever carried on any of the 44s was around 56. The upper deck guns were usually 32pdr carronades, numbering at least twenty. The 36-gun vessels were to have twenty-eight 18pdrs on the gun deck and twenty 32pdr carronades above, and, again, had more ports than ever were filled with guns: 56. It is worth speculating exactly what Humphreys had in mind by 'rating' these ships as 44- or 36-gun frigates when the number of ports certainly did not correspond to the rating, and, in fact, the ships rarely carried their rated batteries, reflecting contemporary European practice.

In any event, once the master plan was agreed upon, copies were made and sent to the various builders and yards. Timber had already begun to arrive from the southern coast and construction was begun. The six vessels' construction was not uneventful and in fact the entire effort was interrupted in 1795 when peace was obtained with Algiers. Congress then authorised the completion of only the three most advanced ships, those being *Constitution*,

This longitudinal diagram shows the location of the diagonal riders installed during the 1990s restoration of *Constitution*. The new version of the riders are of modern wooden laminate construction, in place of the scarphed, three-part riders used originally. [US Navy]

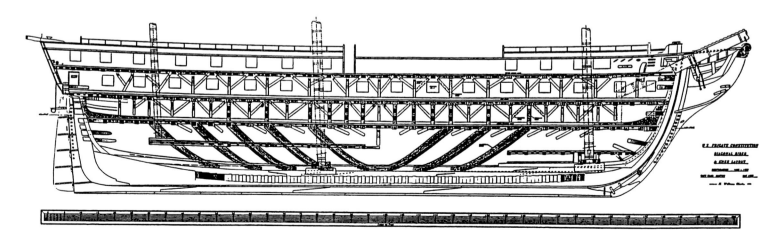

United States and *Constellation*. The other three, *Congress, President,* and *Chesapeake,* were re-instated in 1798 when difficulties arose with France under the Directory, and they were all finally in the water in April 1800.

Constitution

Of the original six frigates, *Constitution* – 'Old Ironsides' – stands unmatched in fame and, of course, longevity. She remains today a national symbol at Boston, site of her construction. It is not an exaggeration to say she is by far the most famous and loved naval vessel in American history. These reasons, when added to the fact that she has, despite several extensive overhauls, retained her basic integrity through the years, make *Constitution* the obvious starting point in looking at these six vessels.

The contract for her construction went to Colonel George Claghorne at the shipyard of Edmund Hartt in Boston, under the naval oversight of Captain Samuel Nicholson. The keel was laid in November 1794. Progress was slow, however, as much of the hull framing depended on live oak, and winter cutting in Georgia was hampered by rains. By December 1795, constructor Claghorne reported the keel completed and both stem and stern nearly ready to raise. Two-thirds of the live oak had arrived and most had been worked into frames. Other than that, all the necessary contracts had been let and a great deal of the other materials, including copper, was on hand. In actuality, there was little to show for a year's work.[28] When peace was made with Algiers in March 1796, Congress deemed it prudent to complete three ships, *United States, Constellation,* and *Constitution,* but work on the remaining vessels was stopped.

By January 1797 Claghorne reported the entire frame of the vessel was raised and ready for planking. The materials for completing the hull were on hand, as well as the masting. Though Claghorne expected to launch her in July, a report submitted to Congress in June revised this estimate to August 1797.[29] In this later report Claghorne specified: 'The various decks are laid; the breast hooks, diagonal riders, and counter timbers, are all in and secured . . .'[30] This appears to be the only extant written evidence that

Constitution had the controversial diagonal riders. But it is noteworthy in this connection that, throughout the construction process, there was much pressure on the builders to adhere to the original instructions. In April 1796, for instance, War Department Secretary Pickering wrote constructor Stodder that the original directions were to be 'exactly followed' and any changes would need to be sent for approval.[31] As will be seen with *Constellation,* it took some persistence on the part of Captain Truxtun to persuade the department to dispense with the riders on that vessel.[32] No such correspondence has been found in relation to *Constitution,* but the fact that *Constitution* was 'hogged' early in her career is taken as evidence the riders were not used. However, it should be noted that, unlike the 1990s 'replica' riders, the original riders were each some 42ft long and *scarphed* together from three timbers. Therefore, the riders were nearly as subject to 'hogging' as the balance of the ship's longitudinal timbers.

Constitution was finally ready to launch in September, though the initial attempt failed when she came to a halt no more than thirty feet down the ways. This was blamed on insufficient declivity of the ways and a second failure, two days later, was due to her stern settling in the interim. Only complete rebuilding of the ways to increase their angle into the water solved the dilemma and she went off successfully on 21 October 1797. One modern writer maintains that the long delay between the first and final launch attempt resulted in her ends settling in relation to her midships, giving her a 'permanent' 14-inch 'hog' even as she began her career.[33] That writer's source for this assertion is not given, but, if true, may have some bearing on the 'rider' question discussed above.

The *Constitution* was commissioned on 22 July 1798. As completed she was finished in typical late eighteenth century fashion: black hull (tarred on the bends and painted above) except for a wide yellow stripe up from the main wales to the channels. Her ochre stripe had one unique feature: the forward end terminated in a semi-circle, about where her bridle ports would later be located. Her figurehead, designed by William Rush and carved by John Skillin, was a seven-foot-tall standing Hercules, brandishing a club. The monumental height of the figure resulted in

The defeat of the British frigate *Guerriere* by the *Constitution*, 19 August 1812: oil painting by Michel Felice Corné. In this and other comparable actions, Humphreys' concept of overwhelming firepower was vindicated. The influence of this design carried through in the US Navy for the remainder of the sailing era. [US Naval Academy Museum]

an unusual 'adam's apple' knee configuration which curved forward and upward to form the figure's pedestal.[34] At the stern, the carving was the most elaborate of her career: the central element was a spread eagle and shield, flanked by nereids, wreaths and cupids.[35]

At his point she had fifteen gun deck ports without a bridle port. As for the arrangement on the upper deck, the earliest representation of the ship (painted in 1803 by Michel Corné) shows bulwarks on the quarterdeck and stanchions with nettings in the waist and forward to the fore mast, leav-

ing the forecastle open for working the anchors. The upper deck arrangement of 1803 is, however, compatible with her original battery, which was thirty 24s on the gun deck and fourteen or sixteen 18pdrs above. The latter cannon were 'borrowed' from Castle Island in Boston harbor, when the 12pdrs ordered for the ship did not arrive.[36]

The *Constitution*'s rig at the beginning of her service was conventional, and had not reached the height seen in most of the illustrations of the vessel in the War of 1812. From earlier contemporary illustrations as well as log entries, it is apparent that she only carried sail as high as royals. It appears, however, that *Constitution* was not to be known for her sailing qualities. Despite the hyperbole surrounding 'Old Ironsides', much of which was read into her popular history after her wartime exploits, the big frigate was hardly a perfect sailer. During her first commissions in 1798 and

1799 her trim was described as faulty and she 'plunged and rowled' in a gale, taking on great quantities of water. Departing from Boston on 21 July 1798, under Captain Samuel Nicholson, she sprung her bowsprit in October, her fore mast in January and again in April; and her main mast in June. Certainly her weak top hamper greatly restricted her operational effectiveness during the Quasi-War with France. Of course, some of her sailing deficiencies might be put down to officers unused to vessels of her size. As to her speed, she was reported to have beaten handily the 36-gun HMS *Santa Margarita* in a day-long contest.[37] But that vessel was not known for her speed, in any event.

Nicholson was replaced by Silas Talbot in June 1799 and she became flagship in the West Indies. Routine patrols marked this cruise, highlighted by a victorious 'race' with frigate *Boston*. By December Talbot was seeing similar top hamper problems: sprung fore mast trestletrees, a loosened bowsprit and weakness in the main mast. Minor repairs held the latter together for six months, and the problem finally forced her into port for sufficient shoring to enable her return to Boston. She decommissioned 18 June 1802 having made only three significant captures.[38]

The Tripolitan wars brought her back into service, this time under Captain Edward Preble. Preparations for sea duty included the onerous job of re-coppering. As there were no drydocks in the US, she had to be hove down for the work. Preble also wished to arm her upper deck with 42pdr carronades, but these were not available and she sailed with sixteen 12pdrs instead.[39] She was flagship of the Mediterranean squadron which bombarded Tripoli in 1804 and blockaded the Barbary Coast. During these years her battery varied somewhat, depending on circumstances, including 'lending' cannon to other vessels, and taking on temporary guns for battering Tripolitan fortifications, etc. At one point she mounted thirty-six 24pdrs and sixteen 12s. Later, she had eight 32pdr carronades on her upper deck, though these probably replaced some of the 12s.[40]

This commission brought two significant alterations to her appearance. First was the planking of her waist, done at Syracuse in February 1804.[41] This left only her forecastle open for working her anchors. Second, an accidental collision with *President* demolished most of her head—

figurehead, rails, and knee were left in splinters. Temporary repairs included a simple billet head and a shortened bowsprit. After two years patrolling the peace, and serving under the command of Preble, John Rodgers and Samuel Barron, she decommissioned in 1807.[42]

May 1809 saw *Constitution* back in commission, responding to increased tensions with the British, signalled by the humiliation of the *Chesapeake* and *Leopard* incident. John Rodgers again took her in hand, and replaced her light upper deck battery with eighteen 42pdr carronades and two 24pdr chase guns. He also rigged her with unusual triangular skyscraper sails. Rodgers was unimpressed with her sailing, however, and soon turned her over to Captain Isaac Hull in exchange for command of the reputedly faster *President*.[43]

Hull now addressed the vessel's poor sailing qualities, first by hauling her down and scraping her bottom. This was a risky proposition, placing much strain on the hull— and, literally, on the crew. The process involved intentionally grounding the ship, and, using block-and-tackle set up on her lower masts, pulling the hull over nearly to the horizontal. In this way, one side of her bottom was exposed. Once the crew had scraped and dislodged the masses of marine growth there and made minor repairs to the sheathing, she was righted again, swung end-to-end, and the process repeated. This was an onerous task, involving not only the hauling out itself, but preparations for the evolution required removing all unnecessary top hamper from the ship as well as everything aboard, such as guns, that could shift when she went over. It was necessary, however, because there was as yet no American drydock available to accommodate her. After every such 'hauling out' there was always uncertainty about how well the hull had stood up to such treatment, and indeed, whether the hull had retained its structural integrity and shape.

The second improvement was to rig the ship with skypoles and their sails, giving her the lofty profile which she retained for much of her active career. Then about a third of her ballast was removed. Next Hull dealt with her battery. By the outbreak of the War of 1812, she had seen two major changes in her armament. For a short time she had shipped an additional six 42pdr carronades, for a total of 56 guns. Hull replaced all the 42s with less massive 32pdrs, giving her a total of 55 guns: thirty 24s, twenty-four 32pdr carronades, and one 18pdr chase gun. By this time her forecastle had been planked in, and her upper battery was situated there and on the quarterdeck, leaving her waist open except for nettings. During this period, Hull also painted her hull black with the familiar white gunport stripe along her side.[44]

Of course, the War of 1812 was the arena in which *Constitution* made her reputation: the dramatic slow-motion escape from the British squadron, the victories over *Guerriere*, *Java*, *Cyane* and *Levant*, the triumphant war-won nickname that epitomised the essence of her sturdiness and

that of her men in the face of the British fleet. However, it is not the purpose of this book to repeat what scores of others have written and sung.

Both the war itself and the decades of post-war active service saw changes in most aspects of the vessel, but none could be described as 'major'. In fact, unlike many ships in the navy of that era which were subject to massive redesigns or even keel-up 'rebuilds'–such as *Constellation*– 'Old Ironsides' maintained her basic original configuration, major and minor dimensions, rate, rig, and fabric: this, despite three major re-builds before ending her active career. The minutiae of every refit cannot be charted here, but what follows is a survey of the most obvious changes made in this era.

During the war itself, modifications were centred around her battery and ports. After her escape from the British

Sail plan, *Constitution*, 1817. Her lofty rig, as shown here, was in place during her War of 1812 actions. Plan is one of several by Charles Ware, a navy sailmaker during the era. [National Archives 15-D-9982]

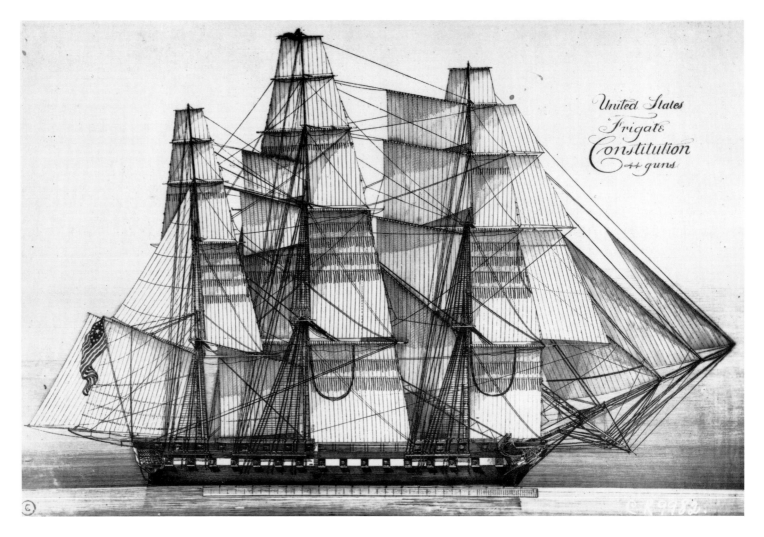

squadron, bridle ports were cut between the forward gun-ports and the stem to facilitate towing. Despite what her commanders might have wished, the confined deck space did not allow using these for gun positions. Shortly after this, three stern gun ports were cut on her quarterdeck. (Hull had had to demolish his quarters as well as the taffrail to run guns out astern during the 1812 chase.)[45] As to her battery, before she met with *Java*, one more 18pdr was added and two carronades were deleted. When she came out again later in the war and defeated *Cyane* and *Levant*, one of the 18s had been replaced with a long 24 and the other 18pdr was landed.[46]

In the post-war decades, until she was converted to a school ship in 1860, she made the rounds of the various cruising squadrons. She made four tours in the Mediterranean, one in the south Pacific, one in the Home squadron, and three years on anti-slavery duties in the African squadron. The highlight of her post-war service was a 30-month goodwill round the world odyssey in the mid-1840s, covering over 50,000 miles. During these years there were various alterations in her rig, battery, and head structure. In the first instance, a ringtail was added in 1815. This was an extension to the spanker comparable to a studding sail. To further improve her performance close to the wind, spencers (gaff trysails) were added to the fore and main masts in 1823. Around the same time, her head rails were closed in, and her gunport stripe was carried forward and around her stem, as was the fashion of the day.[47]

The major alteration to her stem occurred in her 1830s re-build, when she received her controversial Andrew Jackson figurehead. As shown by period illustrations, the curve of the knee was raised considerably higher in relation to the stem, putting the bottom of the trailboards on a line even with the lower edge of the gunports. The result was a rather high, angular knee profile. In her 1848 refit, she reverted to the older profile: with the trailboards meeting the hull below the lower edge of the gunports. At the same time a new Jackson figurehead was carved and fitted, which can be seen in photos of the vessel through the Civil War era.[48]

As for her battery, there were two major re-armings. In

Constitution in the 1860s, showing the angular head supporting the full length carving of Andrew Jackson. This carving was 'beheaded' in a nocturnal visit by one of Jackson's political enemies. [US Navy]

1843-4 four of her gun deck 24pdrs were replaced by 68pdr Paixhan (shell) guns, and twenty 32pdr carronades were mounted on the weather deck. Then, four years later, in accordance with a policy requiring all guns of the same calibre on any given vessel, she was given forty-six 32pdrs—a combination of long guns and carronades—and four shell guns. Another variety of the latter arrangement was seen in 1849 when she mounted eight shell guns and forty-two 32s.[49]

Some contemporary remarks on her sailing and sea-keeping qualities serve to complete the picture of this famous frigate. First, she apparently had a turn of speed, though her logs indicate she actually may have been faster in her post-war commissions. 'Mad Jack' Percival claimed she did 14 knots in the 1840s running free under topgallants—some half knot better than was claimed for her in 1809.[50] However, she was always a heavy roller and very wet forward. To quote an 1853 statement:

Celebrating Washington's birthday at Malta, 1837; *Constitution* in the foreground. Oil painting by J G Evans. [US Naval Academy Museum]

She has always been heavily sparred, and from her peculiar build (tumbling in above the water,) has furnished her masts less angular support from her shrouds than is now obtained in our modern frigates. The latter cause, combined with sharpness of vessel, heavy oak frame, heavy battery, and too much ballast, (which has since been reduced to 7 tons, with a recommendation from her commander, Capt. Percival, that this also be dispensed with,) has generally rendered her wet and uncomfortable in a seaway, hard on her cables, and no doubt was the principal cause of her laboring so much as to roll or pitch one of her long 24 pounders out of her forecastle port,

when on her passage to France in 1835, when she was reported to have labored very heavily, parting several of her chain plates &c. On her passage round Cape Horn labored beyond every thing I had ever witnessed, and gave me a lively idea of what sailors understand by 'working like a basket'.[51]

Other comments were less negative: 'rolls deep and easy'; 'Excellent, very weatherly, works quick, rolls deep, but easy; stands up well under canvas, but not very dry in a seaway'; 'Works within 11 points of the wind; steers, works, sails, scuds, and lies to well . . . and sailing close hauled has beaten every thing sailed with.'[52] These statements need to be treated with care as the ship was practically a monument to American naval prowess, so a little hyperbole was often present in contemporary accounts of her qualities.

In the more than 130 years since her last operational tour, *Constitution* has been a training vessel, a receiving ship, and, of course, a museum ship. Major overhauls were undertaken in the 1870s, 1905, the 1920s, the 1970s, and, recently, in the final decade of the twentieth century. In the last, the objective was to restore the ship to her 1812 appearance and prevent her hull from further hogging. It is a compliment to Joshua Humphreys that the method chosen for the latter objective was that of his 'diagonal riders', a series of which was installed in her hull. The modern riders are laminated and each is a single timber, in contrast to the three-section originals. As to restoring her 1812 appearance, the most obvious change was to eliminate the outsized closed-in head which seems to have been an accretion through several of her rebuilds. A photo of her in 1858 shows the top of her figurehead (the second Jackson carving) significantly lower than an imaginary line straight forward from the top of her forecastle bulwarks. After her 1920s work the line from the top of her bulwarks to the tip of her billet head was nearly straight: the new billet head not only replaced Jackson, but extended high above the level of that figure. The result–the head most people saw in the 1950s–was a

massive wall of timber without the light tracery of her original head. The 'new' head restores the open head rails and their graceful fanning curves. Also, the forecastle bulwarks now terminate at her stem, revealing significantly more of the lower end of her bowsprit and replacing the old straight line with another curve to compliment that of the rails and trailboards.

To complete the circle, USS *Constitution* – 'Old Ironsides' – looking much as she did during her glory days, was put under sail again, although under controlled conditions, for the first time since 1881. On 21 July 1997 off Marblehead, Massachusetts, she was the lead in a two-day media event. Accompanied by two modern naval vessels, each crowded with VIPs, she was first placed in tow, then, on the second day, allowed free in very light winds, moving under six sails (topsails, jibs and spanker) at no more than four knots. Enormous public interest was evident in the hundreds of small boats along her path, as well as massive media coverage, all reflecting the national pride still residing in the old ship and her role in the critical early days of the nation.[53] She remains today the world's oldest naval vessel afloat and in commission, and certainly the eldest able to navigate under her own sail power.

United States

The frigate *United States* was the first of the Congressionally-authorised vessels launched. She went down the ways on 10 May 1797, and was commissioned on 11 July 1798, three months after the onset of the Quasi-War with France and shortly after the launch of *Constellation*. She had been built in Joshua Humphreys' Philadelphia shipyard, under the naval oversight of Captain John Barry. Progress in her construction had been impeded by the temporary suspension ordered by Congress in 1796, an outbreak of 'contagious fever' (yellow fever) at the yard in the summer of 1797, and slow delivery of live oak.[54]

Though her dimensions were as the other two 44s, the general consensus of the time was that she was more heavily built. Augmenting her bulk was a round house (poop cabin) on her quarterdeck–adding significant weight and windage aft.[55] It would be expected that Humphreys would

Constitution under sail for the first time since 1881, off Marblehead, MA. October 1997 saw the 200th anniversary of her launch and the completion of a major overhaul. Thousands turned out for this occasion, marking the American people's continued fascination with the historic vessel. In nearly calm conditions the ship made 3 - 4 knots with her load of dignitaries and visitors. [Photo courtesy Dr Mike Crawford, Naval Historical Center]

have been assiduous in building her according to what were arguably his own specifications, including the diagonal riders. Though these timbers are not mentioned during her construction, they were certainly installed. In 1806, when the vessel was at Washington for refit, Josiah Fox reported that decay in the ceiling had 'caused the whole of the diagonal riders to be removed'.[56] It is unlikely that they were re-installed.

It is assumed she went to sea appearing much the same as *Constitution*: black with the ochre stripe. We do know her figurehead was the 'Goddess of Liberty' but the earliest known representation of the ship was dated *before* she was completed, so is somewhat suspect.[57] Her earliest known battery was fourteen 12pdrs on her upper decks in addition to her thirty 24pdrs.[58] It is worth noting that, despite some poor sailing characteristics of both 44s, it did not prevent their captains from drastically increasing their batteries in later years.

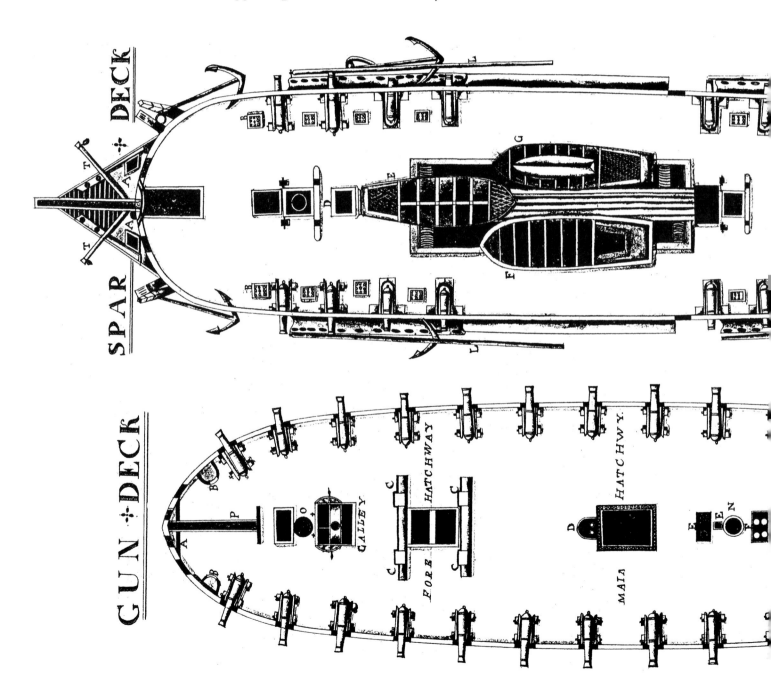

When she went to sea, Captain Barry's glowing report to Joshua Humphreys emphasised her excellent steering, and boasted of leaving Captain Decatur behind in USS *Delaware*. However, he continued with signals that all was not well. He wrote: 'she is rather tender' and 'I hope she will be stiffer'.[59] As she continued in active service, it became apparent that she was plagued with heavy-weather problems similar to *Constitution*'s. Initially, Barry understated the situation to Humphreys: 'if there were a spread of canvas

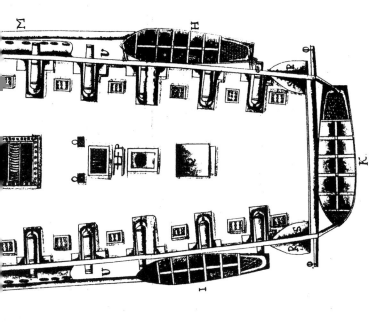

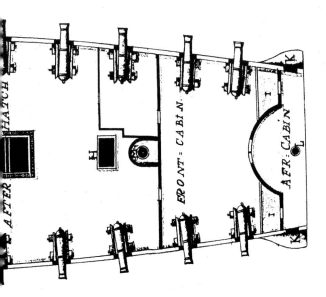

carried on her, it might probably bury her more than it ought . . .' He tentatively suggested moving her fore mast aft and increasing the rake of the masts, the latter to ameliorate her 'pressing' and improve her speed. He then indicated he would add 25 tons of ballast (to the 100 tons already shipped). Finally, he posited that she would be 'a better ship' with a foot or more added to her beam.[60]

Three days after this letter, we find the Secretary of the Navy scrambling to obtain ballast for her – 'immediately'.[61] Less than a month afterward, off Hatteras in a gale, the vessel was reported 'pitching very much' and, in a head sea, she sprung her bowsprit. It is noteworthy that *Constellation* rode out the same storm with ease.[62] Obviously, the problem stayed with her. In 1806, when *United States* was in refit, Tingey wrote of the 'leanness or want of stability in her fore body', and Fox quoted Captain Barron (Barry?) saying she was 'dangerous' and in danger of 'carrying away her fore mast and bowsprit, when on a wind with a head sea', by pitching her bows, bowsprit and 'even flying jibboom under water'.[63] As to her speed, she acquired the nickname 'Old Waggon' by the War of 1812, and was reported to have been outsailed by the damaged and jury-rigged *Macedonian* after the latter's surrender.[64]

United States participated in the Quasi-War with France, though with little distinction. She was laid up in 1801, waiting out the Tripolitan conflict at Washington Navy Yard. During her lay-up, plans were carried out to upgrade her battery and replace the 12pdr long guns with thirty-two 42pdr carronades on her quarterdeck and forecastle. Also, another pair of 24pdrs was added, probably as bow-chasers. As she had 'breastworks' amidships, these were ordered cut down and replaced by stanchions.[65] She went to sea at the outbreak of the War of 1812 under Stephen Decatur, and it was this battery – particularly the long guns – that decimated the British frigate *Macedonian*. During that action, if a contemporary painting by Philadelphian Thomas Birch is accurate, she had two narrow red stripes on her hull, one

Deck plan, frigate *United States*, 1830s. This shows the ship's battery as 54 guns: thirty 32pdrs on the gun deck, twenty 32pdr carronades on the upper deck with four long 32s forward. A drawing by Charles Ware, at Charlestown Navy Yard. [National Archives RG 45 Ware Drawings]

each above and below her gunports. Shortly after returning with her prize, she was blockaded at New London, Connecticut, ending her wartime activities.

The post-war career of the *United States* had its unusual aspects, mixed with the ordinary rounds of cruising on station. First she was in the Mediterranean where she remained until 1819, on patrol enforcing the recently made peace with Algiers. Subsequently she was on the Africa anti-slavery station, in the Pacific, and in the Home squadron. While in the Pacific, one of her sailors was Herman Melville, who wrote *White Jacket* as a result of his experiences. Also, in 1842, under Commodore Thomas ap Catesby Jones, she 'captured' Monterey, California. Unfortunately for Jones, the rumours of war with Mexico which had precipitated the move proved premature by some four years. Appropriate apologies were rendered and Monterey was returned to Mexico.

Much as the *Constitution* seems to have improved her sailing in the post-war years, *United States* also stood her stodgy reputation on end and gained repute as a fast sailer. As early as 1815, her commander was boasting that *Alert* and *Hornet* could 'barely keep up with this ship'.[66] In 1834, in the Mediterranean, she was reported to have beaten all the British fleet. (Though 'beating the British fleet' seems to have been something that happened all too often, particularly in the nationalistic American press.) Some years later, in a trial with the newer *Congress*, she was on a par with that ship on a wind and had the advantage when dead before the wind. She was reported to have logged 10½ knots on the wind and 13 running free.[67]

An article in *Niles Weekly Register* of 18 August 1827 described a 'trial of speed' between 44-gun *Brandywine*, in her second commission, and the thirty-year old frigate: 'the *United States* . . . let the *Brandywine* come up alongside. All sail was then spread . . . The race was only doubtful for a few minutes. The *United States* gained on the *Lafayette* (as she is generally styled in the navy), so fast that she soon shewed her stern; and in an hour clued [*sic*] up her topgallant sails and royals, to let her adversary come alongside, in token of victory.'

There were few external changes in the ship after the war. The first was closing in her head, which was done

before 1833, as she 'set the style' for that of the *Constitution*, rebuilding in that year.[68] Her battery reverted from 42pdrs to 32pdr carronades in 1841, and by 1848 she mounted forty-six 32s and four 8-inch (68pdr) shell guns.[69]

United States was laid up at Norfolk through the 1850s and taken over by the Confederates there in 1861. She was used as a training ship by the Confederate navy until scuttled with the re-capture of the yard by Union forces in 1862. She was broken up in 1864.

President

The third 44-gun frigate was reputedly the best of the three under sail, but had the shortest career. USS *President* was begun at New York in the yard of Forman Cheeseman, then work on her was discontinued in 1796. Construction resumed at that yard in 1798, under Christian Bergh and naval constructor William Doughty. She was launched on 10 April 1800.[70] As launched, she was elaborately carved, carrying a bust of George Washington, supported by the female figures representing Truth and Justice, 'cloathed in light flowing drapery'. The trailboards featured an American eagle and shield, and 'darting thunder and lightning'. On her stern, below the taffrail, was the female figure of 'America', flanked by Wisdom and Strength, both inclined towards the centre. On the quarters were two more figures representing Liberty and Union.[71]

She went to sea under Thomas Truxtun, patrolling for French privateers in the West Indies. She had held up well in a gale on the cruise south, with Truxtun later writing that 'the ship is as kind a sea boat as ever I sailed in.' He did, however, express some trepidation concerning her masts, which were of 'Northern pine [which was] not . . . sufficient for men of war of a large size.' Once on station, he tried her out at every opportunity, outsailing the frigates *Chesapeake*, *John Adams*, *New York*, and schooner *Enterprize* (though the last outsailed the *President* in light winds). With some justification, Truxtun wrote that 'she outsails anything I have seen.'[72] In May 1801 Truxtun wrote that the frigate 'sails very fast by the wind, large & before it, especially if the breeze is fresh, she is kind and good humoured in a gale of wind at sea . . . [in a gale] under main and fore topsails, close

President in European waters by Antoine Roux, 1803. Note planked-in waist. [US Navy]

reefed & lowered down on the cap & never lost a rope'.[73] Later, it was said that Bainbridge offered $5000 to a later commander of *President* to exchange ships with him, when the former was commanding *Constitution*.[74]

Early in her career, *President* carried thirty 24pdrs and twenty-two 12pdrs, and period illustrations of her in the Mediterranean before 1806 show bulwarks and guns on the quarterdeck and waist only.[75] Then, in 1808, in refit, her rail was extended across the bows to stow hammocks. Nine ports were cut on each side of the quarterdeck, and four, plus chase ports, were cut on the forecastle.[76] This was substantially the same arrangement she was to have for the remainder of her career.

After duty in the Mediterranean, participating in the bombardment of Tripoli and subsequently patrolling the

area, she cruised off the US coast as tensions with Great Britain over impressment of American seamen increased. Her claim to fame occurred in 1811, under John Rodgers. Vowing vengeance for the *Chesapeake-Leopard* humiliation, Rodgers unleashed a broadside into HMS *Little Belt*, raising a storm of British protests and further stoking the fires which led to the War of 1812. Controversy remains today over which party fired first, but it is obvious that neither side was reluctant to light the fuse. (Rodgers had in response to threats by the British squadron–which included HMS *Guerriere*–painted 'President' on her topsails in letters that could be 'seen for ten miles'.[77])

Except for a running and indecisive fight with HMS *Belvidera*, *President* accomplished little during the war itself. With much of the navy, she was blockaded for most of 1814. Her escape in early 1815, under Stephen Decatur, was short lived. Coming out of New York, she first grounded heavily, then was hemmed in by *Endymion*, *Tenedos*, *Pomone* and *Majestic* (three frigates and a razee). After a short resistance, Decatur surrendered his ship.

She had been damaged in grounding and a subsequent storm, and was much decayed, so the British reluctantly had her broken up in 1818. Her lines, however, were taken off at Portsmouth Dockyard and used to build a precise copy, which was launched in 1824–and, whenever possible, employed as flagship on one of the trans-Atlantic squadrons.[78] The propaganda value of a captured enemy vessel was immense–and the Americans used *Macedonian* in exactly the same manner.

The British-drawn plans of *President*, as well as contemporary illustrations, give a good idea of the appearance of American frigates during the War of 1812. Of course, the elaborate carving of the head, described above, had given way to a billet head. The head itself was simpler, with only the upper rail curving upward to the cathead, and the curvature was shallower, with the trailboards ending almost on the level of the lower line of the gunports, instead of substantially lower on the hull. Illustrations of her capture also show *President* as having only a narrow stripe along the line

President as she appeared in the War of 1812, giving a good idea of the appearance of the American frigates during the War. British draught of the *President* as captured, taken off at Portsmouth Yard, 4 December 1815. [National Maritime Museum neg 1305]

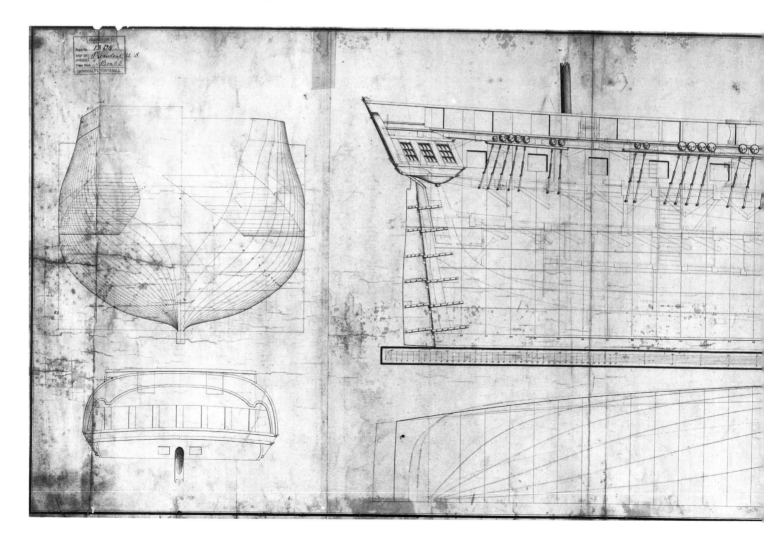

of the lower edge of the gunports, rather than the entire width of the ports.[79]

The American 44-gun frigates had been a humiliation for the British throughout the war, with Captain Broke – who captured *Chesapeake* – having written: 'We must catch one of these great American ships with our squadron, to send her home . . . that people may see *what a great creature it is*, and that our frigates have fought well, though unlucky.'[80] With the capture of *President*, they accomplished this goal.

Constellation

Until the War of 1812, USS *Constellation* was the most famous vessel of the new navy, and her repute continued to rival that of *Constitution* for many decades. That fame continued to cling to the name long after the original frigate had been broken up and replaced by a relatively modern sloop of war. Today, the 'new' *Constellation* remains a historical gem lovingly restored and displayed in Baltimore harbour, carrying on the tradition of her 'Yankee Racehorse' predecessor. The story of the newer vessel will be pursued in a later chapter.

The original frigate was to a plan evidently scaled down from the 44-gun vessels. The two 36-gun ships authorised were to be 163ft 3in between perpendiculars, 136ft on the keel, 40ft moulded beam and 13ft depth of hold. As with the 44s, these ships were larger than their British 38-gun counterparts, which typically measured 150ft between perpendiculars, 125ft on the keel, and 39ft beam.[81] In fact, *Constellation* and *Congress* were re-rated as 38s while under construction. Again, as has been seen, the rate was a fiction: each of these vessels eventually carried 44 or more guns.[82]

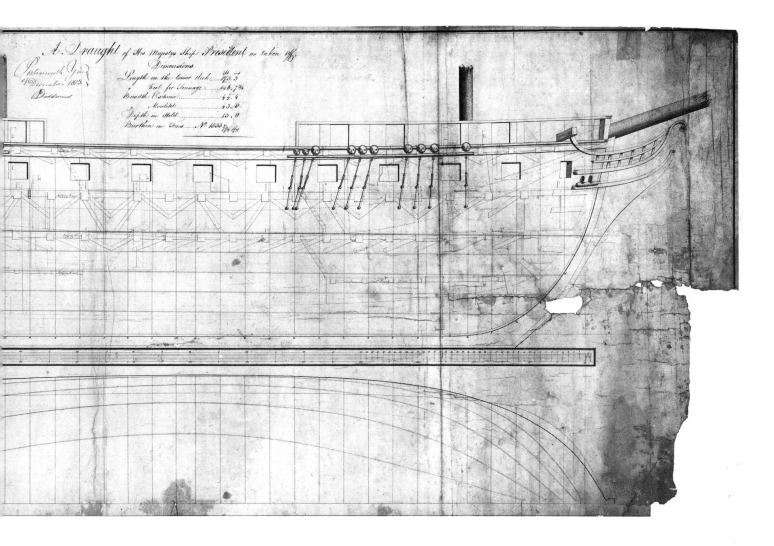

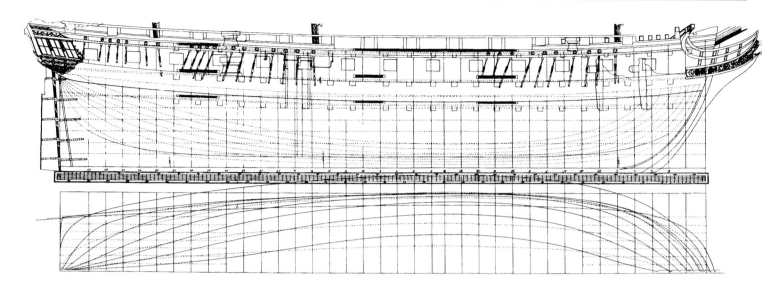

Constellation was built in the Baltimore yard of Samuel and Joseph Sterrett, by David Stodder, under the naval oversight of Thomas Truxtun. Her construction was actually facilitated by the suspension of the other three frigates, in that much of her timber was transferred from the cancelled frigate at Norfolk. Her construction differed from the two first 44s in that the diagonal riders were omitted. As early as April 1796, Stodder had apparently desired to alter the ship, as Pickering had insisted the 'directions' be 'exactly followed'. Then, in November, Truxtun was told that two-thirds of the riders could be retained. Finally, in December, the Secretary of War grudgingly allowed their omission 'resting entirely on your experience'.[83] She was launched on 7 September 1797, carrying a female figurehead representing Nature. She was the second of the six to go into the water.

She was, however, first to go to sea. By 26 June 1798 she was convoying merchant vessels southward. In July, Truxtun reported that the ship behaved 'well in all sorts of weather, and sails fast . . .'[84] By this time, both *Constitution* and *United States* were also at sea, and each was vying for the 'fastest ship' laurels. Truxtun wrote (misspellings included), 'I have seen so much in the public prints of the Sailing of Barry's Ship, and so much bombastical Nonsense of that at Boston, that I am at a Loss to make a report . . . I shall therefore say, that in no Instance of Chace during our Cruize, was half our canvass necessary, to overhawll the fastest sailing vessel we met, some of which were termed

before Flyers.' He then predicted she could outsail both 44s, and she was 'the easiest Ship I ever was in.'[85]

Constellation excelled under Truxtun and became the first vessel of the new federal navy to take a major foreign warship. In February 1799, in heavy blowing weather, she defeated the French frigate *L'Insurgente* off Basseterre. At the time, *Constellation* carried 38 guns: twenty-eight 24pdrs and ten 12s. Though Truxtun called the Frenchman a 40-gun ship, eight of those were 6 pounders, and her main battery was twenty-four 12pdrs.[86] Thus, the broadside of *Constellation* was at least a third again heavier than that of the adversary. A year later, *Constellation* encountered the heavy frigate *Vengeance* in a lengthy, running fight. The enemy vessel was apparently thoroughly mauled, with five feet of water in her hold and hardly a stick standing. Truxtun's command, however, was cut up significantly in the rigging and her main mast went by the board. Consequently, the enemy vessel escaped in the night. By this time, *Constellation* had been rearmed with twenty-eight 18pdrs (a change which Truxtun found made the vessel 'very stiff' when compared to her performance with the 24s in main battery).[87] *Vengeance* mounted 54 guns, with a main battery of 18s.[88]

In April 1801 *Constellation* grounded and was rolled on her beam ends by an ebb tide, resulting in extensive damage. Her commander, Alexander Murray, used the opportunity to alter her, commenting that 'like all sharp built ships [she] will lay over upon a press of sail until she gets to her bear-

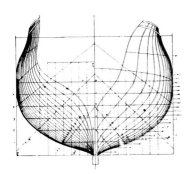

Sheer, half-breadth and body plan, *Constellation*. Note that even the 36-gun Humphreys' frigate design was larger than comparable British vessels. [US Navy]

ings'. He reduced her spars and ballast, but proceeded to add 24pdr carronades to her battery, making her a 44. He commented that she had been 'nearly rebuilt' from the waterline up.[89] After encountering heavy weather in the spring of 1802, Murray wrote that her stiffness, sailing and stowage had improved significantly.[90] After participation in the Tripolitan conflict, *Constellation* was laid up and extensively repaired at Washington Navy Yard. It was probably during this repair that 14 inches was added to her breadth, possibly by additional planking to add longitudinal strength.[91]

Her contribution to the War of 1812 was negligible, having been blockaded for most of the conflict. After the war, her stations included the Brazil squadron, the Pacific, the West Indies, the Mediterranean, and a cruise around the world in the 1840s. In terms of performance during these decades, the ship 'was reported to steer, stay and work well, in her cruise in the Mediterranean in 1833, where she lived through a heavy gale in which a French 80 gun ship was lost . . . Is also reported very weatherly; careens readily to her bearings when she is stiff and easy on her masts.' Her speed was reported, according to her logs, as 10 knots on a wind and 12½ free.[92] By the 1840s she was armed with thirty 18s and sixteen 32pdr carronades. This was to be her final battery.

Constellation in chase of *L'Insurgente*, one of the earliest representations of any of these vessels, during the Quasi-War with France. Engraving by E Savage, published in Philadelphia on 20 May 1799. [Beverley R Robinson Collection, Annapolis]

Above: Constellation in the Mediterranean, pre-War of 1812. Watercolour by Antoine Roux. [Peabody Essex Museum 14509]

Left: Constellation off Port Mahon, Menorca in 1837. Oil painting by N Cammillieri for Commodore Wadsworth, and given by him to Commodore John Rodgers. [US Navy NH 61863]

She was laid up at Norfolk for some eight years and declared 'altogether unworthy of further repairs'.[93] When the extent of the repairs to the *Constellation* precluded economic sense to repair her, it was determined that the old vessel would be broken up, and a new ship, on a new plan, would be constructed, saving only the name. The navy somewhat deceptively called this process 'rebuilding' and in fact legally used stockpiled timbers to build new ships, then re-applied the name of the deceased vessel to the new construction.[94] (An extensive discussion of this controversial issue will be presented later.) In any event, the original frigate *Constellation* was broken up in mid-1853, and her timbers auctioned in September of that year.[95] She was replaced by a thoroughly modern sloop of war of somewhat larger dimensions and with a hull design distinctly different from the 1797 frigate's. See Chapter 7 for a description of the new *Constellation*.

Congress

The sister ship to *Constellation* was easily the forgotten member of this group, having acquired neither fame nor infamy in her career. *Congress* was built at Portsmouth, New Hampshire, by Colonel James Hackett. Hackett and his cousin William had produced four noted vessels during the Revolution, including *Raleigh*, *Ranger*, and the 74-gun *America*; and since 1796 had built *Crescent* (a tribute frigate for Algiers), revenue cutter *Scammel*, and the 1799 sloop of war *Portsmouth*.

This frigate had been laid down by late 1795, and a report in December indicated about 'two-thirds' of the live oak had been delivered to the yard, but that the 'principal framing' was not complete.[96] Work was terminated on *Congress* in 1796, and it appears that some of the collected timbers were utilised to complete the other frigates. The incomplete work, however, may have been retained for the possible re-instatement of her construction. At her launch on 15 August 1799, the local newspaper claimed she had been completed in 258 working days, placing her second keel-laying late in 1798. She was touted as 'equal to the very first stile [sic] of American building', and with carved work by William Deering of 'much taste and simplicity'.[97]

She was armed with twenty-eight 18pdrs and twelve 9s when she went to sea in late 1799, then teamed with *Essex* –also newly commissioned–to convoy merchant vessels southward from Newport, Rhode Island. Her maiden cruise was hardly auspicious: she was 'vastly' outsailed by *Essex* coming out of the harbour, and, less than two weeks out, disaster struck.[98]

As her commanding officer James Sever explained it, 'the first three or four days . . . we had the winds far northwardly, the weather cool, attended with snow and hail. On Saturday the 11th, the wind veered to the southward . . . very fresh, attended by warm rain, and a heavy sea; this . . . produced an astonishing effect on my rigging . . . it stretching so much as to induce apprehensions for the safety of the masts.' First, the main mast was sprung, and before the topmast could be cut away to preserve it, the entire mast went by the board, carrying with it the mizzen topmast, as well as one crew member. With little to steady her in heavy seas, the fore top soon went, followed by the bowsprit and fore mast.[99] Completely dismasted, she wallowed, as one officer put it 'like Noah's ark . . . rolling and straining about'.[100] She struggled under jury rig back to Hampton Roads, and her commander to a court of inquiry.

Captain Sever was completely cleared of responsibility for the disaster, with the cause being laid to foul weather and the 'Badness & insufficiency of the masts'.[101] The question of the role of the weather is somewhat baffling, as the *Essex*, which had been within sight of the *Congress* shortly before the storm, weathered it with no significant damage. Indeed, Preble mentioned the slackness of his rigging and wearing his ship to set it up taut.[102] As to the masting, it may have been the same 'Northern pine' which Truxtun later complained of in *President* (see above).

After re-masting at Norfolk, *Congress* returned to duty on the Santo Domingo station until the spring of 1801 and the end of the French difficulties. She was re-commissioned in April 1804 for Mediterranean duty, where she cruised for eleven months, returning to the US transporting the Tunisian ambassador. During her 1805 to 1811 lay-up she underwent repairs and gained a 'ringtail' for her spanker.[103] By the War of 1812 her armament had been changed to twenty-four 18pdrs and twenty 32pdr carronades.[104]

She made three major cruises during the War of 1812, capturing a significant number of merchant ships. She was in company with *President, United States, Hornet* and *Argus* when they encountered HMS *Belvidera* in 1812. A running fight developed between the fastest of the squadron– *President*–and the British frigate. Relatively slow, *Congress* was well astern, and thus came up too late to participate effectively, and the British vessel escaped.[105] *Congress* spent the last year of the war blockaded in port.

In 1816, she was at Boston and was to carry the new

Sail plan of *Congress* by sailmaker Charles Ware. Note outsized gaff topsails on all three masts. No explanation or other information has been found on these. [National Archives RG 45 Ware Drawings]

American minister to Russia. However, her bottom was discovered to be 'very open under the copper', and USS *Guerriere* eventually was sent in her stead.[106] It was during her lay-up at Boston that a sail plan was made of her, by Charles Ware, sailmaker. It shows her lofty rig–as was common for big American frigates–including skysails. An unusual aspect of the plan are her large gaff topsails, on all three masts. No corroborating evidence has been found confirming she actually carried this rig, however.

She operated against West Indies piracy in the 1820s, and ended her active career in 1824. *Congress* was found unfit for further repair in 1834 and broken up at Norfolk. A few years later, the name was re-used for the last sailing frigate designed by the navy.

Chesapeake

If one vessel of the new navy could be considered a hard luck ship, it was the frigate *Chesapeake*. The superstitious sailor would wink knowingly when told even her name was a source of confusion before she was complete. Then luck eluded her in her short career, as she was humiliated twice by the British–once in peace and the second time in a totally predictable battle defeat in 1813. It is said her name continued to carry the stigma: the second *Chesapeake*, a training ship, was said to have been dogged by misfortune until her name was changed to *Severn* five years into her service life.

The ship itself was originally to have been a 44-gun frigate to be built at Norfolk under John T Morgan. Morgan, however, was sent to superintend timber cutting in Georgia, and Josiah Fox was recommended to replace him at Norfolk (Gosport), beginning in April 1795.[107] No name was chosen for the vessel before work was stopped some three months later, and much of the collected timber was shipped to Baltimore for *Constellation*. When construction was re-instated in August 1798, Secretary of the Navy Stoddert re-appointed Fox to build the vessel.

By this point, the decision had been made to reduce the size of the vessel. The rate (44 guns) remained unchanged: the battery was to be twenty-eight 18pdrs and sixteen 9pdrs. The new dimensions were 'proposed by the secretary of the navy' and were 152ft 6in between perpendiculars by 40ft beam and 14ft depth of hold.[108] As Howard Chapelle indicated, Fox and Truxtun had probably prevailed on the new secretary with their views on the large 'super-frigates'.[109] (By this time the navy had its own leadership and Secretary of War Henry Knox, who had encouraged the big-frigate concept, was no longer in authority.) Indeed, Fox's views on the size of frigates were well known, as a fellow shipbuilder wrote to him: 'the reduced plan of yours . . . [is] in preference to those unwealdy [*sic*] ships of such monstrous drafts.'[110] It is worth noting that reducing the size of the Norfolk frigate was to result in a '44-gun ship' with dimensions *smaller* than the Humphreys design for a 36-gun vessel. Furthermore, the hull design for

Fox's ship is quite distinct from the Humphreys plan, with the latter having significantly rounder bilges. The Fox design was very similar in midship hull form to British practice of the time. In short, the Norfolk frigate was not a sister ship to *Constellation* and *Congress*.

Her keel was laid on 10 December 1798 and she was launched on 2 December the next year.[111] She apparently had significantly less live oak than the others of this group, though some was shipped from Baltimore after the completion of *Constellation*.[112] Some three months into her construction, confusion arose about her name. Fox had thought she was to be *Congress*, then learned otherwise from secretary Stoddert. Only after that misperception was corrected could instructions be given to William Rush for her carving.[113] At her launch, she was described as a 44-gun ship, and had been so described by Fox throughout her construction. In her first year in service she retained that rate and two sources referred to her as such in late 1802.[114] Exactly when she was re-rated as a 36 is unknown, or the reasons for it. She never carried less than 40 guns – and indeed had 48 or 50 on her when captured in 1813.[115]

Her performance at sea was not flawless. After crossing the Atlantic in 1802, her captain, R V Morris, complained of

Chesapeake, the smallest and least lucky of the six original frigates. Josiah Fox, her designer, disagreed with Humphreys' outsized frigate concept. Consequently, though Fox called her a 44, she was actually smaller than *Constellation*. After her launch she was re-rated as a 36. British draught of the *Chesapeake* as captured, taken off at Plymouth Yard, December 1814. [National Maritime Museum neg 7343]

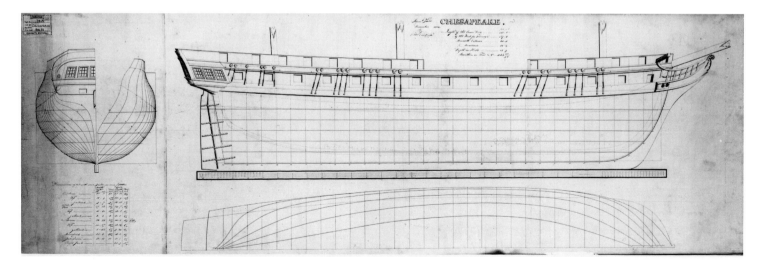

her laboring: 'I never was at sea in so uneasy a ship', and had feared she would roll her masts out. He attributed the troubles to 'injudicious stowage of ballast'.[116] In service, she cruised the coast of the US, and in the West Indies. After the end of the French troubles, she was laid up for a year, then sent to the Mediterranean, participating in the Tripolitan operations. In 1807, she was hailed by the British 50-gun ship *Leopard* and requested to turn over British deserters from her ranks. Captain Samuel Barron refused and *Leopard* fired into her, killing three Americans and wounding many others. This peacetime 'outrage' became one of the major steps in the escalation of tensions which led to the War of 1812.

The War of 1812 meant one short cruise, capturing merchant vessels, for *Chesapeake*. Her second cruise, on 1 June 1813, was into the sights of Captain P B V Broke in HMS *Shannon*. Though the vessels were nearly evenly matched in battery, the outcome was not long in doubt: Broke's superbly trained tars quickly overcame Captain James Lawrence's just-shipped crew and she was captured, with her dying captain voicing the immortal 'Don't Give Up the Ship!' (though James Fenimore Cooper noted that the actual words, spoken in his delirium, were 'Never strike the flag of my ship!'[117])

Chesapeake was repaired, her lines taken off, and served in the Royal Navy until 1820, when she was broken up. At the time of her capture, contemporary illustrators show her painted much like *President*: a narrow stripe at the lower edge of her gunports.

* * *

The influence–both positive and negative–of these six vessels on the ensuing generations of American frigates was immense. First, all but one of the 44-gun sailing frigates built by the US Navy (rather than by private subscription or purchase) through the end of the sailing navy were based on the 1794 design. They were the 'big American frigates' warily eyed by the British for the next forty years. Furthermore, the concept of the big frigate, substantially larger and with a heavier battery than the European coun-

terpart, carried over into the age of steam, with the *Merrimack* and class screw frigates of the 1850s. Conversely, the 36-gun frigate was essentially dead in the US Navy: the only 36 gun-rated vessel built after 1800 was *Macedonian*, the replacement for the captured British frigate, constructed specifically as a 'copy' of the original 36-gun vessel.

A few comments are in order here concerning the American 'super-frigates' in general. Much wordage has been wasted on both sides of the Atlantic and both sides of the question. The tenor of many critics is to castigate the Americans for the 'unfairness' of it all, for disregarding the rules and building larger and more heavily armed vessels than the British counterparts. From the American side, the author has noted something akin to apology for their own temerity–and success.

However, to reiterate the situation in 1794, the American navy's dilemma was how to confront with some measure of success a potential European foe. There was no question of duplicating the Royal Navy, a force of hundreds of ships, created literally over centuries. The only obvious course was the one taken by the nascent navy department: the limited number of ships which could be produced in a short time must each be more than a match for its most likely foe. And the unassailable fact is that the plan worked, as proved by the list of vessels defeated by these ships–*Insurgente*, *Guerriere*, *Java*, *Macedonian*, *Cyane*, *Levant*–and the order that went out to the Royal Navy to always sail in company and for 18pdr-armed frigates to avoid one-on-ones with the American 44s, as well as the subsequent British construction of their own 'super-frigates' to counter the American threat (the *Leander* and *Newcastle*, and others post-war).[118] Even the circumstances of the loss of *President* serve to emphasise the point: she was taken by a British squadron, one of which was the 'super-frigate' *Endymion* (the *Chesapeake*'s defeat can be omitted since, as we have seen, she was not built to the 'super-frigate' design). In any event, it is obvious that intelligent planning, as well as well trained sailors, and officers canny enough to make appropriate use of their vessels, coalesced to bring the results hoped for long before the frigates were in the water.

CHAPTER 3

Subscription, Navy-built and Captured Frigates, 1798–1815

THE CHRONOLOGICAL framework of this chapter is seemingly at variance with the history of the navy through the era. This period saw the birth of the federal navy, under Federalist president John Adams, its decline under the anti-admiralty Democratic-Republican Thomas Jefferson, and its resurrection under wartime exigencies. In terms of the history of American frigates, it is the story of the privately-subscribed and government contract vessels built for the Quasi-War with France, and the three frigates begun during the War of 1812, which were updated versions of the 44-gun ships of 1794. To complete the picture chronologically, the frigates captured from France and England during the two conflicts are included.

The Subscription Frigates

With the national uproar over the 'XYZ Affair' and the appearance of French privateers preying on American commerce, Congress suddenly leapt into action. They re-instated the uncompleted 1794 frigates, called for acquiring another thirteen merchant ships for conversion to war uses, and, on 30 June 1794, approved a measure offering 'stock', at six per cent, in exchange for warships to be built for the government by groups of merchant investors, pooling their funds by subscription.

As pointed out by Frederick C Leiner in *Millions for Defense*, the initiative for the subscription ships was *not* the US Congress. In fact, by the time the bill was introduced, subscriptions were already under way in several cities, led

by the merchants and citizens of little Newburyport, Massachusetts. On 23 May 1798 they had met and determined to raise money to build a proposed 20-gun warship in 90 days and present it to the federal government. They informed their congressman that they would 'accept . . . an interest of six per cent per annum' on their investment.[1] This led to the building of the 24-gun ship *Merrimack* in Newburyport, and nine other vessels in various municipalities from Charleston to Portsmouth, New Hampshire – particularly those port towns whose commerce was the target of French privateering. Of a total of ten warships for the fledgling US Navy, five were frigates mounting 28 to 44 guns, four were ships of 18 to 24 guns, and one was to be an 18-gun brig (the last, built at Newburyport, Massachusetts, was never completed). The ships, *Merrimack*, *Maryland*, *Patapsco* and *Trumbull*, will be considered in the section on sloops of war. The frigates, and their sponsors, were as follows:

Essex – Salem, Massachusetts
New York – New York City
Philadelphia – Philadelphia
Boston – Boston
John Adams – Charleston, South Carolina

The first of the five in service was *Boston*, in July 1799; the last was *New York*, commissioned in October 1800. All participated in some manner in the Quasi-War, four served in the Tripolitan campaigns, and two in the War of 1812. The vessel with the longest service life was *John Adams*, which was broken up in 1829.

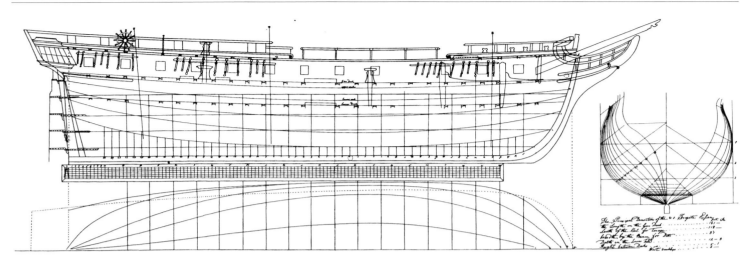

Frigate *Essex*, the most famous of the vessels built by public subscription in the Quasi-War. As with many contract built vessels, the builder's plans were not preserved, or were quite sketchy, as shown here. [US Navy]

Essex

The frigate *Essex* is the most celebrated of the six, because of her eventful career under Captain David Porter in the War of 1812. Her construction was a considerable accomplishment for Salem, a town of 9500 people, but with a noted maritime history.

The 32-gun frigate was built by Enos Briggs of Salem, Essex County, Massachusetts, and designed by William Hackett. Hackett had designed the noted 36-gun *Alliance* during the Revolution and there is some speculation that the designs were similar. *Alliance* was 125ft on the keel, 36ft 6in beam, and 12ft 6in depth of hold; *Essex* was 118ft by 37ft by 12ft 3in.[2] As we do not have a plan of the older frigate, the question cannot be answered definitively. *Essex*'s keel was laid on 13 April 1799, she was launched on 30 September, and delivered to the navy on 17 December. Her carving, including an American Indian figurehead, was the work of Samuel MacIntire, noted for his Federal Style architecture, and particularly his houses in the town of Salem.[3]

Essex, armed with twenty-six 12pdrs and ten 6pdrs, went to sea in company with *Congress*, in late December 1799, under Edward Preble.[4] As noted above, she had no difficulty out-sailing *Congress* coming out of the harbour. They both encountered heavy weather, which dismasted the larger vessel, whereas the Salem frigate weathered it without damage. Preble wrote that she was an excellent seaboat 'and sails remarkably fast. She went eleven miles per hour with topgallants set and within six points of the wind.' Later she out-sailed the British 74 *Arrogant* and frigate *Orpheus*, and her purser noted she 'beat every vessel she has ever had a Tryal [*sic*] with . . .' In another 'Tryal' with the British sloop of war *Rattlesnake*, *Essex* ran her 'Hull down in about four hours'.[5]

She sailed to the Dutch East Indies to convoy American merchantmen, returning in late 1800 and thus becoming the first American naval vessel to double the Cape of Good Hope. After service in the Quasi-War, the frigate was considered useful enough to be retained by the navy in the reductions of the Peace Establishment Act (PEA) of 1801. She was given a complete repair in 1807 through early 1809. Inspection revealed that many of her white oak lower futtocks were rotten and these were replaced by live oak timbers. Much of her decks, beams and knees were replaced. Her wales and thick strakes were raised and her tumblehome reduced, under the direction of Josiah Fox.[6]

Additionally, by the time she was in commission again her battery had been radically altered. She was now armed with forty 32pdr carronades and six long 12pdrs. Captain David Porter was not pleased with this arrangement and wrote Secretary of the Navy Paul Hamilton: 'Considering as I do that Carronades are merely an experiment . . . I do not conceive it proper to trust the honor of the flag entirely with them. Was this ship to be disabled in her rigging in the early part of an engagement, a ship much inferior to her in sailing and in force, armed with long guns, could take a position beyond the reach of our Carronades, and cut us to pieces without our being able to do her any injury.' He requested that four long 18pdrs be used to replace four defective carronades on the gun deck.[7] Secretary Hamilton refused, but Porter persisted, to the extent of requesting a transfer to a ship with a 'due proportion' of carronades.[8] Later, Hamilton relented somewhat and gave permission to replace the 12s with 18s. For reasons unknown, Porter apparently did not implement this change and her battery remained a combination of carronades and long 12pdrs.[9]

Porter, unfortunately, had predicted the fate of his ship. After rounding Cape Horn and playing havoc with the British whaling fleet in 1813 and early 1814, she was set upon by HMS *Phoebe*, 36, and *Cherub*, 18, off Valparaiso, Chile. Initially, at short range, Porter's carronades did significant damage. Then *Essex* lost her main topmast and was forced toward shore. At this point, the *Phoebe*, armed with long 18s, stood beyond carronade range and decimated Porter's vessel. The carpenter's after-action report, a copy of which resides at the Naval Historical Center, reflects the tale: 'The shot were planted so thick in the hull they could not be well counted, but supposed to be upwards of 200 18 [pdrs] through the larb. side below the spar deck . . . The starb. side much injured . . . The head shot away . . . The bullwarks [*sic*] of the ForeCastles nearly demolished . . . Five shot through the center of the foremast . . .'[10] After over two hours in action, the casualty count was over 120. With no other recourse, Porter surrendered. It was a defeat which could well have been avoided.

Essex early in her career: watercolour by Joseph Howard. Her pronounced sheer and delicate head gave her a rather dated appearance for the times. [US Navy]

Essex towards the end of her career. A major rebuild modernised her appearance, including reducing her sheer. Note that the number of ports shown in this drawing is erroneous. [US Navy]

Essex was taken into the Royal Navy and became a prison ship in 1833. She was sold four years later.

Philadelphia

Originally named *City of Philadelphia*, this frigate was the result of a subscription drive which raised $100,000 in one week of June 1798. The subscribers had intended to build two 20-gun vessels with their funds, but were persuaded by Secretary of the Navy Stoddert to build a single large frigate of 36 or more guns.

Construction was at Joshua Humphreys' yard, by his son Samuel, Nathaniel Hutton and John Delavue, but design of the ship was by Josiah Fox. Why Philadelphian Joshua Humphreys himself was not called upon to design this ship is an open question, though the answers are obvious. First, the Humphreys 44-gun design was available, but it appears that someone in authority made the decision that this plan would not do. And, in fact, as has been shown in the case of

the *Chesapeake*, Secretary Stoddert was not an exponent of the 'big frigate' idea. He wrote Jeremiah Yellot, naval agent in Baltimore that 'The Frigates heretofore built have been on a scale too large'.[11] As Josiah Fox was available, and had shown himself equally opposed to the large frigate concept, Stoddert had him provide the design, or at least recommended him to the Philadelphia committee–apparently shortly after Fox consulted with him on the 'reduced' design for *Chesapeake*.

There may have been a financial question involved with the choice of a smaller frigate design. *Constitution*, for instance, cost $302,718.84, some 260 per cent over original estimates, and *Constellation* had consumed about $314,000; *United States*, which had been built in the same yard as the proposed vessel, cost over $299,000.[12] Though these three vessels were just being completed when the subscription drives were under way, it was already a matter of public record that 'extraordinary expenditures' had been invested. A congressional report of March 1798 enumerated the amount, and even at that juncture *Constellation* had consumed over $200,000, and *Constitution* and *United States* over $190,000 and $160,000 respectively.[13] These were daunting sums in 1798, when the typical merchant vessel might be built for around $75,000. Indeed, it appeared that the Philadelphia subscription had run out of steam at $100,000. And the merchants of that city were probably not interested in seeing their funds used for a doubtful cause, particularly if the Secretary of the Navy himself was not behind it. In any event, *Philadelphia* was completed for $179,349.[14]

The Fox design was for a ship 157ft between perpendiculars, 130ft keel, by 39ft moulded beam and 13ft 6in depth of hold. She was six feet shorter than *Constellation*, and six longer than *Chesapeake*. Again, as with *Chesapeake*, she was to carry 44 guns with a gun deck battery of 18pdrs. As with the larger frigates, substantial gangways connected the forecastle and quarterdeck. Another similarity was the use of diagonal riders, apparently of white oak.[15] The *Philadelphia* was launched on 28 November 1799, to the salutes of naval ships *Ganges*, *Richmond* and *Augusta*, in attendance. She was universally regarded as a handsome ship and her carving, including a full length figurehead of Hercules, was by William Rush.[16]

The appearance of the vessel is somewhat uncertain, as the earliest outboard plan was drawn in the 1820s by Henry Allen, a navy department draughtsman. It appears Allen worked from a table of offsets and his draught disagrees with an original sail and outboard plan of the vessel. The latter showed open rails; the Allen plan, solid bulwarks.[17] Also, the Allen plan shows a head configuration more in keeping with the 1820s. However, it is likely that she followed the pattern of the larger frigates in having her rails planked in during this period.

The makeup of her original battery is also of some uncertainty, except for her twenty-eight 18s on the main deck. On the spar deck it was planned that she carry twelve 32pdr carronades, but these were not available when she sailed and only six were mounted. It does appear that six long 12pdrs were substituted for the absent carronades, making her total battery 40 guns.[18] By the time of her loss in 1803, the 12s had been displaced and she had sixteen carronades on her upper decks.[19] As to rate, she was classified as a 44-gun frigate until June 1803, when it was determined that recent alterations had reduced her to a 36.[20]

Philadelphia began her short career in the West Indies, under Stephen Decatur, Sr, and quickly gained a reputation for speed. She was thought to be the fastest vessel there, saving *President*.[21] The impressive list of her prizes and boardings reflects both a zealous commanding officer and a turn of speed. She was laid up for a short time after the close of the Quasi-War, then was sent to the Mediterranean to deal with the Barbary 'pirates'. Her grounding, capture

by the Tripolitans and destruction at the hands of the Americans is a well known and heroic event in the panoply of US naval history. It is obvious that the *Philadelphia* itself had been a ornament to the service and had possessed great potential – a career cut tragically short.

New York

Frederick Leiner refers to the frigate *New York* as the 'squandered ship', and she certainly had a short and undistinguished service life. It is, however, nearly an unwritten rule that Americans unceremoniously dispose of large numbers of otherwise excellent, and sometimes nearly new warships when peace is declared. *New York* actually had a relatively long career compared to the many vessels which were immediately sold at the conclusion of the Quasi-War.

The impetus for building this vessel was not only the patriotic zeal and example of Newburyport, but French audacity: in May 1798 a privateer under the *tricolore* seized the American merchant ship *Thomas* within sight of the Narrows – the entrance to New York harbour. By mid-June outrage had opened local purse strings, and subscription

Frigate *Philadelphia*, designed by Josiah Fox. Again, though a smaller vessel than *Constellation*, Fox rated her as a 44. This plan was made by navy draughtsman Henry Allen around 1820 and, as H I Chapelle noted, is probably incorrect in showing a solid rail on her quarterdeck and amidships. Also the head configuration is more characteristic of the 1820s than 1790s. [US Navy, from *Naval Documents of the Barbary Wars*]

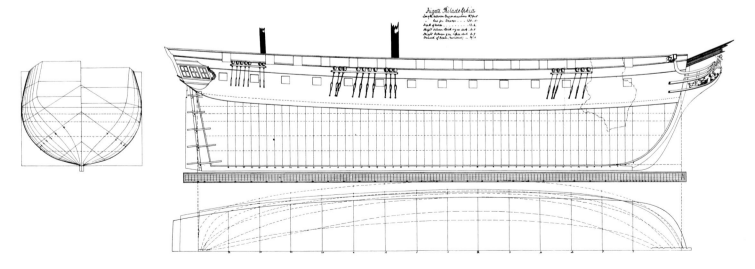

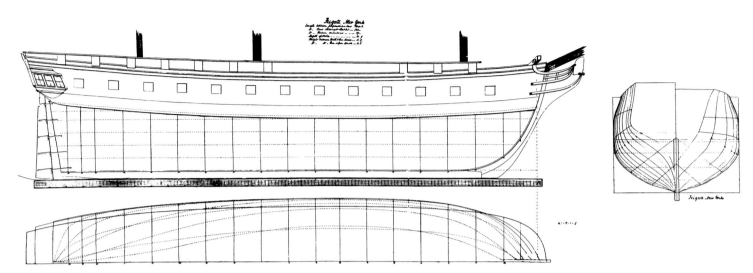

Frigate *New York*. Another Henry Allen drawing containing the same errors as those noted for *Philadelphia*: incorrect spar deck bulwarks and head design. Allen used offset tables for the hull lines, so these can be considered accurate. [US Navy, from *Naval Documents of the Barbary Wars*]

papers were circulating. By the end of the month about $70,000 had been raised.[22]

Secretary Stoddert immediately wrote to the subscription committee and suggested they build at least a 36-gun vessel, rather than the two 20-gun ships which was apparently their first choice. Stoddert noted that Congress was expected to approve subscription 'stock' for major warships from four cities of great 'commercial importance': Philadelphia, Baltimore, Boston and New York, and that the lesser municipalities would likely favour the smaller vessels. Philadelphia, he continued, had determined to build a 44-gun vessel of 1000 tons, and he hoped New York would match that effort.[23] The secretary was obviously counting on a dose of municipal rivalry to assist his quest to obtain warships with relatively little cost to the navy itself.

In anticipation of the committee's next step, Stoddert had Joshua Humphreys forward to them sample dimensions of 44-, 38-, and 36-gun frigates. Significantly, all were to carry 18pdr main batteries. No mention was made of the 24pdr frigates, three of which were nearly ready for sea.[24] It appears that these were truly considered an experiment, not to be repeated until they had proven themselves. The New Yorkers did not meet the implicit challenge from Philadelphia: their decision was to build a 36-gun ship,

measuring 144ft 2in between perpendiculars by 37ft moulded beam, and 11ft 9in depth of hold. The design was by Samuel Humphreys, and she was to be built by Peck and Carpenter on the East River.

Her exact appearance is unknown, as the only extant original plan of the ship is an inboard profile. The earliest outboard plan, presented in the seventh volume of the navy's *Barbary Wars* documents, is also, like the plan of *Philadelphia*, a copy of one drawn by Henry Allen in the 1820s.[25] This shows a solid bulwark forward to about the fore mast, with ten ports on forecastle and quarterdeck. Chapelle's outboard plan shows an open rail in place of the bulwark, and thirteen gun positions, including three in the waist. There are also differences in the head rails and profile of each interpretation of the ship.[26] As the vessel no doubt had her rails planked up early in her service, Chapelle's rendering may be accurate for her original appearance.

The *New York*'s service record was undistinguished. Her completion coincided with the cessation of hostilities with France and she made one uneventful sortie to the Caribbean before being laid up in 1801. She was re-commissioned for the Mediterranean in August 1802, and became the flagship of Commodore Richard V Morris, who was noted for his inactivity during his tenure in that post. During this cruise, the most calamitous event was an explosion and fire in the gunner's storeroom. The fire was threatening the magazine until Captain Chauncey and Lieutenant Porter led the way below and stanched the flames with wet blankets and water. Fourteen were killed in the disaster and at one point Morris had her boats out to abandon ship.[27]

The *New York* returned to the US in December 1804 and was laid up at Washington Navy Yard. Her rotting hulk somehow survived the burning of the yard in 1814, and was allowed to moulder away in the mud of the eastern branch (now the Anacostia River).[28]

Boston

The frigate *Boston* was the product of an enthusiastic outpouring of funds sparked by the actions of the merchants of Newburyport. They raised over $115,000 in two days, and $136,000 in total. The subscriber committee selected Edmund Hartt to design the vessel, and it was built in the yard which had produced the *Constitution*. She was 134ft between perpendiculars and 34ft 6in moulded beam, with depth of hold measuring 11ft 6in. Her original battery was to be twenty-four 12pdrs on the gun deck and six to eight 6pdrs on the forecastle and quarterdeck.[29] In service, in 1800, she carried twenty-four 12s and eight 9pdrs.[30] In 1801, on leaving for Mediterranean duty, twelve 32pdr carronades had replaced the 9pdrs on her upper decks.[31]

She was laid down 22 August 1798, launched 20 May 1799, and cost $119,570. Her copper sheathing, spikes, and bolts had been supplied by Paul Revere. It was said that she was the first American ship built with American-made copper fastenings.[32] Once at sea, her commanding officer,

George Little, reported that she 'exceeded even the most sanguine expectations of Bostonians in sailing.'[33] Though he also commented positively on her speed, *Boston* trailed *Constitution* in two separate trials in late 1799–and *Constitution* had not been noted for her speed in her early commissions.[34]

Boston's Quasi-War service was marked by eight captures, including the French frigate or corvette *Le Berceau*. The latter mounted twenty-two 9pdrs, and two 12s and put up a spirited defence, lasting over two hours, in two separate engagements. Both vessels expended masses of ammunition, but were aiming high–to preserve the prize's hull. In the end, there were seven American casualties and fifty-two French.[35] *Le Berceau* was the second major French naval vessel captured during the conflict, and she was towed and jury-sailed to Boston, where she was repaired. Though purchased through the prize court into the navy, she never served, and was repatriated to France in September 1801.

The frigate *Boston* was retained by the navy during the reductions in force of 1801, and was subsequently re-rated as a 28-gun ship.[36] She was sent to the Mediterranean, with a stop to deliver the American minister, Robert Livingston, to France. Her somewhat routine blockade duty was interrupted by an attack by three Tripolitan gunboats in May

Frigate *Boston*, 32 guns, designed by Edmund Hartt and built at the same shipyard as *Constitution*. [US Navy, from *Naval Documents of the Barbary Wars*]

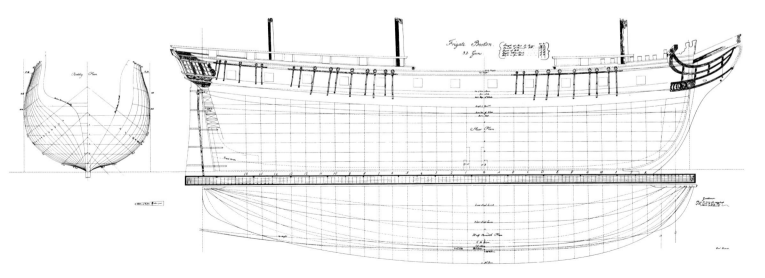

56   SAILING WARSHIPS OF THE US NAVY

1802, when she sank one and drove off the others. She returned in the fall and was laid up in ordinary at Washington Navy Yard. In June 1804, Josiah Fox surveyed the ship, and reported she was in an 'unfavorable' condition. Two years later he stated that it would take the 'cost of a new ship' to repair her.[37] No attempt was made at salvage and the hulk was destroyed at the yard in 1814.

John Adams

From 1799 to 1814 the navy employed the vessels *Adams* and *John Adams*, both 28-gun frigates, in the inventory. Both were in the Quasi-War, both were in the Mediterranean squadron *together* in 1802-3, and both were laid up at Washington Navy Yard in 1804. Additionally, each was commanded by Captain Hugh G Campbell while in the Mediterranean. (Campbell commanded *Adams* from late 1802 until he was transferred directly to *John Adams*, in June 1803.) For the researcher two centuries removed, this creates much confusion. It is probably significant that *Adams* fired upon *John Adams* at one point during the blockade of Tripoli.

Period illustration of 'two sided' frigate *John Adams*, built at Charleston. Due to an error in building, she was asymmetrical, with the larboard side of her hull wider than the starboard. [US Navy]

In any event, *John Adams* was a subscription frigate built in the Cochran yard by Paul Pritchard of Charleston, South Carolina. The city subscription committee raised over $100,000 in late July and early August 1798, with the total coming to $114,000, and plans were made to build a 24-gun ship with the funds.[38] Josiah Fox supplied plans for the vessel, but during construction five feet was added to her length, adding another gunport to her broadside. Another anomaly was the old ' two sided frigate' tradition which held that the vessel was not symmetrical: one side was wider that the other, caused, it was said, by different contractors cutting frames for each side. When she was rebuilt in 1809, Josiah Fox confirmed this, writing: 'From an unknown cause she is wider on the Larboard than Starboard side, and always tends to list starboard, from which circumstance I am inclined to believe she will be considerably stiffer on the starboard than on the larboard tack.'[39] No plans of the ship have survived, other than a body plan, but she was said to have been 127ft 9in on the gun deck and 33ft 3in extreme beam, depth 16ft 10in (ceiling to gun deck). Her carvings were by William Rush and her figurehead was a bust of President Adams.[40]

She was launched in June 1799 and was commissioned on 25 August under Captain John Rodgers. Her battery at that time was twenty-four 12pdrs, two long 9s, and six 24pdr carronades. She was the first American naval vessel with carronades mounted as part of her original battery.[41] At sea, she proved to be overly tender, with poor steering. The weight of her upperworks strained her wales and caused much leakage.[42] Another of her commanders remarked: 'She cannot pass for more than a tolerable sailing merchant ship, and so crank that a ship of 20 guns ought to take her, in what would generally be called a topgallant breeze for ships of war.'[43] However, under Captain George Cross, she was quite active during the Quasi-War, capturing two French privateers and recapturing eight American vessels on her first cruise.

After the end of the French hostilities, and her retention in the down-sized navy establishment, *John Adams* was laid up for a short time at Washington. She returned to duty in October 1802, under the command of John Rodgers, this time in the Mediterranean. Under Rodgers, the *Meshouda*, one of the largest vessels in the Tripolitan fleet was boarded and captured. Shortly afterwards, with the assistance of the schooner *Enterprise, John Adams* fired on a Tripolitan 22-gun corvette which was supported by nine gunboats. After a spirited 45-minute exchange, the polacre surrendered – then suddenly blew up, throwing masts and spars 150 feet in the air.[44] Shortly after this, as noted above, *John Adams* was fired upon by the frigate *Adams* while off Tripoli. The incident occurred when *John Adams* fell in between *Adams* and a group of Tripolitan gunboats. The latter attempted to fire over the former, and in the process the shot passed through *John Adams'* fore topgallant bowlines.[45]

John Adams returned to the US later that year, then was twice sent to the Mediterranean theatre as a storeship in 1804, carrying in one instance over 490 men, most of whom were crew replacements. At the time her guns were housed (*en flute*) to maximise space for men and supplies. She also escorted several of the new gunboats so favoured by Jefferson across the Atlantic.[46] During her Atlantic crossing in June, she was found to be leaking copiously – six to eight inches per hour, and steering badly, so repairs were in order after the end of the war.[47]

The frigate underwent modifications as well as repairs during the post-war years. In 1807 a major repair began at Washington and continued through 1809. Josiah Fox superintended the cutting-down of her upperworks, converting her from a frigate to a corvette. He discovered in the process that her frame – chiefly of live oak – was still sound.[48] At the outset of the War of 1812, she received a quarterdeck, but no forecastle, becoming what was termed a 'jack-ass frigate'.[49] Her armament in the latter state was 24 guns. In 1820, this battery was composed of twenty 32pdr carronades and four long 18pdrs.[50]

She was blockaded in New York for much of the War of 1812, but returned to Mediterranean duty with Commodore Stephen Decatur's squadron in 1815. Subsequently, she served in the West Indies anti-piracy squadron, the South Atlantic, and on the anti-slavery patrol off the coast of West Africa. In 1827, at Norfolk (Gosport), it was obvious she was in dire condition, to the extent that repairs had been suspended. Captain James Barron wrote John Rodgers that a survey of her would result in her condemna-tion.[51] He was correct: it was determined that repairs would require somewhat over $32,000, compared to the cost of a new vessel at $65,000.[52] In a more drastic vein, it was also decided that the 'form of the vessel was objectionable'.[53]

Rather than repair the ship, the decision was made to build a new ship 'in lieu of the old' vessel, but retaining the name *John Adams*.[54] Because of these circumstances, it is not clear when the first *John Adams* ceased to exist, though it was probably early 1830 when the dismantling was complete. The history of the new vessel, as well as the controversy surrounding the 'administrative rebuilding' of naval vessels in this era, will be detailed under the section on the sloop of war *John Adams* in Chapter 6. However, at this point it is sufficient to point out that, at the time, there was no question that the vessel on the stocks in August 1830 was a new hull. Secretary of the Navy John Branch wrote to President Jackson: 'On a partial inspection of the Navy yard . . . I was surprised to find a new sloop of war almost ready for launching.'[55] The contretemps which followed in the department was not concerning whether this was a new ship or not, but rather on the legality of using 'repair' funds for new construction.

The Contract-Built Frigates

As an element in the build up to challenge the French depredations, Congress also allowed funds for building vessels by contract or purchasing them outright. Two frigates and five smaller vessels were built: the former were the *Adams* and *General Greene*; the latter were the ships *Portsmouth, Connecticut, Warren*, and schooners *Enterprise* and *Experiment*. The frigates, which were to carry 28 guns, are presented here, while the other contract vessels will be dealt with in subsequent chapters.

Adams

Not to be confused with *John Adams*, this vessel was built in Brooklyn by John Jackson and William Sheffield, and designed by the latter. She was 113ft on the gun deck, by 34ft moulded beam, and 10ft 9in depth of hold. She was laid down on 30 July 1798 and launched on 8 June 1799.

She was in commission in September of that year. Her carving was by Daniel Train, and figurehead was a full length representation of President Adams. She was originally armed with twenty-four 12pdrs, and possibly four 6s.[56] No plans of the vessel have been found, as was common for the smaller contract-built ships.

She was said to have been a 'remarkably fast sailer'. However, in 1802 when she was being fitted for Mediterranean service, Edward Preble complained that she was 'not well constructed for a frigate', being too narrow and sharp and deep. She was, furthermore, over-masted and required so much ballast that she could only carry three months provisions. At that juncture, he requested permission to *reduce* her battery to 32 guns, indicating she had carried 38 on her previous cruise. Permission was granted for the reduction of her battery.[57]

Adams made two cruises in the Quasi-War, making several captures. In January 1800 she was out-sailed by the *Connecticut* – though that ship was ostensibly the fastest vessel in the navy.[58] A 'rebuttal' to the letter describing the above sailing trial appeared subsequently in a Salem paper, in which the writer claimed *Adams* was in poor condition – out of trim, etc – at the time of the contest. The writer claimed *Connecticut*'s reputation was 'all fudge'.[59]

Following her refit and reduction in battery, *Adams* sailed to the Mediterranean, under Captain Campbell. After blockade duty she returned to Washington Navy Yard in 1803, where she was repaired and refitted. She sailed again in 1805, cruising the east coast and protecting American commerce.

At the outbreak of the second war with England, she was lengthened by 15 feet and converted to a sloop of war. At the same time 10 inches was added to her beam 'to preserve her form'.[60] She ended her career on the Penobscot River in Maine, armed with four long 18pdrs, twenty short 18s, and two long 12s.[61] Severely damaged and leaking after grounding at the entrance to Penobscot Bay, she was moved to Hampden, Maine for repairs. A British expedition pursued and Captain Charles Morris removed her guns to shore and prepared to either defend or burn her, supported by local militia. In the event, the militia scattered and he fired the *Adams*.[62]

General Greene

As with *Adams*, no plans of this vessel are known to exist. Another parallel with *Adams* is that *General Greene* shared her name with a second vessel serving simultaneously. In this instance, the confusion is reduced somewhat by the fact that the second *General Greene* was a revenue cutter sloop of 10 guns, operating with the navy during the Quasi-War.

The frigate *General Greene* was built at Warren, Rhode Island. Her construction was under way by August 1798 and she was launched on 21 January 1799. Her builders were Benjamin Talman and James DeWolf and she measured 124ft 3in on the gun deck, by 34ft 8in beam, and 17ft 3in depth of hold. Her battery was twenty-four 12pdrs and six 6pdrs, and her cost to the government was $105,492.[63] It appears she may have been built to merchant ship lines adapted to naval use as described by the naval agents responsible for re-fitting her in August 1801: 'The *General Greene* is a full built ship with a very round bottom, she was set up for the Canton trade, to carry her Tonnage and sail fast, she is a remarkable buoyant vessel.'[64] Her figurehead was of Revolutionary hero Nathaniel Greene.[65]

Despite a mercantile hull form, she proved quite useful during the war with France, and participated in one of the lesser known aspects of the conflict. Under Captain Christopher R Perry, she was stationed in Haiti during Toussaint L'Ouverture's revolution against the French colonial government. Though *General Greene* served for a time as a safe haven for Americans during the conflict, Perry was less than neutral in some of the vessel's other actions. *General Greene* actively prevented supplies from reaching Toussaint's opposition and lent gunfire support to the rebels in February 1800, aiding their capture of the fortifications at Jacmel. Later, *General Greene* transported Toussaint's representatives to the US to meet President Adams.[66] Perry and his ship later received an official letter of appreciation from Toussaint, for their actions supporting his cause.

She returned to the United States and was laid up at Washington, where she became a sheer hulk in 1805. *General Greene* was destroyed in the yard in August 1814.

Captured Frigates

French engraving by J-J Baugean of a small American frigate, probably *Boston*, in the Mediterranean, about 1802. [US Navy]

In the three conflicts of this era, eight large, frigate-size warships were captured by the US Navy, other than those involved on the lakes. The first two, during the Quasi-War, were *L'Insurgente* and *Le Berceau*. The latter, a 22-gun vessel taken by *Boston*, was repaired, purchased into the navy then returned to France before she could be used by the navy. *L'Insurgente*, captured by Truxtun in *Constellation*, was quickly repaired and commissioned as *Insurgent*. The Tripolitan navy's *Meshouda* was a 26-gun vessel boarded and taken by *Adams*. This vessel was returned without serving in the navy.

In the War of 1812, the *Constitution* defeated *Guerriere*, *Java*, *Cyane*, and *Levant*. Of these, the first two were too badly damaged to bring in and were sunk on the high seas. The *Levant* was re-captured by the British, but the small frigate *Cyane* came home as a prize and was retained by the navy. Finally, *Macedonian* was captured by *United States* early in the war. She was towed home, repaired and remained active in the navy until the mid-1830s, a much touted trophy ship. Only the vessels with active service, *Insurgent*, *Macedonian*, and *Cyane* will be considered here.

Insurgent

The French Republic's frigate *L'Insurgente*, was taken in February 1799, and was the first major foreign warship captured since the Revolutionary War. She had been built at the French navy's L'Orient shipyard and laid down in 1793. She measured 149ft on the gun deck, 37ft 5in extreme breadth, and 11ft 9in depth of hold, and was, therefore, significantly smaller than *Constellation*, and roughly equivalent to the 32-gun *Essex* in dimensions. She carried forty guns when captured, though six or eight were 6pdrs.[67]

Truxtun noted she was 'much damaged' in her rigging, and had her main topmast and mizzen topmast shot away in the engagement. Though the Frenchman had some seventy casualties, she could not have had major hull damage, as repairs were completed in around three weeks at St Kitts. She was actively cruising with *Constellation* by early March.[68] Together they captured the French sloop *Union*, by ruse: the two vessels, one under the American, and one under the French flag, fired on each other in a mock battle, drawing out the French vessel, intending to assist his countryman. *Union* was promptly captured by the two ships. Shortly afterwards, both returned to the United States.[69]

She was purchased through the prize court for $84,500 and sailed again in mid-August 1799 for Europe. She called at Lisbon and was the first American naval vessel to visit that place. She returned to cruise in the West Indies, then to the US in the spring of 1800. *Insurgent* apparently had a turn of speed. She out-sailed the British frigate *Phaeton* in Europe, and the swift sloop of war *Maryland* in a two-day contest off Cayenne. She was, in turn, beaten by the sloop *Connecticut*.[70]

She then underwent major repairs in Baltimore, possibly including replacing her masts and coppering, both of which had been the subject of concern before her previous cruise.[71] In August she sailed again and was lost at sea, apparently in a mid-September storm in the West Indies.

Macedonian

The British frigate *Macedonian*, captured by *United States* in October 1812, was a relatively new vessel, having been launched in June 1810 and, at the time of her capture, fresh from refit.[72] She was a 38-gun ship, with a main deck battery of 18pdrs, but her total battery was 49 guns: twenty-eight 18s, two 12s, two 9s, sixteen 32pdr carronades, and one 18pdr boat carronade.[73]

Macedonian was a standard British design, built of oak and measuring 156ft between perpendiculars, 38ft 9in moulded beam, and 13ft 6in depth of hold. By comparison, she was approximately the size of *Chesapeake*.[74] She was significantly faster and more handy than her victorious adversary, *United States*, and was decorated with a figurehead representing Alexander the Great.

Macedonian was heavily damaged in the engagement. Some one hundred shot lodged in her hull, and her mizzen mast and fore and main topmasts had gone by the board, along with most of her rigging.[75] Two weeks' work was needed to put her in condition to sail safely to the US. In April 1813, after more permanent repairs were accomplished, she sailed under US colours, but was blockaded at New London, Connecticut for the duration of the conflict.

Immediately after the war, she was part of the American squadron sent to end the depredations of the Barbary powers in 1815. Subsequently, while at Charlestown yard (Boston) she was found to need thorough repairs of her decks, though her frame was sound.[76] Once these were completed, she was sent to the Pacific from 1819 to 1821. Her final two cruises were in the West Indies, combating piracy, and another cruise in the Pacific. In 1829 she was reported to need 'thorough and extensive repairs', and, more specifically, 'The whole of this ship, except her lower futtocks and floors, are in a state of decay and requires to be rebuilt.' The cost estimate was over $173,000.[77]

As with *John Adams*, the *Macedonian* was now a candidate for 'rebuilding'. The navy did not want to lose a frigate from the inventory, and certainly did not wish to give up the prestige of a prize captured from the British, but this particular ship was no longer viable. On 6 April 1831, James Barron at Gosport reported she had been 'hauled up on the bank' and was 'in a situation favourable for cutting up'.[78] In February 1833 the keel for a new *Macedonian* was laid, and by August 1834, the old vessel had been broken up.[79] Apparently some measures were taken to re-create the above-water appearance of the old ship, and some of her ironwork was re-used. However, the new hull was begun from the keel up, to a new, modern design, about eight feet longer and over two feet beamier than the old plan. Indeed, both hulls existed simultaneously. Therefore, the 1833 *Macedonian* was a new ship, to be treated in the following chapter.[80]

Cyane

The *Cyane*, by her dimensions and tonnage was approximately the size of a sloop of war. However, she was 'frigate-built', having both gun deck and spar deck (forecastle and quarterdeck) batteries. She had been built in 1805 at Topsham, and was originally intended to carry 22 guns (9pdrs). She measured 118ft by 32ft by British methods, or 120ft 4in by 31ft 6in by the US Navy. With her full-height bulwarks, open waist with nettings, and guns fore and aft, she was 'very imposing in her appearance'[81] – essentially a two-third's length frigate. At the time of her capture, on 20 February 1815, she was also imposingly armed: twenty-two 32pdr carronades, eight 18pdr carronades, two 12pdr carronades and two standard 12s, a total of 34 guns.

The engagement with *Constitution* left *Cyane* a wreck. Her rigging was totally mangled and two masts were on the verge of toppling. She had been holed about ten times between wind and water and had five feet of water in the hold. Her thin scantlings had failed to resist *Constitution*'s 24pdrs.[82] The vessel was purchased through the prize courts and, after repairs, made her first cruise under American colours in 1819. Though recommendations were made in 1819 to cut her down to a corvette, this was apparently not done immediately, as she continued to carry nearly the same battery through 1820.[83] Some modifications were apparently made during her refit in the years 1821-4 as by 1822 she was listed as a corvette and rated at 24 guns.[84]

She made four cruises in her service career: in turn as part of the Africa, West Indies, Mediterranean and Brazil squadrons. By 1829 constructor Samuel Humphreys reported she required 'heavy repairs' and she did not go to sea again.[85] Funds were made available to 'rebuild' *Cyane* in 1831 and 1834, and the result was a completely new sloop

of war, launched in 1837.[86] The original British ship was laid up at Philadelphia and broken up in 1836.[87]

The *Guerrierre* Class Frigates, 1813

After the 'Jeffersonian Revolution' of March 1801, the emphasis in the navy was on defending the nation's port cities with small gunboats manned by a naval militia. Despite growing tensions with the British (and French), which were dealt with in the Non-Intercourse acts, little was done to prepare the navy for meeting any foreign power on the high seas.

Reluctance of the administration to expand the navy, even after the declaration of war in June 1812, was such that no authorisation for new frigate construction was made until 5 January 1813. (Thus the only additions to the frigate inventory between 1800 and 1815, when the new ships were commissioned, were the captured *Cyane* and *Macedonian*). In fact, the timing of this act is instructive: the storied Washington naval ball at which *Guerriere*'s flag was the centrepiece, and, into which Decatur's lieutenant, Archibald Hamilton, muddy from travel, dramatically strode, *Macedonian* flag in hand – and which he gallantly unrolled at the feet of Dolly Madison – had been 8 December 1812.[88]

The Congressional authorisation was for six frigates, only three of which were built during the war. These were named *Columbia*, and – in honour of the *Constitution*'s sunken prizes – *Guerriere* and *Java*. Their design was by William Doughty, who had been hired a full month after their authorisation, but had already written to Secretary of the Navy Jones with ideas for improving the 44s.[89] It is obvious from looking at the respective draughts, that Doughty began with the plans of the 1794 frigates, only slightly altering their dimensions, and dispensing with guns in the waist. Both classes were 175ft between perpendiculars, but Doughty added one foot to the beam, making the new vessels 44ft 6in. Their depth of hold was 13ft 8in, six inches shallower than Humphreys' plan. Externally, the most pronounced differences were in the stem and stern: the new ships showed significantly less rake in both. They also displayed a somewhat straighter sheer.

Their hull lines, both fore and aft, were fuller. The difference between the entrance lines of each class is something in the order of fifteen degrees, with the older ships being the sharper. Aft, the buttock lines of the new vessels were somewhat rounder. These changes, decrease in rake, and increase in breadth and fullness, reflect an obvious response to the criticisms levelled at the *Constitution* and her sisters in service: particularly, as Captain Tingey had put it regarding *United States*, the 'leanness or want of stability in her fore body'.[90]

The ships were rather plainly finished. The early baroque double curves of the stern had given way to a single arch over the stern windows, and billet heads ('fiddle heads') were used in lieu of figureheads. In any event, only two went into service: *Columbia*, though nearly ready for launch, was burned at Washington Navy Yard in 1814. Both remaining vessels went into service too late to participate in the war.

Guerriere

Guerriere, originally to be named *Continental*, was laid down sometime in 1813 at the J & F Grice yard in Philadelphia, and launched on 20 June 1814. John Rodgers mentioned that (Francis) Grice had made some 'alterations' to her during construction, but did not elaborate on his statement. He did recommend arming her gun deck with thirty long 24s, and 42pdr carronades on the spar deck, with a total of 53 guns.[91] Later, in the first year of her service, Bainbridge recommended replacing the 42s with 32s.[92]

As to her appearance, except for Doughty's plan of the class, no published or painted view of *Guerriere* has been found. There is, however, one of the famous Liverpool jugs of the era, showing a port side view of a frigate under sail, labelled 'United States Frigate *Guerriere* Commodore MacDonough'. It is, however, a generic illustration, though the illustration on the reverse is a view of the 'The Gallant Defense of Stonington', lending some credence to the notion that the views may be based on reality. The existence of this piece, as well as another showing the launch of US sloop *Patapsco* (1799), raises some intriguing questions about the sources of the illustrations.[93]

The frigate was ready for sea late in 1814, but was blockaded by the British at one point and later bottled up by ice in the Delaware River. The war ended, and her active service began with participation in Decatur's attack on the Barbary powers in 1815. *Guerriere*, the flagship, inflicted the majority of the damage on the Algerine flagship, the frigate *Meshouda*, in June 1815, including the death of their ranking admiral – victim of a 42pdr shot.[94] The treaty of peace with Algiers was signed on her deck shortly thereafter, and she was the site of the conclusion of peace with Tripoli in August.

The vessel apparently was quite satisfactory in sailing and was recommended by Bainbridge as a 'model' for subsequent 'large 44s'.[95] After another cruise to European waters she became a school ship at Norfolk in 1820, then in 1829 was sent to the Pacific squadron. The last ten years of her existence were spent in ordinary at Norfolk. In 1840 she was surveyed and it was determined that repairs would cost more than a new ship. (Ironically, one of the surveyors was

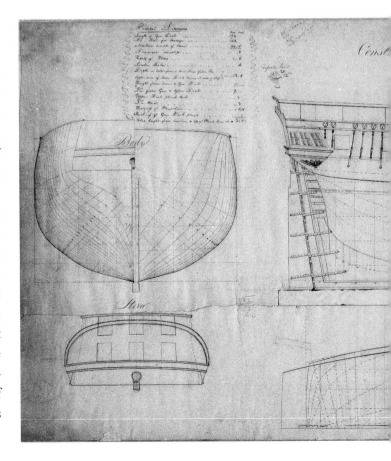

Francis Grice, her builder.) *Guerriere*, lying on the mud flats at Gosport, was cut up in May 1841.[96]

Java

Java had a short, undistinguished career. She was built in Baltimore by Flannigan and Parsons, launched on 4 January 1814, and went to sea in August 1815. Commanded by Oliver Hazard Perry, she was not a favoured vessel. On her first Atlantic crossing, a gale took off a mast, killing five. Perry reported: 'The *Java* does not appear to have been faithfully built, the work in many respects is bad . . . In some of the wales defects have been discovered owing to sap . . . In every part of her the calking [*sic*] was badly performed & she was a little straightened in her launching.' On the positive side, he called her a handsome vessel and admitted that she 'sails & works remarkably well'.[97]

Her career consisted of two cruises in the Mediterranean. The first, from early 1816 to February 1817, ended with her being laid up at Boston. In August of that year, the repairs which were contemplated for her were postponed until the next year, due to their extent. The next summer her 'decayed situation' was mentioned, but by February 1819 Commandant Hull indicated she was prepared for sea duty.[98] However, she did not return to service until 1827, going back to the Mediterranean. In 1831 she ended her active career and was laid up again at Norfolk.

At that juncture, some thought was given to 'procure [-ing] a frame' and rebuilding her, as befitted her 'trophy ship' status.[99] Congress actually authorised funds for this in 1832, but nothing was done.[100] Instead, she became a receiving ship at Norfolk and continued to deteriorate. *Java* was broken up in 1842. Of some twenty-eight years in existence, she had been in active service only about five.

Guerriere class frigates, 1813. These vessels were a variation on Humphreys' 'super-frigates' and were slightly larger, with fuller lines fore and aft. [National Archives 41-9-1B]

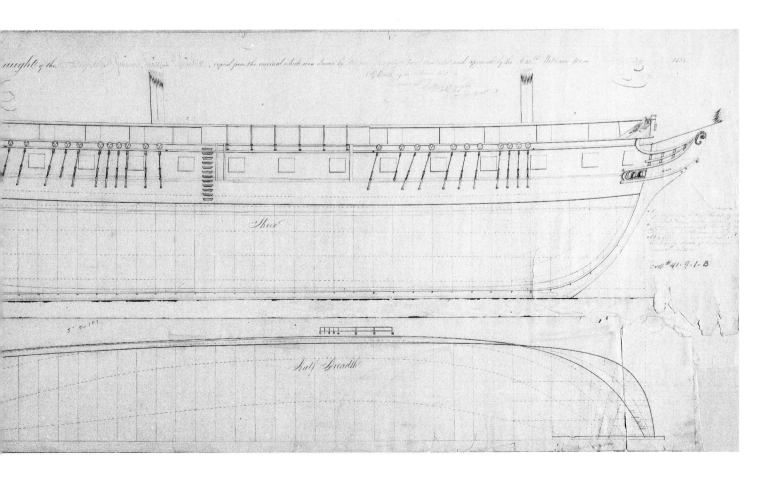

CHAPTER 4

The 'Gradual Increase' Frigates, 1816–1861

IN THE half century from the close of the War of 1812 to the outbreak of the Civil War the navy went about its business in peace. The interruption called the Mexican War scarcely caused a ripple: the Mexican navy hardly existed, so the US Navy provided only blockade, supplies, and amphibious support. Though semi-domestic conflicts–pirates, Native Americans, slavers–provided a rumbling backdrop, the navy's frigates, sloops, and an occasional glowering ship of the line cruised on foreign stations, showing the flag with staunch regularity. In this era, despite the inroads of the sooty, belching steamers, sail was king, and,

Frigate *Brandywine*, off Malta, 6 November 1831. She was the second of the 'Gradual Increase' frigates laid down, but hurried to completion before *Potomac*, to honour Lafayette on his American tour. Also shown is sloop of war *Concord* .[US Navy]

in the US Navy, the sailing frigate was synonymous with the American presence abroad.

With the exception of the Africa anti-slavery patrol squadron, each overseas area typically had a frigate as flagship, and each frigate over the water necessarily required a replacement preparing at home, to succeed the first vessel when she paid off at the close of her two-year cruise. Thus, generally speaking, the navy's quota of frigates was double the number of squadrons–usually six–in being. So the pattern had been set as far back as 1801, which left the navy with thirteen frigates as a 'peace establishment'.

The naval successes of the War of 1812 at least ended the gunboat stranglehold on the service, and paved the way for the 'Act for the Gradual Increase of the Navy of the United States', of 29 April 1816. This legislation called for construction of nine ships of the line and an equal number of frigates, over a period of eight years, with an annual $1 million appropriation. As three of the six frigates authorised in 1813 had not yet been built, there would be a total of twelve frigates built from the date of the 'Gradual Increase' legislation.[1] In 1821 an atmosphere of retrenchment resulted in Congress extending the act for another three years (to 1827), but the annual funding was reduced by half. All the vessels were, additionally, to be built in the navy's new dockyards.[2] The twelve frigates–the last dozen sailing frigates of the US Navy–laid down according to the 'Gradual Increase' act, or in that era, are the subject of this chapter.

Of course, reality modified the regularity of application envisioned in the Gradual Increase act. First, one of the twelve, *Hudson*, by Congressional fiat was purchased from a 'deserving' civilian shipbuilder, disregarding naval opinion on the subject and decreasing by one the number the navy could build according to their own dictates. Second, two of the new ships were actually replacements, under the same names, for the old frigates *Macedonian* and *Congress*. Third, though nine of the twelve were laid down before the act expired, only one (*Brandywine*) was completed. However, it should be remembered that in the naval economy of the times, a ship on the stocks, whether new or being 'rebuilt', was nearly equivalent to one at sea. From a certain point in their construction, finishing a new ship and rehabilitating an old one were identical processes. Furthermore, ships on the stocks were considered as a 'strategic reserve', a policy widely followed in European navies. Beyond a certain point in construction, launching and fitting out could be completed very quickly in times of emergency; and a properly roofed ship on the stocks was regarded as better protected than one afloat.

These nine frigates were laid down in the period 1819 to 1826, as follows: 1819 *Potomac*; 1820 *Brandywine, Columbia* and *Savannah*; 1821 *Santee*; 1823 *Sabine*; 1825 *Cumberland* and *Columbia*; 1826 *St Lawrence*. These frigates formed the mainstay of the pre-Civil War fleet in addition to the venerable *Constitution, United States*, and *Constellation*. The order in which they were laid down had little relationship, however, to the sequence in which they went into service. *Brandywine* led the group, going to sea in 1825, and indeed had the shortest construction time – six years. *Potomac* followed in 1831, twelve years from her inception; 1838 brought *Columbia* – thirteen years from keel-laying. The year 1843 brought three: *Raritan, Savannah* and *Cumberland*, though two of the three were already twenty-three years 'old' at the time. In 1847, in time for the Mexican conflict, *St Lawrence* was completed. *Sabine* and *Santee* (completed in 1858 and 1861, respectively) were afterthoughts of a sort, obsolete before their time and launched essentially to free up building ways for steam men of war. *Sabine* had been building for thirty-five years; *Santee* – the record holder – for forty. The latter had seen from her building ways the entire era of the paddle wheel warship come and go, the introduction of the shell gun, the iron hull, and the armoured warship.

Naturally, other factors had affected the completion of these ships. *Hudson* had been accepted as a 'replacement' for a navy-built vessel in 1828. The newly built *Macedonian* and *Congress* had come along in 1832 and 1842 respectively. Also in the mix was *Independence*, a liner cut down to become a very successful and impressive large frigate (1846). Confusing the issue were the new steamers, vessels such as *Mississippi* (1840), *Susquehanna* and *Powhatan*, of the 1850s. In number and arrangement of guns these were sloops of war, but in size and prestige, they were equivalent to frigates. Of course, the mid-1850s saw the first screw propelled steam frigates, signifying to all that sail – without steam in the same hull at least – was dead.

This group of ships marks the final flowering of the sailing frigate in the United States Navy. The ships of the era included reflections of then-current trends: reduction of tumblehome and thick wales, the round (elliptical) stern, and decrease in sheer and carving. In battery, they marked the summation of the trend which began with the 1794 designs: they were built with guns the full length of the spar deck and the accompanying full-height bulwarks. Further, during this period, the navy adopted a policy of the single-calibre gun throughout the ship – in this instance, the use of various weights of 32pdr weapons. It was not long after this that the shell gun was introduced, leading to a revolution in armament which would come to fruition coincident with the adoption of steam propulsion.

Though obsolete by the 1850s, these dozen ships, with the exception of *Hudson*, generally had long, useful careers. All except *Hudson* survived to the Civil War, though two were burned at Norfolk some few days into the conflict. Four served actively on the blockade of the South, and one, *Santee*, served into the twentieth century, though of course in a training role. Two – *Congress* and *Cumberland*, the former considered the epitome of the sailing frigate – became veritable symbols of the end of the sailing navy: they were lost in battle on 8 March 1862 to the Confederate ironclad steamer *Virginia* (ex-*Merrimack*).

Because of the overlapping and lengthy construction times, and the fact that the already-laid down vessels were modified and modernised during construction, these frigates are presented here in chronological order by the date they went into service. The *Hudson, Macedonian* and

Congress will be dealt with after the nine 'class' vessels. (The razee *Independence* is part of the chapter on ships of the line.)

Brandywine

The frigate *Brandywine* was laid down on 20 September 1821, some two years after *Potomac*. Both were begun under chief constructor William Doughty at Washington Navy Yard, and *Brandywine* was completed during his tenure: launched in June 1825 and commissioned on 25 August of that year. *Potomac* was launched in 1822 but not completed until 1831, during the tenure of Samuel Humphreys.[3]

The original hull design of what is usually denominated the *Potomac* class (based on the earliest keel laying) was another variation on the 1794 frigates. The length between perpendiculars remained 175ft as with the *Guerriere* class, but the breadth became a full 45ft, six inches more than the 1813 vessels. Similarly, an extra six inches was added to the depth, this measurement becoming 14ft 4in. The underwater lines became fuller in the buttocks and, minimally, in the entrance lines. Above water, the rake of the stern was increased significantly, and, to a lesser extent, that of the stem. The most obvious change was the complete, armed spar deck, creating an unbroken sheer. These were truly the much-touted 'double-banked' frigates.

The original design was to undergo various alterations as it was applied to the ships authorised in this period. As will be seen, however, *Potomac* probably received the fewest alterations. *Brandywine* received the most obvious external change: the first elliptical stern in the US Navy.

The elliptical stern and its predecessor, the round stern, were the first major changes in hull design since the disappearance of the beakhead bulkhead in the late eighteenth century. The round stern was introduced by the British Surveyor of the Navy (chief designer), Sir Robert Seppings, and appeared, most notably, in the liner *Asia*, laid down in 1817. This innovation was to eliminate the time-honoured windowed stern galleries, so beloved by senior officers, but which were lightly built and invited devastating raking fire in combat. Furthermore, they were unsuitable for mounting heavy stern-chase guns. Up until this time no effort had

been made to strengthen this part of the hull, and this neglect was no doubt due to the difficulty inherent in designing a suitable replacement. The Seppings design essentially used a variety of the cant timber concept to close in the stern, with vertical timbers continuing past the old transom and continuing in a complete arc around the stern, only broken by small windows, plus gunports. Thus, the stern became as substantial as the sides of the vessel, and the quarters and stern could now mount heavier cannon. However, this structure left the rudder head exposed, and, in its original form, disrupted the officers' head facilities; it was also widely regarded as ugly as well as inconvenient.[4]

The elliptical stern addressed the round stern's drawbacks (particularly its aesthetics), and was a modification introduced in Britain by one of Seppings' successors. In this configuration, the stern was flattened, leaving curved quarters and retaining Seppings' structural concept. In ships of the line, this was first seen in 1832.[5] In the US the British-style round stern was never used. The elliptical stern's American origin dates from April 1820, over a decade before it appeared in British liners, in a plan by William Doughty, intended for the *Brandywine*. The plan is annotated 'invented by' constructor Doughty.[6] As that frigate was commissioned in 1825, she was the first vessel with this innovation – antedating the elliptical sterned sloops of war by a year. Plans do not show the *Potomac* with this new stern, and it is

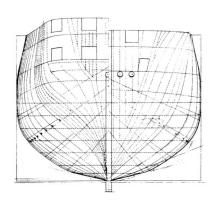

Brandywine again increased dimensions over *Constitution* and *Guerriere*, and was truly a 'double banked' frigate. [National Archives 40-9-5F]

likely that her construction was too far along to allow it to be done to the vessel without major retrofitting.[7] On the other hand, the *Brandywine*'s plans do not show the straighter sheer which was applied to *Potomac* in the course of her building.[8] It is also noteworthy that the Doughty original 'Elliptical Stern Frigate Brandywine' plan shows pencilled-in decorative arches across the stern along with quarter galleries, creating a semblance of the old style stern on the completed ship.[9]

Brandywine was launched and commissioned in 1825, probably armed with 24pdrs on the gun deck and 32pdr carronades on the spar deck. Later, she mounted thirty long 32s on the gun deck and twenty-four 32pdr carronades above. After 1840, four of the 32s were replaced by an equal number of the 8-inch (64pdr) shell guns then coming into the inventory, and in 1847 there were eight 8-inch guns and forty-two 32s on the ship.[10]

We do not know the reasoning behind the completion of this vessel rather than the *Potomac* – particularly since both were built at the same yard, and *Potomac* was begun earlier. However, it may have been to exhibit the thoroughly modern stern in the most favourable circumstances. It is apparent that the completion of this ship was orchestrated to coincide with the end of the Marquis de Lafayette's triumphal visit to the US in 1825 – a date which also celebrated the fiftieth anniversary of the American Revolution.

The ship had been named *Susquehanna* until 1825 and its new designation commemorated Lafayette's first battle in the American Revolution. Lafayette himself noted the name was for a 'brook instead of a river . . . solely to recall my first battle and my wound'.[11] The brand new frigate was selected to receive Lafayette on board with maximum ceremony, and convey him to France. The voyage was of such ceremonial and patriotic moment that twenty-six midshipmen were shipped for the occasion, representing as many states as possible and with as many descendants of Revolutionary veterans as could be found. The ship's fame in this high-profile role was such that she was afterwards referred to as the 'Lafayette'.[12]

The ship proved to be an excellent and fast sailer, and a favourite command. Outward bound with her distinguished passenger, she made 11 knots, and, across the Atlantic, beat a pilot boat off the Needles en route to Gibraltar. Official reports credited her with 10 knots on a bowline and 12 free. In the Mediterranean squadron, she maintained her speedy repute.[13] Matthew Calbraith Perry, commanding the sloop of war *Concord* in 1830, noted that the only vessel in the squadron his ship could not beat 'under press of canvas in a head sea' was *Brandywine*.[14] As has been noted previously, she was only out-sailed by the seemingly rehabilitated *United States*. But it was obvious that she went into that contest with an intact reputation for swiftness, possibly reflect-

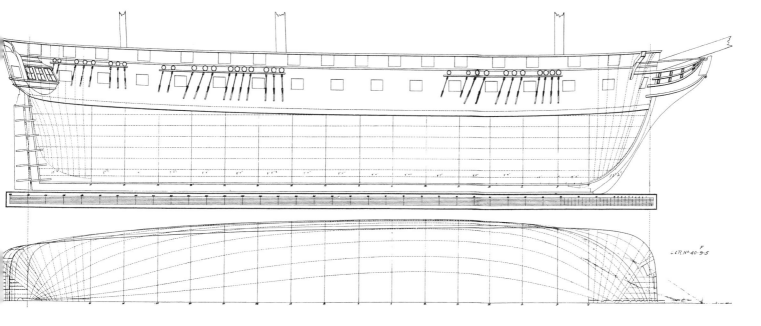

ed by her nickname: 'Roaring *Brandywine*'. Later in her career, her masts were moved, to the detriment of her sailing qualities, rendering her hard on her helm, requiring up to four men to handle her wheel, and with a decided tendency to pitch into a head sea. A reduction in her ballast to some 90 tons resulted in increased leewardness.[15]

The ship made three cruises to the Mediterranean, two to the Pacific, two on the Brazil station, and one each to the Gulf of Mexico and East Indies before being laid up at New York in 1851.[16] When the Civil War broke out she was pressed into service as a stationary storeship for the North Atlantic Blockading Squadron at Hampton Roads. She was

accidentally destroyed by fire at Norfolk on 3 September 1864.

Potomac

Potomac was the first of these ships laid down and the first launched, on 9 August 1819 and 22 March 1822 respectively. She had been in the water over three years when *Brandywine* was commissioned and departed with the Marquis on board. She was finally commissioned on 15 June 1831. During construction she received only one major alteration. In September 1821 constructor Doughty

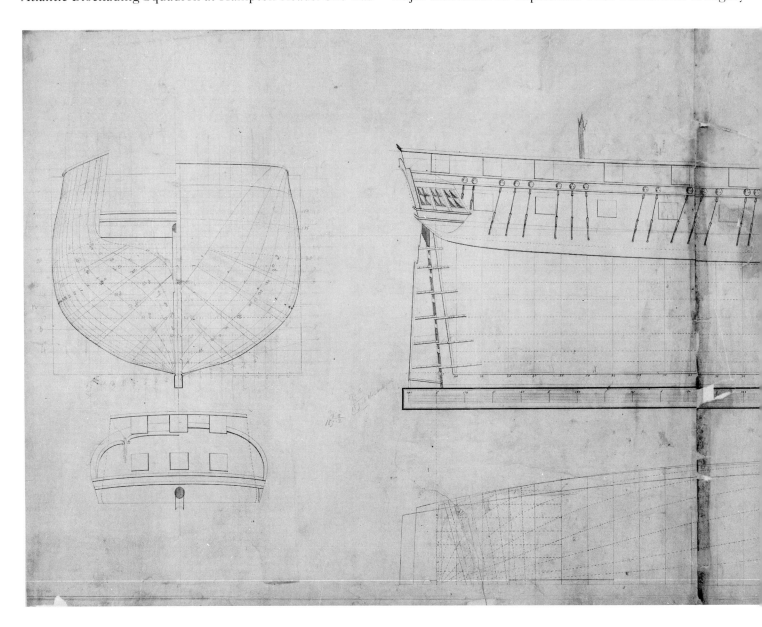

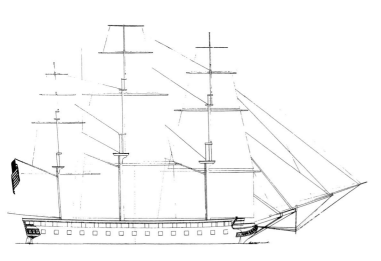

inquired whether she would receive a round (elliptic) stern and a 'straightened sheer', the latter decreased by 10 inches. Lines added later on her plans indicate just such a decrease, and an 1843 sail plan confirms this.[17] Period illustrations also reflect this identifying feature of the vessel. These same plans indicate she retained the old-style square stern.

Left: Sail plan of the frigate *Potomac*. Note marked decrease in sheer from earlier 44s. [National Archives 134-2-10]

Below: Frigate *Potomac*. Though completed after *Brandywine*, *Potomac* retained the old-style stern. [National Archives 134-2-14]

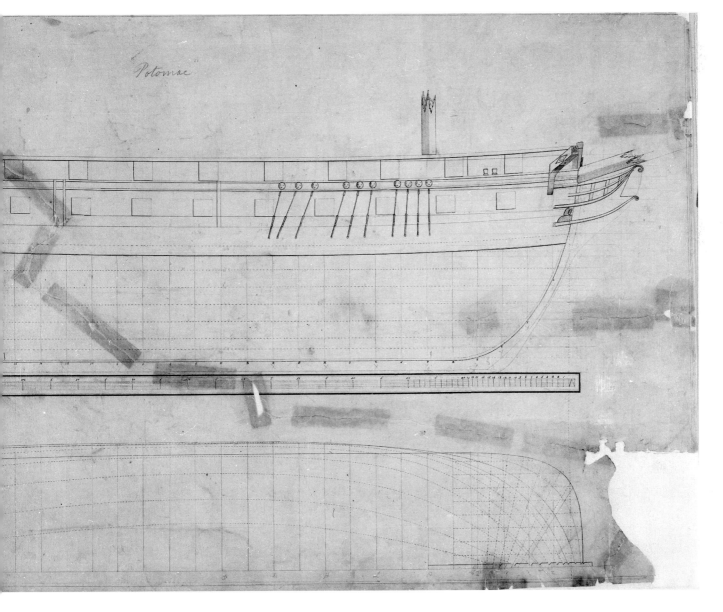

The *Potomac* is best known for her first cruise: in 1831 she sailed for the Pacific via the Cape of Good Hope, thence to Sumatra. There she shelled the natives who had massacred American sailors from the merchant ship *Friendship* of Salem. She returned home in 1834, completing her circumnavigation of the globe. At the end of her voyage, her commanding officer, John Downes, wrote: 'I have never seen so fine a sea boat, or one that was so easy on her spars and Rigging. She works quick and sure, sails well by and large, but her best sailing is with the wind abeam, blowing heavy . . . .'[18] During her third cruise she was beaten by the sloop of war *Decatur* in a variety of circumstances and was reported to have had the advantage only with the wind fresh on the beam.[19] Judging by the tenor of the remarks about her, she apparently was not noted for excessive speed.

Frigate *Columbia*: their length, two tiers of gunports and lofty rig certainly gave these vessels a formidable appearance, an impression not belied by their batteries, which tended to number over 50 guns, usually 32pdrs. [US Naval Photographic Center NH 55282]

Her battery, after 1840, consisted of various combinations of 32pdrs (long guns and carronades) and 8-inch shell guns. At maximum she had 52 guns: twenty-eight long 32s, twenty carronades and four shell guns.[20]

After cruises off Brazil and the West Indies, she provided support for the armies in the Mexican War. She first landed troops in Texas, then participated in the siege and fall of Vera Cruz. After Vera Cruz, the squadron under M C Perry was the largest thus far in American history.[21] *Potomac* next served as flagship in the Home squadron, then, at the outbreak of the Civil War, became part of the Gulf Blockading Squadron. Most of the war she lay with a much reduced battery at Pensacola Navy Yard. She was first a storeship, then was a receiving ship until 1867. In 1877 she was sold at Philadelphia.

Columbia

This frigate is one of the least remembered of the era. She was the second of the name, the first having been destroyed on the stocks when the British burned Washington Navy Yard. The second was laid down in 1825, also at Washington, launched on 9 March 1836, and commissioned by May 1838. No plans have been found of this ship, but she was no doubt built on the very same ways that had held *Brandywine*. Only judging from contemporary illustrations, *Columbia* seems to have had the straightened sheer characteristic of *Potomac*. In 1827 Humphreys wrote William Bainbridge that the only hull difference between her and others of the class was in her 'upper bow', which was 'less full' than the others.[22] No explanation of this has been found.

In service, she proved to be a fine sailer, attaining 10 knots by the wind and 12 knots free. She was stiff, worked well in stays, and steered well. She was reported to be 'easy on her spars and rigging, and in every respect a remarkably fine ship'.[23] Except for a turn of speed, she appears to have been similar to the *Potomac* in her handling at sea. Early in her career she carried 54 guns: four 8-inch shell guns ('Columbiads'), twenty-eight 32s and twenty-two 42pdr carronades. In 1847 four additional shell guns were added and her main battery was forty-two 32pdrs. On her final

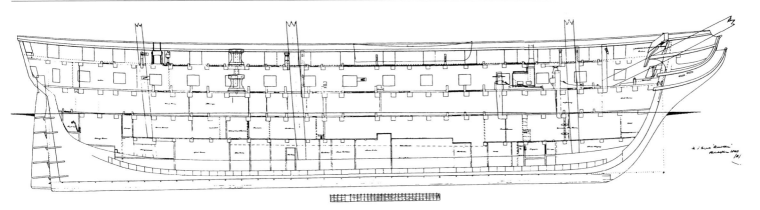

Inboard plan, frigate *Raritan*, note her distinctive and massive head structure. [National Archives 40-14-2E]

cruise, beginning in 1853, she mounted ten shell guns and forty 32pdrs.[24]

Her first commission took her around the Cape of Good Hope to the East Indies and back to the east coast via Cape Horn. Following her circumnavigation of the globe, she lay in ordinary until 1842, when she joined the Home squadron. Her subsequent cruises were twice to Brazil, once in the Mediterranean, and a final stint in the Home squadron. She was laid up at Norfolk in May 1855. She suffered much the same fate as the War of 1812 *Columbia*: she was burned in the yard to prevent her capture, in this instance the enemy being the Confederate army. Her hulk was raised and sold in 1867.

Raritan

Raritan was built at Philadelphia Navy Yard and laid down in 1820. She was launched on 13 June 1843 and commissioned on 1 December of that year. She was built by John Lenthall, who became chief naval constructor in the 1850s. Unlike the earlier vessels of this class, there exists an 'as built' plan for *Raritan*. One can discern some changes made to the original *Potomac* design, and a few alterations are referred to in a letter from constructor Humphreys to the Board in 1839.[25] Both fore and aft hull lines are somewhat fuller, but the most overt change is seen in the head. Between the early 1820s and the completion of *Raritan* the style had changed from the old open rails to a planked-in head. It is also worth noting that the moulding atop the bulwarks now made a continuous line nearly to the billet head.[26] This type of head was not standard with these frigates.

The largest contemplated alteration never occurred: the conversion of the vessel to steam power. Beginning in 1839, Robert F Stockton attempted to persuade the Board to build a steam vessel using John Ericsson's 'pendulum' engine and the screw propeller. At that point both the screw and the engine itself were novelties. The main advantage of both would have been the elimination of the huge paddle wheels amidships. In any event, it was suggested that *Raritan* be modified on the stocks for this innovation, but the board balked at the idea for several reasons: the engines were unproven, the location of the screw might endanger the sternpost, the drag of the propeller would degrade sailing qualities, and the vessel's steering might be effected by the action of the screw. Finally, they objected to converting 'so large and fine a ship', particularly if the installation proved unsatisfactory and further expenses were necessary to rectify the situation.[27] Eventually, the engine and propeller powered the new sloop of war *Princeton*. Also, it is noteworthy that, in contrast to foreign navies, no American naval sailing ships were converted to steam power during this transitional period.

This frigate was armed much as her sisters ships, having gun deck 32pdrs and 42pdr carronades on the spar deck. In her early commissions, she carried twenty-eight 32s and twenty-two carronades, plus four 8-inch (64pdr) shell guns. Later, the number of shell guns was doubled and the balance of the battery was forty-two 32pdrs.[28]

Raritan proved to be a smart sailer, credited with attaining 13 knots, trimmed 30 inches by the stern. In 1845, on the Brazil station, her commander wrote:

> Under topgallant sails & all lower sails with the wind a lit-
> tle before the beam she made a good run from Latitude
> 34 to the line in about 8 days, the greatest daily run was
> 273 miles . . . We beat the *Congress* . . . in a strong topsail
> breeze on a wind. . . . We left December 19th with light
> variable winds and beat the *Congress* easily in smooth
> water by the wind, and after getting to sea ran her Hull
> down. . . . We had the wind to the northward . . . some-
> times blowing fresh & continued beating her under
> whatever sail it was necessary to carry for 10 days succes-
> sively. . . . After beating her every way & in all weathers
> whenever we carried the same sail for 10 days . . . we
> made sail and ran away from her reaching Rio 30 hours
> before her . . .'[29]

Raritan's first commission was on the Brazilian station,
where she out-sailed that nation's squadron, including an

Savannah in the harbour of Rio de Janeiro, December 1854.
Lithograph by A Martinet from a sketch by 'WL'. Note unusual head
configuration. [US Naval Photographic Center NH 001423]

American-built frigate.[30] Subsequently, in the Mexican
War, she participated in the landings at Vera Cruz, Tuxpan
and Tabasco, as well as the siege and capitulation of fort San
Juan de Ulloa. Her post-war stations included the West
Indies, Home squadron and the south Pacific, before being
laid up at Norfolk in 1852. She was burned there in April
1861, to prevent capture by Confederate forces. She was
possibly the best of this class of frigates, which is no mean
statement, as these vessels seemed to have been generally
very satisfactory.

Savannah

Savannah was laid down in 1820 at New York Navy Yard,
under the supervision of John Floyd. By the time she was
launched (24 May 1842) and commissioned (15 October
1843), Floyd had retired and been replaced by Samuel
Hartt. During her construction she was altered from the
original plans in two ways. First was the application of the
elliptical stern; second was the closing in of her head. She
does not seem to have had her sheer straightened.[31] The
only period illustration of the ship before her conversion to
a sloop of war shows a rather unusual head configuration,
with high forecastle bulwarks seemingly extended nearly as
far as the head itself.

At sea, two of her commanding officers agreed on her
outstanding points. One summed it up, writing: 'In fact it
may be said that a ship could not possess better qualities for
general easy movements & rapidity through the water.' He
reported her speed close-hauled under all plain sail as 9
knots. Later, with the wind a bit forward or aft of the beam,
under reefed topsails, courses and fore topmast staysails,
she went over 11 knots. With studding sails and topgallants,
she was 'going 12 to 13 knots'. On a smooth sea, with the
wind directly aft carrying royals and studding sails, she did
over 11 knots. During the passage she was 'easy aloft' and
rolled little and pitched 'easy'. Her only drawbacks seem to
have been a tendency to pitch deeply and violently in a
head sea, and to fall off to leeward.[32]

The *Savannah*'s satisfactory capabilities at sea may have
been a factor in the modernisation of her battery in the mid-
1850s. (*Cumberland* also underwent a similar alteration dur-

ing this period.) The introduction of large shell guns beginning in the 1840s resulted in significant changes in both battery composition and deck configurations. Before the coming of the Dahlgren guns in the mid-1850s, the navy used 8-inch and 10-inch shell guns, developed from the army 'Columbiads', and began mounting them on circular pivot rails fore and aft. The pivot rails facilitated moving these large weapons: the 8-inch barrel alone weighed over 9000 pounds and the 10-inch, nearly 12,000 pounds.[33] This mounting enabled their use on either side of the vessel and allowed as wide a field of fire as the gunports would allow. This resulted in the appearance of wide pivot ports, sometimes fifteen feet long, consisting of several bulwark sections which were hinged from the bottom or simply unshipped for action.

In 1857, constructor John Lenthall recommended the *Savannah* be altered to a sloop of war for carrying 'the heavy guns that are coming into use'. He suggested cutting down her spar deck bulwarks and mounting two 10-inch pivot guns there, and re-aligning the main deck ports for a battery of twenty-two 9-inch guns (Dahlgrens).[34] The general plan was carried out but the former frigate's main deck received eight 8-inch guns, and fourteen 32pdrs in lieu of the Dahlgren 9-inch guns originally recommended.[35] The two 10-inch guns were mounted on pivot rails fore and aft. Forward, there were two large ports on each side: one, about nine feet long, beginning about six feet from the centreline and ending near the cathead; the second was around seventeen feet long on the other side of the cathead. This yielded a field of fire of some 70 degrees for each weapon (though obviously diminished somewhat by the bowsprit and rigging). At the stern, at least sixteen feet of the bulwark was cut down on her sides, as well as an undetermined length across her taffrail. The spacing of the main gun deck ports was broadened from about seven to nine feet.[36] This was the battery arrangement she carried at the outbreak of the Civil War. Before she went into a naval academy training role in 1862, the complement of 8-inch guns was reduced by two, as well as the number of 32s. As a training ship, she carried one of Dahlgren's 11-inch shell guns, two 9-inch guns and four or six 32s.[37]

The *Savannah* first went into service as part of the Pacific

Savannah after her conversion to a sloop of war in the late 1850s. [US Naval Photographic Center NH 2675]

squadron in 1844. At the outbreak of the Mexican war she captured Monterey, California (July 1846). She sailed to the east coast for repairs in 1848, returning to the Pacific the next year. She was part of the South Atlantic squadron until inactivated in 1856 for refit and rearrangement of her battery as noted above. From 1858 to the 1860, she was stationed on the Gulf, returning to New York for repairs. On 22 June 1861 she was ordered to the Atlantic Blockading Squadron, arriving at Hampton Roads in July.[38] She was transferred to the blockade of Savannah, Georgia in October, where she participated in the capture of two Confederate vessels. She returned to Hampton Roads in January 1862 and, in February, was made into a naval academy training vessel.[39]

Savannah remained in a training role until 1870, during which time she made at least one European cruise. One of her more unusual movements in this period was a visit to the military academy at West Point, accompanied by the *Macedonian*. She was photographed there, in 1868, stern to stern with *Macedonian*, and exhibiting eleven gunports, only five of which show weapons. After being taken out of this service, she was laid up and sold at Norfolk in 1883.[40]

Cumberland seen at Portsmouth in the late 1850s. Like *Savannah*, she was razeed in the fifties, and was in fact a sloop of war when lost to the Confederate ironclad *Virginia* at Hampton Roads. [US Navy]

Cumberland

Cumberland was built at Boston (Charlestown Navy Yard) and launched on 24 May 1842. Her first service was in the Mediterranean squadron, from 1843 to 1845. In her original configuration, she carried quarter galleries on the elliptical stern, and her hull lines exhibited little, if any change from

her sister ships. She was quite heavily armed, carrying twenty-eight 32s, twenty 42pdr carronades, and four 8-inch shell guns. By 1847, the 42s had been superseded by 32s, totalling forty-two, plus eight shell guns.[41]

She was part of the Home squadron in 1846, and arrived at Vera Cruz in February of that year. Her arrival at that place was described by her chaplain, F W Taylor and was quoted by Samuel Eliot Morison in his biography of M C Perry. Though not a historically significant event, the description itself paints a vivid picture of one of these magnificent frigates in their heyday.

On a clear winter morning the gleaming white conical summit of Orizaba . . . 18,851 feet above sea level, is sighted a hundred miles away. The wind being fair, Captain [S L] Breese claps on sail in order to reach his anchorage before dark . . . By mid afternoon . . . [T]he church towers and domes of Veracruz can now be made out through a glass and the squadron masts appear over Sacrificios. All hands are aloft or on deck awaiting orders, and some of the old salts are growling, 'What's the old man think he's doing? We'll ground in no time!' The officer of the deck, Lieutenant Hazard, judging the opportune moment, calls through his speaking trumpet, 'Stand by to take in the studdingsails—man the clewlines, sheets and downhauls—stand by to furl royals—man the royal clewlines!' The men quickly take their stations. Then comes the order, 'In studdingsails and royals!' In a moment the little 'kites', fluttering like big handkerchiefs, are pulled into the tops or down on deck, and the royals are clewed up and furled. With topsails and topgallants set, the frigate weathers . . . the outermost reef. . . . 'Man the lee braces—haul taut!' cries the lieutenant. The men brace every yard sharp to weather the last obstacle. She rounds . . . Sacrificios Island . . . the yards are squared again, and *Cumberland* fairly roars down toward the crowded anchorage.

Foretopsail and foretopgallant are thrown back to check her headway, lower courses are clewed up, and the jack is raised . . . to signal for a pilot boat. A boat brings the pilot on board, she fills away again and bears down in gallant style on the anchored ships where hundreds of critical eyes are watching, ready to remark on the slightest mistake. The guns are already charged for saluting, and 1st Luff, after being assured by chief gunner's mate that all rigging is clear, gives the order 'Starboard, fire!' then, 'Larboard, fire!' And so on, until the full 13-gun salute to Commodore [David] Conner is rendered. Flagship *Potomac* replies in kind. *Cumberland* now makes for the berth indicated by the pilot . . . and as her way is checked she makes a running moor, drops her starboard bower anchor and pays out chain while the well-braced yards and close hauled spanker help her to round into the wind. All sails are furled, all lines neatly coiled, and the frigate lies snug to two anchors as the sea breeze dies away and the moon rises from the Gulf.[42]

After participating in the Gulf operations during the Mexican War, *Cumberland* returned to the US in July 1848.

Subsequently she was in the Mediterranean for two cruises, then went in for refit during 1855-7.

At Boston, *Cumberland* was 'razeed' to a spar-decked sloop of war, as described for *Savannah* above. Her high bulwarks were cut down and pivot rails were built into the spar deck for two 10-inch shell guns. Ports for her forward shell gun allowed a field of fire from just forward of her fore mast past her catheads. Her quarter galleries were removed and the gun deck ports re-spaced to mount sixteen 32pdrs and six 8-inch guns. These changes decreased the vessel's weight and windage (height above the water), resulting in a handier and speedier ship.

St Lawrence was laid down in 1826 and completed in 1848 - the last of the 175ft Gradual Increase frigates. In 1861 two rounds from her 8-inch guns sank the Confederate privateer *Petrel*. [Naval Academy Library]

These alterations made, she returned to sea in 1857 on the Africa anti-slavery squadron, followed by assignment to the Home squadron. In 1861 she was laid up at Norfolk, and was the one ship towed out of that place before the yard was burned. As part of the Atlantic Blockading Squadron, the sloop of war was at Hampton Roads on 8 March 1862 when the Confederate ironclad *Virginia* – converted from a vessel which had remained at Norfolk in 1861 – attacked the fleet. The *Virginia's* first target was the anchored *Cumberland*, which she rammed under the starboard fore rigging, while taking point-blank fire from her battery with impunity. *Cumberland*, with a hole in her hull 'wide enough to drive in a horse and cart', sank immediately, with the guns firing and all flags flying.[43] Her casualty list was one of the longest of the Civil War navy.

Plan of frigate *St Lawrence*. Note that original was separated into segments. [National Archives RG 45 Grice Plans]

St Lawrence

The frigate *St Lawrence* was built at Norfolk Navy Yard. She had been laid down in 1826, was launched 27 March 1847 and commissioned 17 August 1848. Lack of funds is often given as the reason for her twenty-two years under construction, but it would be more accurate to say that the funds for her building simply were not a high priority. In fact, in 1842, building had been suspended on the ship, due to heavy expenses in other areas.[44] These expenses were no doubt the completion of three of the other vessels in the class the next year, plus the fallout from the navy's steam vessel program. To be specific, in the navy, the years from the late 1830s to the mid-1840s were dominated by the struggle to adopt a mode of steam propulsion more appropriate to warships than the side-wheel steamer, with its vulnerable paddles and engines placed above the waterline.

Before the adoption of the screw propeller in 1854, a great deal of money and effort had been wasted on a

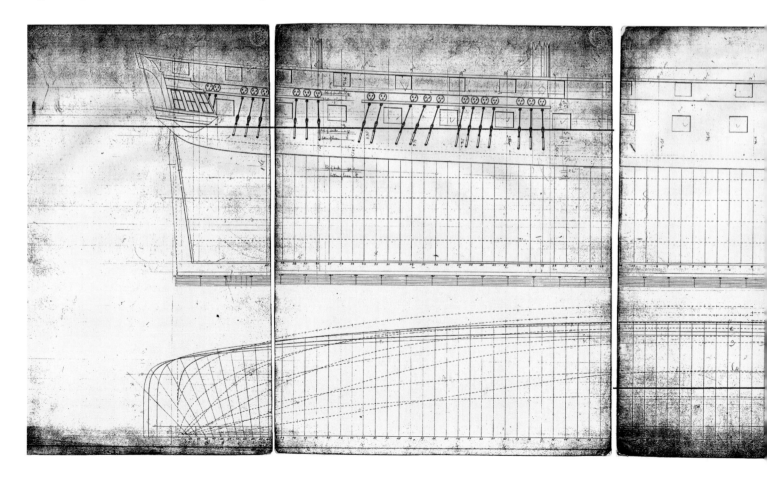

disastrous experimental system called the Hunter's Wheel – a horizontal, below-the-waterline paddle-wheel arrangement. No less than three unsuccessful vessels were built with this machinery between 1840 and 1846, eating up over $450,000 in construction funds, plus significant other moneys attempting to correct their fatal flaws.[45] Though some of this funding, which more than equalled the cost of two sailing frigates, came directly from Congress, the majority was from the Gradual Increase appropriations.[46] The impetus for the completion of *St Lawrence* at this particular time was the Mexican War, as well as the need to vacate space for new construction.

During construction the *St Lawrence* was given the elliptical stern and quarter galleries, but her closed-in head was of the lower, shorter variety – the opposite of the *Raritan*'s head configuration. Where the latter's head reached as high as the top of the forecastle bulwarks, *St Lawrence*'s came up even with the forecastle (spar) deck line. This configuration was somewhat of a throwback to the era before the

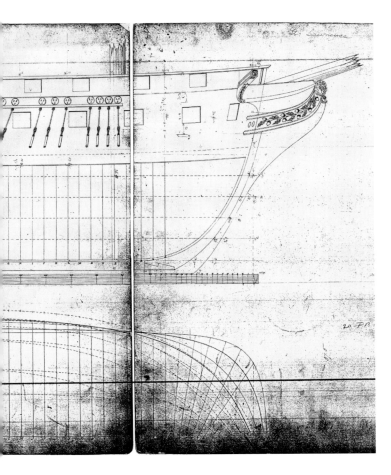

closing in of the forecastle rails. The new style, though presenting a sleeker appearance, obviously used much more timber and thus appears to have had its cost in weight forward.

St Lawrence's first and second cruises were under unusual circumstances. In September 1848, she sailed for northern Europe, calling at the Isle of Wight, then at Bremerhaven. At that German port, Captain Foxhall Parker, detailed by the navy for this purpose, consulted with leaders of the newly established North German Confederation on the specifics of the establishment of a navy. Then, at the request of the Prussian Minister to the US, the *St Lawrence* took on board four midshipmen of the nascent navy of the North German Confederation. These young men remained aboard for a six-month indoctrination in the rules and regulations of the American navy, while sailing to England, Portugal and Spain. They were returned to Germany in July 1849, before the frigate continued on to Denmark – a nation then at war with Germany.[47] After this, *St Lawrence* joined the Mediterranean squadron, returning to Boston in late 1850.

The frigate's second cruise again brought her to Europe. Her main deck battery was removed and she became a transport for American exhibits destined for London's 1851 International Exposition, the first 'world's fair'. In this effort, she carried 300 tons of cargo and 146 tons of kentledge in lieu of her cannon.[48]

During her early cruises, she was reported to have sailed 'very fast off the wind', but did not 'bear her canvass well'. Adding 44 tons of ballast at Bremerhaven markedly improved her stability and sailing qualities.[49]

Between these European ventures and the Civil War, the frigate was assigned to the Pacific and South Atlantic squadrons. During the latter, she participated in the task force detailed to the Paraguay expedition in 1859. This American show of force assisted in obtaining a peaceful settlement of the dispute with that nation.

St Lawrence was laid up in 1859, to be recommissioned on 21 June 1861 as part of the Atlantic Blockading Squadron. Off Charleston in July she encountered the 82-ton Confederate 'privateer' *Petrel*, a former pilot boat and revenue cutter. The chase was short, ending when two shots

from frigate's forecastle battery sank the vessel.[50] She returned to the area around Hampton Roads in March 1862, when the *Virginia* sank *Cumberland* and *Congress*. On learning that the ironclad was coming out, she was towed towards the scene, but arrived after the two ships had been lost. Within 900 yards of the Confederate vessel, *St Lawrence* grounded, but continued to exchange fire with the ironclad. (At this time her battery was composed of ten 8-inch shell guns and at least thirty-four 32pdrs.[51]) *St Lawrence* was damaged, but the ironclad withdrew rather than add the frigate to her tally for the day. Once afloat again that evening, *St Lawrence* retired to Fortress Monroe.

The remainder of her active Civil War service was on blockade duty in the South Atlantic and Gulf of Mexico. She then became a storeship (1863) at Hampton Roads, then Norfolk. After the war, still at Norfolk, she was a marine barracks ship. She remained in this role until 1875, when she was sold.

Sabine and *Santee*

The construction of the *Sabine*, and, to some extent, her sister ship *Santee*, is a conundrum. On the stocks since 1823 and 1821 respectively, they were both patently obsolete before launching. Both had received the elliptical stern, as

Unidentified US frigate, at Portsmouth Navy Yard (Kittery) in the late 1850s, giving an unusual view of her upper deck arrangements. [US Navy]

Plan of *Sabine* and *Santee*, showing their added length and nearly straight sheer. [National Archives 107-11-14E]

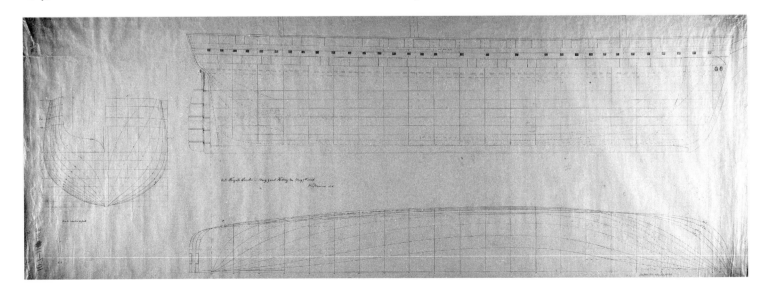

well as the straightened sheer decreed early on. Their construction had suffered from lack of funding as noted in relation to the *St Lawrence*. It is obvious that the department was uncertain how to proceed, not wishing to break up and totally waste these new hulls, nor to launch a vessel identical to a forty-year old design. It is possible that conversion to steam had been considered when the idea was suggested and rejected for *Raritan*. In any event, the Secretary of the Navy's 1854 report on the two hulls noted that their long time in building had been 'taken advantage [of] to improve the form of the fore-end.'[52] Specifically, fifteen feet was added to their bows. In the process they were made significantly sharper in their forward lines. Other alterations were eliminating the rake in the sternpost, increasing the sharpness in the run and reducing the curvature of the sides (though *Sabine* retained the raked sternpost).[53] These were the longest frigates built in the USA, at 190ft between perpendiculars. At 1726 tons, they were slightly smaller than the 1839 *Congress*, which was not as long but was broader in beam.

Sabine, built at New York (Brooklyn) Navy Yard, was

Above: *Sabine* in her later years. Both she and *Santee* were obsolete when launched. [US Navy]

Below: Frigate *Santee* with the old *Constitution* as training vessels at the Naval Academy in the Civil War era. The photo points up the contrasts between the earliest and last 44-gun frigates of the US Navy. [US Naval Photographic Center NH 19890]

launched on 12 February 1855, and commissioned 23 August 1858. She participated in the Paraguayan punitive expedition in 1859, then, after a short refit, became part of the Atlantic squadron, blockading the southern coast. One of her more noteworthy accomplishments was the search and rescue of the crew and 500 marines from the transport *Governor,* disabled and adrift during a severe gale off the Carolinas in November 1861. She also participated in the relief of Fort Pickens early in the war. In 1864 she became a training ship, making cruises to Europe in 1869 and 1870. She was later a receiving ship at Portsmouth (Kittery), and was sold in 1883.

The *Santee* was launched on 16 February 1855 but not commissioned until 8 June 1861, shortly after the fall of Fort Sumter. She joined the blockade on the Gulf coast, in Texas waters, remaining active there until late summer 1862, taking three prizes. After a refit, she, along with the old *Constitution,* became a training ship for the naval academy, which had been moved from Annapolis to Newport, Rhode Island for the duration of the conflict. After the war, she sailed back to Annapolis and continued in this role. For a time she was a gunnery instruction ship, then she was a barracks ship for the remainder of the century and beyond. She sank at her moorings on 2 April 1912 and was shortly thereafter raised and sold. Her hull was burned to recover the copper and bronze in the structure. She was the last of the Gradual Increase frigates.

Hudson

The frigate *Hudson* was unique: the only commercially built frigate acquired by the navy during this era. She was designed by Stephen Smith of the firm of Smith and Dimon, a company noted for its swift packet ships, vessels such as *Independence* and *Virginian.* This New York company, as with many others, built and sold warships for foreign governments. In this instance, Smith and Dimon had already constructed the frigate *Hellas* for the Greek revolutionaries in 1826. This second frigate was named *Liberator* and was intended for the same purpose, but the revolutionaries could not pay for the vessel.

At this point, Smith and Dimon apparently invoked some congressional interest in their plight. In May 1826, the chairman of the naval committee in the House of Representatives wrote the Secretary of the Navy on behalf of the builders, inquiring whether a purchase of the vessel would be possible under the 'Gradual Increase' legislation. Secretary Samuel Southard replied that the Gradual Increase law would not be injured if the construction of one frigate was 'suspended' and one of equal or superior force was purchased in its place. Frame timbers already acquired

Frigate *Hudson,* built by the noted merchant vessel yard Smith and Dimon for Greek revolutionaries. Some packet vessel influence can be seen in her straighter stem and small tumblehome. [National Archives 41-9-1H]

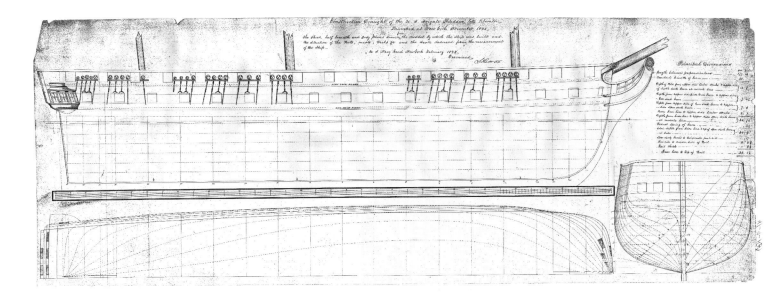

for building the frigate in question would be 'secured' for later use. Shortly thereafter, three senior naval officers were sent to inspect two vessels for sale at New York, one of which was the *Liberator*. The inspectors reported the vessel in question was better adapted to naval use than the–unnamed–other ship. They described her as 'faithfully built' but of white oak and therefore 'greatly inferior' to live oak vessels being built in the navy yards. This inspection seems to have been a formality, as the ship was purchased on 12 August 1826 for $230,570.97.[54]

The calculated purchase price was based on the cost of a white oak frame, by cubic feet ($65,000), labour, masts and rigging, and equipment, including boats, kentledge and guns. At the time of purchase, according to quoted government documents, she carried thirty-two 34pdrs (32s?) and thirty 42pdr carronades.[55] The ship was renamed *Hudson* to co-ordinate with the other 'rivers' in the class, and was commissioned on 27 September 1828. Her dimensions were not far from those of the navy-built vessels: 177ft 10in between perpendiculars by 45ft moulded beam and 13ft 8in depth of hold. Her hull form, however was significantly blunter forward, with much less rake in the stem. Her bilges were harder and lower, and she had a square stern. These characteristics related to merchant vessel practice where carrying capacity was the key criteria. This decade was twenty years before the coming of the clipper ship, and, in fact, American naval vessels of this period tended to be sharper than their merchant counterparts.

The frigate made only one cruise during her service, departing in September 1828 for South America, as flagship of the Brazil squadron. Her short career has been attributed to some prejudice amongst naval officers against commercially built warships, as well as her poor building materials. The latter cause is confirmed by letters from her commanding officer. In June 1830, at Montevideo, she was described as in a 'very rapid state of decay . . . throughout'. The situation was such that stanchions had to be introduced on the berth deck to support the gun deck, and on the latter to strengthen the spar deck beams. Three months later her stern was described as 'very weak'.[56]

She returned to the United States in August 1831, and was utilised as a receiving ship. She was broken up in

Hudson made one cruise and was found to be decaying rapidly. She was of white oak, rather than the long hallowed live-oak of naval-built frigates. [US Naval Photographic Center NH 53598]

1844.[57] *Hudson* was the last commercially built frigate in the service.

Macedonian

As has been described in the previous chapter, by 1829 the captured frigate *Macedonian* had become a candidate for a major 'repair' or, to use the department's term, 'rebuilding'. By the spring of 1831 the tide was ebbing and flowing in her bilges and she was dragged on to the mudflats at Norfolk to prevent her sinking. In July 1832, Congress authorised the 'rebuilding' of the vessel, and on 28 February 1833 a new keel was laid for the ship. By the end of the year, she was 'all timbered' and ready for her gun deck beams. At that point, with the new hull approaching completion, there were two *Macedonian*s in existence at Norfolk Navy Yard. As will be seen, some parts of the old ship were incorporated into the new. However, the old hulk was broken up sometime in 1834, ending the life of the original *Macedonian*. Despite some ethereal notions that the 'spirit' of the old vessel continued and the auspices thereof somehow transformed the new ship into a continuation of

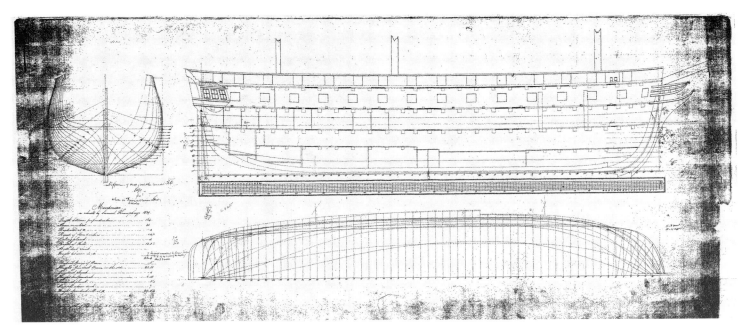

The second frigate *Macedonian*. Though a few timbers from the captured Royal Navy vessel were used in the new frigate and some effort was made to have the new ship resemble the original, documents show that indeed, the hulls of the old and the new *Macedonian* co-existed at one point at Norfolk Navy Yard. [National Archives]

the old warhorse, the undiluted fact is that a second ship had been built and the old vessel was gone.[58] In regards to contemporaries' views of the ship, it is noteworthy that Lieutenant George Emmons, in his *Statistical History* of 1853 called the new ship the *Macedonian 2* and begins her history in 1837.[59]

The existence of a second *Macedonian* was problematic in 1835 because it called into question the method of accounting for the funds. Some authorities contend that the 'rebuilding' of these ships was a fiscal sleight-of-hand, intended to disguise building a new ship as repairing an old one, thus enabling the department to use 'repair' moneys rather than construction ('Gradual Increase') funds. When questioned on this subject by the Board of Navy Commissioners, Commandant Warrington at Gosport replied that 'The frame was placed under "Repairs", as it was neither for the "Gradual Increase" nor "Gradual Improvement". I consider *that* the proper head . . . because replacing in such instances, is of similar import with repair: a deficient vessel in either case [is] renewed.'[60] The ques-

tion had first been raised, officially, five years previously, in the 'rebuilding' of *John Adams*, also at Gosport, but, as will be seen in some detail in the section on that vessel, the practice had been in place in the navy since 1821 with the rebuilding of the sloop of war *Erie*.[61]

It is easy to charge the navy with duplicity and underhanded methods in this question. However, from a strictly practical point of view, when a vessel was brought in for repairs, the original survey, accomplished while the vessel was in the water, may have indicated that only a small percentage of the frame timbers were faulty or rotten; whereas the process of removing the planking and ceiling gradually might have revealed more serious and widespread problems. If, for argument's sake, ninety per cent of the frames were unsound and required replacing, the ship was still considered 'repaired' or 'rebuilt', when in actuality it was virtually a new vessel – possibly the keel and floors were the only tie between the two ships. At what point would the use of 'repair' funds become illegitimate or illegal? Certainly the navy was jealous of the 'new construction' money, and it certainly was not expedient to apply to Congress for funds to replace a vessel already stripped down and in process of repair.

In any event, the design of the replacement for *Macedonian* had been drawn by chief constructor Samuel Humphreys in 1829. Other than her head, which retained the British carving of Alexander the Great, and the old style open rails, the design was completely new. The hull measured 164ft between perpendiculars, eight to ten feet longer than the British ship (the two foot difference was based on British versus American locations for the perpendiculars). More significantly to the contention that it was a new hull, the 1829 ship was 41ft in breadth (moulded), versus 38ft 9in on the original. Above water, the new ship had a complete spar deck battery, rather than the open waist of the old ship, and the new elliptical stern. Finally, comparing body plans reveals a typical turn of the century hull plan for the old ship, including the pronounced knuckles below the two-foot waterline. Humphreys' body plan was distinctly modern, completely shorn of the old-style knuckles and having floors running absolutely straight, and angled upward at about 18 degrees out to over twelve feet from the centreline.[62] Some parts of the British vessel were retained, namely the metal work. Copper sheeting for the magazine and tin sheeting for the bread room was transferred and re-fitted. Anchors, kentledge, the stove and various other fittings were also re-used, as was the figurehead.[63]

The new *Macedonian* was launched on 1 November 1836 and in commission by 11 October 1837, as part of the West Indies and Africa anti-slaving squadron. At sea the ship proved to be a fair sailer, obtaining 11 knots on a wind. In a trial with the sloop *Concord*, the results were mixed – in some circumstances the frigate bested the sloop, and vice versa. She rolled easily and was dry in most conditions. She

The second *Macedonian* serving as a training ship at Newport about 1864. She has the distinction of being the only 36-gun USN sailing frigate built after 1800. [US Naval Photographic Center NH 47093]

was considered a dull sailer in light winds and more so as she rode lighter.[64] Her dull sailing led to some discussions in 1845 which advocated altering her to screw propulsion by adding 66 feet to her length, at the cost of $17,000, plus engines.[65] Nothing came of this idea.

The ship's second cruise, in 1847, was in response to the Irish famine. *Jamestown* and *Macedonian* were detailed to carry relief supplies and provisions – 12,000 barrels – to that country. In an unprecedented move, Congress voted to turn the two naval vessels over to civilian crews and officers specifically for the mission of mercy. *Macedonian* sailed in June 1847, stripped of all but four guns, and carrying 1800 tons of cargo plus paying passengers. She arrived at Cork twenty-seven days later, to the plaudits of the citizenry. Unloaded, it was discovered she was too light for the trans-Atlantic run and over 600 tons of ballast was purchased to bring her down to a safe draught.[66] The return was uneventful.

After returning to the US, it was determined that she should be cut down to a sloop of war. At New York her spar deck battery was removed and she was fitted with twenty-two guns: two 10-inch and sixteen 8-inch shell guns, plus four 32s. After this transformation, her sailing appears to have improved markedly. In fresh gales, under triple reefed topsails and single reefed courses 'which some ships could not have carried' she went off at 10, 11, and even 12 miles an hour', reported one of her commanding officers in 1853.[67]

Her next major assignment was in the Far East. She became an element of Commodore Perry's return expedition to Japan in 1854. Afterwards she served in the Home squadron and in the Mediterranean. During the Civil War she cruised the West Indies and off Portugal, in search of Confederate raiders. This was to be her final active navy assignment.

From 1863 to 1870 the ship was stationed at Newport, Rhode Island, then Annapolis, as part of the training squadron for the Naval Academy. During this assignment, she briefly visited the Military Academy at West Point, on the Hudson River, in company with the frigate *Savannah*. In 1871 she was laid up at Norfolk and she was sold four years later. In a rather bizarre appendix, the hulk was sold

and her timbers found their way into the construction of the Macedonian Hotel on City Island, Bronx. On 9 June 1922, the remains of the ship's American live oak timbers burned to the ground with the hotel.[68]

Congress

The frigate *Congress* was intended to be a new standard for all frigates which followed her. The origin of an improved 44-gun ship can be traced to 1827, with a design prepared by Samuel Humphreys, but not used for actual construction. Then, on 30 June 1834, Congress authorised the 'rebuilding' of the old *Congress*, which had been laid up for ten years and had been declared unfit for further repairs.[69] The next step seems to have been in 1835 when Humphreys was again working on an improvement to his 1827 design. He suggested the beam be broadened to 46ft 6in, to efficiently carry thirty long 32pdrs on the gun deck as well as thirty 42pdr carronades on the spar deck.[70] This dimension seems to have been the starting point for the board, as by March 1838 they reported that the contemplated new vessel differed in form and dimensions from those already built and under construction.[71]

The board then directed the constructors to present alternative designs for the ship. The result was two plans: one by Humphreys and John Lenthall; the other by constructors Francis Grice, Samuel Hartt and Josiah Barker. When the designs were compared, the latter group criticised the former's design as emphasising 'burthen' rather than fast sailing and the Grice group complained that they had been instructed to make use of the timbers on hand, and would have changed the hull shape had that restriction been lifted. In any event, both plans were rejected by the board. It is noteworthy that at this point the design was designated a 60-gun frigate, a complete departure from the old 36-gun vessel.[72] A final plan was in place in late 1838 or early 1839 and the vessel was laid down on 1 June of that year at Portsmouth Navy Yard in New Hampshire.

The new *Congress* was 179ft between perpendiculars and 46ft 6in moulded beam, and depth of hold of 15ft 5in. Thus the dimensions were four feet longer and some eighteen inches wider than the earlier 44s, plus over a foot deeper. At

1867 tons, the completed vessel was over 100 tons larger than the *Potomac* and class. In terms of hull shape, the new ship had a slightly sharper bottom and sharper entrance lines. However, the design exhibited less rake at the stem and a somewhat fuller run. Of course, the elliptical stern was incorporated, and slightly less sheer. Both old and new designs had fifteen gun deck ports, plus the bridle port. On the new ship, the ports and spacing were both wider.

The board was sufficiently convinced of the quality of the vessel's concept that they had already communicated to the Secretary of the Navy their intention to make it the 'first of several that are contemplated to be built by the same moulds . . . if she should prove satisfactory upon trial.' Furthermore, the board wrote that they would prefer to launch the *Congress* 'first instead of those of the previous design on stocks'.[73] At that point, there were still five of the older ships building. *Congress* was launched on 16 August 1841, and went into service 7 May 1842. Through most of

her career she carried some combination of 32pdrs and 8-inch shell guns. In 1845, it was four of the shell guns and forty-eight 32s; in 1855, she mounted ten 8-inch and forty 32pdrs.

The ship first served in the Mediterranean, where she made an instant reputation for speed and handling. She out-sailed *Columbus*, *Fairfield*, and *Preble* 'as if they were at anchor'. She gained high marks for lying to, scudding, steering, staying and wearing. Two years later, the same commander repeated most of his remarks about her handling, but her speed was, admittedly, poor. He attributed this to two years' barnacle growth on her hull gained while off the River Plate, Argentina.[74] After stints in the Mediterranean and the south Atlantic, the ship sailed to the Pacific, where she played a significant role in the Mexican War. She was used in shore bombardment and her crew participated in the engagements ashore. Subsequently, she was stationed off South America, in the Mediterranean, and again in the

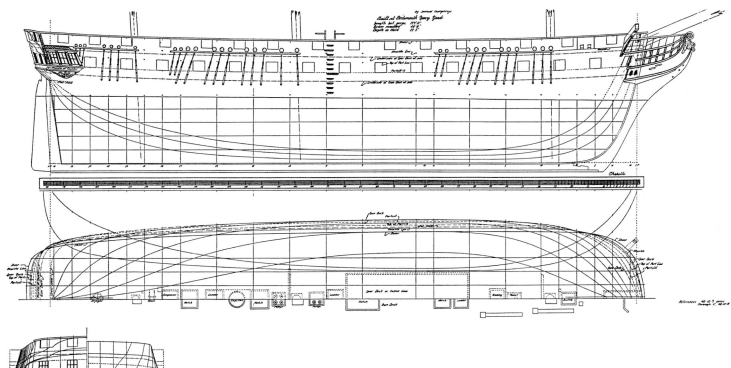

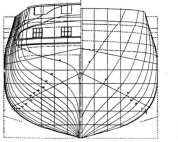

Congress represented the ultimate US Navy frigate design, and, had not steam power intervened, would have been the pattern for sailing frigates to come. She gained a sterling reputation for her sailing qualities during her career. [Plan by Howard I Chapelle, courtesy Smithsonian Institution]

Definitive portrait of *Congress* in the Mediterranean by Tomaso De Simone. She could well have been termed the 'pride' of the sailing fleet when she succumbed to ironclad *Virginia* [ex-*Merrimack*] in 1862. [Franklin D Roosevelt Library]

Brazil squadron before 1860.

At the outbreak of the Civil War she became part of the Atlantic Blockading Squadron, stationed at Hampton Roads, Virginia. On 8 March 1862, she was attacked by the Confederate *Virginia*, shortly after that vessel had rammed and sunk the *Cumberland*. The frigate slipped her moorings, but grounded in the shallows, leaving her vulnerable to the impervious ironclad, which proceeded to destroy the wooden frigate. *Congress*'s guns were unable to bear on the adversary and when they did, the projectiles simply bounced off the iron sides. She surrendered and later burned to the waterline and exploded. There were some 120 casualties, one of the worst single disasters for the US Navy during the Civil War. Her loss—the most modern of the sailing frigates—along with that of the *Cumberland*, marked the final knell for the wooden sailing navy.

As has been seen, the *Congress* was to have been the pattern for later sailing frigates in the US Navy. And it does appear that she had met all expectations, in terms of speed, sea-keeping ability and armament. Of course, history and technology intervened, and there were no more sailing frigates built on her plan. By the mid-1850s steam had invaded the wooden hulls, and the day of her destruction signalled the close of the era of unarmoured sailing warships. *Congress* also marked the end of that remarkable, unbroken line of big American frigates. They had more than fulfilled their purposes and certainly were indispensable in the creation of the American navy we know today.

CHAPTER 5

The Ships of the Line

IN THE pre-dreadnought era, the ship of the line was the ultimate war machine. Not only were they the most powerful agglomeration of weaponry ever concentrated in one mobile entity, the ships themselves were the largest moving objects in existence. Strictly in nautical terms, the 74-gun liner was significantly bigger yet than the largest East Indiaman – the latter being the largest merchant vessel type in existence. In the United States, only one liner had been built before 1815: the 74-gun *America* of 1782, and the largest vessels short of that ship were probably the Revolutionary War frigates.

As the name implies, these vessels were designed for combat as part of the line of battle. For centuries, in a crude contest of broadside throw-weight, this implied two opposing strings of ships, in line ahead, pounding each other, aiming to disable by destroying the enemy's will to fight by overturning guns and killing men, with the coup de grace often the act of boarding. Neither speed nor particularly fine handling was required here, merely the ability to carry weaponry and withstand enemy shot. This was not a battle of manoeuvre. In European fleets, the liner mounted no less than 64 guns, and the prestige and power of a seafaring nation was virtually proportional to the number of liners on hand. Britain's oaken walls had long held sway, with a maximum of over one hundred ships of the line at the close of the Napoleonic Wars.[1] The French, Spanish, and Russian fleets trailed in this numbers game, with other European nations aping the major powers, as far as their naval budgets allowed.

In the United States, three liners had been planned during the Revolution; but two of them were not finished and the third was transferred to France without ever seeing service in the Continental Navy. When it became necessary to re-establish the navy in the 1790s, it was originally a measured response to the Barbary powers' commerce depredations – an adversary with no line of battle fleet. This circumstance, plus the opposition from the anti-navalist Jeffersonian Republicans, discouraged any move to construct ships of the line in the original 1794 naval bill.

By 1799, however, France had become the dominant concern. As Trafalgar was some years hence, the French fleet was a threat not to be dismissed easily, particularly given the French colonial interests in the West Indies. Thus, on 25 February 1799, Congress authorised construction of twelve 74-gun ships, in addition to frigates and smaller vessels, 'a force sufficient to ensure our future peace with the nations of Europe'.[2] Of course these ships were never built, the war with France being settled before their construction was begun. There had been time, however, for a design to be executed. In March 1799 Samuel Humphreys completed a copy of a 74-gun plan made by his father shortly beforehand. The vessel was to be 183ft between perpendiculars, 48ft 6in moulded beam by 19ft 6in depth of hold, to carry seventy-four 32pdr guns on two lower decks and forecastle and quarterdeck. (See plan 40-15-6J.) The ships would have had the old-style beakhead bulkhead, and were relatively sharp forward for liners of the period. They were likely to have been, according to H I Chapelle, 'comparatively fast sailers', though probably 'unable to bear the armament proposed for them.'[3] Though the moulds were made for the ships, and there was some gathering of timbers for their hulls, no actual construction took place.

Naval cutbacks during the Jeffersonian era prevented any actual work on 74s until the War of 1812. The act of 2 January 1813, which authorised three frigates, also called for four 74-gun ships to be built. Only three of the four were constructed: at Philadelphia, Portsmouth (Kittery), and Boston.[4] The *Franklin* was designed by Samuel Humphreys and built by Humphreys and Penrose at Philadelphia Navy

Yard. The *Washington* was built by Hartt and Badger at Kittery, supervised by yard commandant Isaac Hull. The *Independence* was built by Hartt and Barker at Boston. The latter two were based on the 1799 design with some major alterations made during construction.

Franklin

The *Franklin* was the first ship built at Philadelphia Navy Yard. She was laid down and launched in 1815. Like the others in this group, she was built for the War of 1812, but was completed too late to see action. Her plan, by Samuel Humphreys, called for a ship 187ft 10¾in between perpendiculars by 50ft moulded beam. The vessel exhibited some changes in ship of the line design since the 1799 plan had been promulgated. Unlike the older draught, *Franklin* no longer had the vulnerable beakhead, so long a standard in line of battle ships. This feature was one in which the sides of the upper gun deck (on a 74) ended just forward of the first gunport. There an athwartship bulkhead was built, in which were passages to the head facilities. This resulted in another area similar to the square stern, where weak framing and bulkheads made the ship vulnerable to raking fire. This 'beakhead bulkhead' had been superseded by a design where the bow cant frames, hawse pieces and planking were extended upward to the forecastle deck and bulwarks, thus closing in the bows and making them theoretically as strong as the sides of the ship. This feature was seen in British liners by 1814, and had become standard practice in smaller warships long before that time.[5] Also, unlike the 1799 design, the *Franklin* had complete bulwarks on the forecastle.

As will be shown, the dimensions of this vessel and the other two 74s laid down this year, were very similar. However, the hull lines of *Franklin* vary considerably from those of the the other ships, indicating a new design was made by Samuel Humphreys within the dimensions set down by the Secretary of the Navy for the Boston and Philadelphia ships (see below).

Comparing these first three American 74s with European contemporaries, it is evident that the idea behind the big frigates was carried over to the liners. From 1783 to 1815,

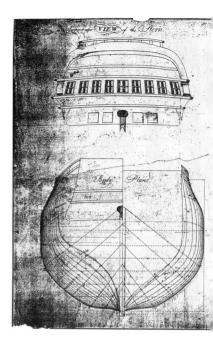

Joshua Humphreys' 1799 ship of the line plan. Timber was gathered for twelve 74-gun ships but construction was never begun. The material was stored and used for the War of 1812 liners. [National Archives 40-15-6J]

British 74s ranged in length from 173ft to 182ft (on the main deck) and 47ft to 49ft in beam. The only exception was *Rochfort* of 1809, which was 192ft 8in by 49ft 4in. By way of contrast, the 80-84 gun *Canopus* class (1816-1825) was about 194ft in length, by 52ft 4in. Also, the batteries were significantly larger, both in number of guns and weight: no British liners had entire batteries of 32pdr weapons, the majority having 18pdrs (or in a few cases 24s) on the upper deck, and 32pdr carronades on the quarterdeck and forecastle.[6]

The *Franklin* was in commission in late 1815, but her first cruise was to the Mediterranean two years later, by way of England, where she transported the American ambassador to his post. There she was inspected and reported to be 'built of seasoned oak, admirable [*sic*] put together, and, like the generality of Philadelphia ships, highly finished in every part.'[7] She became flagship of the Mediterranean squadron, and was the third American ship of the line seen in those waters, following *Independence* and *Washington*.

Her 'model' was much admired while on the Mediterranean station, as was, no doubt, her battery: eighty-seven 32pdrs, of which twenty-four were carronades. This gave her a total throw weight of 2784 pounds, some 650 pounds greater than that of *Albion*, a typical British 74.[8] However, as common with the other two first generation American liners,

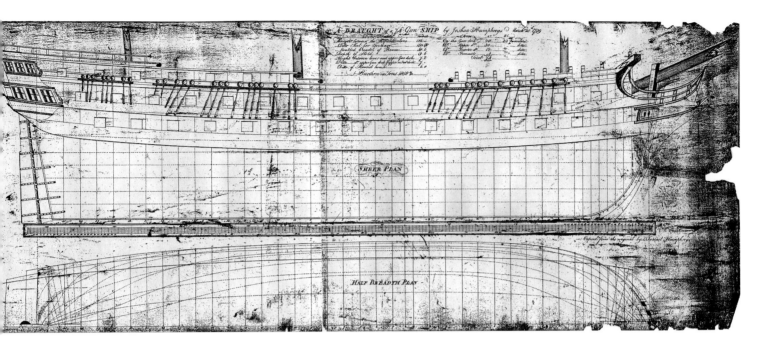

when loaded her midship lower gunports were only four feet from the waterline.[9] Therefore, when she heeled over in a breeze, her lee lower gunports were likely to be unusable. Though the three ships were reasonably good sailers, they were considered failures: if their lower battery was useless in any kind of seaway, they were little more effective than a frigate, if not less so, as the frigate was speedier, handier and required a smaller crew—something around 400 as opposed to over 750 men on the ship of the line.

Franklin served on the Mediterranean station until 1820, then, after refit, became flagship of the Pacific squadron in 1821. Her tour, and active duty, ended in August 1824 and she became a receiving ship at Boston. In 1852, she was

Though a good sailer, *Franklin*'s lower deck guns were useless in a seaway. She served from 1815 to 1824, and was considered for conversion to a frigate, but instead was broken up in the 1850s. [National Archives 40-15-5]

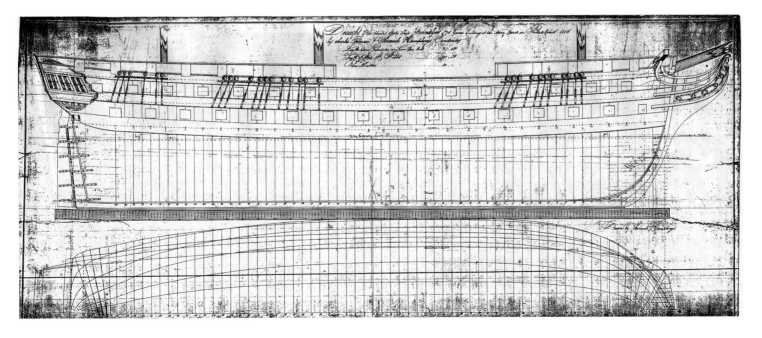

Ship of the line *Franklin*, drawing by W A K Martin. These American liners followed the example of the Humphreys' frigates in being larger than their European contemporaries. At one point she carried 87 guns - all 32pdrs. [US Navy: original at Independence Seaport, Philadelphia]

towed to Portsmouth, New Hampshire where she was used to test the new floating dock. The next year she was taken in hand to be razeed to a frigate. The concept for this no doubt had been the cutting-down of the *Independence* in 1836-7 (see below). The idea was kicking around as early as 1850, when John Dahlgren proposed a two-decker with 32pdrs on the lower deck and 10-inch shell guns, in broadside, above. *Franklin* was an obvious candidate for this, given that she was significantly broader in the beam than the frigates. Existing plans for this project are dated 1853, indicating that the project was short-lived, as a committee recommended 'substituting' a steam frigate for the old liner in August of that year.[10] It is not known whether the project was ever actually begun. In fact, the old ship was completely dismantled and, according to Bureau of Construction and Repair records, 'no part of the old vessel was used' in a new vessel: the steam frigate *Franklin*.[11] The steamer measured some 75 feet longer and 3 feet wider than the old liner.[12]

Independence

Independence was built at Charlestown Navy Yard at Boston, under the superintendence of Captain William Bainbridge, who obviously had his own ideas on warship design. It does appear, however, that there was no new plan drawn for these 74-gun ships. The 1799 Humphreys draught mentioned above (40-15-6J), is annotated 'Independence' on its reverse, and 'Indep.' can be made out in the stern section of its body plan. Furthermore, a letter from Bainbridge as early as 31 March 1813 indicates there was already a plan in

existence, for the naval commander suggested that the 'beam is narrow by two feet' and that the change could be made by altering the floor timbers. Bainbridge justified his suggestion with the observation that deficiency in beam was 'evident' in 'almost all the vessels of our navy'.[13]

Secretary of the Navy Jones agreed in principal with Bainbridge, and authorised adding 18 inches to the beam, indicating a change in the original from '48ft 6in to 50 feet'. At the same time he mandated increasing the length by five feet, straightening the sheer by raising it amidships and dropping it fore and aft, and reducing the tumblehome. The increase in beam was possible because Jones had consulted with Joshua Humphreys and learned that the original timber had been cut with enough excess to support the enlargement.[14] The fact that Humphreys was consulted (he had been out of federal service since around 1801) is a further indication that his 1799 plan was indeed the basis for *Independence* (and, by extension, the nearly identical *Washington*). The 1799 plan had called for a beam of 48ft 6in and length of 183ft. The *Independence* as completed had a 50ft beam and was 188ft between perpendiculars. Thus, the secretary's alterations tie the dimensions of the old design to that of the new ship. Even a cursory comparison of the body plans of the 1799 design and that of the (razeed) *Independence* further confirms the identification of the two.

With alterations in place, including the round bows, *Independence* was launched on 20 June 1814 and commissioned about 3 July 1815. She was armed with a combination of long 32pdrs on the lower gun deck and 24pdrs on the upper decks.[15] Subsequently, this was changed to all 32s, totalling eighty-seven, twenty-four of them carronades.

She was detailed to the Mediterranean under Captain Bainbridge, becoming the first American 74-gun ship seen in European waters. His report emphasised her good points, which were many. She was 'a ship of the line possessing in a very eminent degree the valuable qualities of sailing, steering, and working and without exception the easiest and best sea boat I have ever sailed in.' The encomiums continued: she was the 'fastest sailing ship in our navy. She greatly outsails the frigate "Con—-[illegible]" & all others in company.' Bainbridge noted a tendency to pitch and roll but these he considered 'inconceivably easy even in rough weather . . . there is not the least strain or work in the hull or wear and chafe in the rigging.'[16]

However, the negative aspect had already been seen: even as she departed for duty, when fully provisioned and stored, her lowest gunports were only three feet above the water. She had departed for her initial cruise in July 1815, and by September there was already talk of razee-ing the ship. Bainbridge would have none of that, though his alternatives were weak, and one senses he was a bit tender on the subject as he had shepherded her construction. He complained on general principles that she was too shallow for her dimensions, then said he had fitted 'very close half ports' on the lower gunports 'which can be kept in in time of action and raises her 14in, to 4ft 10in'. He also suggested reducing her sheer by raising her decks amidships.[17] However, it is puzzling why the navy simply did not reduce the battery from eighty-seven to her rated armament.

With or without the use of her lower gunports, she made a fine, and impressively militant show, particularly aimed at the Barbary powers, which had recently been the target of a British bombardment. The American squadron, headed by *Independence*, provoked sufficient trepidation amongst the Algerians to result in a treaty signed in late 1815, drawing to a close decades of troubles with these venal North African powers.[18]

This was the *Independence*'s only cruise as a ship of the line. She returned to Boston in late 1815 where she was laid up. Two years later, Samuel Humphreys and the Board of Navy Commissioners revisited the razee question, with the constructor estimating that removing her upper deck would increase the height of her sills to 4ft 11in above the water.

Ship of the line *Independence*. No 'as-built' hull plans of this vessel as a 74-gun ship exist, though evidence indicates that Humphreys' 1799 plan was the starting point for *Independence* and *Washington*. This plan was drawn by navy sailmaker Charles Ware. [National Archives RG 45 Ware Plans]

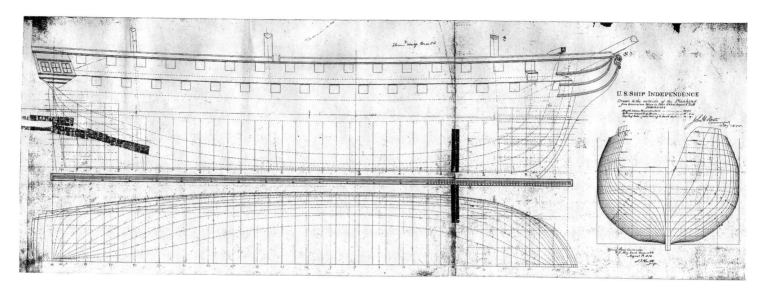

Plan of the razeed *Independence*. After her upper deck and its battery was removed, she proved a very satisfactory frigate - the largest in US Navy service. [National Archives 28-5-34A]

The board agreed, but no action was taken.[19] No doubt some desultory work was done on the ship in the ensuing years at Boston, but the final push was at the behest of the

Independence as a razee. In this iteration, rated at 54 guns, she proved a useful vessel. [US Naval Photographic Center NH 6078]

President, who in early 1836 inquired how long it would take to 'cut down' the two 74s at Boston and have them ready for sea. In any event, work on transforming the ship into a very large frigate was completed in 1837 and she was back at sea on 21 May of that year.

The razee *Independence* justified the expenditures involved in her alterations. She retained the masting and rigging of the 74: main and fore masts over 115 and 105 feet in length, respectively, and a main yard of 101 feet—in each instance about ten feet longer than those of a frigate of the era. She was reported to be quite fast—10 knots on a wind and 13 free. She was stiff under canvas and sure in the stays, but with a tendency to gripe when close-hauled. She now carried her ports at least seven feet above the water.[20]

Her career began with a fast Atlantic crossing, carrying the American ambassador to Russia, then sailed south to become the flagship of the Brazil squadron. She served in the Home squadron, then joined the American forces on the west coast during the Mexican War. After a stint in the Mediterranean, she was again posted to the Pacific. She went out of commission at Mare Island, California, in October 1857.

She became a fixture at Mare Island as a receiving ship for naval recruits. She was sold in 1914 and there was a plan to convert her to a restaurant for the upcoming Pan-Pacific Exposition. Nothing came of this and she was burned in September 1919 to recover the metal in her hull.[21]

Receiving ship *Independence*, at Mare Island, California in 1881. She was over a century old when she was finally disposed of. [US Naval Photographic Center NH 7706]

Washington

As with the original *Independence*, there are no 'as built' plans of *Washington*. However, as with the *Independence*, secretary Jones directed Isaac Hull, newly appointed commandant of the Portsmouth (Kittery) yard, to have the sheer straightened on the ship, then added 5 feet to her length and made the breadth 50 feet.[22] Then, in October 1813,

Hull wrote Jones asking whether to follow Bainbridge's instructions or the 'draft' of the 74-gun ship.[23] As the final dimensions of both ships were much the same, it appears that one plan was used for both *Independence* and *Washington*.

Washington was built under the direct supervision of William Badger, a local shipbuilder of some reputation, hired in April 1813. Though most of the frame timbers from the cancelled 1799 ship were still on hand, Hull had much to accomplish before the ship could be started, including building the ways and a smithy; and, once the timbers were inventoried, it was determined that there were some shortages to be made up. Bringing in materials and timber from

Gloucester and Portland was hampered by the British blockade, and December 1813 brought another impediment: much of the town of Portsmouth was destroyed by fire. Adding to the delays was Hull's perception that the location was too vulnerable to British incursions. He balked at building the ship if she was likely to be destroyed by the enemy before she was completed. Consequently, Commandant Hull attempted, with little success, to gather forces to defend the yard in the event of a possible incursion.[24]

In any event, the keel was finally laid in March 1814. And, despite the tightened blockade and the invasion of Maine in September, the hull was launched on 1 October,

Ship of the line *Washington*, painting by Roux. [US Navy, Keller Collection]

decorated with a figure of George Washington at the head. The war ended before she was ready to go to sea, however, and she was finally commissioned on 28 August 1815.

Her career was a short one. She was initially sent to Annapolis, where she played host to a plethora of dignitaries who were anxious to view the first available American ship of the line (while her sister ship was over-awing the Barbary powers in the Mediterranean). The ship sailed for the Mediterranean in June 1816 and remained there until returning to New York in mid-1818. In July of that year she was ordered to be dismantled at New York Navy Yard but kept at her moorings with a small maintenance crew aboard.[25] The *Washington* remained in ordinary there until broken up in 1843. There does not appear to have been any plan to make further use of the ship, either as a liner or as a

razee, though periodically reports were made on her condition and the cost and time required to put her in service.

Though the expense of keeping 74s in commission was later to limit their use, this consideration apparently was not applicable in the case of these three ships, as plans for new classes of 74s were already in the works by 1816. Their inability to carry their main deck guns sufficiently above water led directly to their failure as effective ships of the line.

The 'Gradual Increase' Ships of the Line

The 'Act for the Gradual Increase of the Navy', of 29 April 1816, in addition to the frigates previously covered, called for nine ships of 'no less than 74 guns'.[26] These nine vessels can be divided into three groups: five which were completed as ships of the line, two which were completed as storeships, and two that were never launched. For the purpose of this volume, the first five will be covered in some detail.

The five active liners were to four different designs. *Columbus*, the first ship completed, was the smallest of the five, and was designed by naval constructor William Doughty. *Ohio* was designed by Henry Eckford, a noted designer of merchant vessels. *Delaware* and *North Carolina* were sister ships by William Doughty. (Their plan was also used for the two storeships and two uncompleted ships.) Last, but far from least, was the 120-gun *Pennsylvania*, possibly the largest ship of the line ever built, designed by naval constructor Samuel Humphreys.

Columbus

The design of the *Columbus* is almost literally a middle point between the wartime ships and the *Delaware* class. Not only was this ship longer and beamier than the earlier ships, she was also deeper, all of these increases reflecting corrections in the wartime ships' inability to carry their lower guns high enough. *Columbus*, built at Washington Navy Yard, was 191ft 10in between perpendiculars, 52ft moulded beam and 21ft 10in depth of hold. All three of

these dimensions were at least two feet larger than those of her predecessors. Her tonnage as completed was 2480, up from 2259 for *Independence et al*. Her lines were a bit fuller fore and aft than the earlier ships' and she exhibited less rake in the stem and stern.

The increase in dimensions and displacement may have been aimed at improving her ability to carry the armament required. However, the battery itself – rather than remaining at the already substantial 86 guns seen previously – was also increased significantly. In her first commission, *Columbus* carried no less than 92 guns. The main battery was sixty-eight 32s, plus twenty-four 42pdr carronades. Later, this was reduced to 86 and the 42s replaced by 32s, but eight of the total were 8-inch shell guns.[27] *Columbus* was within inches of the size of the British liners of the *Canopus* class (80-84 guns) mentioned earlier in the chapter.

The ship was laid down in June 1816, launched on 1 March 1819 and commissioned on 7 September of that year. Her service life was curiously bisected: her first commission ended in 1821 under adverse circumstances and her second began over twenty years later, and this time she was a significantly improved vessel.

Her first duty station was the Mediterranean as flagship for William Bainbridge. At the time her sailing was 'not very good, makes great leeway'.[28] The problems were severe enough to warrant an extended lay up, and she was not at sea again until 1842. In the interim, 'the injuries [were] removed that hindered her qualities on the first cruise.'[29] Indeed, after this point she became known for her far flung cruises. Her initial assignment was in the Mediterranean in 1842, and from thence sailed to join the Brazil squadron. She returned to the US for refit in 1844, then sailed to Canton, China, carrying copies of the first US treaty with the Chinese. She remained in the Far East to carry Commodore James Biddle on the first American attempt to open Japan to the west. Biddle's effort met no success, however, and *Columbus* returned to the west coast, though the ship was too large to be of significant use in the Mexican War.

Her performance was much improved during these commissions. Her speed was 12.4 knots under the best circumstances, and she was reasonably stiff under canvas. Her

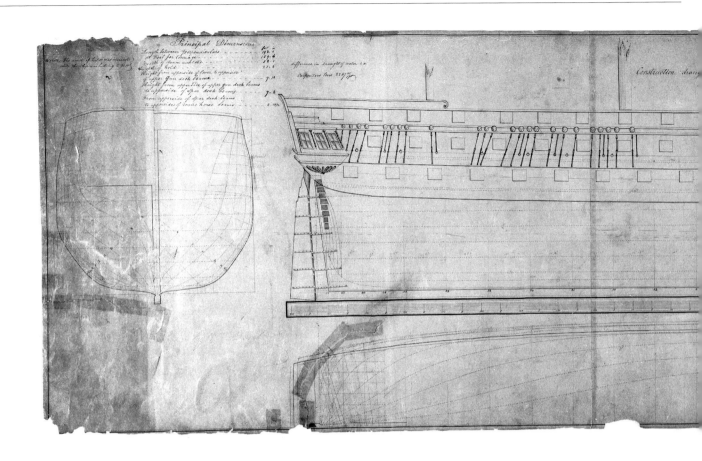

Above: The 74-gun ship *Columbus*, designed by William Doughty. The larger dimensions of this ship were intended to correct problems with the earlier three 74s. [National Archives 40-11-6]

Left: Sail plan of *Columbus*, by navy sailmaker Charles Ware. [US Naval Photographic Center NH 38993]

Right: Liner *Columbus*, with sloop of war *Vincennes*, departing Jeddo Bay, 29 July 1845, after an unsuccessful attempt to open Japan to the west. [US Naval Photographic Center NH 6178]

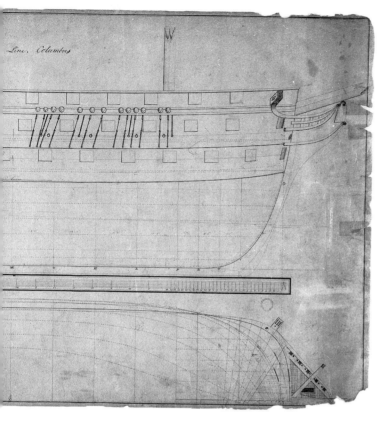

major drawback was a tendency to steer wildly under a press of canvas with the wind on the quarter.[30]

She was laid up at Norfolk in March 1848 and there ended her career. On 20 April 1861 she was burned at Norfolk Navy Yard to prevent her falling into Confederate hands.

Ohio

Henry Eckford had a shipyard in Brooklyn and had begun designing and building ships around 1800. He was probably best known for his prodigious efforts in building a naval force on Lake Ontario during the War of 1812 –warships built from keel to truck in the wilderness in 1814. Afterwards, he returned to his own yard in New York and continued designing and building merchant vessels.

In 1816 John Rodgers, head of the Board of Navy Commissioners, asked Eckford to submit a model and plan for a 74-gun ship, 193ft by 53ft beam. The board's purpose in extending this privilege to a private builder was to avail themselves 'of the most approved professional skill of our country'. Eckford's design met the board's approval, though

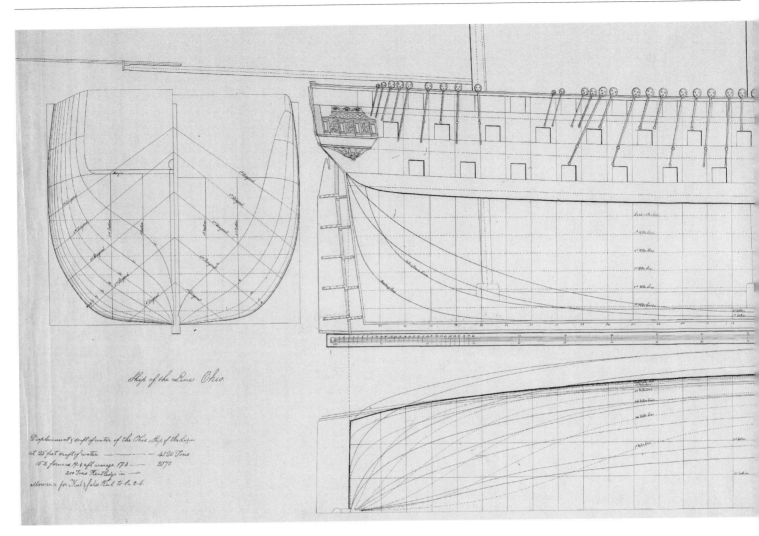

Ship of the Line Ohio.

Displacement & draft of water of the Ohio, Ship of the Line
at 25 feet draft of water ———————— 4130 Tons
15 2 forward 19.4 aft average 17.3 ——— 2170
200 Tons Kentledge in ——
allowance for Keel & false Keel to be 2-6.

with some minor exceptions, and he was appointed naval constructor at Brooklyn to superintend the building of the ship.[31] Eckford's vessel, the ship of the line *Ohio*, was considered the best American liner and possibly the best 74 in the world. She was laid down in November 1817 and launched on 30 May 1820. Her dimensions were 197ft 2in between perpendiculars, by 53ft 10in beam, somewhat larger than the Board's requirements.

It was, however, seventeen years between her launch and commissioning, on 11 October 1838. She had been laid up in Wallabout Bay in the yard since her launch and coppering. Keeping, but not completing her, was, among other things, a money-allocation device. The department's object seems to have been to allocate the 'Gradual Increase' funding incrementally to bring as many ships as possible to a point where they could be fitted out for active service in a short amount of time. The Secretary of the Navy's 1835 report, which listed twelve ships (seven of them liners) on the stocks under 'tight houses', stated the rationale succinctly: 'it is believed they can be completed and equipped by the time that crews could be collected for them.'[32] The result was an increasing number of ships on the stocks or in ordinary, but which were theoretically available, given a specific expenditure of funds and time.

The preservation of the *Ohio* involved having her bulkheads removed to 'admit the free circulation of air' and building a roof on her in 1830. Also, by 1831, most of the materials to fit her out, including guns, canvas, tanks, and ballast, had been gathered. However, even by this latter date, it was estimated that over $170,000 was necessary to complete her.[33]

When the decision was made to place her in service, she

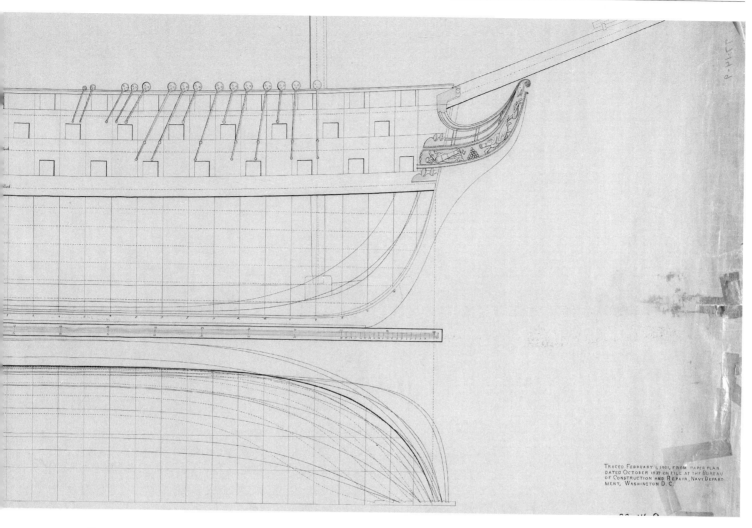

was sent to Boston to utilise the drydock there for re-cop-pering. That passage provided a preview of her capabilities. The *Naval Magazine*'s article was glowing. The ship 'realised the fullest expectations of those who had so confidently predicted her good qualities as a sea-boat—fast sailer, etc. She proved to be perfectly easy in all her motions, steered like a pilot boat, worked quickly, and sailed at the rate of 12 knots 7 fathoms, with a whole sails breeze, off the wind, under double reefed topsails.' All this, said the writer, despite having a set of sails too small for her, and seventeen years of growth on her bottom. The article went on to decry the state of the navy and the poor design of their ships, using the obvious qualities of the *Ohio* to support their contention that more 'progressive' merchant vessel builders such as Eckford should supplant the 'stodgy' naval constructors in the design of American warships.[34]

The 74-gun ship *Ohio* was the only US Navy liner designed by a non-naval constructor, Henry Eckford. Many considered her the best American 74 and she was much admired at home and abroad. [National Archives 77-14-9]

It is not clear whether the ship was completely outfitted, armed—originally with 32pdr long guns and carronades—provisioned or ballasted when the above was written. However, it appears that much of the above was accurate. Her commanding officer wrote a detailed report on her with such minutiae as complaints about the height of the waist boat davits and catheads (all too low), width of the hammock nettings (too narrow), and the inconvenience in having the galley on the lower deck. He also mentioned that the half-ports on the lower gun deck were not well fitted, making the deck wet in heavy weather.

As to sailing qualities, the report was complimentary:

In a severe gale, which continued and with some violence for thirteen hours, she was [*sic*] scud under close reefed Main Topsail and Foresail, with perfect safety. She is stiff, lively and buoyant, steers with ease and is as dry as could be expected. She rolls deep but easy, straining nothing below or above. In a 'head beat sea' she pitches quick and h– [illegible] this I attribute to the construction of the ship, her floor being too short and the foremast being placed too far forward . . . In tacking she is rather sluggish in her movement . . .

He went on to describe crew accommodations as generally comfortable.[35] The latter statement may have been a bit optimistic for during her first cruise the officers were board-ed on the orlop deck, a deck lower than was traditional, and there was something of a rebellion against the 'exceedingly uncomfortable' conditions there.[36]

Later reports on the ship's sailing characteristics echoed much the same story. She logged up to 13 knots (11 knots on a wind) and, in one instance, rode out a heavy norther off Vera Cruz, a storm in which some thirty merchant ships parted their cables and went ashore.[37]

The *Ohio*'s original 32pdr battery was altered later to a combination of 42pdr long guns (thirty-two), 42pdr carronades (twenty-four) and 32pdrs (thirty-four), totalling 90 guns. With the introduction of shell guns, she was re-armed with twelve 8-inch, twenty-eight 42s, and sixteen 32s (1846).[38]

Ohio's first commission took her to the Mediterranean, as flagship under Isaac Hull. She returned to Boston in 1840 where she was a receiving ship until called back into service for the Mexican War. She rode out a heavy gale, as mentioned above, in early 1846 off Vera Cruz. Ten of her guns were taken off for the siege of that city, and over 300 of her

Ohio is a good example of the navy's policy toward line of battle ships: she lay in ordinary for seventeen years between her launch and commission. It was less expensive to preserve her stationary than in commission. [US Naval Photographic Center NH 59576]

crew participated in the Tuxpan River operation of 1847. However, her deep draught limited her usefulness during the operations in the Gulf of Mexico. In 1847, she was sent to the Pacific squadron, remaining there until 1850, overseeing American seagoing commerce in the first years of the California gold rush. At Boston she was decommissioned and became a receiving ship in 1851. The career of the *Ohio* ended when she was placed in ordinary in 1875, and she was sold in 1883.

The ship had had a significant effect on the British when she appeared in European waters. In the 1820s the Controller of the Navy was asked if more ships like *Ohio* were needed in the British fleet. He replied that the British vessels would prevail, but the First Rates ought to be broader and more heavily armed. The upshot was three new two-decker 90-gun vessels, designed by Robert Seppings, slightly larger than *Ohio*, carrying 92 guns.[39]

Ohio was one of the favourite commands in the pre-steam navy, and became part of 'old salts' stories and legends. Herman Melville in his long poem *Bridegroom Dick* mentioned her:

'Twas Jack got up the ball at Naples,
Gay in the old *Ohio* glorious;[40]

North Carolina

The *North Carolina* was the first of an eventual class of six, only two of which saw active service as ships of the line. All were laid down between June 1816 (*North Carolina*) and May 1822 (*Virginia*). The design was by William Doughty, and was obviously a slight enlargement of that of his *Columbus*, which was laid down the same month as *North Carolina*. The latter was about three feet longer (196ft 3in), one foot wider (53ft), but two inches less in depth of hold (21ft 8in). The lines and body plan of the two ships were, except for the enlargement in dimensions, nearly identical. By the time both ships had been laid down, the inadequacies of the *Franklin* and her sisters (all of which had been in the water in 1815) had been manifest and it appears Doughty prepared two versions, one larger than the other, to ensure that one or both would obviate the problems with the earlier design.

The *North Carolina* was first of the six commissioned, by 18 December 1824, sporting a figurehead representing Sir Walter Raleigh. She was pierced for 102 guns, but her earliest battery was said to have been 94, consisting of 42pdrs and 32s.[41] Later, in 1841, she carried thirty-two 42pdrs, thirty-four 32s, and twenty-four 42pdr carronades. Her most impressive battery was listed in 1845 when eight of her 32s were replaced by the same number of 8-inch shell guns.[42] This amounted to a broadside of 1798 pounds.

She was a magnificent sight, and comparable to a British Second Rate of the times. A sail plan of the era yields some impressive dimensions. From waterline to truck she measured about 230 feet, with the main stick about 100 feet above the deck. (She was about half the height of the Great Pyramid at Khufu.) From flying jib to ringtail boom was about 380 feet. Other statistics and descriptions from her first commission round out the picture of a pre-Civil War battle ship. She carried a crew of 960 men and had a ship's library of over eleven hundred volumes–purchased through volunteer contributions by officers and crew. Lieutenant Alexander Slidell Mackenzie described the pomp on deck when Commodore John Rodgers went ashore at Gibraltar:

The sailors were drawn up before the main mast, looking with respect toward the hallowed region of the quarterdeck. Upon this spacious parade-ground, flanked by a double battery, a company of fine-looking soldiers, with burnished and well-brushed attire, were drawn up . . . A splendid band of music, dressed in Moorish garb, was stationed at the stern, and the officers were all collected for the same purpose upon the quarterdeck, in irregular groups of noble-looking young fellows . . . At length the Herculean form and martial figure of the veteran commodore was added to the number . . . a thousand eyes were fixed upon him, a thousand hats were raised; and as he passed over the side, the soldiers presented arms, and the music sent forth a martial melody. I thought I had never seen any array so soul-inspiring, so imposing.[43]

There were consistent positive reports on the ship's

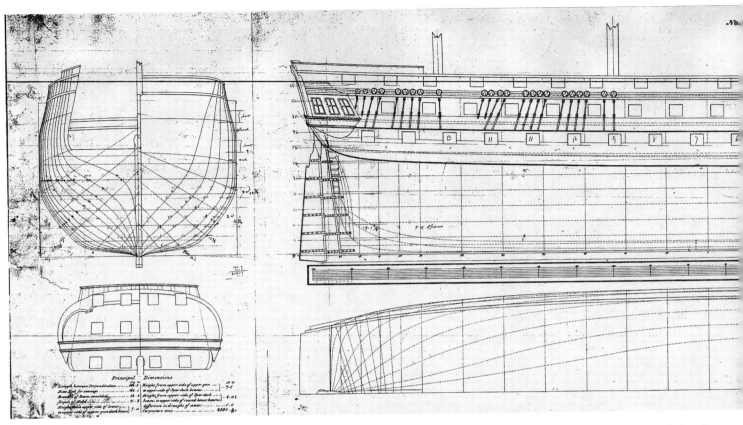

Above: North Carolina was constructor Doughty's enlargement of the *Columbus* design, used also for *Delaware*. [National Archives 40-5-17B]

Left: Spar plan by Ware of uss *North Carolina*: her mainmast measured 100ft above the deck, and waterline to main truck was 230ft. [US Naval Photographic Center NH 38993]

Right: Watercolour by Cammillieri of the *North Carolina* in service, 1827. She carried an impressive battery, ranging from 90 to 94 guns. [US Naval Historical Center]

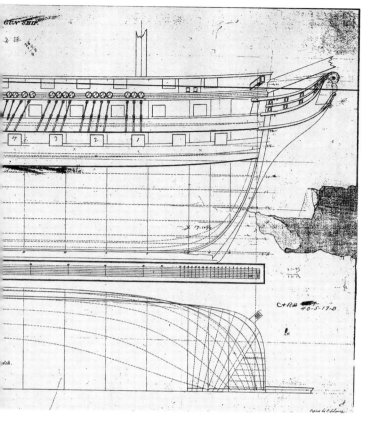

sailing qualities. She was relatively fast for a 74, logging 10 knots on a wind and 12 running free. At sea she was stiff and capable of laying to and scudding satisfactorily. Though she rolled deep and lurched quickly in heavy seas, her spars showed little strain.[44] It appears her lower deck gunports were sufficiently high above water.

Her first duty station was as flagship in the Mediterranean, under Captain John Rodgers (where he apparently used the wide latitude allowed in those days for uniforming his crew – particularly the band). The Mediterranean, was, of course, the prestige assignment in the navy, and the *North Carolina* was an appropriate 'showboat' to display American naval prowess, or at least martial polish, before the critical eyes of the major European fleets.

She was in ordinary or decommissioned from around 1827 to 1836, then fitted out for the Pacific. She remained on station there until 1839 when she returned to the US and was again taken out of active service at New York. She was a receiving ship there until final decommissioning in 1866, and sale in October 1867.

North Carolina was not only the 'showboat' for the Mediterranean squadron, she was noted for her sailing qualities and speed. [Naval History Center]

Delaware

The *Delaware* was nearly identical to *North Carolina*. She was laid down in August 1817 at Norfolk, and launched on 21 October 1820. Her figurehead was a formidable looking Delaware Indian, still to be seen on the campus of the US Naval Academy. As was common practice during this era, there was no haste in putting her into commission, and she was roofed over for preservation. The order for her commissioning was dated 27 March 1827 and she sailed for the Mediterranean on 10 February 1828, replacing *North Carolina* on that station.[45]

The ship's battery listed in 1833 consisted of 92 guns: thirty-two each of 32pdrs and 42pdrs, and twenty-eight 42pdr carronades. In 1841, when shell guns were authorised, she carried 98 cannon: eight 8-inch shell guns, twenty-eight 42pdrs, thirty 32s, and twenty-two 42pdr carronades.[46]

Her sailing characteristics were similar to those of the *North Carolina*. She was stiff in a wind, and steered and worked efficiently. She was considered safe on a lee shore as long was she could carry close reefed topsails. Both *Delaware* and *North Carolina* trimmed by the stern from 14 inches to 2 feet, and carried significant ballast: the former 270 tons, the latter 100 tons less.[47]

Delaware was in the Mediterranean until 1830, then returned for refit at Norfolk. She was again in the Mediterranean from 1833 to 1836, carrying the American ambassador to England on the outgoing voyage. On her return to the US, she was the victim of a 'white squall' knock-down, but quickly recovered. From 1841 to 1844 she was on the Brazil station. On 22 March 1844 she was decommissioned at Norfolk and laid up. She was at Norfolk and was burned to prevent her capture in April 1861.

Vermont and *New Hampshire*

These two vessels were identical in their hull lines to *North Carolina*. Both were completed for auxiliary roles and were never armed as ships of the line. *Vermont* was laid down in September 1818 and launched in September 1848. *New Hampshire*'s keel was laid in June 1819 and she went down the ways in January 1864. These dates are misleading because it leads to the conclusion that the delay was due to insufficient funds. In fact, the navy had no need for these ships, particularly after steam became practical for warships. It is apparent that the navy could have completed any one or

Left: Figurehead of *Delaware*, a formidable looking Delaware Indian. The original was a fixture at the Naval Academy for many years. [Courtesy US Naval Academy Museum]

Below: Lithograph of *Delaware* en route to France, 25 August 1833. *Delaware* was built on the same plan as *North Carolina*. Her career was uneventful excepting a knock down in a white squall in 1838. [US Navy]

more of these ships at will, if there was a need. They were all in excellent state of preservation throughout the pre-Civil War era – as was evident by the long careers of both these vessels.

Vermont was launched to free up the ways for new construction as well as for fire safety considerations. She lay in ordinary until 1862, when she was needed as a storeship at Port Royal, South Carolina, the headquarters of the South Atlantic Blockading Squadron. While under tow southward, a violent gale blew up and the tow was dropped. She broached to, lost all her sails and her rudder was wrenched

Vermont in her role as a receiving ship. Launched in 1848 she was never commissioned as a warship, but became a store ship in 1862. [US Naval Photographic Center NH 2102]

in two, leaving her adrift for two days in the storm. Rescue vessels did not reach her until some days later. With a jury rudder, she sailed on to Port Royal, arriving on 12 April, over six weeks after setting out from Boston. She served at Port Royal as hospital, ordnance, stores and receiving ship until 1864, when she was replaced by *New Hampshire*. Subsequently, she stayed at New York Navy Yard as a receiving ship until 1901, then was sold the next year.

New Hampshire was originally named *Alabama*, but in 1863, when selected to serve in southern waters, the name was changed. Her hull had been essentially complete by 1825, but she was not launched until 23 April 1864. She was commissioned on 13 May as a storeship, in which capacity she replaced *Vermont* at Port Royal, South Carolina on 29 July and remained on station until June 1866. From then

until 1876 she was a receiving ship at Norfolk, followed by another five years at Port Royal. From 1881 to 1892 she served in various training roles at Norfolk, Newport, Rhode Island, and New London, Connecticut. In 1893 she was loaned to the New York Naval Militia as a training ship, and was there when her name was changed to *Granite State* in 1902. She caught fire and sank on 23 May 1921 at her Hudson River pier. She was sold and eventually sunk off Massachusetts in July 1922. She was just short of a century old at the time.

Virginia and *New York*

Another pair of hulls identical to *North Carolina*, these two were never launched. *New York* was laid down in May 1820 at Norfolk; *Virginia* in May 1822 at Boston. *Virginia* was broken up on the ways in 1884. *New York* was on the stocks at Norfolk and was burned to prevent her falling into Confederate hands when the yard was abandoned by Federal forces in April 1861. Coincidentally, the navy's next *New York*, a steam frigate laid down during the Civil War, also was never completed. Her hulk was sold in 1888.

Although having these huge hulls on the stocks for so many years seems a waste, it should be kept in mind that retaining them on the stocks was significantly less expensive than maintaining them in the water. This reasoning was apropos up until the mid-1850s, but after the advent of the ironclad, it made no sense at all.

Pennsylvania

Pennsylvania was the largest sailing warship built in the United States and possibly in the world up to this time. Samuel Humphreys, who apparently prepared a draught for the 74s which was not used, was assigned the task of designing this ship. Though she was not laid down until November 1822 at Philadelphia, Humphreys had begun the process as early as February 1820. At that point, there was some secrecy involved, as John Rodgers directed Humphreys to avoid divulging the fact that the ship's dimensions were to be different from the other 74 building at Philadelphia (*North Carolina*).[48]

Humphreys had in his possession the plans for the Spanish *Santisíma Trinidad* and the British *Royal Sovereign* at the time he was designing *Pennsylvania*.[49] Both vessels had been at Trafalgar, and the former was widely regarded as the largest ship in the world at the time, carrying about 134 guns on four decks. She had been built in 1769, however, and exhibited the exaggerated tumblehome characteristic of that era. Her dimensions were approximately 190ft (pp), by 58ft moulded beam, by about 24ft depth of hold.[50] *Royal Sovereign* was a 100-gun First Rate, 183ft by 52ft, launched in 1786.[51] Humphreys apparently used these as benchmarks rather than patterns for the ship. He also built a full hull model of the design and immersed it to determine the new ship's displacement, a figure he put at 4994 tons.[52] The ship's stern and head were designed by William Rush and were rather more elaborate than other contemporary warships. Over the stern arched the requisite gods of antiquity, including, on one side, a view of the Parthenon. This was balanced by a stone fortification and the stern third of a three-decker, apparently on the stocks. This design element may well have been unique to this vessel. The ship's head was a god-like figure, probably Hercules.

The ship was not launched until 18 July 1837, but had already been the subject of some foreign scrutiny. A British naval officer looked at her in 1826 and noted the following: 'She is a beautiful model, remarkably well put together. Frame live oak. Planked with white oak. A long, low floored ship; fine entrance, clean run; full flaring bow; rounds in at the main deck ports; round stern with a counter; no poop.' At that time he estimated four months would be required to launch her and estimated her displacement at 5141 tons, and counted 148 gunports, though her spar deck was yet unfinished.[53] She was completed and in commission by November 1837, when she made her single cruise. This was from her launch site on the Delaware River to Norfolk Navy Yard, departing on 29 November and arriving on 2 January 1838, with stops en route to ship gun carriages and other equipment.

She was reported to be cumbersome, leewardly and crank, but capable of 'surprising' speed when in trim. These judgements were based on the single passage, however, and it is not certain she had more than thirty-four guns

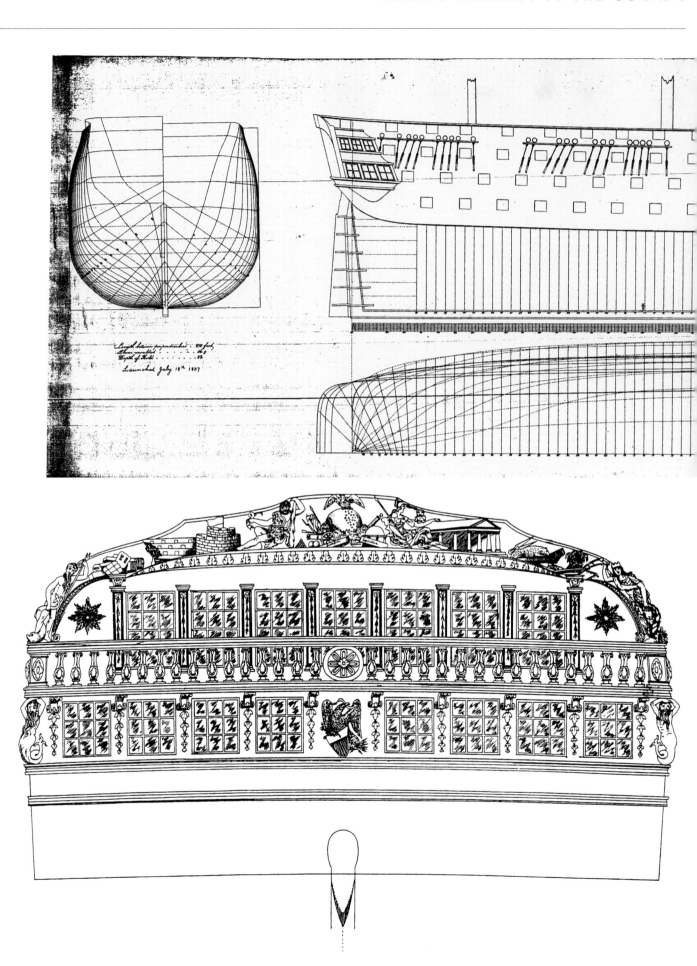

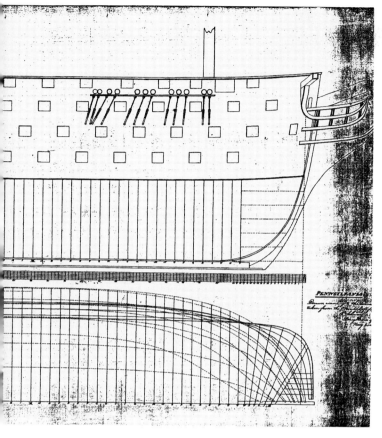

aboard at the time.[54] If so, she would have been high in the water, contributing to her leewardlyness. In any event, excessive speed and handiness were not generally characteristics of large liners.

The *Pennsylvania* was larger than any British First Rate (120-gun ship) of the time, both in size and potential battery. Her broadsides were pierced for 138 guns, plus bridle ports. If she received the standard 32pdr battery, her broadside would have been something over 2200 pounds. As to her actual armament, an 1846 listing gave her 90 guns: four 8-inch shell guns and thirty-two 32pdrs on her lower gun deck; four 8-inch and thirty 32s on the middle gun deck, and four 8-inch and twenty-eight 32s on the upper gun deck. No broadside weapons were on the spar deck at the time.[55] Vessels of the *Caledonia* class First Rate of this era carried 122 guns, ranging from 32s to 12s.[56]

In terms of size, *Pennsylvania* was 210ft between perpendiculars, 56ft 9in moulded beam, by 23ft depth of hold, and about 3100 tons burthen. This dimensions are substantially larger than the *Caledonia* class (broadened) of 1819 to 1823, which measured 205ft 5in (on gun deck), by 54ft 6in and 23ft 2in depth, measuring 2694 tons.[57] The only compara-

Above: The120-gun ship *Pennsylvania*. Arguably the largest sailing warship ever built, she could carry 138 guns. [National Archives 8-3-4]

Left: Stern carving of *Pennsylvania*, 'designed and executed by William Rush Esq of Philadel in August 1824'. Note depiction of the stern of a ship of the line on the upper left. [National Archives 4-14-7]

Right: Model of the *Pennsylvania*, giving an idea of her substantial freeboard (and windage) resulting from her four decks. In keeping with the US Navy's reluctance to fund such large vessels in commission, the ship was simply preserved at Norfolk Navy Yard against the eventuality of hostilities. She was destroyed there in 1861. [US Naval Historical Center NH 60687]

ble ship of the era was the *Queen* rated as a 110, which was about 3100 tons and 204ft by 60ft, launched in 1839.[58] These dimensions and comparisons certainly place the American liner among the largest in the world.

Some idea of her masting can be gained from dimensions published in 1833, produced by Charles Ware, sailmaker at Boston Navy Yard. Her main mast would measure 178 feet from step to truck; her main yard, 110 feet. Her total sail area measured 18,341 square yards and the main topsail measured 1531 square yards. Her rigging included shrouds measuring 11 inches in diameter and mainstay 19 inches across. *The Military and Naval Magazine* published these statistics along with those of the RN ship of the line *Neptune* 'represented as being the largest British vessel that has ever floated.' The American vessel was larger in all of the comparable listed dimensions.[59]

As mentioned, she made one cruise, then was coppered at Norfolk Navy Yard. She remained there, first in ordinary (to 1842), then as a receiving ship. She was among the vessels destroyed to prevent their capture in April 1861. (A total of three other 74s were lost in the conflagration: *Delaware*, *New York*, and *Columbus*.)

The First American Battle Fleet

The American blue-water battle fleet is generally agreed to have come into existence with the emergence of the steel navy and vessels such as the battleship *Texas* of the 1890s. However, it is worth considering this group of line of battle ships of the pre-Civil War era.

Their origin, in 1799, during the Quasi-War with France, made that nation the most likely adversary, especially considering their colonial interests in the West Indies. The act by which they were authorised specifically mentioned 'ensuring peace' with European powers. Though the first three liners were built during the British blockade in the War of 1812, their origin and design certainly predated that blockade, calling into question the theory that they were strictly built as large blockade breakers.

It is the belief of this author that the ships were intended to form a classic line of battle fleet, a contention based on several factors. First of all was the fact of their retention over the decades after their initial construction. Though many say they lost favour as cruising vessels on overseas stations because of their high operating expense, it was obvious even before the vessels were built that such ships would be more costly to operate than frigates. So the question is, if they were so expensive why were they retained, whether on the stocks or in ordinary, for literally decades?

Second is the condition in which they were kept, again for decades. There was much discussion about preserving these ships, and they usually were roofed over when in 'ordinary'. The preservation efforts were effective, whether the ships were in ordinary or on the stocks. These examples suffice: *Columbus* went some twenty years between commissions, and indeed was considered a much improved ship in the 1840s than she was in the early 1820s. The same can be said of *Ohio*, which was in the water seventeen years before commissioning. On the stocks, there were *Vermont* and *New Hampshire*, which went thirty and forty-five years, respectively, between keel-laying and launching, and both survived into the twentieth century. The point here is that regardless of whether in ordinary or on the stocks, these ships were accessible in relatively short order when needed.

Specifically, the Secretary of the Navy's annual reports usually listed the vessels on the stocks and in ordinary, and often cited estimates of the time and cost required to ready them for service. In the report of 1831, for instance, there were five liners being built. Four—*Alabama*, *Vermont*, *Virginia*, and *New York*—would require sixty to ninety days each to launch, and would require funds ranging from $37,000 to $79,000 each to complete. *Pennsylvania* was the exception. She would require six months and $33,000 to get into the water.[60] Note that two of these four were never completed at all. In the same report were similar statistics on the liners in ordinary: *Columbus*, *Independence*, *Ohio*, *Delaware* and *North Carolina*. The cost of refurbishing them ranged from $100,000 to $171,000. The latter two would require sixty days and four months respectively for the work.[61] In total – theoretically – the cost would be less than $1 million to have all ten of these vessels in service, in not more than six months time. As wartime experience showed, it would take longer than that to recruit their crews.

These statistics point up the state of these vessels. They

illustrate how forward was the construction of the vessels on the stocks, and how quickly they could be launched. Second, they show the same for those ships laid up in ordinary. The figures also point up the fact that repairing a ship was more expensive and time consuming than getting one launched. Therefore, it was also more fiscally responsible to retain a vessel on the stocks than to send her to sea. It is worth noting here that this policy of keeping vessels long on the stocks was also typical French practice.

Thus, it is obvious that at any given time from around 1825 (when all of the 1816 vessels were either in the water or within months of launching), to the mid-1840s, the United States had on hand, available in no more than six months notice, no less than eight capital ships. In 1831, as seen above, there were ten, five each in ordinary and on the stocks.

As to the question of whether these ships comprised a legitimate line of battle, it is informative to compare the fleets of some of the smaller European powers at the end of the Napoleonic Wars. The following had fewer than twenty line of battle ships: Denmark (2), Netherlands (19), Portugal (11), Sweden (13), Kingdom of Naples (2), Austria (3) and Spain (16).[62] It should also be noted that, though Britain and France had large numbers of liners, their colonial responsibilities required their forces to be widely dispersed, militating against their ability to concentrate their forces against an American foe.

Of course, another consideration is whether there was an American battle plan for these ships. As far as this author has been able to determine, there was none–but there appears to have been no formal 'war plan' as such, nor any large body of policy in this area, in any case. It is informative in this regard to look at the Secretary of the Navy's statements when he proposed the original twelve 74s, in a letter to the committee chairman in the House of Representatives (29 December 1798): 'If twelve ship [*sic*] of Seventy-four guns are added to our Navey [*sic*] . . . an invasion of our country [by France] . . . would be rendered so difficult, that it would scarcely be attempted . . . She would be obliged to employ more than double the Number of ships of equal force, to convoy her armies, provisions, and Stores, and to keep the communication open

between her armies and her own country.'[63] The implications of this statement are clear: a wartime scenario wherein a French force–troopships plus battle fleet escorts–attempted to invade the US. The success of the venture could be obtained only when the defending fleet of American 74s was neutralised. Regardless of whether there was a formal battle plan in place, the upshot would be a classic line-of-battle engagement on the high seas. Given the state of Franco-American relations in 1798 and their truculent high-handedness when dealing with Americans, the possibility of an invasion was a distinct one. It would not be until 1802 and the failure of the LeClerc Santo Domingo expedition that Napoleon finally foreswore his western hemispheric ambitions. In these circumstances, it is clear that the 74s were intended to check a European interloper on the high seas.[64]

As to the somewhat ancillary question of the viability of twelve American 74s against the French fleet, it is worth noting that there were only eighteen French liners at Trafalgar and seventeen at the Battle of the Nile. And, should actual war have been declared, the Americans would have been, by virtue of a common enemy, allied with the British, who would never willingly have allowed a French squadron to escape the blockade, whatever their intended target.

It is also worth noting here that, in the Jefferson administration, Secretary of the Navy Robert Smith also favoured a fleet of a dozen 74s. In this instance the potential enemy was Spain. Such a force might prevent her from gaining control of the Gulf, and enable American seizure of the Floridas. Of course, the general anti-navy attitude of that administration prevented any such expansion of the fleet.[65]

Three possibilities occur for the possible wartime roles of these ships: (1) as Chapelle speculated, they may have been tasked to break a blockade; (2) they may have been used for convoy escorts; and (3), they could have composed a battle fleet to check an invasion. In actuality, their use may have been a combination of the above. In any event, these ships would have been a powerful element in any strategic operations, and certainly would have been a strong factor in any decision by a foreign power intent on exerting undue influence in the western hemisphere.

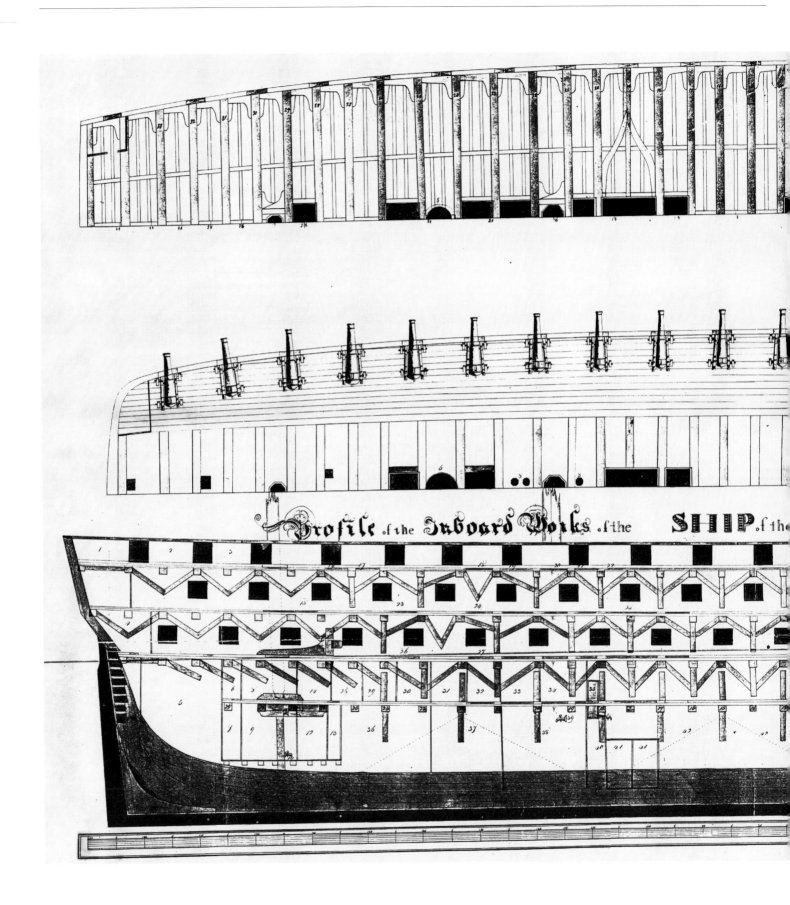

Profile of the Inboard Works of the SHIP of the

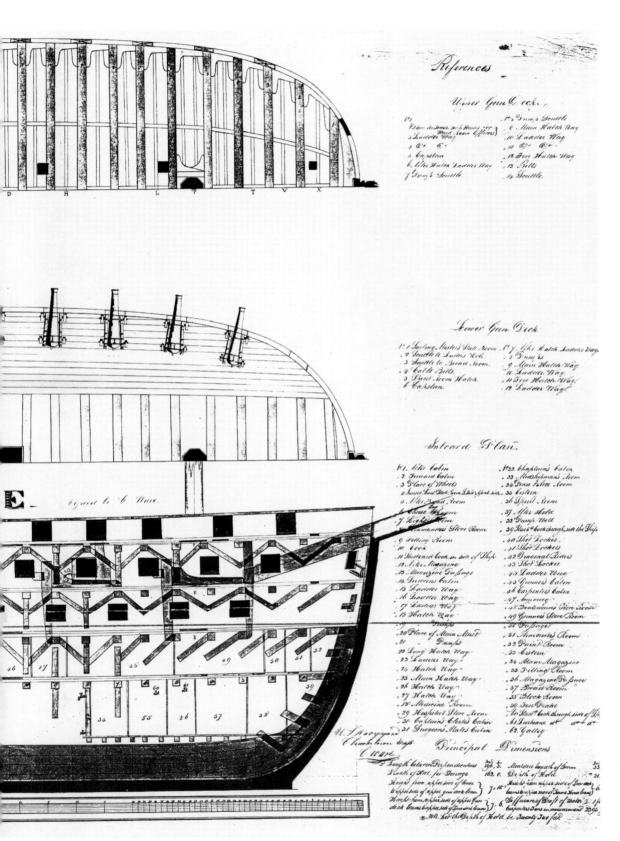

Inboard plan of an unidentified US liner, by sailmaker Charles Ware. Many have wondered at the navy's persistence in not only building but keeping these huge vessels in ordinary. In fact, until steam power superseded sail, these ships could have been fitted out and at sea in about six months – becoming, in theory – the first American sailing battle fleet. [National Archives RG 45 Ware Plans]

CHAPTER 6

The Sloops of War, 1798–1831

T HE TERM sloop of war refers to a ship-rigged warship smaller than a frigate with all the main battery guns on a single deck, usually the weather deck. The French used the term 'corvette' for this type vessel. A major variety of the type was the spar-decked sloop, which had a light weather deck to protect the gun-deck crews. The distinction between this ship and a frigate was, again, the concentration of main deck battery below the weather deck. Both frigates and sloops were likely to carry chase guns on the forecastle, whether a separate raised platform or on the forward portion of the main deck.

This chapter covers these ships from the re-establishment of the navy in 1798 to 1831, the latter date being tied to the completion of the first large class of these vessels in the US Navy. Included in the Quasi-War portion are a few ships for which we have little concrete information or plans, leaving only conjecture concerning their battery layout, other than the number of guns. Contemporary accounts often simply refer to these vessels as 'ships'–appropriate for their rig, but not enlightening as to their battery. It appears that some of these 'ships' may have built to modified merchant vessel plans. In any event, they are included here, rather than in the section on frigates, due to their size alone.

Quasi-War Contract and Subscription Sloops

Seven sloops of war were built in the era 1798-1800 for the undeclared war with France. Three were built by public subscription: *Merrimack, Maryland,* and *Patapsco.* The ships built by private contractors for the government were *Portsmouth, Warren, Connecticut,* and *Trumbull.* Apparently

Congress appropriated a designated amount for all the ships, and left it to the discretion of the Secretary of the Navy as to the method of acquiring them – purchase, subscription or contract. Of course, the larger the number of ships which could be financed through public subscriptions, the larger the amount available for other uses. On the other hand, the advantage of the contract method was that there was no need for a time-consuming citizens' fund-raising effort, nor was it necessary to negotiate with the local committee on the size and design of the vessel to be built. It is also worth noting that there was some leeway wherein 'public' (federal) money was available to compensate for shortfalls in funds raised by subscription.

There is some disagreement on the financing of the ship *Trumbull.* The navy's documents of the Quasi-War lists her as built by 'citizens of Norwich, Conn', as does Chapelle. However, Gardner Allen's book on the Quasi-War indicates she was not subscription built.[1] Furthermore, correspondence on the subject in the Quasi-War volumes mentions no citizens' group, merely that the Secretary of the Navy engaged Joseph Howland of Norwich, Connecticut, to build an 18-gun ship 'for the Public'.[2] This is not typical with the subscription vessels: usually the local committee was involved in selecting the builder.

Merrimack

The citizens of Newburyport, Massachusetts began the subscription movement with this vessel. She was built by the firm of Cross & Clark and designed by William Hackett. She was laid down 9 July 1798, launched on 12 October, and was in service by early January 1799. Though rated at 24 guns, she carried twenty 9pdrs and eight 6pdrs, the latter probably on her quarterdeck.[3] Despite having quarterdeck guns, the ship was never referred to by contemporaries as a frigate; she was usually termed a sloop of war or ship. Such vessels had a similarly anomalous position in the Royal Navy, where they were, in formal terms, called 'post ships', because they were too small for frigates but large enough to be commanded by a post captain.

Other than her tonnage (467), no dimensions of the ship have survived. Her figurehead was 'composed of an Eagle perched upon the Globe' supported by figures representing Commerce and Justice, and carrying the arms of the United States.[4] As to dimensions, an approximation can be seen in an otherwise unidentified contemporary plan of a 20-gun vessel cited and traced by Howard Chapelle. This vessel measured 106ft between perpendiculars, 29ft beam and 13ft depth of hold.[5] The department either suggested dimensions or sent actual examples of plans to the communities intending to build for the government, but obviously had no direct control over the builders. In the case of Newburyport, it appears William Hackett had the design in hand before the city's subscription proposal came to Philadelphia (then the capital of the United States).

Only one contemporary illustration purports to represent this vessel. This broadside view shows her with significant sheer, no quarter galleries, a relatively long quarterdeck with the latter showing four gunports. She is rigged to topgallants on the fore and main, but carries only a topsail on her mizzen. The accuracy of this illustration is doubtful: it was also used on the famous Liverpool jugs of the era, and another of the transfer ware designs, labelled 'Ship Caroline' (supposedly circa 1837) shows a three-masted vessel with a line-for-line identical rig (and flags) to that of the *Merrimack*. There are differences in the hulls of the two ships: the merchant vessel has no gunports, for instance, but has quarter galleries. The general sheer and outline of both hulls is the same, however. It seems that the artist began with a generic ship-rigged vessel and modified it as needed.

She went to sea early in 1799, under the command of Moses Brown, a noted local sea captain. She had cost $46,170, and was significantly less expensive than others of her rate.[6] Her crew numbered 105 plus 20 marines and a marine lieutenant.[7] Crew size was determined by number

Illustration purporting to be the subscription-built sloop of war *Merrimack*. Unfortunately, the same picture, with minor variations is seen on various of the famous 'Liverpool jugs', and was apparently a generic one – with minor alterations to illustrate other vessels of the era. [US Naval Photographic Center NH 560]

of guns in the main battery: five men per gun. Another manning convention of the day was that there should be one marine for each gun.

She was immediately assigned to convoy duty and gained some reputation for swiftness. In August 1799 the ship *Ganges* – not a dull sailer by all reports – was said to have been faster than 'even the *Merrimack*'.[8] One officer was somewhat less enthusiastic about her, and complained that she carried less than two month's provisions – certainly a drawback in terms of extended cruising.[9]

She cruised for two years, for the most part escorting convoys on the Atlantic and in the Caribbean. She captured four French vessels and re-captured several American and British merchant ships from the French. In September 1800, along with *Patapsco*, she bombarded a French army force on Curaçao, driving them off.[10] She was sold out in early 1801 for less than half of her construction cost and converted to merchant service under the name *Monticello*. Shortly afterward she was lost off Cape Cod.

Maryland and *Patapsco*

These two sloops of war were of the same rate, but differed slightly in (carpenter's) tonnage. They were the product of a citizens' subscription drive yielding over $100,000, the majority of which was raised in less than two weeks in June 1798.[11]

With money in hand, negotiations with the Secretary of the Navy began on the character of the vessels to be built. Stoddert, with an eye towards the future of the navy, preferred a frigate, while the Baltimore merchants insisted on providing two smaller sloops.[12] Given the character of the conflict at hand, it seems obvious that the smaller ships were of much more utility in dealing with the French privateers and in handling commerce-protection tasks.

The navy did not provide plans for the ships. Instead, Stoddert, a Marylander himself, wrote only broad guidelines. Speed was essential, of course: 'they should be fine sailors [he wrote], so as to suffer nothing to escape them, & be taken by nothing. This can be done at Baltimore, if any where.'[13] As with the *Merrimack*, no authentic plans have been found of these ships, nor has the identity of their designer or designers surfaced. It would not be inconceivable, however, that they were designed by their builders, William Price and Lewis de Rochbrune. William Price, who built *Maryland* in his Fells Point, Baltimore, yard, had been building pilot boats and schooners for several years, and went on to become noted for his designs for the naval schooners *Experiment* and *Vixen*, and sloop of war *Hornet*. His name is prominent in association with the development of the Baltimore clipper.[14] Lewis de Rochburne had been building ships since at least 1794, on Maryland's Eastern Shore. By 1798 he had a yard at Fells Point, Baltimore, and it was there that the second of the navy vessels was built: the *Patapsco*.[15] This ship was originally to have been called *Chesapeake*, but the name was changed to avoid confusion with the frigate of the same name being completed at Norfolk.

Contracts for the ships were signed on 24 July 1798 and construction began immediately. Construction was facilitated by the navy's agreement to allow use of timbers left over from construction of the frigate *Constellation*, at cost. The government also provided the copper sheathing, fastenings and cannon for one of the vessels.[16] The first of the sloops to be launched was *Maryland*, which went down the ways to much acclamation on 3 June 1799. Surprisingly, given the wartime exigencies, she was elaborately carved, by a 'Mr Brown', a student of William Rush of Philadelphia. The figurehead, with pedestal, measured over eight feet high and was of the goddess of 'commerce and plenty', over trailboard designs representing the emblems of the arts and sciences, including agriculture and shipbuilding. At the stern was the seal of the state of Maryland flanked by figures of the 'genius' of literature and the arts.[17]

Her commanding officer, John Rodgers, was a Marylander, as were many of her other officers and midshipmen. The crew numbered some 160 men, of which about 20 were officers.[18] She was armed with twenty 9pdrs and six 6pdrs. The only dimensions available for the ship were those recorded at her sale in 1801: 114ft long (probably on the gundeck), 30ft 4in beam (extreme), and 464 $^{4}/_{95}$ tons (the latter is tons burthen, or 'carpenter's' measure, a crude calculation of the cubic capacity of the hull, as opposed to displacement tonnage).[19]

Though no plans survive of this ship, there were contemporary indications that she had been endowed with some elements of the Baltimore clipper design, to the extent that emphasis on speed was detrimental to her warfighting capabilities. Even before she was fitted for sea, Thomas Truxtun had written navy agent Jeremiah Yellot advising against overloading her with guns. He commented that overloading 'sharp-built vessels' made them 'laborsome and crank' as well as too deep in the water, and, consequently, wet. He recommended adding a light spar deck to relieve crowding and any possible health consequences.[20]

Later that year, another critic, who described *Maryland* as a 'Charming little ship', noted significant faults in her. First was the complete spar deck, which he deemed unnecessary – as all foreign vessels of her size were open in the waist. The second problem: she was 'Swimming too low in the water', making her lowest gunport sills only 3ft 10in above the waterline. Finally, he complained that her 'Mettall' was excessive: British vessels of her size carried 14 to 16 guns, compared to the *Maryland*'s 26. By the same token, her crew was at least 60 hands larger than the comparable RN vessel.[21]

Rodgers took her to sea in September 1799, convoying vessels to Surinam on the north-east coast of South America. She joined the American squadron there, where she had a 'fair trial of sailing' with the *Portsmouth*, another of the newly built contract ships. One of her officers wrote that she out-sailed the *Portsmouth* 'shamefully', and was of the opinion that only the captured frigate *Insurgent* was capable of keeping pace with the Baltimore-built sloop.[22]

Maryland's wartime career was uneventful. Rodgers found few Frenchmen in his vicinity and much of late 1799 through the summer of 1800 was spent convoying merchant vessels to safe latitudes. The winter of 1800-1801 was spent in refit, and by that time the war had wound down. *Maryland*'s final task was to carry the treaty ending the conflict to France. This she did in March 1801, returning in August to Baltimore. Her usefulness was now over and on 1 December 1801 she was sold for about $20,000.[23]

Patapsco was launched on 20 June 1799, about three weeks after *Maryland*. The usual festivities and speeches accompanied her descent and the inevitable florid newspaper account described the event, as well as her figurehead. In this case, it was a 'Neptune-like man' with long beard and holding an urn, a figure 'emblematic of the water from which she derives her name'.[24] Of *Patapsco* we know less than her sister ship. Though listed at the same nominal tonnage as *Maryland* (380), her carpenter's measure was 418 ⁴/₉₅ tons, and her complement was 140 men, 20 fewer than *Maryland*'s. Her battery was given as 24 guns in an 1800 listing, two less than that of *Maryland*.[25]

The ship was commanded by Captain Henry Geddes, an older gentleman with naval experience in the Revolutionary War. He was commissioned on 24 September 1799 and, after some prodding by Stoddert, finally got his ship to sea in mid-November.[26] Her initial task was to convoy General James Wilkinson and staff to New Orleans. Once this was accomplished she returned to New Castle, Delaware for re-caulking. From thence she sailed for the West Indies. On station there through December 1800, she made two captures and assisted *Merrimack* in dislodging a French

force at Curaçao, providing shore bombardment, musketry from the ship's marines, and a substantial landing force. She returned to the United States and was sold in June 1801.

Portsmouth

This sloop of war was built at Portsmouth, New Hampshire by James K Hackett, to a design by Josiah Fox. The contract was let sometime before 22 June 1798, under the auspices of naval agent Samuel Higginson, for a price of $30 per ton.[27] Little is known of her construction, other than a letter from Secretary Stoddert naming the vessel and acquiescing to having a head built on her, despite his opinion that it was a 'useless ornament'. Her launch date was 11 October 1798.[28]

She was armed with twenty 9pdrs and two 6pdrs, and manned by 115 men, plus officers and a marine contingent consisting of a lieutenant and 21 privates. Her tonnage is listed as 590, significantly greater than that of similar sized ships of this group.[29] Of course, no plans or exterior descriptions have been found for this vessel.

She went to sea under Captain Daniel McNeill, sometime late in January 1799, in company with the frigate *United States*. The officers of the ship gave 'a good account of her' but indicated that she was not a fast sailer, 'except in fresh breezes'.[30] As noted previously, she was out-sailed 'shamefully' by the *Maryland*.[31] *Portsmouth* sailed for the West Indies, joining a squadron commanded by John Barry, in *Constitution*. She was stationed off Surinam and acted as convoy escort during this period. Her major capture was the French 20-gun vessel *Hussar*. *Portsmouth* and the revenue cutter *Scammel* blockaded her in the Surinam River for over a month, forcing her surrender. Unfortunately for the captors, a British fleet appeared at the same time, causing the capitulation of Surinam. The valuable prize, no doubt to the chagrin of the American crews, was consequently turned over to the Royal Navy.[32]

In the spring of 1800 she was selected as a truce ship to sail to France and await the return of the American diplomats negotiating a peace with that nation. On return, she made a second cruise to the Caribbean and was sold in Baltimore in 1801.

Trumbull

Trumbull was the second to the last of the sloops contracted for by the navy. On 30 March 1799 Secretary Stoddert wrote Joseph Howland of Norwich, Connecticut: 'Being informed that you have a quantity of seasoned timber on hand . . . I have the honor to request that you will be pleased to cause a Ship, or brig to be built.' He directed that the vessel carry 'eighteen twelve pound cannon' and measure 360 tons. In this instance, the navy's 'agent' and builder were the same –Howland–and he was to be compensated at a rate of two per cent. Howland was also given permission to design the vessel, with the concurrence and consultation of Captain David Jewett, who was to command her.[33]

Stoddert further directed that the ship carry provisions for six months for 100 to 120 men and that the weight of the battery not 'impede' her sailing qualities. He requested that her plan should be sent to the department with the expectation that, if she proved successful, her lines might be applied to subsequent vessels of this type.[34] However, the plans for *Trumbull* are among those which have not been found. Most of the vessels built during this emergency had such brief service that no reference draught was needed for any refit or major repair. Furthermore, neither the contract-built nor the subscription ships were necessarily designed by navy-employed constructors, so the navy had little control over the pertinent paperwork and plans.

The *Trumbull* did not get to sea until February or March of 1800, with some delays apparently caused by recruiting difficulties. She measured 400 tons, was ship-rigged and carried a crew of 86 sailors, 21 marines, and 26 officers.[35] *Trumbull*'s first mission was as escort for the storeship *Charlotte*, carrying provisions for the American squadron in the West Indies. In her subsequent patrols in the Caribbean, *Trumbull* made three captures, one in May and two in August 1800. She then escorted the captured French vessel *Vengeance* to New London, and returned to Santo Domingo in October. After a patrol off Puerto Rico, she returned to the United States and was sold at New York in early 1801 for $26,500, some $30,000 less than the government had paid for her.[36]

Connecticut

The building of the sloop of war *Connecticut* was initiated by Secretary of the Navy Stoddert in July 1798, in a letter to naval agent Nehemiah Hubbard of Middletown, Connecticut. A 24-gun ship was needed, to be built of live oak or red cedar, and white oak. He suggested dimensions of 93ft on the keel, 31ft beam and 13½ft depth of hold, to be pierced for 20 guns on the main deck plus bridle ports and two additional ports on the quarterdeck. The agent's remuneration was to be two per cent on all expenses, and the government was to supply all copper sheathing and fastenings. Stoddert hoped to see the ship completed in ninety days.[37] Shortly after this letter, Seth Overton of Chatham, Connecticut was selected to build the vessel, at a price 'not exceeding 30½ dollars per Ton'. Tonnage was to be in 'carpenter's' measure.[38]

In August, there was an exchange of letters regarding the design, with the constructor suggesting greater depth of hold. Stoddert replied that the builder should use his own judgement, as 'All knowledge of the subject of ship building is not confined to Philadelphia.' The same letter indicated that the size of the ship 'being reduced', she would only carry 9pdrs on the main deck and 6s on the quarterdeck, and that she should have quarter galleries.[39]

By the end of 1798 Captain Moses Tryon had been selected to command the vessel, but completion was not expected before May of 1799. Even this date proved optimistic. Though we do not know when she was launched, she had sunk at her moorings and attempts were being made to raise her in July of that year. Troubles continued through August, with Stoddert testily writing 'I regret extreamly that *Connecticut* has not yet crossed the bar.– My letter of the 7th inst will inform you how much I have been disappointed by this ship' [Underline in original]. She finally went to sea in October.[40]

The ship quickly gained a reputation for speed. She beat *Insurgent*–a ship already known for her swiftness–'most shamefully', according to *Insurgent*'s commanding officer. The latter judged her a 'fine ship' and 'well calculated for a cruiser'. When she beat *Adams* and the account appeared in public print, a rebuttal appeared from an *Adams* officer, carping at the 'fairness' of the contest (pleading bowsprit sprung, masts too short, out of trim, etc). The correspondent called *Connecticut* 'an uncommon looking thing, no ways warlike'.[41] Though there was obviously a bit of pique operating in this statement, it is an intriguing description of the vessel.

Her speed proved a great asset on station off Guadeloupe in the Caribbean. She captured four privateers and recaptured seven American merchantmen in her year of active service. *Connecticut* arrived at New London, Connecticut on 18 October 1800 and was sold out at New York in 1801.

Warren

The last sloop to be built for the Quasi-War was *Warren*. On 4 April 1799 Secretary Stoddert wrote Nicholas Johnson of Newburyport on the subject. Johnson had been one of the major investors and leaders in that town's drive to build the *Merrimack* and Stoddert was recruiting him to act as the navy's agent in building an 18-gun vessel of 360 tons.[42]

Stoddert's requirements for the ship included 'fast sailing', the capacity to carry eighteen 9pdrs, 'agreeably to such model, and dimensions, as you approve', carry six months' provisions for 100 to 120 men, and be copper-sheathed. In this initial communication, she was to be brig-rigged. The secretary requested that her plans be forwarded to the department when finished.[43] Johnson accepted the proposal and shortly afterwards suggested the vessel be ship-rigged. Stoddert agreed to that and to naming her *Warren*. Little else is known about the period of her construction, other than the appointment of Captain Timothy Newman as her commander. Sources indicate the actual construction site was in Salisbury, Massachusetts, and her builder was a Mr Webster.[44]

Recruiting began sometime late in the year, with Newman authorised to gather 88 men and boys. This number, plus 22 marines and ship's officers would be her complement. She was launched on 26 September 1799 and sailed to Boston in October, to finish fitting out. In particular, she was short two guns, which were to be supplied by the navy agent there.[45] She sailed from Nantasket Roads the last day of 1799, after dealing with significant problems getting her into proper trim.[46]

The vessel escorted the storeship *Trio* southward, with the latter carrying supplies for the American squadron off Cuba. She remained on duty in the Caribbean escorting merchant convoys until mid-1800. By this stage in the war French vessels were rarely seen in the waters around Cuba, and she spent some time in Havana harbour, despite instructions to the contrary. *Warren* then made passage to Vera Cruz at the behest of an American diplomat, before returning to Havana. It was on this cruise that, on 15 June, the first case of yellow fever appeared on the ship. Between 30 June and 13 July, thirteen men died on board and the disease raged in her through August. At one point twenty-five of her crew were stricken on board, and another two dozen were hospitalised ashore. Some thirty-eight men died – over a quarter of her crew – including her commander and his son, a midshipman on the vessel.[47]

She was ordered back to Boston, along with the *Ganges*, whose crew was also dropping from the disease. *Warren* was 'cleansed', re-provisioned and made a second cruise, a relatively uneventful one, to the West Indies late in 1800. She was in Commodore Barry's squadron there when the Quasi-War ended in February 1801. She then returned to Boston where she was sold according to the provisions of the Peace Establishment Act.

Authorisation of 1804: *Hornet* and *Wasp*

The Peace Establishment Act of 1801 severely reduced the size of the navy, despite the fact that peace with France had no bearing on the continuing conflict with the North African Barbary powers. Ironically, most of the vessels sold out of the navy as part of the reduction were smaller vessels which might have been useful on the North African coast. Within three months of the end of the French difficulties, Tripoli declared war on the United States, and by August 1801 American warships were blockading the Tripolitan coast. The war rumbled on until 1806, with a major American naval presence almost constantly in the Mediterranean.

Despite the navy's war footing during these years, in that time only seven vessels were added to the American seagoing fleet, none larger than a sloop of war.[48] *Hornet* and *Wasp* were two of the seven. (Besides these, the only other additions were the dozens of Jeffersonian gunboats, the first of which went into service in 1804.) These two vessels were near sister ships and were designed as brigs. *Wasp*, however, was converted to a sloop of war while under construction and *Hornet* was similarly altered in 1811. Therefore, they are included here, rather than with the smaller vessels.

The Tripolitan war was, of course, the rationale behind Congressional actions to strengthen the navy, in particular, with vessels suitable for inshore operations. Their first action was the authorisation, in 1803, of four vessels: two schooners and two brigs. Then, on 26 March 1804, appro-

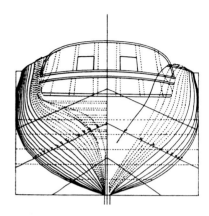

Right: Sloop of war *Wasp*, 1807. Originally designed as a brig (as shown here), she was turned into a sloop of war before completion. [US Navy, from *Naval Documents of the Barbary Wars*]

Below: Sail plan, sloop of war *Wasp* as a ship. Her short War of 1812 career ended with capture by the 74-gun HMS Poictiers while repairing battle damages sustained in her successful action with the Royal Navy brig *Frolic*. [National Archives 109-8-2D]

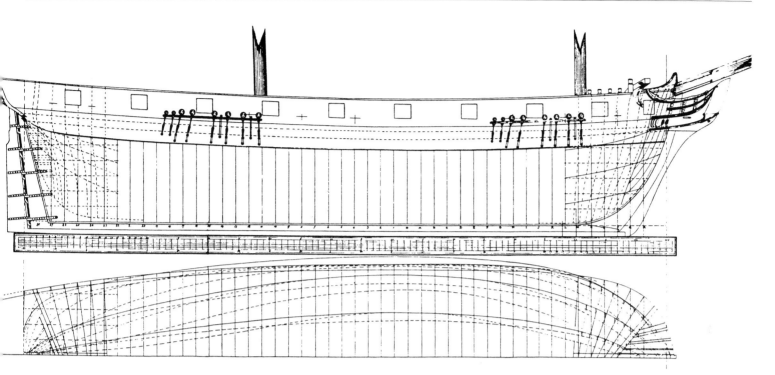

priation was made for two additional 16-gun brigs, which would become *Wasp* and *Hornet*. In contrast to most of the previous generation of sloops, these two vessels are thoroughly documented. Josiah Fox, naval constructor, was called on to provide their design, and both plans and detailed building instructions are still extant. Though the vessels were to be given the same battery as the 1803 brigs, Fox made them significantly larger: 105ft between perpendiculars and 30ft beam as opposed to about 95ft and 27ft respectively for the earlier ships (brigs *Argus* and *Syren*). The latter were about 300 tons; the new ships, 387³⁵⁄₉₅ tons. They were to be 84ft on the keel for tonnage.

The hull design, wrote Fox, was based on an 'English Cutter', and obviously emphasised speed. They were given much deadrise and were sharp in fore and after bodies. He wrote: 'The general construction . . . is calculated . . . to Embrace buoyancy without losing the advantage of Holding a good wind and general ease: for which purpose her Body is pretty evenly balanced, and to prevent her droping [*sic*] to [*sic*] low abaft by reason of her clean run, a good spread of Wing transom hath been given.'[49] The *Wasp*, according to Fox's notes, was built mainly of white oak, with substantial portions of live oak and cedar. The stem was of black walnut, and deck beams and planks of

yellow pine and Maryland eastern shore yellow pine. The keel was in two segments: the forward 64ft was of hickory, and the remaining 20ft was white oak.[50]

Wasp was built at Washington Navy Yard, superintended by Fox, while the second vessel was constructed at the yard of William Price in Baltimore. *Hornet* was launched first of the two, on 28 June 1805, and her dimensions were somewhat different from Fox's plan: she measured 14ft depth of hold, five inches narrower in beam and 85ft 9in keel for tonnage, making 440⁶⁴⁄₉₄ tons.[51] She was apparently given an eagle figurehead, which was designed to be unshipped and replaced with a billet head for the winter months.[52] She was commissioned in October 1805, was to carry a complement of 150 and mounted a battery of fourteen long 9pdrs and two long 12s.[53]

Captain Isaac Chauncey, her first commander, was well pleased with her: 'The *Hornet* . . . is one of the finest vessels of her class I ever saw. She sails uncommonly fast, steers and works well, and is an excellent sea boat.' However, off Frying Pan Shoals, in December, 'in a very heavy gale . . . I sprung my main mast and received considerable damage.'[54] Late in 1807 heavy weather again wreaked havoc on her main mast, and parted a few of her shrouds. Shortly thereafter, her commander suggested her

Sloop of war *Hornet*. Wash drawing by W A K Martin. Martin, working in Philadelphia in the mid 1800s, was said to have measured the naval vessels he depicted, though his rationale for the vestigial 'spar plan' which is common in his drawings, is not known. [US Naval Historical Center NH 86236: original at Independence Seaport Museum, Philadelphia]

channels be raised (according to Chapelle, they were originally about mid-gunport level) to increase the protection for her masts. In the event, it was found structurally impracticable to raise them when she went into repair at Charleston late that year.[55]

Her first commission was coastwise cruising, followed by joining the Mediterranean squadron in 1806. She was repaired in Charleston from late 1807 to December 1808, then cruised enforcing the Embargo Acts until November 1810. When she was repaired at Washington Navy Yard in 1810-11, she was re-rigged as a ship-sloop—as had been done to *Wasp* previously. Her battery was altered also, with her gundeck now carrying two long 12s and eighteen 32pdr carronades. To accommodate these guns, another port was added to her broadside by the expedient of making all of her ports more closely spaced. At this time she was also given quarter galleries.[56]

Hornet was carrying this battery when she defeated HMS *Peacock* during the War of 1812. The action was astoundingly short and destructive for the *Peacock*, which was found in a sinking condition 14 minutes into the fight. In contrast to the American emphasis on shooting for the hull, nearly all the British hits were above the *Hornet*'s rail. As Roosevelt observed, the fact that the British vessel only mounted 24pdrs had little bearing on the inaccuracy of her gunnery.[57] Three Americans, sent over to assist in the attempt to save the brig, went down with *Peacock*.

Late in the conflict, after running the British blockade, she encountered HMS *Penguin*, a vessel nearly equal her size, with similar results. In some 22 minutes, the *Penguin* surrendered and was found so cut up in her hull that she was later destroyed by her captors. Again, most of the damage to *Hornet* was in her rigging.[58]

The post-war career of the *Hornet* was for the most part based in Pensacola and Key West where she was assigned to anti-piracy duties. She departed for the last time from Pensacola on 4 March 1829 and was sunk in a storm off Tampico on 29 September 1829.

Wasp was still under construction when the first incident with *Hornet*'s main mast occurred. This must have been part of the rationale for the January 1807 decision to alter *Wasp* to a ship-rigged sloop of war before she was completed.[59] She was also finished with quarter galleries and channels located above the gunports. Her original armament was sixteen 32pdr carronades and two long 12s. She went to Europe in the summer of 1807, and her commander wrote favourably of her 'staunchness, stiffness, and fleetness' during the passage.[60] She cruised in American waters until the

War of 1812, and by that time had been re-armed identically to *Hornet* with eighteen 32s and two long 12s. Presumably the same requisite alterations were made to her gunports.[61]

Her war career was short. In October 1812, off the east coast of the US, she fell in with the 18-gun *Frolic*. The British brig was taken after a vicious 45-minute engagement in heavy seas. Again, the Americans fired low and the British fired high, resulting in both an American victory and a wide disparity in crew losses–some sixty British casualties versus ten Americans. The triumph was short-lived with the arrival of a British 74 on the scene, taking *Wasp* and re-taking *Frolic*. *Wasp* was taken into the Royal Navy as *Loup Cervier* and later re-named *Peacock*. She was lost at sea in 1814. *Frolic*, on the other hand, was found not worth repairing.[62]

Ontario Class, 1813 and the Second *Erie*, 1822

January 1813–six months into the War of 1812–brought Congressional authorisation for three frigates and six sloops of war. William Doughty, recently installed as naval constructor, provided two designs for the latter, both using the same basic dimensions, but featuring radically different hull lines.

Of the two designs, that used for *Ontario*, *Erie*, and *Argus* was the more radical, showing pilot-schooner lines. Two of them, *Erie* and *Ontario*, were constructed by Thomas Kemp, at Fells Point, Baltimore; the third was supervised by Doughty himself at Washington Navy Yard. The most obvious pilot-boat characteristic was the extreme drag in the keel: these ships were 4ft 8in deeper at the stern than forward. Further evidence of an emphasis on speed was great deadrise and sharp lines forward and aft. As documentation for these vessels is sparse, it is not beyond the realm of possibility that Doughty collaborated with Kemp and William Price on this design. Price, as mentioned before, was one of the foremost practitioners of the Baltimore schooner/pilot boat design that was later to be heralded as the Baltimore clipper. In 1811 Price had built a ship-rigged armed merchant vessel, originally named *Hannibal* but re-

named *Andromeda* after her capture by the British in 1812. Plans of that ship, though she was larger in dimensions, show some resemblance to the *Ontario* class: significant drag (approximately three feet) and sharp lines generally.[63]

A comparison between the 1813 sloops and the 1804 naval brigs (later sloops) *Wasp* and *Hornet* show few similarities. The later design was significantly larger: 117ft 11in between perpendiculars, 31ft 6in beam, 14ft 6in depth, versus 105ft, 30ft and 13ft 9in respectively. The older design showed little keel drag, less deadrise and more rake in both the stern and stem. The new vessels were to be rated as 18s, versus 16 for the 1804 ships. Of course, in the event, the latter carried 20, the former, 22 guns.[64]

Ontario

The first of the class completed, *Ontario* was launched in 1813 and commissioned or completed on 25 October 1813. She was blockaded in Chesapeake Bay until the end of the war, however, and did not get to sea until March 1815. Her performance, according to her commander, was outstanding: 'the finest vessel ever built in Baltimore, both as to beauty, comfort of accommodations, and swiftness of sailing.'[65] Four years later, the question of a major repair for the ship was addressed. It was estimated that this would cost over $20,000, as opposed to around twice that much to build a new ship of her class. As she was considered 'a good model', she was repaired rather than replaced.[66]

Towards the end of her long career, another commander detailed a more considered report on her qualities. He regarded her as a fair sailer under most circumstances, without extraordinary speed (she had been out-sailed by *Erie* and *Natchez*). He complained of her lack of stowage: she had only sufficient space for four months' cruising. The vessel was unduly crank, made much leeway, and was noted for missing stays in moderate seas. She was apparently quite wet as he mentioned opening the mid-ship gunports to allow exit for the seas she shipped, and, in heavy weather, keeping her hatches battened as the coamings were too low to keep water out.[67]

Ontario first went into service in the Mediterranean, participating in the actions against the Barbary states and the

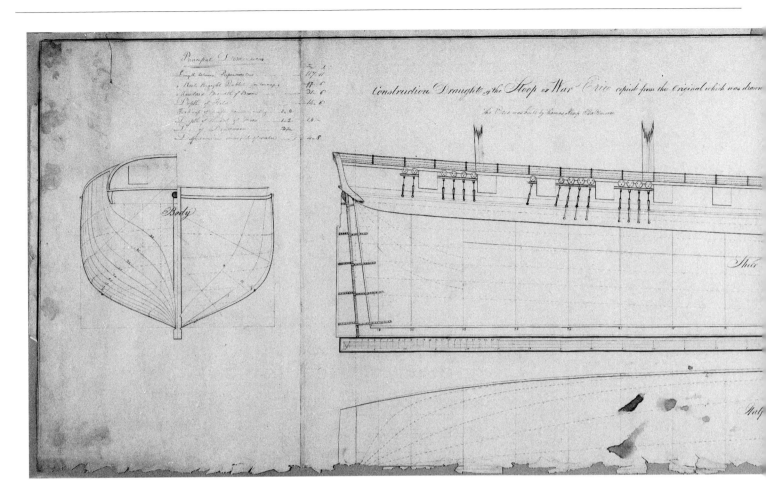

Below: Sloop of war *Ontario*, watercolour by A Carlotta. Her commander called her the 'finest vessel ever built in Baltimore'. [US Navy]

Above: Sloop of war *Erie*, built at Baltimore by Thomas Kemp. Note the pilot boat lines and drag of keel. [National Archives 41-5-6E]

capture of the Algerian frigate *Mashouda*. Her second commission took her to the Pacific, where she was the first naval ship to visit what would become the states of California, Oregon and Washington. The remainder of her service was divided between the Mediterranean and the coast of the US, the latter on anti-piracy patrol. She was decommissioned in July 1843 at Baltimore and remained there until June 1856 as a receiving ship. She was sold by auction on 15 July 1856.

Erie

Erie was launched on 3 November 1813 at Baltimore, but was prevented from escaping to the open ocean by the British blockade. However, after trials on Chesapeake Bay her commander wrote of her apparent stiffness and easy

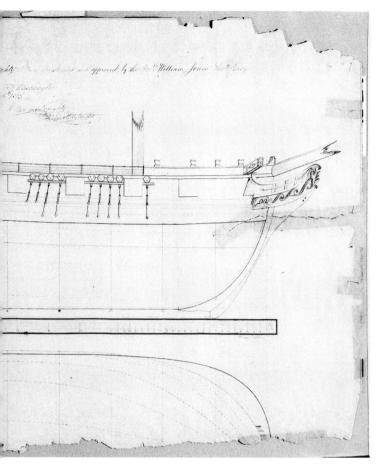

began for repairing the ship 'or building a new vessel of similar class' (wrote navy board commissioner John Rodgers to the Secretary of the Navy). Little else was done until April of 1821, when Rodgers wrote that 'rebuilding' would begin soon and all that was needed was a 'draft'. He further stated that 'any new vessel' could not be started until new ways were constructed.[69] The 'draft' was apparently completed about that time, as Doughty wrote in May mentioning the 'construction plan' and that the 'moulds are progressing'. He sent the inventory of moulds late that month. Finally, in June, Rodgers listed timbers needed for the 'repairs'. These included three pieces of 14ft by 22ft oak, totalling over 135 feet, for the keel, and six 14ft by 14ft timbers for keelsons.[70]

These communications leave little doubt that a new ship was built. Even extensive repairs would not have required a new construction draught, nor a complete set of moulds for the frame timbers. That timbers for new keel and keelsons were ordered rounds out this case of what Chapelle

The second sloop of war *Erie*, painting by Nicholas Cammilieri, 1824. An early example of building a new vessel as a 'repair' of the old. The new ship was longer and some 50 tons heavier. [US Naval Historical Center NH 54259]

steering, plus her efficiency in working: '. . . she works very quick and shoots ahead on stays as much as a frigate.' He was anxious to get her out to sea, however, to put her qualities to the test of blue water.[68]

Her career was a short one. At the close of the war, she went to sea and joined the Mediterranean squadron, remaining there to enforce the peace until 1819. She returned to New York Navy Yard for repairs on 20 January 1820. The repairs to this vessel were the first in a long series in which the navy department, using the term 'rebuilding', actually constructed new ships to replace the originals. The new *Erie*, though very similar in appearance to the old one, and with minimal differences in dimensions (an addition of five feet to the length and one foot to the beam), was, in fact a new ship. Evidence for this is easily followed in the departmental documents.

First, in July 1820, it was determined that the cost of repairs for the ship would be within $1000 of building a new ship. Shortly afterwards, the process of gathering material

called 'administrative rebuilding'. Contemporary acknowledgement of this can be found in a letter from John Rodgers defending the 'rebuilding' practice to Secretary of the Navy John Branch when the subject arose in relation to the reconstruction of the *John Adams*. Rodgers listed *Erie* as the first of the navy vessels which had been 'rebuilt' (or 're-' built) using funds designated for ship 'repairs'.[71]

The new *Erie* was laid down sometime in 1821 and commissioned in 1822. (Though chronologically after the *Wasp* class, she is placed here for convenience sake.) She was 121ft 11in between perpendiculars, 32ft 6in moulded beam, with a 14ft 9in depth of hold. She measured 559^{65}⁄₉₅ tons (compared to the first *Erie*'s 509^{21}⁄₉₅ tonnage).[72]

The ship's first assignment was in the Mediterranean, from 1823 to 1826, followed by a turn in the West Indies, and another in the Brazil squadron. Her final service was in the Gulf of Mexico and the West Indies, returning to Boston in July 1840. On 9 February 1843 the armed storeship *Erie* sailed from Boston for the Pacific. There is disagreement over whether this vessel was a new ship or yet another 'rebuild'. Chapelle contends that the old ship was broken up at this time, and replaced by another whose measurements were nearly identical to the *original* sloop of war: 117ft 11in by 32ft 4in extreme beam, 14ft 6in depth of hold.

Certainly there was much discussion at the time concerning the fate of the sloop of war. A proposal was made to convert her to a storeship and transport and add six feet to her length. Samuel Humphreys complained that this would cost about $36,000 and she was not worth it. Three months later, however, Humphreys and constructor Foster Rhodes proposed converting her by altering her lower decks, adding a light spar deck and eliminating all but three ports on each side.[73] This writer is not certain which path was taken. The 4-gun storeship *Erie*, however, remained in the inventory until November 1850 when she was sold.

Argus

The sloop of war *Argus*, the third vessel of the *Ontario* class, was built at Washington Navy Yard and laid down in 1813. She was still on the ways when the British entered the city and she was burned there on 24 August 1814.

Wasp Class, 1813

These three ships, *Wasp*, *Frolic*, and *Peacock*, were also designed by William Doughty and were of a more conventional hull design than the *Ontario* class. All were built by contract. The *Wasp* was constructed by William Cross and Orlando Merrill at Newburyport, Massachusetts; the *Peacock* by Adam and Noah Brown of New York City. Josiah Barker built the *Frolic* at Boston.

The Browns had, by 1813, gained a considerable reputation as shipbuilders. Though self-taught in the trade, the Browns' privateers *General Armstrong* and *Prince de Neufchatel* had both been noted for their speed and seaworthiness. Barker had been in the business since 1795 and became a naval constructor after the War of 1812. Merrill had built privateers and the revenue cutter *Pickering* in 1798.[74]

The above-water hull design of these three was nearly indistinguishable from the other design, except for quarter

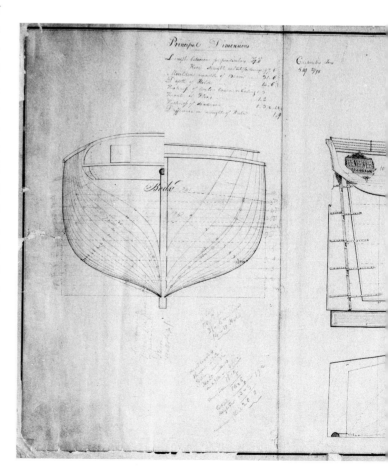

galleries incorporated on the *Wasp* class. Below the water-line, the latter displayed less than half the drag in the keel, and appreciably less deadrise and sheer. Two of the three, *Peacock* and *Frolic* varied somewhat from Doughty's design. Both, according to the lines taken off later, were about a foot and a half longer between perpendiculars.

Wasp

Launched on 21 September 1813 and in commission by 1 May of the next year, *Wasp* was armed with three 12pdrs and nineteen 32pdr carronades when she got to sea under Captain Johnston Blakeley. In her five-month career she blazed a trail through British shipping probably unmatched during the war. Taking station in the western approaches to the English Channel, she captured eight vessels between 2 June and 6 July, including the naval brig *Reindeer*. In a vicious point-blank exchange of 19 minutes, the latter lost 33 killed and 34 wounded – over 56 per cent of her crew of

118. The American loss was 26 of a crew of 173.[75]

Wasp repaired at Lorient from 6 July through 27 August, then returned to her duties. She took seven more British vessels between that date and 21 September, including the Royal Navy brig *Avon*. In less than 45 minutes, the brig was in a sinking condition, having lost 42 men, compared to 3 on the *Wasp*.[76]

The *Wasp* was last seen on 9 October 1814 and was assumed lost in a storm. By that date she had been at sea no more than four months (she had been repairing for over a month at Lorient). In round numbers, she taken an average of one British vessel for each week of her known active career.

Copy of William Doughty's plan for the *Wasp* class sloops, 1813. Built at the same time as the *Ontario* class, this design showed less drag of keel, sheer and deadrise. *Peacock* and *Frolic* were about 18 inches longer between perpendiculars. [National Archives 41-5-6]

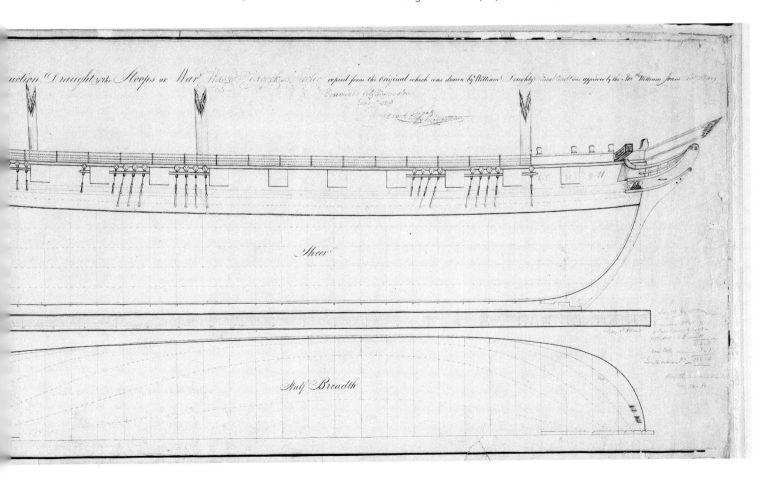

Frolic

Built at Boston, *Frolic* was slightly larger than *Wasp*. She measured 119ft 2½in between perpendiculars, 31ft 5½in moulded beam, and 14ft 2in depth of hold. This was a bit over one foot longer than Doughty's original dimension. Comparing the original lines to that of *Frolic*, taken off by the British in 1816, it is apparent that the extra length was used to sharpen her forward lines, particularly below the waterline.

Frolic was launched 11 September 1813 but did not get to sea until February 1814, out of Portsmouth, New Hampshire. She sailed southward. Off Cuba she was overtaken by the British frigate *Orpheus* and schooner *Shelburne*, the latter the Baltimore-built former pilot boat *Racer*.[77] She surrendered on 20 April and was taken into the Royal Navy as HMS *Florida*.[78]

Peacock

This ship also was a bit longer than *Wasp*, measuring 119ft between perpendiculars. Her underwater lines were slightly sharper forward, and she exhibited a bit more sheer and forward rake than called for in the original plan. It is noteworthy that this class was some twenty feet longer than the typical brig-sloop counterpart in the Royal Navy – the *Cruizer* class – enabling the American vessels to mount additional guns on each broadside.[79] Again, one can see the design concept of the 1794 frigates carried down into American sloops of war.

Peacock was launched at New York on 23 September 1813 and was at sea by 12 March 1814. She quickly gained a reputation for speed, as evidenced by a string of captures in three wartime cruises. Her qualities were detailed much later in her career, and under unusual circumstances, but are remarkable enough to quote at length. Her commanding officer, Thomas ap Catesby Jones, who had for a time re-rigged her as a barque, reported:

> . . . when not going over five knots, I consider her dull, from 6 to 8 knots, very fair, her superiority of sailing increases with the wind forward of the beam. I have seen her take twelve knots off the reel before the sand run [*sic*] out of the glass, nine, ten or eleven according as the sea is rough or smooth as close as the topsail yards will trim when the sails are double reefed, is her usual rate, with the wind two points off the beam . . . in smooth water, with a fresh breeze, she actually took fourteen knots off the reel whilst there was yet sand to run out . . .

Even more remarkably, in this instance Jones 'supposing some error in the glass or line' had both measured, then repeated the process. The result was 'the whole line of fourteen knots taken off while there remained a full second of sand in the glass, hence her actual rate could be but little short of fifteen knots'.[80] Jones expressed his admiration of the ship's capability to stand up under a press of sail. In a gale with heavy cross seas off the Falklands, 'at no time did she ship water enough to fill the lee scuppers'. Further, he was impressed with her steering, noting that she was a deep roller, but with little strain on her hull or rigging.

In a series of letters Jones also related his dissatisfaction with the vessel rigged as a ship. This stemmed from the location and size of her main and mizzen masts, particularly the short distance between the two masts, which made the square sails on the mizzen 'worse than useless' by limiting the angle at which the yards could be braced. This also had negative consequences on the ship's efficiency in wearing and tacking. He recommended she be permanently re-rigged as a barque, along with some relocation and resizing of her masts and bowsprit. In trials with two other noted sailers, *Peacock* demonstrated to his satisfaction that his alteration significantly improved her sailing. He continued his justification by noting that while ship-rigged she was considered very wet and to labour and pitch dangerously in a seaway.[81] Unfortunately, because Jones was obviously intent on convincing the department of the merits of his re-rigging scheme, there is some suspicion that he exaggerated both the negative characteristics of the vessel as a ship, and the positive aspects of the *Peacock* as a barque.

On the *Peacock*'s first cruise she encountered and defeated HM Brig *Epervier*, in an action of less than an hour. The British vessel sustained forty-five shots in the hull and 25 casualties. There were two minor injuries to American crewmen, and miscellaneous damage to *Peacock*'s rigging. Though much has been made about the size and armament advantage for the American vessel, it is obvious that the number of guns on the enemy vessel had little relationship to its demonstratively poor gunnery.[82] Her second cruise netted fourteen merchant prizes, and her final wartime sortie resulted in three merchant captures as well as the East India Co brig *Nautilus*. The latter engagement occurred in the East Indies after the end of hostilities, and the prize was released.

After the war, the ship took stations in the Mediterranean and the West Indies, the latter as part of the anti-piracy squadron. As noted above, she was on the Pacific station in the mid-1820s. It was there that she bested the frigate *United States* – hitherto unbeaten – in a trial of sailing. She also was matched with the sloop of war *Vincennes*, with mixed results: in light winds the latter prevailed; in stronger breezes the *Peacock* soundly trounced the newer ship. In both instances, it appears that *Peacock* was barque-rigged.[83]

An unusual incident contributed to her end. In March 1827, while going over 8 knots 'a large spermaceti whale . . . apparently trying our speed . . . suddenly turned and ran directly at the ship, which he struck rather obliquely on the starboard bow and stem, with so much force as for the moment to check the ship's way . . .' The damage caused a major leak and materially effected her sailing.[84] She returned to New York and was broken up in 1828. The ship was 'rebuilt' that year to a new design. Though records indicate a few items from the old vessel made the transition to the new one, the intention was obviously to replace the old ship.[85]

The *Peacock*, and to some extent the entire class, was a resounding success. A modern historian wrote that they '. . . proved almost perfect commerce raiders. They were fast and powerful under sail, with a low flush-decked hull that made them weatherly; although fairly sharp in hull form, they could stow enough provisions to make long-distance cruises.' Furthermore, their long hull enabled mounting a battery superior to the most common British brig-sloops of the era.[86]

It is questionable, however, how much the design of these vessels influenced later US sloops of war. As will be seen, the sloops authorised in 1825 would be similar only in that they were large vessels for sloops of war. In fact, the new vessels would be significantly larger and carry a totally different battery.

Boston Class, 1825

By the 1820s the US Navy was an unusual mix of vessels. The first of the 74s were coming into commission, and there were several schooners and smaller vessels of 12 or fewer guns, built or purchased for anti-piracy and anti-slaver operations. The bulk of the fleet comprised 44-gun frigates, with more on the stocks as called for in the Gradual Increase legislation of 1816. However, there were few vessels of medium size: by 1824 there were only four sloops of war in the inventory.

With the 1820s came a vast expansion of American trade, spurred on by loosening of British ocean commerce restrictions and growth of new American industry, particularly in New England. These factors brought increased naval responsibilities around the world. Closer to home, the decline of the Spanish empire created a void being filled by pirates and freebooters, making American trade with Spain's former colonies an exceedingly hazardous proposition.

The navy's response was the establishment of new squadrons to protect America's world-wide trade and commerce. In addition to the continuing presence in the Mediterranean, the era saw establishment of squadrons in the West Indies (1822), the Pacific (1822), Brazil (1826) and West Africa.[87] It is also noteworthy that 1823 brought the Monroe Doctrine, with its obvious implications for American naval forces in the entire hemisphere. Thus, naval vessels were needed which were substantial enough to cruise anywhere on the globe, but – in an era of naval retrenchment – do so with economy.

With this need in mind, in January 1825 Secretary of the Navy Samuel Southard wrote the naval committee in Congress requesting funding for ten sloops of war, of no less than 20 guns each. The upshot of this was an act of 3 March 1825, authorising $500,000 to be used for that purpose.[88] Naval constructors Francis Grice, John Floyd and Samuel

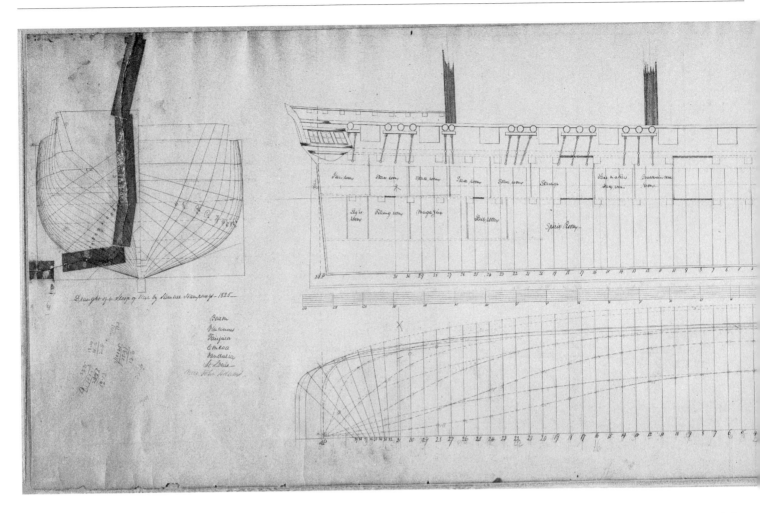

Boston class sloops, designed by Samuel Humphreys, 1825. Seven vessels were built to this plan. [National Archives 108-10-11]

Humphreys each prepared a proposed design for the vessels, which were to carry 24 guns. The dimensions of the three ranged from 119ft by 32ft 6in to 136ft by 42ft. Humphreys' plan was selected and the vessels were to be 127ft between perpendiculars, by 34ft moulded beam and 15ft 3in depth of hold.

However, William Doughty and Josiah Barker were allowed to introduce some variations in the actual construction of some of these ships. Barker, at Boston, built *Falmouth* to a length of 127ft 6in, with significantly less freeboard and rounder bilges. Doughty's vessels were 3ft narrower in beam and fuller in their forward and aft lines. Annotations on the plans indicate his design was used for *Warren* and *Natchez* (there is some indication *Lexington* was

also to Doughty's plan). Humphreys' plan was used for *Boston*, *Vincennes*, *Fairfield*, *Concord*, *Vandalia*, and *St Louis*. As noted previously, the *John Adams* (officially 'rebuilt', but actually a new vessel) was constructed on Humphreys' design.[89]

It is worth noting that it did not necessarily follow that the same building plan would be used for vessels built in the same yard. The three built at Charlestown Navy Yard were to three different designs: *Boston* (Humphreys' design) and *Warren* (Doughty's) were constructed simultaneously, followed by Barker's ship, *Falmouth*. Similarly, there were three built at New York: two (*Vincennes* and *Fairfield*) from Humphreys' plan, though sequentially. The third was Doughty's *Lexington*, built simultaneously with *Vincennes*. In fact, in this class, no two identical ships were building (*ie* on the stocks) at the same yard at the same time. The explanation for this may lie simply in the avail-

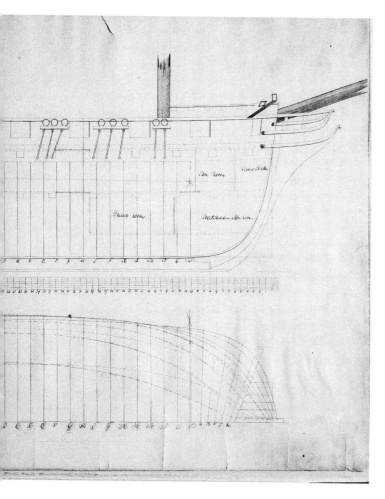

ability and allocation of building ways to the various vessels being constructed, and, as always, the political desirability of spreading the work fairly among the yards.

The 24-gun rating for these vessels would prove questionable at best, given their dimensions. On a length of about 125ft between perpendiculars were a dozen gunports, compared to the typical American 44-gun frigate, which carried fifteen broadside ports on a length of 175ft or more. It is also noteworthy in this regard that the previous wartime sloops (like *Argus* and *Wasp*), which had been about 117ft in length by 31ft, though carrying twenty to twenty-two guns, had batteries of carronades only, while the new class, though significantly larger, was slated for twenty-four 24pdr long guns. (It was felt that the short-ranged carronade was not effective for commerce raiding.) The weight differential was substantial: a 24pdr long gun was over 5200 pounds compared to the 32pdr carronades typical of the

wartime sloops, which weighed something over 1700 pounds.[90]

Barker's *Falmouth*

The single example of Barker's design was built at Boston (Charlestown) Navy Yard and commissioned by 20 January 1828. Her original battery was – in accordance with her rate – twenty-four 24pdrs. Her dimensions were 127ft 6in between perpendiculars, 33ft 9in moulded beam and 15ft 3in depth of hold. Unlike her nine (ten including *John Adams*) semi-sister ships, she had no quarter galleries on her elliptical stern. She also had at least a foot less freeboard and shorter forecastle and poop decks than the others.[91]

As will be seen, the typical problem with this class as a whole was a rate too large for their displacement. *Falmouth* was not atypical. In 1840, when she was in for refit, Samuel Humphreys recommended the number of her ports be reduced to eleven per side. Indeed, even during the Mexican War years, she carried no more than twenty-two guns.[92]

The vessel seems to have given general satisfaction, as reflected in a report on her condition in 1831. Though 'much decay' was in evidence, Humphreys recommended repairing her.[93] Her commander described her as 'very weatherly, and in all respects a very safe and comfortable ship, sailing 10 knots per hour on a wind and 12 free.' It is noteworthy that he reported her fore mast was raked aft more than usual during that particular cruise. Later, she was termed a 'dull sailer before the wind', but 'good under most circumstances'.[94]

Her career began with cruises in the West Indies and the Pacific, followed by extensive repairs in 1840 to 1841. She was an element of the Home squadron afterwards, including the Mexican War years, when she was flagship under Commodore D Conner. After the war she sailed for the Pacific, returning to the east coast in 1852. Her final cruise as a sloop of war was in the West Indies from 1854 to 1857. The vessel was afterwards converted to a storeship, carrying two guns. After service during the Paraguayan expedition, she became a stationary storeship at Panama. *Falmouth* was sold in October 1863.

Doughty's *Lexington, Warren* and *Natchez*

These three vessels were built to Doughty's draught. They were 127ft between perpendiculars, 33ft 6in moulded beam by 15ft 3in in the hold. Visually they could be distinguished from the Humphreys vessels by an extra port between the bridle port and the first broadside port, plus a more pronounced elliptic curve at the stern. They also displayed a bit more rake in the stem, and fuller waterlines both fore and aft.[95] However, these three were generally much less satisfactory than the Humphreys vessels and two of the three had the shortest active careers of the class: *Natchez* was broken up in 1840 and *Lexington* became a storeship in 1843.

Natchez was built at Norfolk and commissioned by 9 July 1827, carrying twenty-four 24pdrs. A measure of her effectiveness can be deduced by her employment before she was broken up in 1840. First, she was never sent beyond the West Indies and the Caribbean, making three cruises in that area during her career, one of which was curtailed by an outbreak of yellow fever. Her only other employment was during the Nullification crisis when she was essentially a floating battery at Charleston for three months in 1833.

In 1840, when she was in need of considerable mainte-

nance and repair, there was little sentiment for spending the needed funds. It was first suggested that she be lengthened at a cost of $65,000 (hinting that her problem was related to overloading). Humphreys replied in the negative, referring to her 'few good qualities'; then a committee report by M C Perry, Humphreys, Hartt, Lenthall, Benjamin Cooper and Stringham concurred, also mentioning her 'objectionable model'.[96] She was broken up shortly thereafter.

Warren was built at Boston, and commissioned on 14 January 1827. As early as 1829 she was reported in a 'very defective state' along with the observation that she was 'not ... so well built as the other sloops'.[97] Her sailing qualities were 'not as favorable as several of the [other] sloops' though no specifics on her shortcomings have come to light.[98] Her early conversion to a guardship and auxiliary duties possibly indicate major problems in carrying her armament.

Her initial commission was in the Mediterranean, followed by cruises on the Brazil station and in the West Indies. She joined the Pacific squadron in 1843 and began duties as a guardship at Monterey during the Mexican war. She subsequently became a receiving ship and a storeship and was sold at Panama in 1863.[99]

Lexington was launched at New York (Brooklyn) Navy Yard in March 1826, then commissioned on 12 June 1826. She was possibly the first of the class to go to sea, and carried twenty-four 24pdrs in her initial commission. Her sailing qualities were reported to the department in 1834. Her com-

Copy of William Doughty's plan for the 1825 sloops: used for *Warren*, *Natchez* and possibly *Lexington*. Though differences seem slight between the designs, these three vessels had short service lives. [National Archives 40-8-4A]

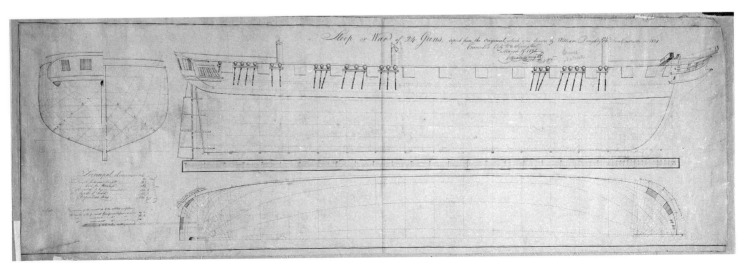

manding officer stated that she did well in smooth water, but 'with even a moderate head sea, in consequence of the leanness of her Harping, she performs badly.' Though she worked well and laid to 'admirably', he attributed these qualities to her recently raked masts and having 'her bow guns put below'. She made 11½ knots going free.[100]

Her career began with a tour off the east coast, ending with the return of the body of Oliver Hazard Perry, who had died while on duty in the Caribbean in 1819. Following this she cruised in the Mediterranean, South Atlantic and Pacific. She was converted to a storeship while in repair at New York in 1840 to 1843. She continued her service in that capacity until sold in 1863.

The Humphreys design

The sloops of war built to the design of Samuel Humphreys were demonstratively serviceable – 'good sea boats' – though unspectacular. One, *St Louis*, was used into the next century, and another, *Vincennes*, was possibly the most widely travelled, having circled the globe four times in the course of her career. These vessels – *Boston*, *Vincennes*, *Vandalia*, *Fairfield*, *Concord*, *St Louis*, and, built later to the same plan, *John Adams* – measured 127ft between perpendiculars, 34ft moulded beam, 15ft 3in depth of hold and about 700 tons ('carpenter's as opposed to displacement tons). Each was originally armed with twenty-four 24pdrs. The cost of each of these vessels was around $100,000; as examples the *Vincennes* ranged upward to $115,889, and *Vandalia* cost $98,699.[101]

The sloop of war *Boston* was possibly the first laid down, at Charlestown Navy Yard on 13 May 1825. She went into service in January 1826. On her initial commission her captain reported she worked admirably and during one stretch averaged 11 knots. Before a strong wind, under single reefed topsails, fore sail and main topgallant, she made 10.[102]

In 1839, while she was under repair, Captain Charles Ridgely suggested reducing the number of broadside ports to eleven, as they were too close together and 'too many', as well as altering her after body. Constructors Humphreys, John Lenthall and Samuel Hartt agreed with the former.

Sloop of war *St Louis*. Her claim to fame was in intervening on behalf of Hungarian revolutionist Martin Koszta at Smyrna on 12 July 1853, as celebrated in this lithograph. [US Navy]

But they disagreed with the latter, noting that her 'sailing and stability has always stood high'.[103] After this date she carried twenty 42pdr carronades and two 24pdrs. In 1846 she was further reduced to 20 guns: sixteen 32s and four 8-inch shell guns.[104]

She began her career on the Brazil station, then joined the Mediterranean squadron. Subsequently, she served in the West Indies, East Indies, and again, on the South Atlantic. In 1846 she was ordered to join the squadron blockading the Mexican coast and was lost in a squall off Eleuthera Island.

The second of the Humphreys-designed sloops of war laid down was *Vincennes*. She was built at New York, where she was launched in April and commissioned on 27 August 1826. Early descriptions of her sailing qualities were positive. In fresh or strong breezes she sailed best with reduced sail: topsails and courses, but under 'lofty sail' she tended to bury herself in head seas. Her best sailing was with the wind abeam or thereabouts, while she was 'but ordinary' with the wind abaft or on the quarter. She was a deep roller, but relatively easy on rig and cables. Her best point was 'the great facility with which she performs all maneuvers and the capacity to carry a great deal of sail without strain'. Of course, the size of her battery was mentioned with the comment that 'in heavy weather the removal of guns from forward and aft is a great relief and advantage to the ship.' Furthermore, in action or practice the firing of the battery would 'wreck the ship to pieces'. However, despite a list of minor faults, the ship's first commander considered her a 'Nonpareil'.[105]

Vincennes's career certainly justified her commander's confidence. Her first commission set an extraordinary pattern. She departed from New York, rounded Cape Horn to Hawaii, then crossed the Pacific. She returned to New York via the Cape of Good Hope and became the first American naval vessel to circumnavigate the world. Her next commission was more mundane: a cruise in the West Indies, marred by an outbreak of yellow fever. She then returned to Portsmouth yard for overhaul. In June 1833 she departed for her third cruise, which again took her to the Pacific. Her route took her further south than previously and she was the first American warship to visit Guam. She returned to Hampton Roads in June 1836 after her second circumnavigation.

Having proved her hardihood, she was selected as the flagship for Lieutenant Charles Wilkes' 'South Sea Surveying and Exploring Expedition'. Preparations for this epic undertaking included additional accommodations and work spaces for the scientists in a large stern cabin, and reduction of her battery to eight 24s and two 9pdrs.[106] The five-ship expedition departed in mid-1838, carrying nine selected scientists and their equipment and books. In their four-year odyssey they surveyed 280 islands, mapped the Oregon coast, and explored 1500 miles of the Antarctic continent, returning with masses of natural history specimens which became an important seed bed for the fledgling national museum, now the Smithsonian. By the time of

their return in 1842, *Vincennes* had made her third world circumnavigation, not to mention crossing the Pacific three times and the Atlantic twice.[107]

Subsequently *Vincennes* joined the West Indies squadron, then returned to the Far East in 1845. In yet another remarkable cruise, she joined the ship of the line *Columbus* in an abortive first attempt to open Japan to the west. She returned to New York in 1847. After a period of refit, *Vincennes* joined the Pacific squadron in 1849, returning to New York in 1852. She was then given another round of modifications, including reduction of her battery, in preparation for yet another exploring expedition. In this case, the areas of interest were the China seas, the North Pacific and the Bering Straits, under Cadwalader Ringgold. She returned in 1856, by way of Cape Horn. This was circumnavigation number four. By the end of this voyage she had also become the first American naval vessel to cruise in the Arctic as well as Antarctic zones.

The remainder of her career was anticlimactic. Late in the 1850s she was assigned to the anti-slavery patrol off Africa, then she became part of the Gulf blockading squadron during the War between the States. From 1865 to 1867 she was in ordinary at Boston, then was sold on 5 October 1867. She no doubt had had the most extraordinary peacetime career of any vessel in the old sailing navy, and epitomised the sturdiness of this class of vessels.

The sloop of war *Fairfield* was the second of the Humphreys design built at Brooklyn Navy Yard. She was laid down early in 1828, launched on 28 June and commissioned around 20 August of that year, carrying the usual twenty-four 24pdrs. The *Fairfield* was considered an excellent sailer and sea boat during her first decade of service. In an 1836 letter her commander wrote that she was faster than any vessels they had sailed with, except *Vincennes*, which had a clean bottom at the time. Her handling under various conditions was not faulted in any way.[108]

Later, while on the Brazil station, another officer was less generous. She was, he wrote, overloaded, a condition which manifested itself particularly when running before the wind. She would pitch violently and was exceedingly wet. The writer ascribed this to both the heavy weight of her guns and to her newly installed water tanks—which had replaced the traditional casks. Where the latter could be disposed of and were relatively light, the iron tanks were a permanent weight–regardless of the amount of water being carried.[109]

The vessel had a relatively short and uneventful career. She sailed in the Mediterranean, West Indies, Pacific, South Atlantic squadrons, ending her career with a second cruise in the Mediterranean. She was decommissioned at Norfolk on 3 February 1845 and was broken up in 1852.

St Louis was the only sloop of this class built at Washington Navy Yard. She was laid down on 12 February 1827 but not launched until 16 August 1828 and commis-

sioned 20 December of that year. John D Sloat, one of her early commanding officers, was particularly impressed by the vessel, which he described as 'the safest and most manageable ship I have ever been in'. He considered her too 'lean' in the bows, however, causing her to 'press down forward' in a fresh breeze. She would do 9 or 10 knots easily, but then would be retarded by this characteristic. He did

Sloop of war *Vandalia*. She was lengthened by 30ft in the 1840s and was 'rebuilt' as a steam sloop in the 1870s. A sketch by Midshipman Henry K Davenport, who served aboard the sloop from April 1838 to October 1839. [US Naval Historical Center NH 43842]

u. S. Sloop of War "Vandalia". Commander John Gwinn U.S.N. + A.J. Dallas u.s.n.

report she would do 11½ knots at times, with skysails and studding sails rigged out and wind on the quarter.[110]

St Louis first served in the Pacific, then the West Indies. Her third cruise took her to the Pacific again, where she was the first American warship to visit San Francisco (1839). A tour in the East Indies followed, then refit at Norfolk, where she was lengthened by 13ft. After service in the South Atlantic, she was assigned to the Mediterranean. While lying at Smyrna, her captain intervened to free Hungarian revolutionist Martin Koszta, who was being detained on an Austrian warship in that harbour, but who had previously announced his decision to become an American citizen. With the support of the American consul, the American captain delivered an ultimatum, cleared his vessel for action, and won his point.

Her next cruise was on the African station, followed by duty on the South Atlantic Blockading Squadron during the Civil War. *St Louis* was also one of several ships detailed to hunt down Confederate cruisers in the Atlantic. After the war she ended her active service at Philadelphia, where she became a receiving ship. She remained in this role until lent to the Naval Militia of Pennsylvania as a training ship. She was renamed *Keystone State* in 1904 to free the name for a new cruiser, and was finally sold for scrapping in 1907.

Vandalia was built at Philadelphia, launched on 26 August 1828 and commissioned on 6 November 1828. She was first assigned to the South Atlantic squadron, then the West Indies station. In the latter she worked with land forces against the Seminole Indians of Florida as well as against the slave trade in the area.

While laid up at Norfolk in the mid-1840s, she was lengthened by 30ft. Her next duty was in the Pacific, and she accompanied Perry's squadron to Japan in 1854. During the Civil War she served on the blockade, but was sent north in 1863 for decommissioning. She was a receiving ship at Portsmouth, New Hampshire for the balance of her career and she was broken up around 1871.

Concord had the shortest career of this group of ships, excepting *Natchez*. She was built at Portsmouth, New Hampshire with her keel laid in March 1827. She was launched on 24 September 1827 but was not commissioned until 7 May 1830, carrying twenty-four 24pdrs.[111]

Her first commanding officer was Master Commandant M C Perry, who took her to Russia with the new American ambassador, then joined the Mediterranean squadron. Perry described her as 'an admirable vessel in every particular' and noted that she sailed 'well under any sail, but her best is on a wind in smooth water, under single or double-reefed topsails'. She out-sailed all vessels in the squadron, saving *Brandywine*. Her only major drawback was a deep waist, which allowed green water over the hammock rails and down her hatches in heavy weather.[112]

Concord's second cruise was in the West Indies, followed by two years on the Brazil station. She was then detailed to the coast of east Africa to protect American whaling interests, but in October 1843 ran aground in the mouth of the Loango River and was a total loss.

The 'rebuilt' *John Adams*, has been alluded to previously, in the chapter on frigates. The genesis of the new sloop of war of the same name came in December 1828, when John Rodgers (senior member of the Board of Navy Commissioners) ordered Samuel Barron, commandant of Norfolk Navy Yard, to 'commence those [repairs] of the Jno. Adams, taking one of the frames of the sloops of war which have been delivered under the appropriation for Gradual Improvement'. Later Rodgers explained to the Secretary of the Navy that the 'form of the ship was objectionable' and a contract was made for a 'new live oak frame' for her. Furthermore, a draught was sent to Norfolk for the new ship. This was necessary because none of the other sloops of this class had been built at that yard. Later, in justifying to Secretary Branch the use of 'repair' funds for the ship, Rodgers would rationalise that repairing a vessel could easily include new sails, rigging, and boats, and indeed, the hull itself was only 'one third the value' of the entire vessel. Besides, he explained, the terms 'repairing' and 'rebuilding' had been 'synonimous' [*sic*] in the navy yards, and that similar 'rebuilding' had occurred previously with *Peacock*, *Erie* and *Ontario*.[113]

In any event, Samuel Humphreys provided further evidence that the 1831 sloop was a new vessel. First is the listing of the vessels written on Humphreys' original plan (NARA 108-10-11) for the class. This clearly lists the 'new John Adams' at the end of the list of the other sloops.

The launch of the sloop of war *John Adams*, built to the plans of Samuel Humphreys. Note the obvious similarities to the others of the Humphreys sloop design. Other evidence makes it obvious that the original 1799 *John Adams* was replaced by a new sloop of a modern design. [US Naval Historical Center NH 20236]

Furthermore, a letter dated 1835 finds Humphreys remarking on the stories he had heard from various officers that *John Adams* was 'superior in sailing & working to any vessel of the same class', owing, it was said to the alterations made in her by constructor Francis Grice. Humphreys was anxious to know 'what, if any, alterations were made . . . from moulds sent to him.'[114] The reply to Humphreys' somewhat affronted inquiry was that no liberties had been taken with his original plans.[115]

It is evident that, at the time, there was no question that the sloop of war *John Adams* was a completely different ship from her namesake. Particularly convincing is the fact that the letter of 'explanation' from Rodgers to Secretary Branch quoted above is not an attempt to justify the building of a new ship, but merely to defend the use of 'repair' money for the project. As to the question of the use of timbers from the old ship in the new one, that well could have been

done. However, the intention was to build a new ship and the 'frame' itself was for a totally different vessel than the original. Therefore any use of timbers from the old ship becomes merely incidental.

The sloop of war *John Adams*, armed with her two dozen 24pdrs, went to sea as part of the Mediterranean squadron in May 1831, and was there off and on through 1837. Subsequently she made passage to the Pacific and East Indies. She joined *Columbia* in bombarding the Sumatrans in 1839 and returned via Cape Horn, completing a circumnavigation of the world. She later served in the South Atlantic, by this time carrying 32pdr carronades in lieu of

A painting of the sloop *John Adams* (left) passing the frigate *Brandywine* off the entrance to Valletta harbour, Malta in 1832. [Maryland Historical Society]

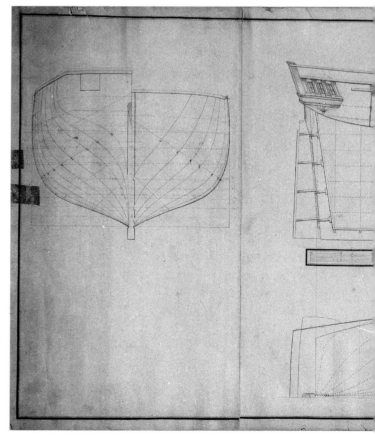

her long guns.[116] Later she was in the Gulf of Mexico (during the Mexican War), and in the Africa squadron. From 1853 to 1861 she operated in the Pacific and Far East. Her first assignment during the Civil War was as a training ship for the Naval Academy, and in 1863 she was transferred to the South Atlantic Blockading Squadron. After the war she was decommissioned at Boston, and sold in 1867.

The final sloop of war built in this era was another old vessel 'renewed'. In this instance, it was the aged, but highly regarded and fast *Peacock*, which, as has been noted above, had sustained significant damage towards the end of her final cruise. A new design was made for the ship, which lay at New York, and there was apparently no intention of actually 'repairing' the old vessel. Samuel Humphreys wrote in April 1828 that 'The sloop *Peacock* is completely laid down on the mould loft floor and instructions for cutting the frames are made out.'[117] The fact that a new plan was drawn, table of offsets made, and complete set of moulds done clearly indicates there was a new vessel in the works. Mere repairs required none of the above. A later report specifically listed the portions of the old ship re-used in the new. 'The hull [was] all renewed except 10 berthdeck knees, the cross piece of the cable bitts, drum head and pall [*sic*] heads of the capstan. A part of the old iron & copper were used in the repair. Joiner work, masts, spars & boats all new.'[118] This indicates that probably 99 per cent of the ship was new. (Berth deck knees were relatively generic in configuration and in similarly sized vessels could well have been interchangeable, simply by measuring vertical and horizontal dimensions.) Note also that John Rodgers had listed this vessel as one which had been rebuilt as a new vessel, in his letter of explanation to Secretary Branch in 1830, quoted above in the section on *John Adams*.

Further, though the new vessel's dimensions were within inches of the old ship's, the hull form was unrecognisable. The new ship was significantly sharper forward and aft, had less sheer, less rake in her stem and stern, less drag to her keel, and had an elliptical in lieu of the old square stern. She measured 118ft between perpendiculars, 31ft 6in moulded beam and 14ft 10in depth of hold.

The ship was commissioned on 1 November 1828 and joined the West Indies squadron. She was listed as carrying 18 guns, though by 1831 she had 22: twenty 32pdr carronades and two 12s.[119] The new *Peacock*'s career was a short one. After three years in the Caribbean, she was assigned to the Brazil squadron, then voyaged to the Far East, carrying the American envoy to Siam. She returned to the Far East in 1835, visiting Siam, Muscat and other Asian ports. After some alterations and reduction in armament, she was attached to the Wilkes expedition in 1838. She accompanied the *Vincennes* squadron in the Pacific and in Antarctic waters, but was lost at the mouth of the Columbia River in 1841.

The second sloop of war *Peacock*, 1828. Note differences between this plan and the earlier *Peacock*, indicating this was a completely new vessel when completed. [National Archives 41-5-6A].

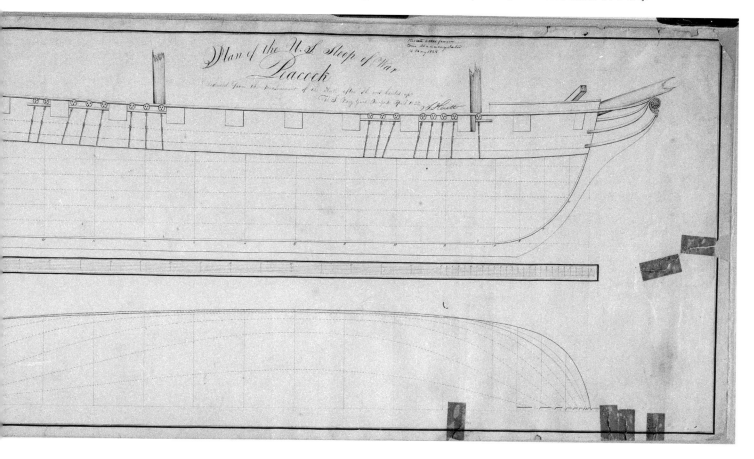

American Sloops of War, 1837–1855

WITH THE completion of *John Adams* in 1831, construction of new sloops of war ceased until 1837. In the interim, the navy built up its inventory of smaller vessels, more suitable for close-in operations in southern waters—in the anti-piracy campaign as well as in support of the army in the Seminole War. Congressional authorisation for new sloops of war came in 1832 and 1834, with funding to build a replacement for the old British prize *Cyane* and another to be called *Levant*[1] (named for the sloop captured by *Constitution* but subsequently re-taken by the British). From these ships, which went into the water in 1838, to the close of the sailing ship era, the navy built one class of small sloops of war, in 1838 and 1839, and a series of 'First Class Sloops' commencing with *Saratoga* in 1841 and ending with the commissioning of the new *Constellation* in 1855.

Cyane and *Levant*

Samuel Humphreys designed these vessels with an obvious intent to rectify the shortcomings of the 1825 sloops. The new ships were somewhat larger, both in dimensions and tonnage. At 132ft 3in between perpendiculars by 35ft 3in beam and 792 tons they were some five feet longer, a foot beamier and ninety tons larger than the *Boston* class ships. Above the water they resembled the older class in rake fore and aft and sheer. Beneath the waterline, they were significantly finer in their stern lines, and exhibited less drag in their keels.

Though using the same hull plan, it appears that the two differed in the number of gunports. The original sheer plan for the two shows twelve ports plus a bridle port, but below the half-breadth plan is sketched a diagram showing eleven broadside ports. A later sail plan of *Cyane* confirms her eleven ports.[2] A contemporary painting of *Levant* on station in the Mediterranean, by an artist noted for accuracy, shows her with twelve broadside ports. The artist also accurately

Lines plan of the sloop of war *Cyane*. This vessel and *Levant* mark a mid-point in the size and development of USN sloops of war. [National Archives 41-3-20B]

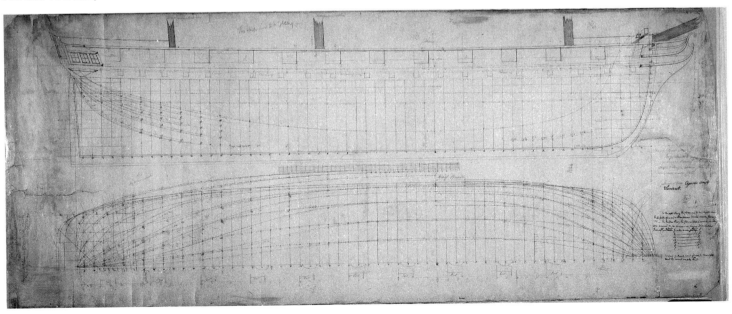

Sloop of war *Levant* off Naples. Painting by Francisco De Simone. [Naval Historical Center NH 18402]

portrayed the ship's rig: these two were among the earliest American naval vessels to have spencers on fore and main masts. These were gaff-headed fore-and-aft sails comparable to the spanker, but hoisted on their own 'sticks' located immediately abaft and attached to the main and fore masts. These sails effectively made these ships three-masted schooners when necessary.

Cyane was launched on 2 December 1837 and commissioned around June 1838. Her original battery was four 24pdrs and eighteen 32pdr carronades. Her first commander was not impressed by this ship, or at least as she was at that time. She was extremely stiff, dry and comfortable, but she pitched deeply and suddenly, causing him to move two of her guns aft (though this did not significantly alleviate the problem). He recommended her masts be moved aft

slightly, as well as her catheads, the latter to move the weight of the anchors aft. The ship was not particularly fast (11½ knots running free), and carried a strong lee helm.[3] The ship's second commander–though on the same cruise –had a thoroughly different view of the *Cyane*. Though she had not been altered in the least since the date of the report quoted above, he deemed her 'in all respects, a very fine and safe ship'. It appears, by comparing the two reports, however, that the second commander had not encountered the kind of rough weather which is mentioned in the earlier report.[4]

Following her tour in the Mediterranean, *Cyane* served in

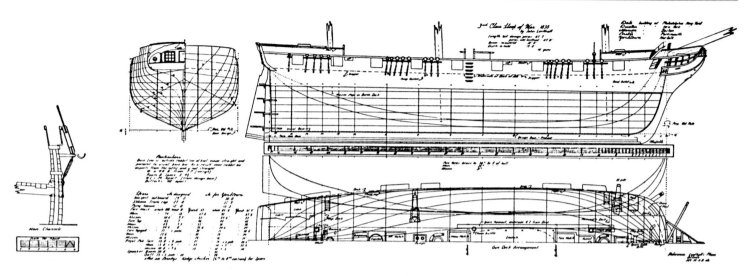

Building draught for the 1838 sloops of war, as redrawn by Howard Chapelle. These vessels were smaller than *Cyane* and *Levant*, were to carry 18 guns, but in the end were given 16. [By courtesy of the Smithsonian Institution]

the Pacific, where she participated in the seizure of northern California during the Mexican War. Along with two other US naval vessels, she captured Mazatlan in 1847. From 1851 to 1857 she was employed in the Home squadron cruising as far south as the isthmus of Panama. From 1858 to her decommissioning in September 1870 she was stationed on the Pacific Coast. She was finally sold in July 1887.

Levant was built at New York, launched on 28 December 1837 and commissioned on 17 March 1838. She was reportedly slightly faster than her sister ship (12 knots). Otherwise, she reflected some of the same characteristics: a 'comfortable' sea boat and very stiff, but steered badly and worked slowly.[5]

Levant was initially part of the West Indies squadron, then, in 1843, was sent to the Pacific. With *Cyane* and *Savannah*, she seized Monterey, California in 1846. Her next cruise was to the Mediterranean, where she loaded sculptures by Horatio Greenough for transport to the United States. She then joined the Far East squadron and participated in taking the 'Barrier Forts' below Canton in 1856. Men from her crew, plus those from USS *Portsmouth*, stormed and captured all four fortifications. She was close in during the action, taking twenty-two hits in her hull and rigging and seven casualties.

She made two more cruises afterwards, the first on the west coast, the second to the Hawaiian Islands. She departed from Hawaii in September 1860, en route to Panama, and was never heard from again.

Dale Class, 1838

The Congressional act of 3 April 1837 authorised the construction of six 10- to 18-gun warships. One of this group became the *Princeton*, the navy's first screw steamer.[6] The other five became the 'Third Class Sloops' *Dale*, *Yorktown*, *Preble*, *Marion* and *Decatur*. These vessels were built to a design by John Lenthall, 117ft 7in between perpendiculars, 32ft beam, by 15ft depth, and 566 tons. This was slightly larger than the 1828 *Peacock* design, which in turn was not a great deal different from that of the 1813 *Peacock*.

The small size of the 1838 sloops is a puzzle, and certainly reflected a reversal of the trend shown in the 1825 sloops and in the *Cyane* and *Levant*. That they were an aberration is particularly plain in light of the burgeoning dimensions which would be seen in the 'First Class Sloops', the first of which was laid down in 1841. And, though the authorisation for the new class was for 'up to 18 guns', the navy, uncharacteristically, armed them with only sixteen. It appears that the Board was in search of a turn of speed for these vessels, probably in reaction to the stodgy reputations of the 1825 sloops, as well as of the 1837 vessels. (It also can be noted that the three ships built for exploration purposes and tried in 1837 had also been embarrassingly slow.) These factors may explain the reversion to a design recalling that of the original speedy *Peacock*.

It is noteworthy that these vessels saw increased use of iron in their fittings, a trend which of course would continue apace through this era. The *Decatur*, for instance, was fitted with iron futtock shrouds secured by iron bands to the masts, and chain topsail ties, with the latter run through sheave holes in the mast head. Also, iron plates were employed for the gaffs to work on, in place of the trysail (spencer) masts.[7]

Yorktown was built at Norfolk and launched on 17 June 1839. She was commissioned around 13 December 1840 and went to sea armed with fourteen 32pdr carronades and two long 12pdrs. On her first cruise, to the Brazil station, her commanding officer called her the 'dullest ship I have ever sailed in – 10 knots is her utmost, and then she requires little short of a gale of wind on her quarter.' She proved to be a heavy roller and exceedingly wet: at 10 knots with the wind on the quarter she rolled her waist hammock rails under water. She proved significantly slower than *Dale* when sailing in company, with the latter periodically having to lay her topsail aback to maintain her station relative to the *Yorktown*.[8]

Her commanding officer proceeded to increase the rake

Sail plan of 1838 sloops. [National Archives 107-14-21]

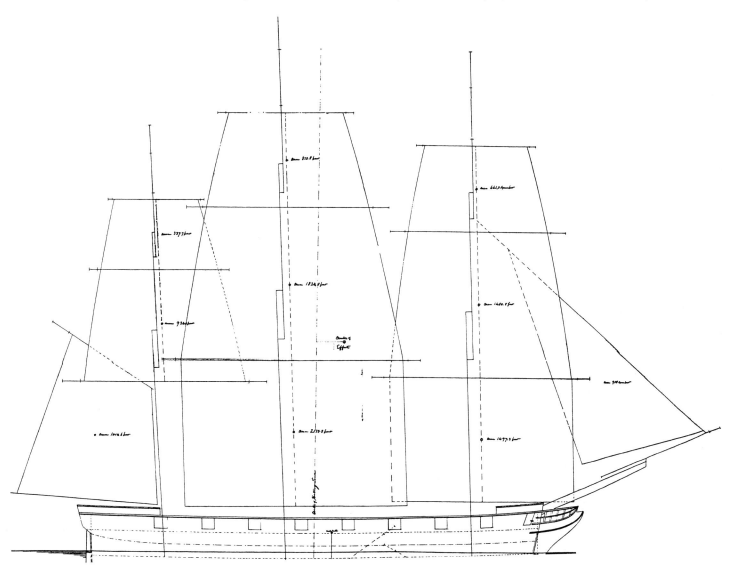

in her masts and rearrange her ballast, distributing the latter further aft. Afterwards she was appreciably drier and pitched less severely into head seas. Additionally, her speed improved significantly, enabling him to report attaining 12 knots in a fresh gale with a heavy press of sail. However, she

An excellent pre-Civil War view of one of the 1838 sloops, probably *Decatur*, at Boston. A carved bust can be seen between the stern windows. A view by Southwark and Hawes. [Peabody Essex Museum neg 23977]

still remained substantially slower than *Dale* in light and moderate breezes.[9] Another drawback for this and others of the class was their limited stowage – only carrying provisions and water for 3½ months at sea.[10]

The ship had a short career, with a cruise in the Pacific and two in the African squadron. In September 1850 *Yorktown* was wrecked on an uncharted reef in the Cape Verde Islands.

The sloop of war *Decatur* was built at Brooklyn Navy Yard and launched on 9 April 1839. She was also armed with sixteen guns: two 12s and the balance 32pdr carronades. The ship was not a fast sailer, with her commanding officer noting no more than 11 knots, with the wind. Her speed and handling gained appreciably as she lightened and she brought her head up in the process of a cruise. With a strong gale on her quarter she only required one man on the helm and sailed 'without shipping a particle of water'. However, she was 'so short that under her lofty sails she [is] easily buried.' She also had a pitching problem, exacerbated, according to her captain, by the stowage of her anchors far forward, as well as the extreme flare of her bow above the line of her deck. He was of the opinion, however, that she could easily carry a 'much heavier armament' than fitted with at the time.[11]

The pre-war career of the *Decatur* was colourful and varied. She began in the Brazil squadron, then was part of the anti-slavery patrol off West Africa. She supported army operations against Mexico in the Gulf (armed with sixteen 32s), then returned to anti-slaver work. After a stint in the Home squadron and another defending American fishing interests on the Grand Banks, she was sent to the Pacific Coast. In 1856 her gunfire support was decisive in quelling a Nez Perce Indian uprising in Seattle, Washington territory. She was decommissioned at Mare Island, California in 1859 and made into a harbour battery in 1863. *Decatur* was sold there in August, 1865.

Preble was launched on 13 June 1839 at Portsmouth Navy Yard, New Hampshire. She was commissioned around 2 June 1840 and entered service with the same battery as her sister ships: 12pdrs and 32pdr carronades. This vessel was typical of the class: not particularly fast and prone to heavy rolling. She sailed, worked and steered well, though not as

Sloop of war *Dale* in her post-war training role. The 1838 sloops, though small, proved quite serviceable for peacetime roles. *Dale*, renamed *Oriole*, became cadet housing for the Revenue Service as late as 1906, and was returned to the Navy in 1921. [US Navy NH 61572]

efficiently in light winds. Her provision stowage, for a crew of around 150 men, was about 3½ months, significantly less than the standard in the cruising navy which was for six months at sea.[12]

The ship's pre-Civil War career included cruises in the Mediterranean, off Africa, and in the Pacific. After returning from the East Indies in 1851 she was made into a practice ship for midshipmen, with her battery reduced to ten 32pdrs, then further to eight guns in 1853.[13] She participated in the Paraguayan punitive expedition in 1858, then joined the Gulf Blockading Squadron at the outbreak of the war. She was a store- and guardship at Pensacola when she caught fire and was destroyed on 27 April 1863.

Dale was built at Philadelphia Navy Yard and launched on 8 November 1839. On commissioning in December 1840, she carried 16 guns. She apparently was the fastest vessel of the five, with one source crediting her with 13 knots. As mentioned above, sailing in company with

Yorktown resulted in rather baffling results, considering their identical hull lines. In one pre-arranged trial between the two, both were put under the same sail – royals and all below – and braced sharp by the wind. In six hours the *Yorktown* ran 33 miles '. . . at the end of which the *Dale* was 4½ miles ahead'. (The difference was some 5 .5 knots versus slightly over 6 knots.) Later in the same cruise, against a head sea, *Yorktown* was 'laboring along under topmast and topgallant [studding] sails, pitching and struggling . . . the '*Dale* taking it quite easy, keeping ahead of her station with one reef in her topsail and no [studding] sails set.'[14]

The career of the *Dale* began with extensive cruising on the Pacific coast, including capturing privateers during the

Mexican War. In the 1850s she was employed for the most part in the anti-slavery patrol, returning for decommissioning in May 1859. In 1851, while in the Africa squadron, she logged 28,313 miles and 252 days at sea–an average of 112 miles per day.[15]

At the outbreak of the Civil War she was assigned to the Atlantic Blockading Squadron, capturing two schooners in her passage to Port Royal, South Carolina. She was utilised as a store- and guardship at Port Royal, then Key West, until July 1865. From 1867 to 1884 she was a training ship at the Naval Academy, then became a receiving ship at Washington Navy Yard. In 1895 she was transferred to the Maryland Naval Militia and renamed *Oriole* in 1904.

In 1906 she was transferred to the Revenue Service at Curtis Bay, Baltimore, where she became a barracks ship for the cadets in training there. By this time the hull of the veteran vessel had become so porous that if her pumps were left unattended overnight, she would sink at her shallow moorings. This created some rather vivid memories for the young men in training for the Revenue Service. In 1921 she was returned to the Navy and sold.[16] She had survived eighty-two years.

Marion was built at Charlestown Navy Yard, Boston, and launched on 24 April 1839. She was commissioned on 4 October 1839 carrying 16 guns and a crew of about 150. She was comparable to the others of her class in her speed and characteristics at sea. She would make 11½ knots running free and 9 close-hauled. She was, however, significantly faster than *Yorktown*, a circumstance which was attributed by the commanders of both vessels to greater rake in her masts and the distribution of her ballast farther aft.[17] It is noteworthy that in her cruise ending in 1853, her ballast was reduced from 16½ tons to 5 tons. She was then able to carry five months' provisions. (The other vessels of this class carried from 7 to 25 tons ballast.) This reduction apparently did not adversely effect her sailing.[18]

Marion was first assigned to the Brazil station, departing from Boston in November 1839. In 1842 she sank while hove down at Rio de Janiero. She was re-floated and returned to Boston under her own power. Subsequently she was part of the anti-slavery patrol, the Mediterranean squadron, and the East Indies squadron. During the Civil War she participated in the search for the Confederate cruiser *Jeff Davis*, then joined the blockade in the Gulf of Mexico. After May 1862, she was a practice ship for the Naval Academy, remaining in that role until 1870. She was taken out of service in 1871 at Kittery (Portsmouth Navy Yard). She was subsequently broken up.

In probably the most egregious example of the navy's administrative 'rebuilding' fiction, the *Marion* which reappeared at Portsmouth in 1876 was a 1900-ton steam vessel, measuring about a hundred feet longer and five feet wider than the 1839 sailing sloop of war.[19] It was obvious that there was no resemblance whatever between the old and new *Marion*.

The 1838 sloops obviously did not fulfil the speed expectations of their designers. They were, however, well built and competent sea boats. It is unlikely that they would have been efficient in wartime, however. Because of the their light battery, a reasonably well armed merchant ship could have given them a stiff fight. To make matters worse, a merchant vessel with a turn of speed could have out-ranged the sloops' carronades. By the same token, the carronades combined with their lack of speed would have spelled disaster in action against speedier vessels armed with long guns. Therefore, it appears the Board obtained exactly what they were in search of, rightly or wrongly, an economical vessel for peacetime cruising. In fact, the resulting hull was about as small as would support the full three-masted ship rig requisite for extended cruising on station.

The First Class Sloops of War, 1841-1846

The administration of Secretary of the Navy Abel P Upshur was marked by great progress and dynamic change in the navy department. One of the major institutional changes was the replacement of the Board of Navy Commissioners with the bureau system in 1842. Six of these seven 'First Class' sloops of war were authorised under the new regime. These six, begun in 1843, were to be built in the six yards, and the respective constructors were allowed much scope in their approach to the design, in the hope that competition among the constructors might yield better results than was had in the 1838 sloops.[20] The seventh vessel, *Saratoga*, was begun in 1841, and, in fact can be viewed as the generic prototype for the other six.

These vessels were significantly larger, obviously, than the 1838 Third Class Sloops, and in fact were the largest sailing sloops of war constructed in the US, excepting the 1853 *Constellation*. Though none was less than 146ft in length, they were designed for only 22 guns. Two factors seem to have been operating in the development of this design: extra length for its advantages in attaining speed, and sufficient displacement for a battery of substantial guns: eighteen medium 32pdrs and four 8-inch shell guns. These two types of guns were becoming the standard ordnance on all US Navy ships in this era.[21]

Saratoga

The sloop of war *Saratoga* was laid down at Portsmouth Navy Yard in August 1841, to a design by Samuel Humphreys and Samuel Pook. The similarities between this hull design and that of the *Cyane* and *Levant* are sufficient to indicate the new ship was an improved version of the older vessels. At 146ft 4in between perpendiculars, she was fourteen feet longer than the previous design, but was identical in moulded beam (35ft 3in) and, at 16ft 3½in, very similar in depth of hold. It is obvious that the additional length was utilised to sharpen the hull lines, particularly aft,

and increase the rake of the stem, compared to the older ships. It is interesting to note the progression of designs beginning with the 1825 sloops–though of course disregarding the small Third Class ships of 1838.

It appears that great expectations were entertained for this ship. Indeed, a new pattern of 32pdr cannon, weighing 4500 pounds was designed specifically for the vessel, with twenty-four being cast by Cyrus Alger. This was a medium weight gun in the continuum of 32pdrs in service at the time. (The navy's other 32pdr guns of this era were classed as 27cwt, 32cwt, 42cwt, 46cwt, 51cwt and 57cwt.) The new shell ('Paixhan') guns, recently tested on the steamer *Fulton II*, were also included in her battery: these were 8-inch guns of 60cwt, firing a 64-pound projectile, first cast in 1841.[22]

The ship was launched on 26 July 1842 and commissioned on 7 January the following year. Her earliest battery was 20 guns: sixteen 32s and four shell guns, but the number of the latter ranged from two to six throughout her career. Annotations on her hull plan indicate these guns–when she carried six–were located in ports amidships, immediately aft of the fore mast and forward of the mizzen. Certainly the size of the weapons warranted placing them in the open (or under the grating deck) rather than beneath the forecastle and quarterdecks, and their weight precluded

Sloop of war *Saratoga*, designed by Samuel Pook and Samuel Humphreys, first of seven very large sloops, all of which were quite successful. [National Archives 108-13-11B]

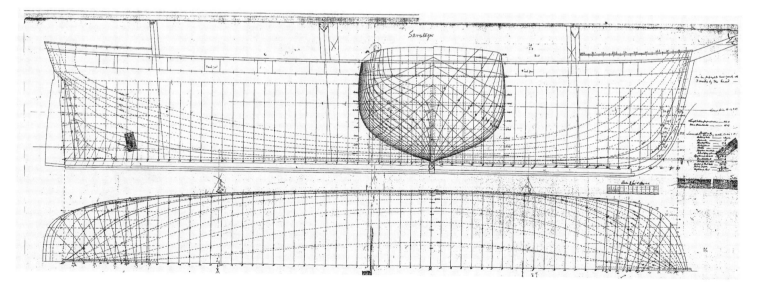

concentrating them forward or aft.[23] The vessel was originally built with a grating spar deck, but this was removed before January 1845, reducing her top weight by some five tons.[24] The grating was re-built in the 1850s, possibly in connection with the Japan Expedition.

She went to sea under inauspicious circumstances in March 1843. The second day out from Portsmouth she was caught in a strong gale and completely dismasted. Two months later, with a new complement of masts, she sailed for duty on the African anti-slavery patrol. Her commander, Josiah Tatnall, was generally positive about the vessel. He reported 10 knots close-hauled and 12.6 knots with the wind on the beam or quarter. He had out-sailed *Macedonian* and *Porpoise*, and, on one occasion, the brig *Truxtun*, running the latter 'courses down' in twelve hours.

It is worth noting that in these performance reports 'out-sailing' was not defined as an 'absolute' speed contest. It might have been understood as how well the vessel performed in given conditions of wind, current, swell, etc. In the above-mentioned trial with *Truxtun*, the two ships were in trim and going free, maintaining 6 to 9 knots. Shortly thereafter, with the *Saratoga* newly provisioned and out of trim, the *Truxtun* ('with a clean bottom & great advantage from the quality of her sails') out-sailed Tatnall's vessel. It should also be kept in mind that the term 'fast' was also a relative one. The commander of *Decatur*, for instance, once reported: 'I consider her a fast ship, up to eight or nine knots, but it requires much pressing to make her sail at a higher rate.'[25] In other words, a 'fast' ship was one which could maintain high velocity in any given wind condition. As to the *Saratoga*'s handling, Tatnall noted she was slow 'but sure' in stays, and steered remarkably well. She rolled easily and with little strain on her rigging, in part due to the removal of her grating deck. Tatnall complained, however, that she was not 'as stiff as the *Fairfield*' and that her gunports were too small for the 64pdrs.[26]

The career of the *Saratoga* was a long one. After her dismasting she was repaired and joined the Africa squadron, serving for a short time as flagship of Matthew Calbraith Perry. In addition to anti-slave trade activities, the vessel took part in defending the freed-slave colony at Liberia against local aggressors. Subsequently she was part of the Home squadron, under the command of David G Farragut. During the Mexican War she served in the Gulf of Mexico, participating in the blockade of Tuxpan. After an outbreak of yellow fever she returned to the United States, and was decommissioned at Boston in 1848. After another short term with the Home squadron, she was selected to join Commodore Perry's expedition to Japan, visiting that nation in 1853 to deliver the American treaty terms, and in 1854 to obtain the Japanese response. Her last completed cruise prior to the Civil War was in the Gulf of Mexico, then was again on the anti-slavery patrol from 1860 to the outbreak of the war. Early in the conflict she performed guard-ship duties at the Delaware capes, before being assigned to active duty in the South Atlantic Blockading Squadron.

After the war she lay in ordinary for much of the period until 1875 when she was re-activated as a gunnery ship for the Naval Academy. This duty ended in 1888 and in 1890 she was transferred to the state of Pennsylvania as a marine school ship. It is noteworthy than in mid-1902 a report was made on her condition with recommendations for repairs.

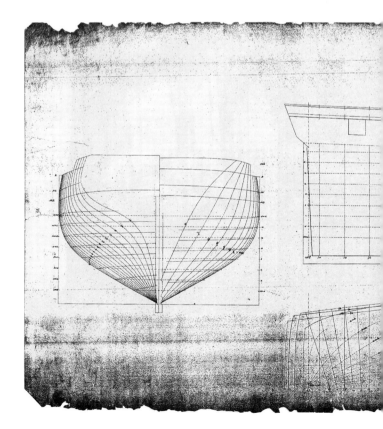

Though she had not been overhauled in some thirteen years, she was still in fair condition, and her hull was sound, only needing new copper. The total cost was estimated at about $40,000. Later, in 1907, another survey indicated the cost to repair the vessel and keep her in service as a school ship – which included extensive cruising at sea – was estimated at not more than $10,000. Supporters of continuing her funding pointed out that she was the last surviving vessel from Perry's Japan Expedition and had been commanded by Farragut before the war. Despite these appeals, funds were not forthcoming and she was finally sold out on 14 August 1907.[27]

Albany

Albany was the first of the main group to be laid down, sometime in 1843 or 1844. It is probably significant that the first of the First Class Sloops, Saratoga, had gone to sea early in 1843, so the general parameters of these sloops had been tested before the subsequent sloops were begun. Francis

Grice's objectives in her design were speed, stability, good sea-keeping and space to work her guns. Thus he enlarged on the Saratoga's dimensions, making her 147ft 11in in length and 38ft 6in moulded beam. His original plan was to make her a barque, possibly with the speed of the original Peacock, when a barque, in mind. His suggested rig was to have the same centre of effort as a ship rig and same quantity of canvas, and exhibited much rake in her masts.[28] However, the barque rig was apparently – and not unexpectedly – overruled by the department. She may have had the same rake early in her service, but If contemporary illustrations are accurate, later she was given a very tall ship rig, with much less rake in it.

Grice also objected to the idea of installing a light spar deck on the ship. He maintained that it would increase her draught significantly, confine gun smoke between the

Sloop of war Albany, designed by Francis Grice, had the greatest deadrise and sharpest ends of this group of ships. [National Archives 108-8-4K]

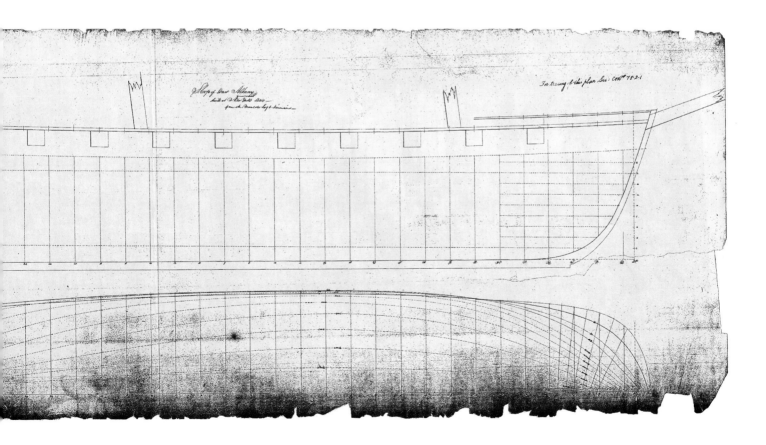

decks, and obstruct the clear view of all the guns from the poop and forecastle. Furthermore, her speed would benefit from carrying deeper courses. It is interesting that William Shubrick agreed with Grice, adding that the rather unkempt appearance of the typical crew was an embarrassment which would be somewhat mitigated if they were not exposed by the spar deck's low bulwarks: 'the fewer men visible in the working of a ship, the higher is the idea entertained of her discipline.' Shubrick was head of the Bureau of Provisions and Clothing at the time.[29]

The hull of this vessel was the most extreme of the First Class Sloops, exhibiting sharp ends and greatest deadrise – about 28 degrees from the horizontal – of all these ships. The Baltimore clipper model comes to mind, as well as the naval ships of Sir William Symonds in England. Certainly this vessel was one of the largest American warships to incorporate such extremes in her design. It is noteworthy that Symonds' vessels were criticised for their relatively small stowage and as unstable gun platforms. Of all the ships in this group, *Albany* was the most 'clipper' like in her appearance. Her low freeboard – a result of not having a spar deck – raking stem and tall masting all contributed to give her a rakish look indicative of speed.

She was launched on 27 June 1846 and commissioned on 6 November that year. Her original armament was four 8-inch shell guns and eighteen 32pdrs. Her first commander, S L Breese, was not particularly pleased with her, indicating

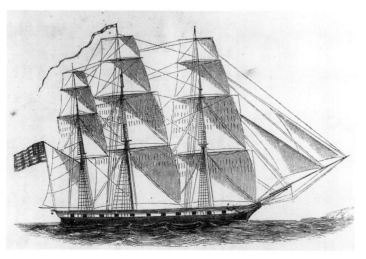

Albany's low freeboard and generous stem rake, plus tall rig, made her the most 'clipper' like of these sloops. [US Navy NH 200]

her best speed was 11½ knots with the wind abeam or just abaft it. He thought she was 'overhatted', which, combined with her sharp lines, caused her to pitch heavily and pull up hard, considerably impeding her progress and working her bowsprit and jibboom. She rolled heavily, but was relatively easy on her spars and steered well. Breese also complained of her inadequate stowage and lack of quarter galleries.[30] Some alterations in her rig were made before 1853, among them shortening her lower masts and reducing her canvas on the fore mast. Her speed benefited from these changes, reportedly achieving 10 knots on a wind and 13 running free.[31]

The *Albany's* first service was in the Home squadron, then the sloops was occupied in operations against the Mexicans at Anton Lizardo. She later landed troops at Vera Cruz and participated in the Alvorado and Tuxpan operations. She was active in the blockade but her deep draught prevented close-in action. After the war she was assigned to the Caribbean and West Indies areas as part of the Home squadron. She departed from Aspinwall, Columbia in September 1854 and was never seen again. She was the first of this group lost, and the only one whose career was terminated before the outbreak of the Civil War.

Portsmouth

The sloop of war *Portsmouth* was laid down at Portsmouth (Kittery) on 15 June 1843 and designed by Josiah Barker. The design was somewhat larger than that of the Portsmouth-built *Saratoga*, measuring 151ft 10in between perpendiculars, 37ft 3in moulded beam and 16ft 9in in the hold. Above the waterline there was significant rake in her stem, but less overhang at the stern than *Saratoga*. Below, she had less deadrise and showed some hollowness in her floors. The result was a tonnage of 1022, significantly larger than that of *Saratoga*. An early source claimed her lines were an enlarged version of a fast War of 1812 privateer, *America*,[32] but this seems unlikely, as *Portsmouth's* lines are in no way extreme, and in fact are not at great variance from *Saratoga's*.

Her length encouraged the builder to employ an intriguing stratagem to prevent hogging: her keel was laid with a

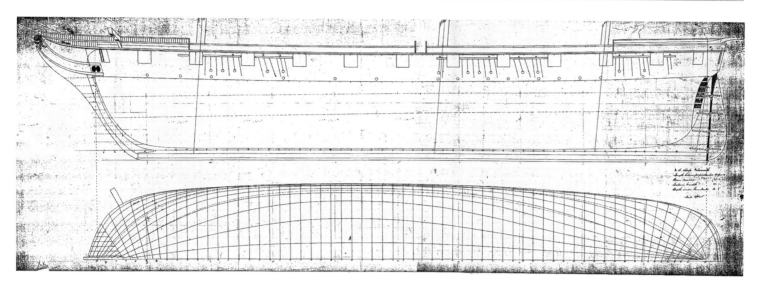

Plan of the sloop of war *Portsmouth*, by Josiah Barker. In her original state she did not have a spar deck. [National Archives 77-13-4]

built-in 3-inch 'rocker' or curve. After launching she was measured using 'sight ranges' and it was determined that she had straightened only ¾-inch.[33] It should be remembered that this vessel was not significantly smaller than a typical 36-gun frigate of an earlier date. She was launched on 23 October 1844 and commissioned 10 November 1844.

She carried four 8-inch guns and eighteen 32pdrs, and was not originally given a full spar deck. This was added later in her career. She went to sea in December and sailed southwest.

First reports of her qualities set the tone for her career. Under courses and topsails with the wind free, she made over 12 knots, and she averaged 11 over twelve hours. Scudding in a strong gale and high seas, she made 11 knots. When the gale increased again, she hove to easily and

Right: Portsmouth in a training role. She remained active until 1915. [US Navy]

Below: Portsmouth in her early career, before the adding of her spar deck; illustration dated 1863. [US Navy NH 000514]

remained dry and under control. Though she rolled 'considerably' it was not deeply nor in such a manner as to strain her rigging.[34] Later reports confirmed her good qualities, with one recording her speed as 14 knots running free. One of her commanders wrote, she 'rolls as easy as a cradle, and stands up under her canvas like a church'.[35]

Her pre-Civil War career included duty off Mexico, in the Pacific, off Africa, and off China. She participated in the attacks on the Barrier forts in 1857. After a refit she was assigned to the Gulf Blockading Squadron and was towed as part of the fleet attacking New Orleans in April 1862. After the Civil War she was variously employed as a quarantine ship, in the Brazil squadron and as a survey ship in the Pacific. She decommissioned on 14 July 1878 and became a training ship for boys. She continued in training roles for another three decades, and was easily distin-

guished by her two narrow white stripes above her ports. From 1911 to 1915 she was on loan to the Marine Hospital Service and was sold on 17 April 1915.

Jamestown

Jamestown was designed by Foster Rhodes and built at Norfolk. She was laid down in 1843 and launched on 16 September 1844. She was the longest (163ft 5in) of these vessels, but, at 35ft, was not as beamy as several of the others. She was quite sharp in her forward lines, and had straight rising floors. Above water, she had a complete spar deck from the outset, and vertical stem. She was given a deep, ornately carved head and quarter galleries.

She was commissioned on 25 January 1845 and went to sea in company with *Portsmouth* to try the vessels side by

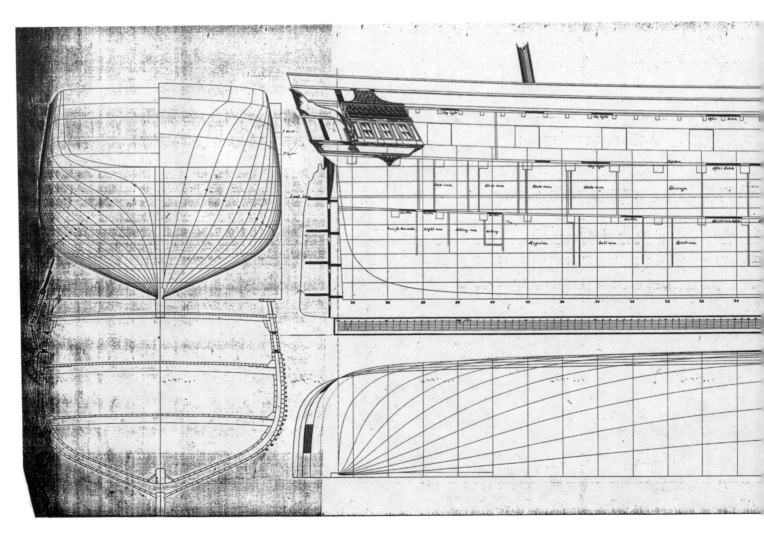

Left: The sloop of war *Jamestown* in a lithograph by A W Atkinson published in January 1847. [US Naval Historical Center NH 001421]

Below: Lines plan of the *Jamestown*, the longest of these sloops, which had sharp lines forward and rising floors. Note ornate head and straight stem. [National Archives 28-1-8]

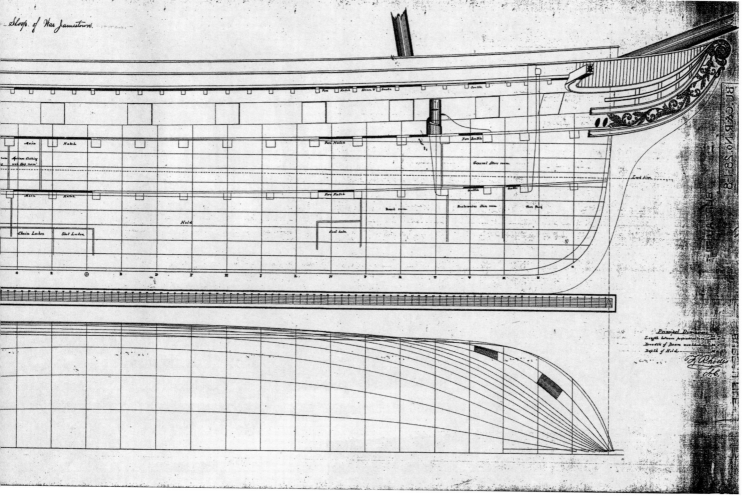

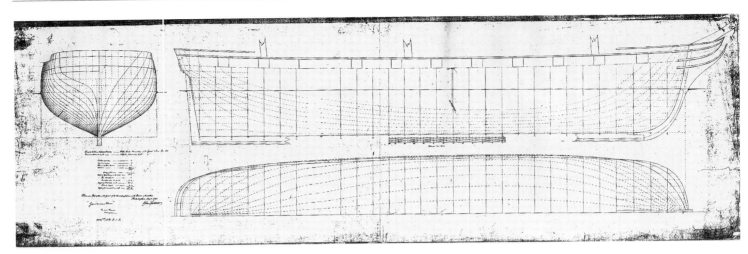

Germantown, designed by John Lenthall, was a favorite command, but became part of the Union debacle at Norfolk in 1861. [National Archives 109-8-1A]

side. Winds and conditions did not allow the close trial envisioned but it was determined that the two ships were 'matched in every way'. *Jamestown* was more weatherly by the wind and stood up well to her sails. She made 11 knots on a wind and 13 running free. Complaints were noted on her pitching, which seems to have been exacerbated by her heavy head.[36] Her masts were originally raked but they were straightened around 1848, then subsequently returned to their original angle.[37]

The ship's first assignment was as a unit of the anti-slavery patrol off the west coast of Africa, returning to Boston in August 1846. She was available when Congress voted funds to send aid to Ireland that year. A civilian crew and captain (R B Forbes) manned her and her guns were landed for the mission. Eight hundred tons of relief supplies were delivered and she returned to Boston only 49 days later.[38]

Subsequently she returned to the Africa station, then transferred to the Mediterranean. Before the Civil War she was again off Africa, then part of the Home squadron. As part of the blockade of the Atlantic coast, she captured five blockade runners, then was transferred to the Pacific for the balance of the conflict. She remained in the Pacific until 1882, supporting the acquisition of Alaska and sailing as far west as Tahiti and Fiji Islands. After decommissioning at Mare Island in 1871 she was made into a training vessel, serving in this capacity until 1879. She then was assigned to survey Alaskan waters until 1881. From 1882 to 1892 she

was again in a training role, this time in the Atlantic. Her final duty was as a marine quarantine vessel at Hampton Roads where she caught fire and was destroyed in January 1913.

Germantown

The sloop of war *Germantown* was designed by John Lenthall, and laid down on 7 September 1843. She was 150ft between perpendiculars and 36ft moulded beam, with 16ft 8in depth of hold. She was built without a spar deck and with a slight rake to her masts. With a more pronounced sheer, low sides and raked stem and stern, she was one of the more graceful vessels of this group in the water. Her hull lines were sharp forward and aft, but no more extreme than the other sloops of this class. Her floors were some 25 degrees from the horizontal – nearly as extreme as *Albany*'s.

The ship was built at Philadelphia and commissioned on 9 March 1847. However, the vessel had been to sea as early as December 1846 – she had been sent to Hampton Roads to complete her fitting out and avoid the Delaware River winter ice. On this initial cruise she made 11 knots 'with great ease' under topgallants, and her commander indicated she worked easily, even with her small crew.[39] Her later commanders reported her speed at 12 knots going free, though also noting she beat *Albany* 'in every way', indicating 12 knots was not her maximum. She rolled deeply, was weatherly, but wet in a seaway.[40]

Germantown proved a favourite command and was quite active in the Mexican War. She was the flagship of Matthew

C Perry for a short time and participated in the operations at Tuxpan and Alvorado. Afterwards, she was stationed in the West Indies, then was part of the African anti-slavery patrol. Her final two cruises were to the South Atlantic and the Far East. She put in to Norfolk and was decommissioned on 18 April 1861, shortly after the firing on Fort Sumter and onset of the Civil War. Though completely equipped for sea, she was scuttled two days later when the Navy Yard was fired and abandoned to Confederate forces. Two months later she was raised by the Confederates and became a floating battery for the protection of Norfolk. She was scuttled a second time in May 1862, as an underwater obstruction in the Elizabeth River. Federal forces raised her again in April 1863 and she was sold in February 1864.

Plymouth

The sloop of war *Plymouth* was Samuel Pook's follow-up to *Saratoga*, which was already considered a successful design. Comparing the two designs reveals that Pook took to heart

Decks of *Plymouth*, including her spar deck. Though not shown here, in 1857 she was fitted out for testing Dahlgren's 9- and 11-inch shell guns. [Peabody Essex Museum 2289]

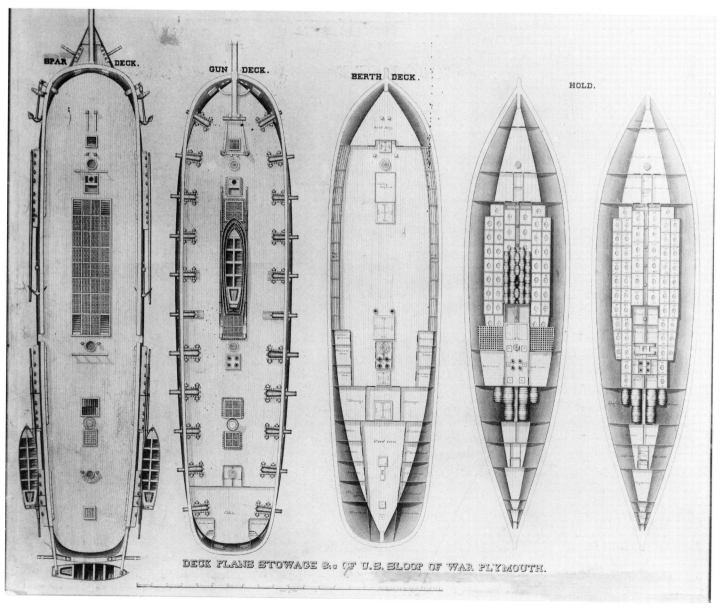

DECK PLANS STOWAGE &c OF U.S. SLOOP OF WAR PLYMOUTH.

the fact that *Saratoga* had needed her spar deck removed, an alteration which greatly improved her stiffness. Thus, to achieve stiffness while retaining a complete spar deck, the major difference in the new design was an increase in beam by two feet (from 35ft 3in to 37ft 3in) with a slight decrease in deadrise and an accompanying hardening of the bilges. The length of the ship was 147ft (4 inches short of the *Saratoga*), reflecting a decrease in the rake of the stem in the new ship. The new ship exhibited less sharpness in her forward lines but finer lines aft. At 974 tons, *Plymouth* was about 100 tons larger than *Saratoga*.

She was built at Charlestown Navy Yard in Boston, with

keel laying in 1843 and launch on 11 October the same year. She was commissioned before 3 April 1844, carrying the requisite 22 guns: four shell guns and the balance in 32pdrs.

Her performance at sea was little short of extraordinary – if not for speed, for handling and seaworthiness. In her first cruise in the Mediterranean her commander praised the ship without stint, noting fast passages and performances that 'astonished the Pilots and every person on board'. Pook's object in adding beam was effective: she stood, according to her commander, 'well under her canvas. Almost to a fault; lays to well, rolls quick and easy without strain to rigging.' He remarked on her 'great breadth of beam and space between her guns' and 'fine light spar deck'. The latter was good for 'the comfort of the crew and . . . safety in case she was knocked down'. In action it would prevent falling spars from interfering with the guns. Her

Lines plan of the sloop *Plymouth*, Samuel Pook's follow-up to *Saratoga*; she proved an outstanding sailer. [National Archives 31-9-411A]

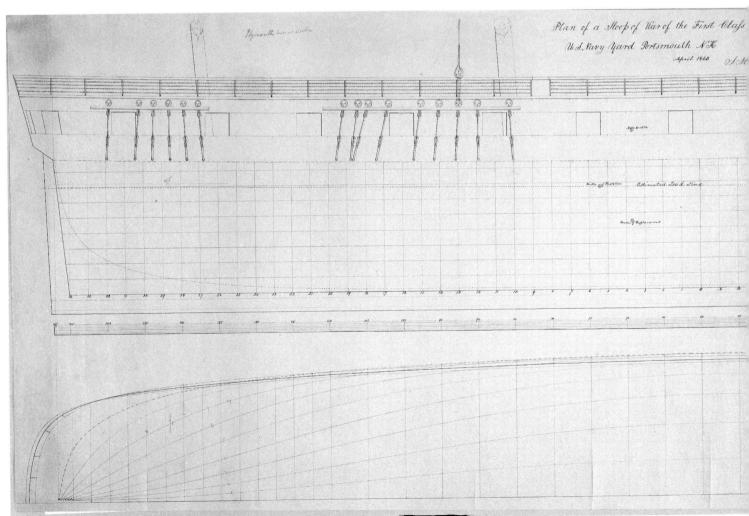

size, plus the spar deck gave her the 'comforts of a frigate'.[41] As to her speed, she made 10 knots on a wind and 12 running free.[42]

Her initial commission was in the Mediterranean, as noted above, then she was sent to the Brazil station, followed by duty in the East Indies. She was selected for Perry's Japan expedition, served successfully and returned to the east coast in 1855. For the balance of the decade she was used for midshipmen training and ordnance testing. In the latter role, she came under the command of John Dahlgren and became a 'test-bed' for the Dahlgren shell guns which were to become standard ordnance during the Civil War. In 1857 she was fitted out with four of the 9-inch guns and one 11-inch. The object of this testing was to allay the fears of many that the weight and size of these weapons were such that they would be impossible to handle in a sea-

way. Indeed, they were the largest guns ever mounted on a US naval sailing vessel. The 9-inch gun (tube only) weighed about 9000 pounds; the 11-inch 15,700 pounds. The size of the latter precluded mounting in broadside with standard carriages. Instead, they were mounted on specially designed carriages and stowed fore-and-aft on the vessel's centreline on pivot rails let into the deck. Using roller hand-spikes, the gun could be manhandled on the circular rails to fire on either side of the ship, through wide gunports.

The *Plymouth* trials, in the summer of 1857, had her crew practising with the guns in various weather and sea conditions during a transatlantic cruise. The 9-inch gun was fired at a rate of one round every 40 seconds, using handspikes to return the guns to battery. As for the 11-inch gun, 121 rounds were fired without 'any of the difficulties' expected due to its mass.[43] These results were satisfactory enough to

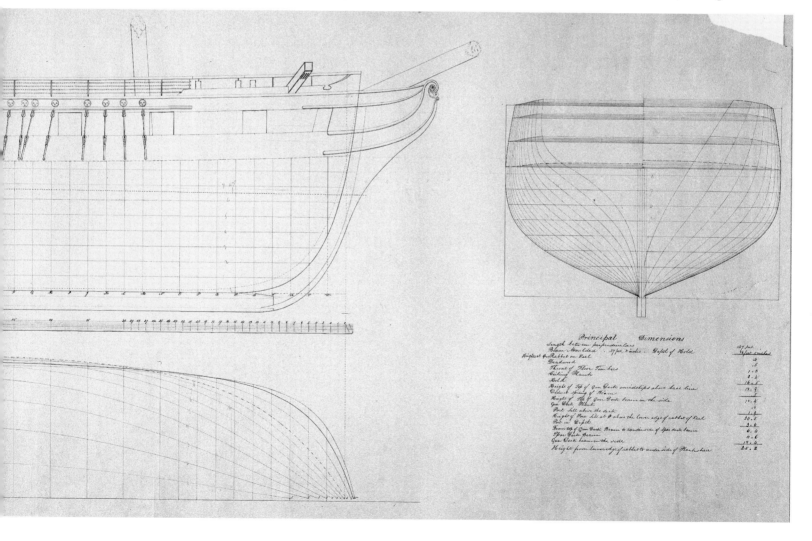

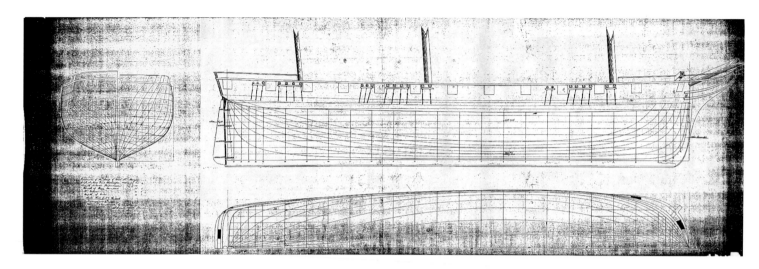

Lines plan of the sloop of war *St Mary's*, designed by Charles Brodie. [National Archives 8-3-6]

and she was one of the ships burned and scuttled to prevent capture by the Confederates in April 1861.

St Mary's

cause the navy to standardise the use of these guns on most of the vessels of the Civil War era–from the famous '90-day gunboats' up to the *Merrimack* class frigates. *Plymouth* returned to Norfolk in 1860 after another practice cruise,

Lithograph of original drawing by W A K Martin of the sloop *St Mary's*, dated 1851. Note high bulwarks and spar deck. [US Naval Historical Center NH 1367]

This sloop was built at Washington Navy Yard and designed by Charles B Brodie; she may have been the only major ship by this constructor. Her hull was given marked deadrise and a straight stem. As built she had only forecastle and quarterdecks and measured 150ft by 36ft 6in, but a spar deck was added at an undetermined later date. At 958 tons she was in dimensions and tonnage in the middle of this group of vessels.

She was launched on 24 November and commissioned on 13 December 1844. Her performance was unremarkable, at least in comparison to some of the others of this group. Her sailing was described as: 'indifferently well; steers easily, but rolls and works badly and stands up well under canvass [*sic*]'.[44] Apparently, some time later in her career, a report characterised her as 'dry and able and . . . unusually fast in light weather'.[45]

Her initial duties were as part of the American forces employed against Mexico in 1845 through 1848. Subsequently, she was transferred to the Pacific, remaining there through the pre-war years and participating in the surrender of the filibuster General William Walker in 1857. She continued duties on the Pacific coast during the Civil War and was laid up at Mare Island after the end of the conflict. She returned to the east coast of the US in 1873, when

Photograph of the sloop *St Mary's* under sail. [US Navy]

she was again laid up at Norfolk. From 1875 to 1908 she served as a school ship at New York, then was sold and scrapped.

* * * * *

The sloops of war of 1841-3 were a remarkable group of ships. They were the conclusion of decades of evolution, going back to the War of 1812 *Peacock*. With each successive generation there were lessons learned and improvements made. The sequence was marred only by the unusually small sloops of 1838, though even those vessels were competent for peacetime cruising. Then *Saratoga* set the pattern for the subsequent six: a substantial battery of 32pdr long guns and sufficient dimensions and displacement to

carry them with ease and some speed. Then the even more noteworthy decision was made to allow six naval architects free reign in their design for their respective versions of the formula. In a remarkable *tour de force* for the American constructors, every single vessel proved to be not only competent for the job in terms of sea-keeping, handling and carrying the battery and crew required, but the ships usually exhibited a turn of speed thrown in for good measure. All proved solid and long lasting. Six had useful careers before the Civil War, and four survived into the twentieth century. Only *Albany* succumbed to the elements, being lost at sea in 1854. These vessels marked a high point in the history of the American sailing navy.

The *St Mary's* in drydock, 1874. [US Naval Historical Center NH 2090]

US Sloop of War *Constellation*

After the completion of the seven sloops described above, construction of new sailing sloops of war ceased until the laying down of *Constellation* in 1853. In the interim, a single 'new' sloop was added to the inventory: the 1832 frigate *Macedonian* had been 'razeed' to a 22-gun corvette with

complete spar deck. She went to sea to join the Japan Expedition in April 1853, and proved to be an excellent sailer. This vessel became the precursor of a series of over-size sloops of war, both steam and sail, in the US Navy, all armed with main batteries of 8-inch or larger shell guns.

Of course, the story of the sloop of war *Constellation* has become entwined with that of her predecessor, the 1790s frigate of the same name. And the controversy over the identity of the vessel now afloat in Baltimore's Inner Harbor has only recently been resolved. A summary of the story follows.

The original frigate was laid up in 1845 at Norfolk (Gosport) Navy Yard. With the growing number of steam vessels in the navy, fewer sailing warships were required and, indeed, by the late 1840s the old-style 32pdr batteries were becoming obsolete, being replaced by large calibre shell guns. Thus there was no real use for the old frigate. These considerations, plus the deteriorated condition of the ship, sealed her fate. On 22 February 1853, she was hauled out of the water and dismantling was begun. By July a local newspaper was reporting that she had been 'literally torn to pieces preparatory to the building of the new *Constellation*.'[46] On 12 September 1853 permission was asked to auction off her timbers.[47] At this point, the old ship had ceased to exist.

In the meantime, John Lenthall, assisted by B F Delano, had prepared a new design for a sloop of war to carry on the name. The preliminary drawing was done in June 1853, followed by a half-hull model. Tables of offsets were worked out at Gosport and moulds made for the timbers. The keel of the new ship was laid on 25 June 1853. This consisted of nine pieces, cobbled together from various storage areas in the yard: ship of the line, frigate, and sloop timbers. The stern and stem were raised in late August and early September, and framing up the hull ensued. According to storekeeper's records, some 204 white oak knees were drawn from the 'used' stock of white oak timbers—but official sources do not indicate transfer of material directly from the old to the new ship. Newspaper accounts of the time made much of the preservation of some of the old timbers in the new vessel.[48] Even had the old timbers been utilised, as one paper insisted, they were little more than a

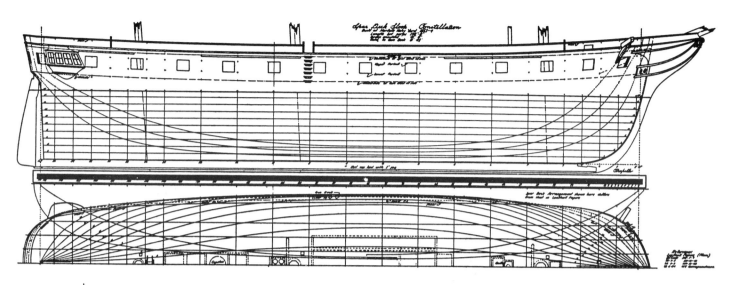

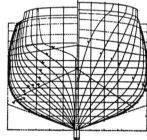

The sloop of war *Constellation*, built at Norfolk Navy Yard in 1853-4. Comparing this plan with that of the original frigate of the same name graphically shows the contrast between this modern hull design and that of the old ship. Note particularly the straight rising floors here compared to the hollow garboards of the original frigate. [Plan by H I Chapelle, Courtesy Smithsonian Institution]

token effort to retain the old vessel's identity – and in keeping with an older and obscure British tradition of carrying over a small number of timbers from the old to the new vessel in order to 'carry on the name'.[49]

The new sloop of war was launched on 26 August 1854. The ship was 176ft between perpendiculars and 41ft moulded beam, with 21ft depth of hold. This compares with 163ft 3in and 41ft for the original frigate. The new hull exhibited straight rising floors, little tumblehome, and moderately raked stem. Probably the most significant, by way of comparison to the old ship, were the straight floors: this was in distinct contrast to the old-style slightly hollow garboards of the frigate. The completely differing configuration of the lower hull shape, and thus the lower futtocks

Original half-hull model of the sloop *Constellation*, used by Navy researchers to confirm the origins of the still extant sloop of war. [US Naval Academy Museum 19181-07-91]

confirm that a new hull was constructed in 1853. Of course, above water, the differences were manifest. The rake of both stem and stern was significantly less than that of the old frigate and the spacing, size, and number of ports was now commensurate with larger but fewer guns. Finally, the new sloop carried no broadside guns on the upper deck.

Constellation was commissioned on 28 July 1855 and departed for the Mediterranean. She was armed with sixteen 8-inch and two 10-inch shell guns, plus four 32pdrs; this was identical to the battery on *Macedonian* at this time. She was considered an excellent sailer and was credited unofficially with 14 knots.[50] Her performance on her first cruise is exemplified by a letter from a marine on board:

Painting of *Constellation* in the Mediterranean in the late 1850s, by Tomaso De Simone. One of three paintings of the vessel by the artist. [USF Constellation Foundation]

We left Leghorn in company with the Flagship *Congress* . . . the Commodore wishing to try the speed of the two vessels, kept us in company until the evening of the 23rd, during which time we convinced him effectually that there was no use in trying to sail with us. We ran away from him several times with considerably less sail on than the *Congress* had, we ran around her twice, and beat her so bad that the crew of the *Congress* were ashamed to come on board . . . at 9:00 PM the light in the *Congress* top was barely perceptible, we had run so far ahead of her . . . The morning brought us . . . a heavy gale . . . We were obliged to close reef our top sails, haul up courses, and let the storm stay sails and stand out to sea . . . During the gale it was a pleasure to see the way our ship stood up to it and ride the seas mountains high. I never saw a vessel act better than she does . . . [51]

After three years in the Mediterranean, she was re-assigned

to Cuban waters, protecting American vessels from unlawful search at sea. In 1859, as flagship of the Africa squadron, she patrolled sea lanes and captured three slavers: *Delicia*, *Triton* and *Cora*. The last, taken in mid-1860, carried 705 slaves, all of whom were returned to Liberia. After the outbreak of the Civil War she was again sent to the Mediterranean, remaining there until May 1864. With the exception of special missions, she was relegated to training roles from 1865 to the 1930s.

The special missions were a diverse lot. The first was to transport American displays to the Paris Exposition in 1878. Another was to carry relief supplies to Ireland in March 1880. A third was to bring works of art from Gibraltar to the US for the Columbian Exposition of 1893. In 1914 she was towed to Baltimore to celebrate the role of that city in the War of 1812 and the centennial of the 'Star Spangled Banner'. At that time there was no controversy about her origins and the assumption was that her 1850s rebuilding was a simple conversion from a frigate to a sloop of war.

During one of her training assignments as a gunnery ship, *Constellation* carried a unique battery. In the early 1870s she was armed with a 100pdr Parrot rifle, eight 9-inch shell guns, a 20pdr rifle and one 11-inch Dahlgren smoothbore. The large guns were mounted on the gun deck, on pivot rails, designed to fire from either broadside. Because of the size of the guns, and also to allow a wide field of fire, two of her midship gunports on either side were knocked into one, measuring about ten feet long. She carried these guns from 1871 to about 1880. She was one of the few US naval vessels which carried the 11-inch gun between decks. She may have been the only sailing sloop to carry an 11-inch gun – save the old *Plymouth* as a gunnery platform. After about 1888 her battery was altered to ten 8-inch shell guns and two modern breech-loading rifles, one a 60pdr, the other a 20pdr. By 1900 all her major guns were eliminated and she only carried a saluting and signalling battery of 6pdrs.[52]

Re-designated IX-20 in 1941, President Roosevelt selected her as a shore-based relief flagship for the Atlantic Fleet, and later for Battleship Division Five. This was her last official assignment. In 1955 she was decommissioned and towed to Baltimore where a group of citizens planned to preserve her and open her to the public; she remains in

Constellation as a gunnery training ship in the 1870s. Note wide centre gunport specifically cut for use with a 100pdr Parrot rifle. [US Navy]

Baltimore to this day. The selection of Baltimore for her berth and preservation is a reflection of the long-standing, but ignored question concerning her identity. Of course, Baltimore was interested in obtaining her because the *original* frigate was built there. In fact, official doubts about this did not surface until the late 1940s, when proposals were being made to raise funds for her restoration. Until this time no one had seriously studied the pertinent plans to determine to what extent she had been 'rebuilt' at Norfolk in the 1850s. And, of course, the technical nature of the question was much more difficult to understand than the time-honoured traditions surrounding this historic icon.

The first to write in detail about the differences in the two ships was Howard I Chapelle, who was researching his work on the sailing navy. Though he indeed published these findings in that work, those who interpreted and wrote about the vessel in Baltimore continued to claim she was the 'oldest' American naval vessel in existence. In any event, the controversy simmered for decades and spawned an occasional article and one book: *The Constellation Question*, by Chapelle and Leon D Polland. Finally, in the late 1980s as the vessel began to show great deterioration and something over three feet of hogging, the question of her identity became more critical. If indeed she was an 1850s vessel built at Norfolk, then Baltimore's historic interest in the vessel truly would be called into question, and might well determine whether sufficient funds could be raised in that city to sustain a major restoration of the vessel. In order to settle the question, a research team led by Dana Wegner, the US Navy's curator of ship models, instituted a thorough study, using computer technology as well as extensive research in the records. The results of their efforts were published in a book entitled *Fouled Anchors: The* Constellation *Question Answered*, published under the auspices of the navy in 1991.

Computer modelling techniques applied to the plans and an original half-hull of the sloop of war proved that the hulls of the 1797 frigate and 1853 sloop of war were distinctly different in design. Furthermore, scientific examination of some of the documentary evidence which purported to 'prove' the continuous existence of the 'one' *Constellation*, showed that many of the documents crucial to the case were doctored or were outright forgeries. There was even evidence that a faked 'National Archives' rubber stamp had been employed by overly zealous individuals to 'authenticate' trumped up documents.

The upshot of these findings was to inject realism into the identity of the ship at Baltimore. She is now properly identified and interpreted as the last sailing vessel built for the navy and the last intact survivor of the Civil War. As such, she has been rebuilt, this time utilising a modern laminate technique called 'cold moulding'. This method was employed when it was found that her original frame could

Constellation after the Civil War. [The Mariners' Museum]

Recent photo of the *Constellation* at Baltimore's Inner Harbor, after her major restoration in the 1990s. [Photo by author]

not support new fastenings and that the replacement of the entire frame would have been prohibitively expensive. Furthermore, the latter would have resulted in a hull which would have had a relatively short life span before extensive maintenance would again be necessary.

'Cold moulding' involved laying planks of douglas fir in four layers over the original frame: the inner and outer layers were laid fore and aft and the inner two laid on opposite diagonals. The layers were glued in between. The same layering technique was applied to the gun deck. The whole result was a solid structure relatively impervious to the elements. It is estimated that the hull is 30 per cent stronger than the original and the use of this technique allowed for the preservation of over 50 per cent of *Constellation*'s historic fabric.

The total cost of the project has been nearly $9 million, and, at the time of writing, though she is again open to the public, work is still ongoing. Topgallant yards, a jibboom, and replacement of her faux 18pdrs with 8-inch shell guns are all items still to be added. After drydocking and restoration she returned to Baltimore in 1999 as the centrepiece of that city's Inner Harbor, and she now has a staff well qualified to care for and preserve the ship for posterity.[53]

CHAPTER 8

Brigs and Schooners, 1798–1843

AROUND THIRTY brigs and schooners were built for the US Navy during the sailing ship era, over a space of about fifty years. Because of their small size they were less useful for cruising on overseas stations than frigates or sloops of war, and, of course, the prestige value of a frigate in the eyes of foreign observers was much greater than that of a smaller vessel. These vessels were suitable for commerce raiding, convoy escorts and specialised tasks requiring shallow draught and handiness. Schooners, particularly, were useful in certain situations – usually involving

coastal operations – due to their ability to sail closer to the wind than a square-rigged ship. On the other hand, the schooner-rigged vessel was at a disadvantage vis-à-vis a square rigger in battle: the square-rigger's capability of backing her sails was considered a useful manoeuvring tool in close action.

Revenue Cutters

The sole naval force available to the United States at the outbreak of the Quasi-War with France was the small fleet of revenue cutters belonging to the Treasury Department. The first cutters had been built, on an extremely tight budget, in 1791-3: nine schooners and a sloop, armed only with swivel guns and each manned by ten men.[1] Then, in 1797, in the same act which provided for the completion of the first three frigates, Congress authorised increasing the 'strength of the revenue cutters so that the number of men

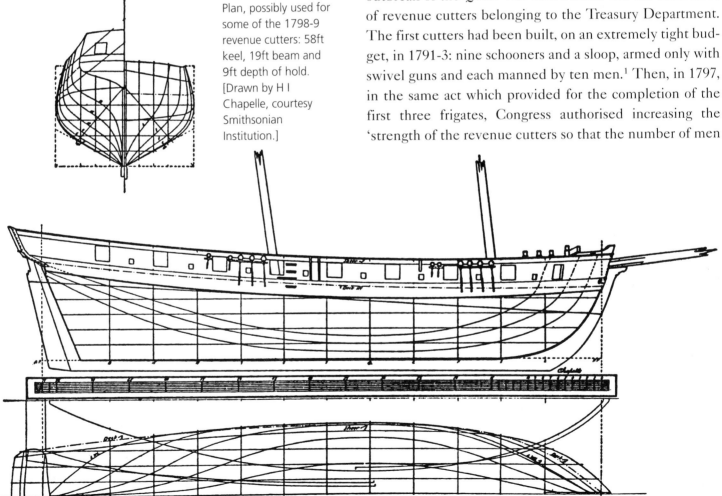

Plan, possibly used for some of the 1798-9 revenue cutters: 58ft keel, 19ft beam and 9ft depth of hold. [Drawn by H I Chapelle, courtesy Smithsonian Institution.]

employed do not exceed thirty marines and seamen . . . and cause the said revenue cutters to be employed to defend the Sea Coast of the United States'.[2]

With this directive as authority, a total of eight revenue cutters would come under the direction of the navy during the Quasi-War with France. All of these were two masted vessels–schooners or brigs–except one, the *General Greene*, which was a sloop. The seven two-masted vessels were: *Virginia*, *Diligence*, *Eagle*, *Governor Jay*, *Pickering*, *Scammel*, and *South Carolina*. Of these, four were returned to the revenue service before the end of hostilities, to assume duties protecting the revenue. *Eagle* served with the navy until June 1801, *Scammel* until December 1801, and *Pickering* was still under navy control when she was lost at sea in August 1800. Another brig, *Pinckney*, was begun as a revenue cutter, but was said to have been taken over by the navy before she was completed. Details for her are given below.

Unfortunately, the information existing about these ships is sparse and contradictory. It should be noted that one of the reasons for the paucity of information about them is the lack of Treasury Department documents for this era. Two fires, one when the British burned Washington, the other an accidental blaze in 1832, destroyed the majority of departmental records, including revenue cutter material. The remains of the pre-1832 material amounts to one bound volume (now in the archives' Record Group 26). How much there was to begin with is also questionable, given the decentralised nature of the department. Fortuitously, the three cutters retained by the navy are also those for which a substantial amount of information exists.

Pickering was built by Nathan and Orlando Merrill at Newburyport, Massachusetts. She was laid down sometime after February 1798, when Secretary of the Treasury Wolcott directed the collector at Boston to have a 'swift sailing schooner' built, with a coppered bottom. Wolcott passed along dimensions from a 'leading' naval constructor: 58ft keel, 20ft beam and 9ft in the hold. The vessel was completed in July 1798 and sailed for Boston to ship her guns: fourteen 4pdrs. She had a crew of 90 men and boys.

This vessel is the only one of these cutters for which a period illustration exists. It shows her with a plain stem, and ten ports (eight of which have guns). Of particular interest

Revenue cutter *Pickering*. Note the unusual 'jack-ass brig' rig–square and fore and aft sails on both masts. [US Coast Guard]

is her rig. She is a cross between a schooner and a brig: fore and aft sails, plus topsails and topgallants on both masts. She has studding sails and her fore sail is loose-footed. This configuration is consistent with a list of masts and yards for the cutter *Scammel*–of the same hull dimensions–found in Joshua Humphreys' Mast and Yard Book, dated June 1799.[3] Howard I Chapelle referred to this as a 'jack-ass' brig. Its combination of features is sufficient to explain why contemporaries used the terms schooner and brig interchangeably for some of these vessels.

Pickering was under the command of Edward Preble in 1799, convoying merchantmen for protection against French privateers. Preble considered her a 'remarkable fast sailer', but noted that she was incapable of carrying over six weeks' water and provisions without being too deep and out of trim.[4] Her speed was invaluable, however, and she made a significant number of captures in the course of the war. *Pickering* sank with all hands in the West Indies sometime after August 1800.

Scammel was built by J K Hackett at Portsmouth, New Hampshire and was launched on 11 August 1798. Her dimensions, according to the Humphreys mast book, were 58ft keel, by 20ft by 9ft 6in in the hold. When first at sea she was found to be quite tender and it was suggested she be made a brig. However, the Secretary of the Navy objected, noting that an increase in weight in her tops would aggravate the condition. Instead her masts and spars were reduced proportionately.[5] In December 1801 when sold, her main deck was measured at 75ft, and her beam at 21ft 2in. Much of the beam dimension discrepancy is probably explained by 20ft being the moulded, and 21ft 2in the extreme beam to the outside of her planking. She was measured at 131$\frac{89}{95}$ tons.[6]

Eagle was laid down on 4 August 1798 at the shipyard of William and Abra Brown in Philadelphia. Her dimensions, as taken off in 1801, were 77ft on deck, 23ft 8in beam and 9ft 2in depth of hold; her tonnage was 143$\frac{41}{95}$.[7] She carried fourteen 6pdrs.[8] During the war she made five captures of armed French vessels plus recapturing four American merchantmen.[9] She was sold on 17 June 1801.

The four two-masted vessels returned to the treasury department at their request in 1799 were *Virginia*, *Diligence*, *Governor Jay* and *South Carolina*. Of these, *Governor Jay*, *South Carolina* and *Diligence* are believed to have been built to the same plan as *Eagle* and the others. The *Governor Jay* was built in New York; the *South Carolina* in Charleston; *Diligence* had been built at Philadelphia by Joshua Humphreys, also in 1797. *Virginia*, built at Hampton, was of a different design, measuring 70ft on the keel but with a narrow 18ft10in beam and 8ft6in depth of hold. She had been in service as early as 1797.[10]

The sole surviving plan which might shed light on any of these cutters is reproduced here. According to H I Chapelle, who redrew it for publication, the original was no longer to be found at the National Archives, and was, indeed, a rough working drawing. The dimensions of this schooner were 77ft between perpendiculars, 58ft straight rabbet, 19ft moulded beam and 9ft depth of hold. Chapelle regarded the plan as unlikely to be the actual one for these schooners because of the one foot narrower beam (19ft *vice* 20ft).[11] However, given the variations in the dimensions of the completed vessels, as shown above, a one foot discrepancy on a rough plan would not be of great significance. The plan was annotated 'July 1798', after most of the cutters were in the water;[12] but that date may have been when it was received from the Treasury Department. In any event, lack of solid evidence hampers any conclusive

judgements. Comparing this plan with the illustration of the *Pickering* seems to confirm that the drawing is a fairly good representation of her and other cutters of her dimensions (*Diligence*, *Governor Jay*, *Eagle*, *South Carolina* and *Scammel*).

Another cutter is sometimes listed as coming under naval authority during the war. This was the brig *Unanimity* which operated out of Charleston, South Carolina in 1798. This vessel, however, was never under navy control, and was commanded by Robert Cochran, a revenue service officer. The vessel was run ashore by her captain in an attempt to escape from a vessel significantly smaller than his own. The adversary proved to be a British sloop, and Cochran's repute was severely tarnished by the incident. The result was that Cochran lost any chance he had had to command the new cutter (*South Carolina*) being built at the time.[13]

Pinckney

This vessel (also called *General Pinckney*) was referred to initially as a brigantine, then as a brig. Her dimensions were 62ft on the keel, 23ft beam, 10ft 6in depth of hold and 195 tons. As such she would have been the largest of this group of ships, and seems to have been armed with as many as 18 guns early on. Later she was rated at 14. She was intended to be a revenue cutter and was built by William Pritchard in Charleston, South Carolina. She was begun in mid-1798 and was to go to sea in December 1798 to join the sloop of war *Ganges*. However, it is not clear that she actually sailed at that time as she is not mentioned in connection with the cruise of the *Ganges*. She was taken over by the navy's agent in January 1799.[14] The vessel served in the West Indies and in the protection of the trade with Havana through 1799. She returned to the US in early 1800 and was sold around April of that year.[15]

Enterprise Class, 1799

These two schooners, *Enterprise* and *Experiment*, were authorised in April 1798. In common with many of the Quasi-War emergency vessels, no plans have survived of these very successful ships. The only primary visual evi-

Half-hull model of *Enterprise*, 1799. Note significant drag in her keel. No plans survive of this vessel. [US Naval Historical Center NH 16850]

dence we have is a half-hull model and two illustrations. There is even uncertainty about the actual builder of one of the vessels.

It is known that Secretary Stoddert wrote Jeremiah Yellot, the naval agent at Fells Point, Baltimore, with instructions to have a 'fast' vessel built there, as 'only fast vessels could be effective against the French'. He continued: 'there is no person on the Continent better able to direct the construction of these kind of vessels'.[16] Yellot, as has been mentioned, was known for his advocacy of the so-called Baltimore clipper pilot boat design.

Yellot, in turn, employed William Price as constructor and work was begun on the ship. Then, a month later, Stoddert requested that Yellot have a second one built 'as quickly as possible'.[17] According to recent research by Geoffrey Footner, the first vessel was built at Baltimore and was the schooner *Experiment*. As Price's yard was busy with the sloop of war *Maryland* as well as the schooner, a Maryland Eastern Shore yard was selected for what would become the *Enterprise*. Though the builder for this schooner is listed as 'Henry' Spencer, Footner notes that there was no 'Henry' Spencer building ships in Maryland at this time. Alternatively the first name may have been mistakenly copied and was actually Hugh or Perry Spencer, both of whom were active builders at the time. Financial records indicate the masts and spars for *Enterprise* had a drayage charge added, indicating these may have been transported to the Eastern Shore from the mast-maker in Baltimore. After the vessel was masted and launched, she was moved to Baltimore for fitting out.[18]

In any case, the schooners were probably built to the same plan, with dimensions of 60ft on the keel, 84ft 7in on

deck, 22ft 6in moulded beam, and 9ft 6in depth of hold. The vessels mounted 12 guns and may have had sweep ports (oars are mentioned in one of *Experiment*'s action reports).[19] The half-hull model shows little rake in the stem, rather more in the stern, moderate sheer, considerable drag in the keel, and no cutwater knee. The painted gunports on the model are rather large and out of proportion to the hull. There are no illustrations of the *Experiment*, but two have been found of the *Enterprise*. These, however, purport to show her in 1806, after she had undergone two substantial rebuildings. The first was in early 1805, at the Arsenal at Venice, and the second, in late 1806, was necessitated by damage received in a gale off Leghorn.

While she was rebuilding at Venice, significant changes were made, including increasing her length on deck to 92ft 9in, breadth to 23ft 9in (extreme) and depth to 10ft 10in. Both stem and stern were replaced, with the square tuck being taken out of the latter and possibly some rake added to her stem. However, her keel remained the same length.[20] Comparing the post-rebuild images of the vessel with the half-hull shows the significantly increased stern overhang. It is also of note that she was re-rigged sometime in 1806 from a schooner to a brigantine.

Plans of a vessel purporting to be *Enterprise*, of the same dates as her rebuild, have been located by researchers at the Arsenal in Venice. However, above the waterline the vessel has no resemblance to the US Navy ship shown in the 1806 illustrations. The vessel has an exaggerated sheer, equally outsized knee-head with rails, and greater rake to the stem.

Enterprise after rebuilding in the Mediterranean, around 1806. Note increased stern overhang and increased rake of her stem compared to the half-model. This view shows a more substantial rig than the companion view [below]. Illustration by French engraver Jean-Jerome Baugean. [US Naval Historical Center NH 5119]

Further, she has what appear to be swivel mounts on her bulwarks. Her keel length (around 70ft) is significantly longer than that of the American vessel.[21]

The *Enterprise* proved as speedy as her lineage implied. In crossing the Atlantic in 1801, the squadron encountered heavy weather and she was falling badly behind. However, after Commodore Dale allowed her to make her own way, light winds prevailed and *Enterprise* beat the squadron to Gibraltar by five days.[22] Her speed is reflected in the number of prizes taken during the Quasi-War—over thirteen,

according to one of her commanders. She was so well thought of that her plan was solicited as a pattern for the next navy schooner: *Vixen* of 1803.[23]

The vessel served in the Quasi-War, the Barbary conflicts, and the War of 1812. Her most famous engagement was against HM Brig *Boxer* in September 1813. The ships were nearly matched in battery, *Enterprise* (now rigged as a brig) being armed with fourteen 18pdr carronades and two long 9s against *Boxer*'s twelve 18pdr carronades and two 6s. The 30-minute fight resulted in twelve American casualties and twenty British. The *Boxer* surrendered after having her main topmast and much of her rigging shot away.[24]

Later in the war *Enterprise* captured *Mars*, a formidable British privateer armed with 14 guns. Afterwards, she managed several escapes from enemy frigates and in 1814 was made a guardship. After refitting she made a cruise in the Mediterranean and another in the Caribbean, capturing thirteen prizes in the latter. She underwent a major repair in 1819, then returned to the West Indies.[25] She grounded and broke up on Little Curaçao Island in July 1823, without casualties.

Experiment had a much shorter, but equally lively career. She went to sea in late 1799 and cruised against the French privateers in the Caribbean, taking several valuable prizes. On 1 January 1800 she participated in one of the most horrifying sea-fights of that era. While escorting three small merchantmen in a strait off Santo Domingo, she was becalmed and attacked by over 400 armed brigands or 'picaroons' in eleven barges. In a battle lasting over six hours, which included three separate attacks, two of the barges were sunk by the guns of *Experiment* – one by a judicious shot between the masts of one of the merchantmen – and the pirates driven off. *Experiment* had one man wounded: Lieutenant David Porter. The only other American casualty was the captain of one of the merchant ships, who was murdered after the brigands had captured and boarded his vessel. Two of the convoyed vessels were lost in the engagement.[26]

Subsequently, after a short refit, *Experiment* returned to

Enterprise, also in the Mediterranean, though apparently at an earlier date than the picture above. It may show her prior to her rebuild. Watercolour by Antoine Roux, dated 1806. [US Naval Historical Center NH 18756]

the Caribbean. After recapturing several American vessels and taking a number of armed privateers, she returned to the US where she was laid up at Norfolk. *Experiment* was surveyed after the end of the war and found to be in sound condition. Despite this finding, she was sold out in October 1801 at Baltimore.[27] This was in accordance to the retrenchment policies of the Jefferson administration.

The Brigs and Schooners of 1803

The outbreak of hostilities in the Mediterranean in 1801 forced the Jefferson administration to reverse, or at least modify, their anti-naval policies. These policies had deprived the navy of most of their smaller ships, classes of vessels now seen as crucial in dealing with a conflict on the North African littoral. Indeed, at the outset, the navy's only vessel smaller than a frigate was the schooner *Enterprise*. Admission of this shortage was implicit in the authorisation for the commander on scene to acquire necessary smaller vessels locally. This led to Edward Preble borrowing gunboats and bomb vessels from Sicily in 1803.[28]

The first congressional attempt to remedy the situation was the 1802 act authorising privateers to act against

Argus, from a painting by Felix Corné, of the American attack on Tripoli. [US Navy]

Tripolitan vessels. This action, however, was ineffective, given the small size of the adversary's merchant fleet. Finally, when it was obvious that the conflict was not abating, Congress acted, calling for the acquisition of four 16-gun vessels and ten gunboats (28 February 1803).[29] The four 16-gun vessels were to become *Argus*, *Siren*, *Vixen* and *Nautilus*. Secretary of the Navy Robert Smith initially intended to have the four built at Norfolk, Philadelphia, Baltimore and Portsmouth, New Hampshire, by contract – and quickly. Builders at Norfolk and Portsmouth, however, were unable to promise quick completion.[30] Consequently, Smith resorted to construction of one of these two at Boston. After some hesitation, Smith purchased the other at Baltimore.

The dimensions for the two brigs were recommended by 'Gentlemen of professional skill' and were to be 94ft on deck, 76ft straight rabbet, 25ft 6in moulded beam and 12ft 6in depth of hold. They were to have 'narrow, light yards' and be equipped for sweeps 'as rowing fast will be of importance'.[31] Shortly after these dimensions were disseminated to the shipyards, Commodore James Barron suggested that a foot and a half be added to their beam, and this was passed along to the respective builders.[32] The two brigs were *Argus* and *Syren* (sometimes rendered *Siren*). They were two distinct designs, the former by Joseph and Edmund Hartt at Boston, the latter by Benjamin Hutton at Philadelphia. *Argus* was referred to as *Merrimack* during the early stages of her construction.

Argus was laid down on 12 May 1803 in the yard where *Constitution* had been built, and she was launched on 21 August. As completed she was 94ft 9in between perpendiculars, 27ft 4ft moulded beam, and 12ft 8in depth of hold, measuring 298 63/94 tons. She mounted sixteen 24pdr carronades and two 12pdr chase guns. Her model was somewhat fine both fore and aft, with moderate deadrise and slight hollows in her floors.

Her appearance excited some admiration among contemporaries. Preble noted that she was 'without exception the handsomest vessel of her rate that I have ever seen. She is very much and very justly admired by every officer.'[33] A period depiction of her at the bombardment of Tripoli, by Felix Corné, is somewhat misleading, however. (It should

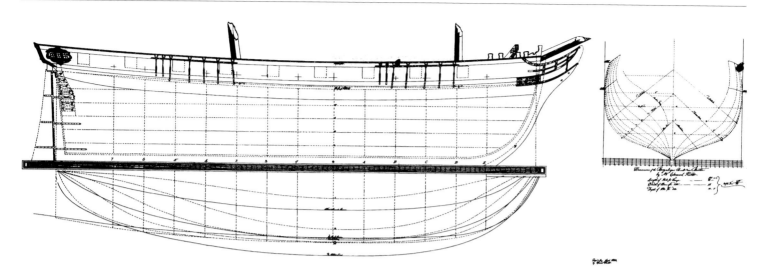

Plan of *Argus*. She was very fast and noted for the 'most destructive cruise of any US warship' in the War of 1812. [US Navy, from *Naval Documents of the Barbary Wars*]

be pointed out also that in the official *Naval Documents of the Barbary Wars* volume the captions of the illustrations of this vessel and schooner *Nautilus* are reversed.) No quarter badges and only nine ports are shown, whereas plans indicate she had quarter badges and ten ports, including the bridle. It should be noted that Chapelle reduced the steeve of her bowsprit as well as the height of her head for his redrawing of her plan. This is in keeping with the vessel's appearance in the Tripoli scene.

Stephen Decatur reported as follows on her qualities: 'The *Argus* sails fast, is very stiff & scuds well, but in lying to she pitches remarkably heavy.'[34] In two trials, she easily out-sailed *Syren* and, in a heavy blow, held her own considerably better than the other vessel.[35] After her duty in the Mediterranean, she was laid up and underwent repairs in the United States. In 1811 the only major change in her battery occurred, with the addition of another pair of 24pdr carronades. She retained this battery until her capture.

During the War of 1812 she made three cruises, the third of which put her in the English Channel to harass British commerce, which she did exceedingly well. In what has been called 'the single most destructive cruise of any US warship during this war' she destroyed about twenty merchantmen, including six on one day. Her rampage was terminated by the British brig *Pelican*, which carried 32pdr carronades, thus outgunning her opponent. *Argus* struck her colours after a 45-minute fight and loss of sufficient rigging to make her unmanageable.[36]

The dimensions of *Syren* varied somewhat from *Argus*

and their hull forms also diverged significantly. She was designed by Benjamin Hutton, Jr and measured 93ft 3½in between perpendiculars, 27ft moulded beam and 12ft 6in depth of hold. Comparing her lines with those of *Argus* shows the former with a sharper hull with straight rising floors, more tumblehome, and fuller lines forward and aft. She also exhibited more sheer and a bit more rake in stem and stern. As one authority pointed out, the vessel's sharpness, combined with tall rig and slack bilges would have made her quite tender and easily overladen. As seen above, she was out-sailed by *Argus* and, in a blow that roughed up the latter, the same conditions threw *Syren* on her beam ends.[37]

Syren was launched on 6 August 1803 and commissioned by 27 August, immediately sailing for the Mediterranean. Her armament was originally as *Argus*. Her plans show a male figurehead, though after she was captured in 1814 the carving was reported as a mermaid. Given her name, the latter is more likely.[38]

Syren served first in the actions against the Tripolitan corsairs, finally returning to the US in 1806. She was laid up until 1807 when she carried dispatches to France. In the War of 1812 she was armed with twelve 24pdr carronades, two 42pdr carronades and two 9pdrs.[39] These had little impact on her fate: she was captured by the 74-gun HMS

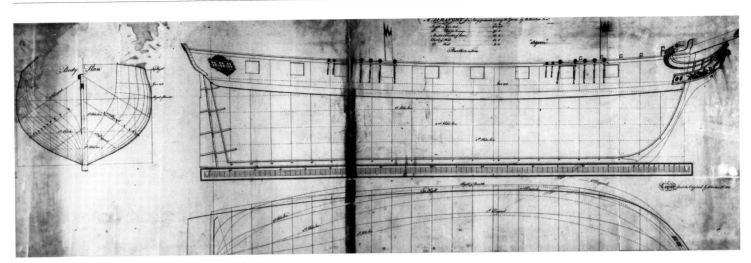

Syren was designed by Benjamin Hutton Jr and was of a much more conservative hull form than *Argus*. [National Archives 40-10-2A; courtesy Robert Gardiner]

Medway after an 11-hour chase, in which she jettisoned virtually everything – guns, spars, anchors – all to no avail. She was used as a prison vessel by the British after her capture.[40]

The third vessel of this group was the schooner *Vixen*, built by William Price at Baltimore and designed by Benjamin Hutton, Jr of Philadelphia. Her dimensions, as mentioned previously, were to be exactly as those of *Enterprise* and there was an attempt to obtain a draught of the previously built vessel on which to base the work.[41] However, apparently an entirely new design was promulgated as the plans for *Vixen* show a much less extreme design than that evident in the existing half model of *Enterprise*. Furthermore, the tonnage discrepancy – 135 for *Enterprise* and 170 for *Vixen* – indicates a much more capacious hull for the newer vessel.

She was launched on 25 June and commissioned by 3 August 1803, carrying twelve 18pdr carronades and two 9pdrs. Her figurehead was a female fox. Her lines were somewhat akin to those of Hutton's *Syren*: with straight rising floors, and significant tumblehome, though she had much more rake in her stern post and stem.

She went to sea as part of the Mediterranean squadron in the Tripolitan war. As early as October 1804 while at Malta, she was re-rigged as a brig.[42] It is noteworthy that her re-rigging occurred after the major bombardments of Tripoli, indicating the brig-rigged vessel sometimes identified as

Vixen was somewhat more capacious than *Enterprise* and built at Baltimore. [National Archives 109-4-15; courtesy Robert Gardiner]

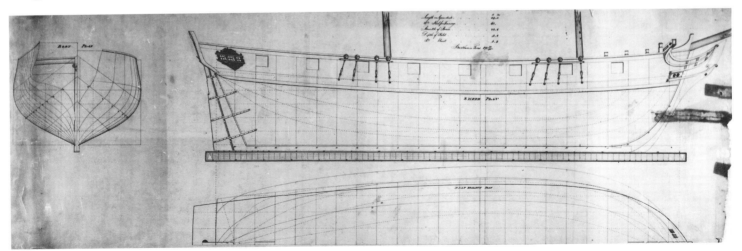

her in the Corné painting of the event was not. After the war she returned to the US, where she was laid up for a short time, then cruised the east coast until the War of 1812. Her war career was brief: she was captured by the British frigate *Southampton* on 12 November 1812 and wrecked on Conception Island, along with her captor, shortly afterwards.

The schooner *Nautilus*, as noted above, was purchased in the stead of a fourth contract-built vessel. Unlike other purchased vessels, this ship is included because of its significance in the service's attitude toward schooners in general.

The vessel is said to have been built by Henry Spencer, of Maryland's Eastern Shore, who also was responsible for *Enterprise*. The purchase was not without its controversy. William Bainbridge criticised her as 'too sharp' and unlikely to hold more than five weeks' provisions. Further, he feared her great rake weakened her extremities. Later, Richard Somers described her hull as 'just like a wedge' and said that her accommodations were too small. Despite these opinions, the Secretary of the Navy purchased her, writing that 'the Schooner Partisans' insisted on it, and, in any event he could not get the vessels he would rather have had built quickly enough.[43] She was purchased in early May 1803 and measured 87ft 6in on deck, 23ft 8in beam and 9ft 10in in the hold (for about 105 tons). Her armament was twelve 6pdrs and two 12pdr carronades.[44]

She was predictably fast. On her trials and crossing the Atlantic, Lieuteant Somers reported that she 'beat everything plying to windward, including Baltimore pilot boat', and that she 'sails fast, is easy, strained nothing, tight & strong'.[45] Her rig, as shown in the Corné painting of the attack on Tripoli, was as a two-topsail schooner–akin to the jack-ass brig used earlier by the revenue cutters. In 1806 she was a fore topsail schooner and in 1811 she became a brig. The painting shows a plain stem also, with no knee or figurehead.

Naval opinion of the vessel was not improved by her near destruction in a gale in April 1804. Preble wrote that she was 'near being lost . . . having all one side of her waist stove in . . . and three of her guns carried overboard & lost . . . She is very rotten, and never was strong enough for a cruiser.'[46] She did prove useful in the actions against the Barbary

Nautilus was very fast, but lightly built. Note her double topsail schooner rig. From a painting by Felix Corné, in which she was mislabelled *Argus*. [US Navy]

pirates, remaining with the American squadron until the end of that conflict. She returned to the US in 1806 and was laid up until 1808. She was repaired in 1810-11, when she gained her brig rig as well as a main battery of twelve 18pdr carronades. Her initial cruise during the War of 1812 was her last: she surrendered to a three-vessel British squadron off New Jersey on 17 July 1812, thus becoming the first vessel captured by either side during the war.

Brigs of 1814

Between the authorisation of 1803 and the War of 1812, as has been seen, the sea-going navy was neglected in favour of the Jeffersonian gunboats. An interesting and anomalous addition to the fleet during this interregnum was the *Ferret*, a vessel for which plans have not survived. Her origins are also unclear. Though some say she was purchased, Chapelle believed she was built by the navy at Norfolk Navy Yard.[47] She was commissioned in April 1809 and her dimensions were 73ft on deck, 23ft 8in beam and 7ft 8in depth of hold. Chapelle speculated she was built with

Sail plan of brig *Chippewa* by Charles Ware. [US Naval Historical Center NH 57007]

gunboat funds, and it appears from her small dimensions—particularly her depth of hold–that she may have been begun as a gunboat. Her designer was said to have been Josiah Fox, who indeed provided the draughts for a number of the gunboats. However, this is based on a letter from Fox dated 1799 and his 1827 letter defending his role as naval architect, in which Fox erroneously listed her as being built at Washington.[48] She was originally rigged as a cutter, then was re-rigged as a schooner. In 1810 she was again re-rigged, this time as a brig, and her name changed to *Viper*. She served on the east coast before the war and was captured by the frigate *Narcissus* on 17 January 1813, seven weeks out of port.[49]

Other than purchases, lakes vessels and wartime captures, the next brig-rigged vessels authorised by Congress were *Chippewa*, *Boxer* and *Saranac*. These were the result of an act dated 15 November 1814 for the purchase or construction of fast, commerce raiding schooners and brigs.[50] The three did not get to sea until after the end of hostilities.

Chippewa (also called *Chippaway*) was built at Warren, Rhode Island under the supervision of Oliver Hazard Perry, and named for one of his captures on Lake Erie. Perry had been designated to command a 'flying squadron' of four vessels, including *Chippewa*, intended to harry British commerce and convoys. The builder was Caleb Carr, and the design was, according to Chapelle, by William Doughty. A second opinion is found in Morison's biography of M C Perry, where O H Perry himself is credited with the design.[51] A Doughty design for a brig, dated late 1815, was presented by Chapelle as a possible candidate for the plan of *Chippewa*. This plan was 108ft by 29ft 9in and 13ft 9in depth of hold. Given the late date of its approval–five months after she was commissioned–it is somewhat doubtful that this was her plan.[52]

Chippewa was 410 tons and carried fourteen 32pdr carronades and two long 18s. She was launched on 25 March 1815 and O H Perry wrote of her: 'a very superior vessel . . . built of excellent timber, although green; of a beautiful model . . . [she] appears to sail uncommonly fast, particularly by the wind.'[53] She sailed for the Mediterranean with the squadron on 3 July 1815. After a short cruise showing the flag she returned to the United States. She departed on a second cruise in November 1816 and was wrecked on Caicos Island on 12 December of that year.

Boxer and *Saranac* were both built by Beldin and Churchill at Middletown, Connecticut. Their dimensions were 115ft on the keel, 29ft beam (extreme) and 12ft 6in depth of hold. (These dimensions do not correspond with either of the Doughty plans presented in Chapelle for these vessels.) One of them was 360 tons, the other 370, though it is unclear which applied to which. Both were launched in May 1815. Their rig included skysails and ringtails on their spankers.[54]

Saranac also joined the squadron in the Mediterranean in 1815, then returned to the US in November of that year. She next sailed south on anti-piracy duties, where her green timbers deteriorated rapidly. She returned in a leaking condition to New York City and was condemned and sold on 12 December 1818.

Boxer sailed to the Mediterranean in 1815, returned to join the squadron in the Gulf of Mexico, and was lost off Balize (near New Orleans) on 25 October 1817.

Other brigs added during the War of 1812 were the British vessel *Epervier* captured by *Peacock* in April, and three 14-gun vessels purchased in New York. The latter were initially built as privateers and were *Firefly*, *Flambeau* and *Spark*. *Epervier* was lost in the North Atlantic sometime after 14 July 1815; *Firefly* and *Flambeau* were sold in April 1816. *Spark* remained in the inventory until 1826.

Schooners purchased for war service were the *Eagle*, *Prometheus*, *Spitfire* and *Torch*. All were out of service by 1819.

Schooners of 1820

These vessels were the result of a recommendation by the Board of Navy Commissioners in 1819. They noted that most of the smaller vessels acquired during the war were wearing out or had been sold off, and the fleet ought to be balanced with the addition of fifteen schooners. The smaller vessels were necessary for the anti-piracy squadron in the West Indies and the anti-slavery patrol off West Africa. Congress responded by authorising five vessels of no more that 12 guns each.[55] The resulting ships were *Grampus* and, to a second design, the sister ships *Alligator*, *Dolphin*, *Porpoise* and *Shark*.

William Eckford's design for *Grampus*. [National Archives RG 19]

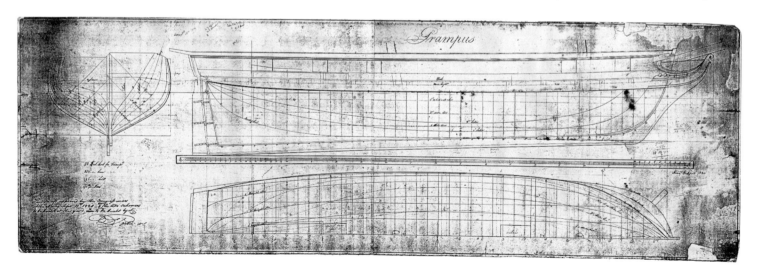

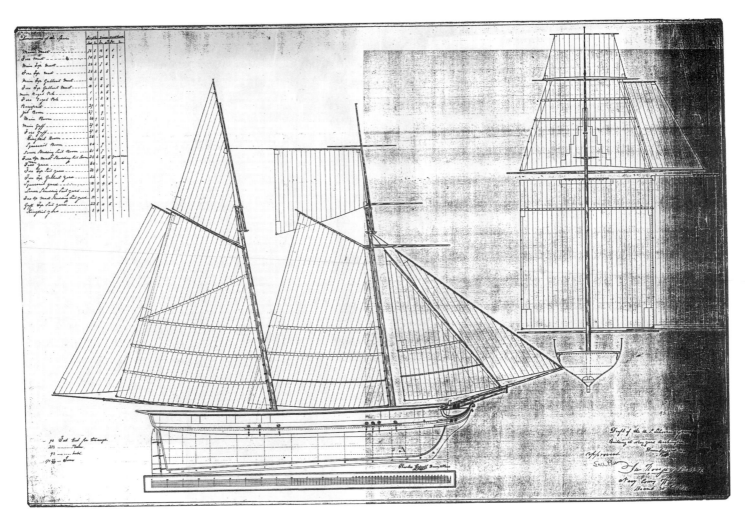

Sail plan of *Grampus*. Note huge sail area, including large fore course and ringtail. [National Archives RG 19]

Grampus was designed by William Eckford and built at Washington Navy Yard. She was to be a light draught design and measured 92ft 6in between perpendiculars, 24ft 6in beam and 9ft 6in depth of hold. As will be seen, her hull displayed less drop in her keel but considerably finer lines than the four others of this group. Her general appearance, lines and dimensions are suggestive of the brig *Spark*. Indeed, the Board of Commissioners had, in 1819, requested that Eckford supply them with *Spark*'s plan, apparently for reference.[56]

The armament for this and the others incorporated a high-mounted pivot gun amidships, designed to fire over either rail. On *Grampus*, this was an 18pdr, with the balance of her battery made up of eight to ten 12pdr carronades.[57] Because of the space taken athwartship by the gun and pivot carriage, no ports were provided amidships on her. The origin of this centreline pivot can be seen in the design of several of the 'Jefferson' gunboats.

The sail plan of all these ships was the 'topsail clipper schooner' rig. The most prominent feature of this was the incorporation, in addition to the square top- and topgallant sails on the fore mast, of a huge square fore course. All three fore mast square yards had studding sails and the mainsail was also fitted for a ringtail. A sliding gunter was provided for the gaff topsail. The lowest reef of the fore sail was actually a lacing, allowing the removal of that portion of the sail. This decreased the bulk of the sail for furling as well as allowed clearance for use of the pivot gun. Another point of interest was the use of a jack-yard, laced to the top of the fore course. This yard could be lowered by halyards, thus bringing the sail on deck for stowage. This reduced the top weight otherwise incurred if this huge square sail was furled to its yard in place.[58]

Grampus was launched on 21 August 1821 and went to sea later that year, joining the anti-piracy squadron in the West Indies. She was considered one of the fastest schooners of her day, and her speed was an important element in the ultimately successful anti-piracy campaign of the 1820s. In August 1822 she engaged and demolished a Puerto Rican pirate, the *Palmyra*, in less than five minutes. Her assignments included the Africa squadron, the Brazil squadron and, finally, the Home squadron. She foundered in a gale off Charleston in March 1843.

The *Alligator*, *Dolphin*, *Porpoise* and *Shark* were designed by William Doughty. They measured 86ft between perpendiculars, 24ft 9in moulded beam, 10ft 4in depth of hold, and 198 tons. Their hull lines exhibited considerably more drag in the keel than Eckford's vessel, as well as more rake in the stern and stem posts. Unlike *Grampus*, they were given gunports the length of their broadside, though they also mounted a centreline pivot gun.

As Chapelle points out, there were detail differences among the five vessels. *Alligator* was given a simple gam-

mon knee carved at the end with an alligator head. *Porpoise* and *Shark* received a complete naval billet head with rails. The channels of the latter pair were half-way up the gunports; *Dolphin*'s were below the ports; *Alligator*'s were below the rail cap. *Alligator* and *Dolphin* had mouldings the length of the hull just below the port sill level; the other two omitted this. All the vessels were given the topsail clipper schooner rig described above.[59] These vessels carried ten 6pdrs and an 18pdr on the pivot. This arrangement was soon changed and the latter was replaced by a pair of broadside 18s. *Shark*, by 1840, had two 9s and eight 24pdrs.[60]

Alligator was built at Boston and launched on 2 November 1820. She went to sea in April 1821 and became part of the anti-slavery patrol off the west coast of Africa. *Alligator*, however, under Robert F Stockton, was instrumental in locating and acquiring a new site for the re-settlement of former slaves from the United States (the original parcel's climate proved poorly suited for a permanent settlement), under the auspices of the American Colonization Society. Cape Mesurado was selected and was the germ of the nation of Liberia. Her second cruise also was on the

Schooner *Grampus*, drawing by W A K Martin, after removal of pivot gun. [US Naval Historical Center NH 86236: original at Independence Seaport, Philadelphia]

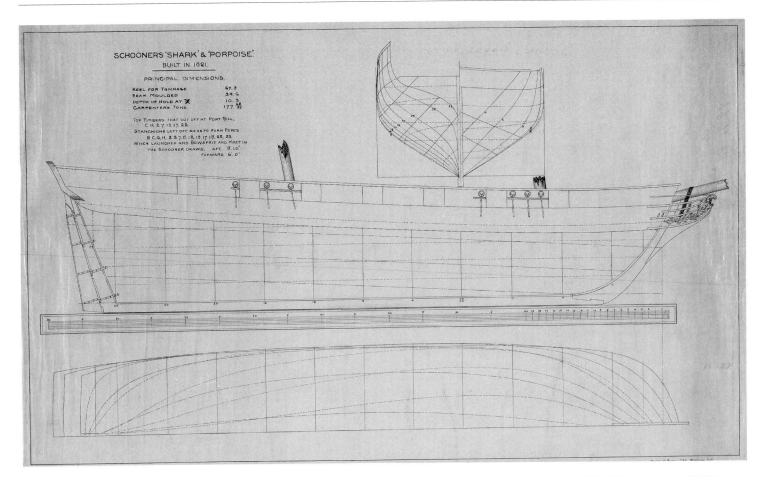

SCHOONERS 'SHARK' & 'PORPOISE'.
BUILT IN 1821.

PRINCIPAL DIMENSIONS.

KEEL FOR TONNAGE   67.3
BEAM MOULDED   24.6
DEPTH OF HOLD AT   10.3
CARPENTER'S TONS   177.95

TOP TIMBERS THAT CUT OFF AT PORT SILL,
    C.H. 2, 7, 12, 17, 22.
STANCHIONS LEFT OFF, SO AS TO FORM PORTS
    B, C, G, H, 2, 3, 7, 8, 12, 13, 17, 18, 22, 23.
WHEN LAUNCHED AND BOWSPRIT AND MAST IN
    THE SCHOONER DRAWS, AFT, 8.10"
                    FORWARD, 6.0"

Above: Plan of *Alligator*, *Dolphin*, *Porpoise* and *Shark*. [National Archives RG 19]

Right: Sail plan of schooner *Alligator* by Charles Ware. [US Naval Historical Center NH 57010]

African station, followed by a stint in the West Indies on anti-piracy patrol. Her career there was brief, as she ran aground on Carysfort Reef in the Florida Keys and was lost on 23 November 1822.

Dolphin was launched on 23 June 1821 at Philadelphia Navy Yard. With the ship of the line *Franklin*, she inaugurated the new Pacific station for the US Navy. By the early 1830s she had passed her prime and it was suggested her deck be raised and she be re-rigged as a brig. As early as 1832 she was such a 'dull sailer' that it was recommended that she be sold.[61] She remained in the Pacific until 2 December 1835 when the above recommendation was implemented.

Porpoise was built at Portsmouth, New Hampshire, and launched on 2 December 1820, being commissioned on 30 March the following year. Her first cruise was part of the West Indies squadron, involved in the suppression of piracy in that quarter. Following this she was part of the West African squadron, then the Mediterranean squadron. She returned to the West Indies station in 1830 and was wrecked in 1833 off Point Lizardo.

Shark was built at Washington Navy Yard, and launched on 17 May 1821. She was initially under the command of M C Perry, who wrote the following concerning her qualities:

... we have contended against bafling [*sic*] adverse winds, but during the whole time the Schooner has behaved in a manner highly satisfactory, not only as regards her sailing, but the ease with which she carries her guns, her stiffness and buoyancy, are equally the subject of admiration ... speaking in admiring terms of her appearance, good accommodations, and excellent fitment. . . . I regret that I cannot give so favourable a representation of her spars, her lower masts complain at the slightest puff, particularly the Foremast, which indicates a serious weakness a

Schooner *Shark*, designed by William Doughty: watercolour by François Roux, done in Marseilles 1843. [US Navy]

little below the hounds, her topmasts are by no means to be depended on . . . we sprung our Fore top mast in three places, when . . . going but 4½ knots . . . [62]

Perry commanded her on a cruise to West Africa, delivering the head of the American Colonization Society to Sierra Leone, then joining the anti-slave trade squadron off that coast. Later, as part of the West Indies squadron, Perry landed on Key West to take possession of that site after the cession of Florida to the United States by Spain. *Shark* remained in the West Indies until 1833, with the exception of one patrol of the Grand Banks fisheries in 1827.

After 1833, she served in the Mediterranean, then the Pacific. On 10 September 1846 she grounded at the mouth of the Columbia River, while surveying that treacherous bar and confluence of ocean and river current. The ship was a total loss, but her crew was saved.

Schooners of 1831:
Boxer, Enterprise and *Experiment*

In 1830 Secretary of the Navy John Branch wrote that the anti-piracy squadron in the West Indies was still necessary, and certainly could not safely be reduced. It consisted at that point of four sloops of war and three schooners. However, he suggested that one of the sloops of war be replaced by an additional three schooners. He reasoned that 'they would . . . [result in] multiplying . . . the chances of discovering the enemy, while their structure and inferior size would diminish the risk of being known in their approaches.'[63] Their lighter draught would also be advantageous in negotiating the shallow inlets of the area. The need for these vessels was in part due to the phasing out of most of the small schooners and barges purchased in the early 1820s for this work.[64] Congress responded by authorising the three schooners on 3 February 1831.[65]

All three were to be 88ft between perpendiculars, 23ft 6in moulded beam, and 10ft depth of hold, designed to draw no more than 12ft. Their battery was to be carronades and two long 9pdrs. All were apparently to be built to the same hull lines, penned by Samuel Humphreys, but the

hull of one, the *Experiment*, was constructed according to the experimental ideas of William Annesley.

Annesley had published his ideas in London in 1822 in *A New System of Naval Architecture* and had presented proposals for their use in a naval vessel as early as 1816. The ideas had been tried in practice in four small vessels, the largest of which was a 256-ton bark built at Deptford in 1819. When the three schooners were authorised, John Rodgers, president of the Board, suggested that his plan be used on one of them, with Annesley himself superintending its construction at Washington Navy Yard.[66]

Annesley's plan was to reduce the weight of the hull by eliminating the frames, relying entirely on layers of planking to provide longitudinal and transverse strength. Also absent in this 'system' was the keel or any other major longitudinal structural member, though the designer recommended bilge keels. Construction began with temporary 'moulds' set up in lieu of the frames, onto which the first layer of planking was laid. (The moulds were removed after construction was finished.) The first layer was laid longitudinally and covered with pitch and oil. The second layer was laid transversely, gunwale to gunwale, and covered with pitch, oil, and a layer of oiled paper. Layer three was longitudinal; layer four transverse, and layer five longitudinal. The seams of the inside and outside layers were painted with white lead and oil. Instead of caulking, the planking seams were sealed with wooden wedges. The fastenings for the interior four layers was of iron, and the completed hull was copper sheathed, with the latter providing the final security for the outer layer. It was estimated that the hull—all five layers—was about 5½ inches thick. [67]

In like manner, the decks were three layers thick, two athwartships, one longitudinal. Oak beams were incorporated at each hatchway and the masts, but apparently there was little else securing the deck to the ship's sides. She had a round stern and Annesley claimed she weighed about one-third that of her registered tonnage.[68] The description of this method of construction, plus characterisations of Annesley's designs as being based on elliptical forms, added to the fact that the vessel had a 'round' stem and stern, lead to the conclusion that the hull lines may have deviated significantly from Humphreys' design. It would certainly have been difficult to make sharp curved forms as are found in the run and buttock lines of a sharp schooner, with five layers of planking. But it is impossible to be certain, as no plans of this vessel have been found.

The ship was launched on 14 March 1832 and made trial runs on Chesapeake Bay. It appears that before she made her first run, beams and knees were added, as Humphreys later stated, 'to prevent the deck from falling in to the hold'. Early on, caulking replaced the wedges on the outside planking.[69] In sailing she was at her worst working to windward, barely making 6½ knots and making considerable leeway. Going before the wind she did much better, 'working like a pilot boat'. However, her commander, William Mervine, after another trial wrote: 'The most indifferent bay craft . . . worked dead to windward of us in a few hours', and, conclusively, 'she will prove to be unfit for a vessel of war'.[70]

Some alterations were made subsequently. Her masts and spars were reduced, ballast was added, and 6pdrs were substituted for the two long 12s on board. She was sent north, and was found somewhat stiffer, in part due to the alterations. In 1833 she went to the Gulf coast and weathered a gale satisfactorily. Mervine was satisfied with her toughness but regretted that her sailing was unsatisfactory, particularly close-hauled (he at one point suggested a centreboard for her).[71] He also complained that officers were

hard to find, citing 'much prejudice' against the vessel; doubts about her safety, and her continual leaking did not improve her status in the navy. She was relegated to coast survey work from 1835 to 1839, then became a receiving ship at Philadelphia. She was sold in 1848.

Boxer and *Enterprise* were built to a clipper schooner model, despite opposition from some quarters. John Rodgers wrote John Branch in April 1831 that 'Baltimore built schooners' were fast and weatherly, but were 'lightly built', having small timbers, long room and space and frames of white oak (which weighed about 56 pounds per cubic foot, as against over 76 for live oak.).[72] It is noteworthy that these vessels would be the last schooner-rigged vessels built for the US Navy.

Their model was typical of the Baltimore clipper: sharp rising floors, fine forward and aft lines, considerable drag in the keel and much rake fore and aft. They carried eight 24pdr carronades and two 9s. They were fast but considered tender–Chapelle described them as overloaded with guns and boats. By 1840 *Boxer* had been altered to a brig, and her commander regarded her as a 'dull sailer', though a good sea boat: that is, she handled satisfactorily, and stood up to her canvas well, but was not excessively fast.[73]

Plan of schooners *Boxer* and *Enterprise*, designed by Samuel Humphreys. Their light draught was for use in coastal anti-piracy duties. [National Archives 40-9-1]

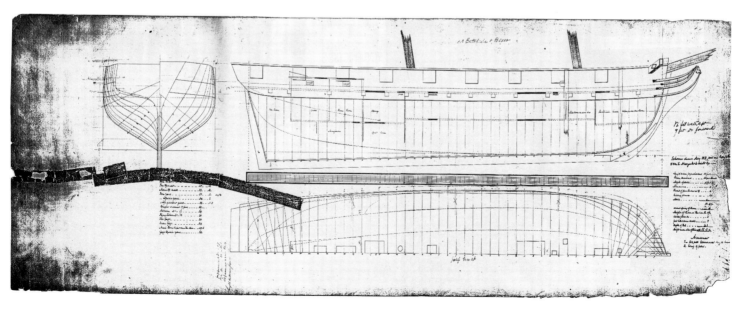

Enterprise was built at New York. She was launched on 26 October 1831 and commissioned on 15 December that year. Her initial assignment was as part of the Brazil squadron, then she cruised with *Peacock* to the Far East, finally taking station on the west coast of South American until 1839. After another cruise on the Brazil station she was decommissioned in 1844, and sold in the following year.

Boxer was launched on 22 November 1831 at Boston (Charlestown) Navy Yard and commissioned the next year. She cruised as part of the Brazil squadron, in the West Indies and on the Pacific through 1840. After being altered to a brig, she became part of the Home squadron, then, in 1846, joined the African anti-slavery patrol. She was found unseaworthy and sold at Philadelphia in 1848.

Dolphin Class Brigs, 1836

These two vessels, *Dolphin* and *Porpoise*, were designed by Samuel Humphreys, and obviously were based on the 1831 schooner design. Their dimensions were 88ft between perpendiculars–the same as the previous vessels–but were 25ft moulded beam and 11ft depth of hold, compared to 23ft 6in beam and 10ft depth for the 1831 schooners. The

Plan of the 1836 vessels *Dolphin* and *Porpoise*. These marked the service's move away from schooner to a brigantine rig. [National Archives RG 19]

new vessels were to be brigantines –square rigged on the fore mast but without the brig's square course on the main mast. The increased beam and depth would tend to improve the vessel's stability under the added canvas of a square rig. The hull design actually showed a bit more deadrise than the 1831 schooners, slightly sharper stern lines but less rake at the stern post. They would carry ten 24pdr carronades and two long 9pdrs.

A S Mackenzie wrote of his experience with the *Dolphin* in 1838 and 1839. Before Mackenzie began redistributing her weight, he described her movements as:

> more violent than those of any vessel I ever sailed in, she plunged violently, tore everything to pieces forward and made some very old sailors seasick, she griped badly, too, was very apt to fly into the wind and come round against her helm until the head yards were braced aback . . . she was given up to me with the character of being unsafe and incapable of lying to.

After rearranging her ballast and trim, Mackenzie wrote, 'her sailing and working improved astonishingly, she no longer shipped water forward or tore away her head rails.' After modifying the location of her fore yard and moving the headstays further forward on the bowsprit, he also improved her windward sailing performance. She now

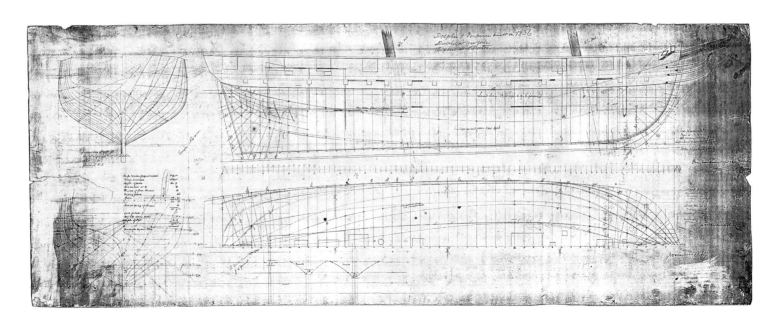

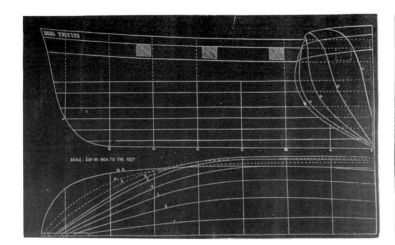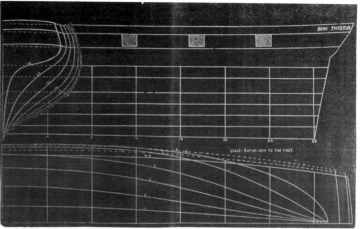

Plan of brig *Truxtun*, published in *US Nautical Magazine and Naval Journal* in 1856. Her rig included skysails and measured over 9700 square feet of canvas. [Author]

would do over 9 knots with royals set within 5½ points of the wind, and in smooth water, went 10 knots on the same point of sailing.[74]

He reported her to be uncommonly stiff under all sail, capable of lying to 'in the most perfect manner being dry, safe and easy'. He reported out-sailing eight men-of-war, including *Fairfield* and *Independence*, and she had never been beaten. In all, he considered the vessel the 'best and safest' vessel he had sailed in.[75] Later Mackenzie wrote that making her into a 'full' brig would unquestionably improve her sailing.[76] It appears, however, that she remained a brigantine, though *Porpoise* was made into a brig in 1840.[77]

The only reports on the sailing qualities of *Porpoise* are dated 1853, after she had been outfitted for arctic exploration. It is possible that the alterations made in her for this service radically altered her trim and thus her sea keeping capabilities as she was called a 'horrible rolling' brig and a 'man-killer' by the crew.[78]

Dolphin was built at New York, launched on 17 June 1836 and commissioned on 6 September 1836. Her first cruise was to the coast of Africa, after which she joined the Brazil squadron. Subsequently she was again part of the anti-slavery patrol, then of the Home squadron. Following a refit, she re-joined the Africa squadron, then was transferred to the Far East, via Cape Horn, returning to New York in 1851 by way of Cape Horn. The remaining years before the Civil War were spent again in the anti-slavery patrol, as well as the squadron sent to Paraguay in 1858. One of her more noted captures was the slaver *Echo*, taken in the West

Indies in 1858, with a cargo of 318 blacks, all of whom were returned to Africa. She was laid up at Norfolk in December 1860 and was burned when the yard was abandoned to the Confederates in April 1861.

Porpoise was built at Charlestown Navy Yard, Boston. She was launched on 31 May 1836 and commissioned on 29 August. Her initial cruise was on the east coast, in a surveying role. This was followed by service with the anti-piracy squadron on the Gulf of Mexico. This short cruise was followed by the arduous Wilkes expedition, which departed in 1838 and returned over four years later, after extensive world circling survey and exploration. She later was part of the anti-slavery squadron, the forces against Mexico in the Gulf, and, again, in the anti-slavery unit. In 1853 she was selected to be part of Cadwallader Ringgold's exploration of the western Pacific. She separated from the squadron in September 1854 near China, and was lost at sea with all hands.

Brigs of the 1840s

The construction of small vessels languished in the late 1830s, with the attention of the department, and particularly the constructors, consumed with the first of the navy's steam vessels. Though Secretary of the Navy James K Paulding submitted a request to build five brigs or schooners in 1837, no congressional authorisation result-ed.[79] Despite this, in 1841 the Board ordered four brigs built, two to be designed by Samuel Humphreys, and two by Francis Grice. These and the *Lawence* of 1843 were to be the last sailing brigs in the US Navy.

Truxtun was the first laid down, late in 1841, and her con-struction was superintended by her designer. Grice wrote an interesting letter regarding her design in May 1842, after her launch. He indicated that the Board had requested he build a vessel by 'Mr Grice's draft' measuring 100ft between perpendiculars, 25ft beam and 11ft depth, but said he had not submitted a plan corresponding to those dimen-sions, so he built 'as best he could'.[80] This letter was in response to the fact that the Board noted *Truxtun* deviated from the others in dimensions.[81]

The vessel measured 100ft between perpendiculars, 27ft 4in moulded beam and 13ft depth of hold. The hull was sharp but with less drag in her keel and less forward rake than the Humphreys design (see below). As built she was given spencers on both masts and rigged to skysails, totalling over 9700 square feet of canvas.[82] She was armed with ten 32pdr carronades and two long guns, probably 12s. She was reported to be fast. One of her officers wrote: 'The *Truxtun* is . . . a fast sailer, and fine sea boat. We have beat-en everything we have met; and the *Saratoga*, considered

one of the fastest . . . of any nation, has . . . [yielded] us the palm . . . after a long trial of speed.'[83]

The brig was launched on 16 April 1842 and commis-sioned on 18 February 1843 at Norfolk. Her first assign-ment was to the Mediterranean squadron, then she spent two years on the anti-slavery patrol off West Africa. With the outbreak of the Mexican War she was sent to the Gulf of Mexico to blockade the enemy coast. On 14 August 1846 she grounded off Tuxpan in a gale. She remained hard aground but refused to surrender to a Mexican demand. While still aground, her cutter boarded and seized a Mexican vessel with the intention of having the prize assist in re-floating the stranded brig. This did not prove practica-ble and the American vessels *Princeton* and *Falmouth* were dispatched to assist her. They arrived on the 20th, to find she had been surrendered three days before. Crews from the two ships set the captured brig on fire and she burned to the waterline on 22 August 1846.

The second vessel designed by Francis Grice was the brig *Perry*, laid down on 13 February 1843, also at Norfolk. Her dimensions were 105ft between perpendiculars, 25ft moulded beam and 11ft 6in depth of hold. Note that this was longer but narrower and shallower than *Truxtun*. She had somewhat harder bilges, however. Her battery was ten 32pdr carronades.

She was launched on 9 May 1843 and went into service on 13 October. She was reportedly 'very fast (except in light winds), and weatherly; steers and works to perfection; rolls

Brig *Perry*, like *Truxtun*, was designed by Francis Grice. [National Archives 40-8-10C]

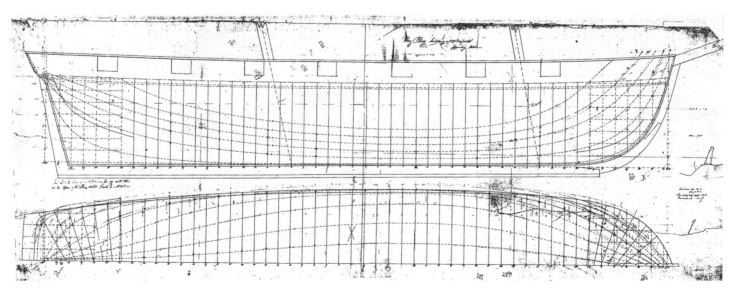

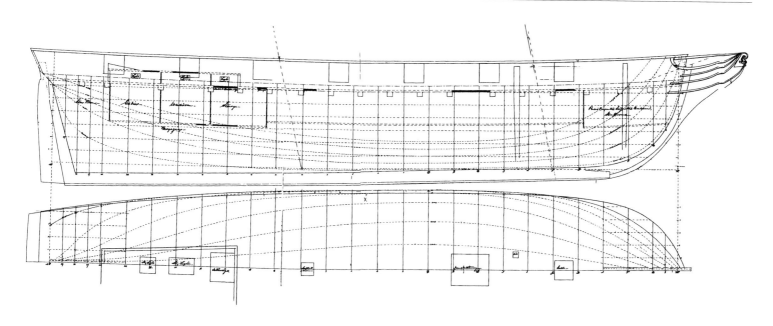

Plan of brigs *Somers* and *Bainbridge*, by Samuel Humphreys. [National Archives 38-3-10]

deep and easy'. On her first cruise she was thought to be unsafe: she had 'lost four of her boats, and threw overboard 2 of her guns' on passage to the East Indies. Subsequently her masting was altered and number of boats and guns reduced, the latter to six carronades and two longer 32s. Her ballast was significantly increased also, from around 3 tons to over 6, then 8½ in 1847.[84] All of this indicated she was originally rather tender and over-hatted.

Perry sailed to the East Indies in 1843, returning via Cape Horn two years later. At the outbreak of the Mexican conflict, she sailed southward, but was dismasted and driven ashore in a hurricane in October 1846. She returned to service in May 1847 and joined the Brazil squadron. Subsequently she was in the anti-slavery patrol until 1854, and later participated in the expedition against Paraguay in 1858 and 1859. Her Civil War service included duty in the Atlantic Blockading Squadron, the Potomac Flotilla, and the South Atlantic Blockade Squadron. She was decommissioned on 29 April 1865 and sold on 10 August.

Bainbridge and *Somers* were designed by Samuel Humphreys and their beam and depth measurements were the same as that of the Humphreys-designed *Dolphin* and *Porpoise*: 25ft and 11ft, respectively; but 12ft was added to the length, making them 100ft between perpendiculars. Their hull lines, particularly forward, were finer than those of their predecessors, but it is obvious that the new plan

was derived from the older one. Both ships were built simultaneously at Boston. *Somers* was launched on 16 April 1842; *Bainbridge*, ten days later. The former was commissioned on 12 May; the latter on 16 December 1842. They were armed with ten 32pdr carronades.

Bainbridge's sailing was described as 'good, very stiff and weatherly'. Though her speed was noted as 11 knots free, she 'kept company with the *Portsmouth* in light winds and was beaten whenever it freshened.'[85] This was no mean feat, given the sloop of war's reputation for speed (see above). Chapelle noted they were both over-sparred and *Bainbridge* was reported to 'need all her ballast'. Given that both met the same fate – capsizing – it is probable their centre of gravity was higher than safety allowed.

Somers' name is linked inextricably with the 'mutiny' which occurred on her first voyage, which was as an apprentice training vessel. Returning to the US in late 1842, three of her crew were charged with mutiny and hung from her yardarms. One of the three was an apprentice, Philip Spencer, 19-year-old son of the Secretary of War. The controversy over this episode remains to this day. Following this cruise, she was assigned to the Home squadron, serving both on the Atlantic and in the West Indies. During the

She capsized and sank off Cape Hatteras on 21 August 1863, with the loss of all but one crewmember.

The origins of the brig *Lawrence* are rather obscure. She was built by contract with Langley B Culley of Baltimore in 1843, though the contract has not been found. Her builder was noted for his fast vessels, and the hull of *Lawrence* was an extreme Baltimore clipper design, with great drag in her keel and sharp lines fore and aft. With a length of 109ft and breadth of 26ft 2in, she had the longest length to breadth ratio of all these brigs. Her depth of hold was 13ft 3in and draught was 16ft 6in. The latter was extraordinarily deep for a vessel of her size.

She was armed with ten 32pdrs, eight of them carronades, and went to sea on 19 September 1843. She first cruised on the Atlantic coast, then was transferred to the Gulf before the outbreak of the Mexican-American War. Though she participated in the blockade and was a good sailer, her deep draught prevented close-in work and her shortage of stowage space limited her usefulness as a blockader.[86] She returned to the US in September 1846. She was surveyed and condemned by a board of officers and sold late in 1846. She subsequently became a merchant vessel.[87]

Brig *Bainbridge*. Both vessels of this class were probably over-hatted– and both were lost to capsizing. [US Naval Historical Center NH 1231]

Mexican War she served on the blockade, then capsized and foundered on 8 December 1846 in a sudden squall off Vera Cruz.

Bainbridge's first duty was in the Home squadron, followed by the Brazil and African squadrons. She took part in the operation against Paraguay and was decommissioned in November 1860. During the Civil War she was active in pursuing blockade runners while part of the East Gulf Blockading Squadron and the cruisers in the West Indies.

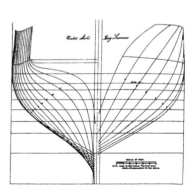

Brig *Lawrence*, an extreme example of naval application of the Baltimore 'clipper' design. Note: the gaps in her lines on this plan are due to tears in the original. [National Archives 38-2-11B]

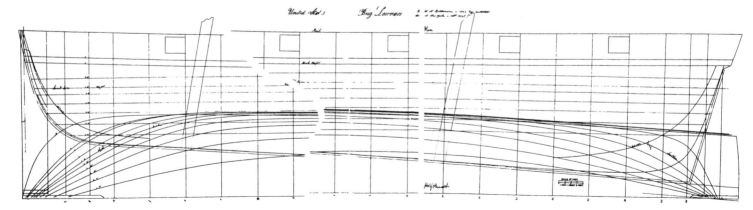

CHAPTER 9

Vessels on the Northern Lakes

BY THE War of 1812, the American northern frontier extended westward to include all the Great Lakes, with growing populations on both Lake Ontario and Lake Erie, and British Canada continued to hold an implicit threat to those areas. In addition, Lake Champlain was, as it had been in the Revolution, a possible invasion route for an enemy from Canada. As tensions grew with Great Britain, particularly after the *Chesapeake-Leopard* affair, the United States had taken only minor measures to provide a naval armament on these lakes, amounting to a brig on Lake Ontario and two small gunboats on Lake Champlain. It was not until war had broken out that serious naval construction was begun and, indeed, there was a veritable race between the opposing sides to out-build the other in terms of both number of ships and their size. The following is a survey of this construction, presented in lake-by-lake sequence.

To some extent the character of the lakes determined the types of vessels which could be used on them. Lake Erie was relatively shallow while Lake Ontario was quite deep, allowing vessels on the latter to be built much like ocean-going vessels. Furthermore, given the short distances involved in navigating these bodies of water, warships could dispense with extensive stowage room for provisions and water. It should also be kept in mind that the squadrons on Erie and Ontario were not interchangeable, nor mutually supportive: the lakes were separated by Niagara Falls.

Lake Ontario

The first American warship constructed on the lakes was the brig *Oneida*, built on Lake Ontario. The vessel had been authorised by Congress in December 1807 and was expected to enforce customs laws on the lake as well as Jefferson's Embargo, which had been instituted the same month.[1]

The vessel was to carry a 32pdr on the bow and twelve 18pdr or 24pdr carronades (or, alternatively, twelve long 9s) in broadside. Two New Yorkers, Christian Bergh and Henry Eckford obtained the contract with the latter providing the design. The vessel was built near Oswego, launched on 31 March 1809, and commissioned shortly thereafter. The design was very conventional in terms of hull lines: she had little deadrise and rather blunt lines forward, though with a long run. The gun arrangement, as mandated by the Secretary of the Navy, included a single large bow gun. In this instance it was a 32pdr mounted on a pivot carriage on her forecastle. In broadside were sixteen 24pdr carronades.[2]

She was heavily sparred and at the start of her career was reported to be fast, but early in the war she was considered so slow that when the British squadron appeared, she was hauled out of the water and her guns used for a shore battery.[3] Later, in 1813, when going into battle, she was towed by the sloop *General Pike* because 'she [sailed] badly'.[4] She served through the War of 1812 and she was sold in May 1825. *Oneida* has the distinction of being the only American lake-built vessel of this era for which there are original plans still extant.

It was not until August 1812 that Captain Isaac Chauncey was ordered to 'purchase, hire or build' vessels for the defence of Lakes Ontario and Erie, and was authorised to take munitions and men from the navy yards for the purpose.[5] By 4 September Chauncey had hired Henry Eckford and carpenters and sent them to the lakes, and had written to Lieutenant Melancthon Woolsey, already on site, to find a spot at Sackett's Harbor to build gunboats and a 300-ton brig.[6]

By the time Chauncey himself arrived from New York City, on 6 October, the keel for the brig had been laid. Given the timing, no doubt Eckford had provided the design. As Chauncey had only written Woolsey to find a 'spot' for it on 4 September, and communications between

New York City and the lakes required about ten days, a keel laying date of 11 September (as found in some sources) is unlikely. We know that on 8 October Chauncey wrote of the vessel being 'on the stocks' to be launched in 'six weeks'.[7]

The *Madison*, designed as a 'corvette-built ship', was launched on 26 November 1812. According to Chauncey, she had been built in forty-five days, 'nine weeks since the timber that she is composed of was growing in the forest'. However, this timing would have had her keel down on 12 October, some four days after he arrived. He put her dimensions at 112ft on the keel, 32ft 6in beam, 11ft 6in depth of hold, and 580 tons.[8] As no plans of this ship have been found, little else is known about *Madison*'s particulars, saving her armament. This was four long 12pdrs and twenty 32pdr carronades. She was commissioned by 24 April 1813.[9] She was flagship of Chauncey's squadron and participated in the capture of York (Toronto), and attacks on Fort George, and engagements with the British squadron on Ontario. She was laid up after the war and sold in 1825.

The spring of 1813 brought more new construction on

Ontario. The corvette *General Pike* was laid down on 9 April, and rushed to launch in sixty-three days, despite being set on fire during an attack on 29 May. She was also designed by Henry Eckford and was quite large, measuring 145ft between perpendiculars, 37ft beam, and 15ft depth of hold. Though no hull plans have been found, a sail plan indicates she was heavily sparred, up to skysails. The accuracy of this plan is questionable, as she is shown with quarter galleries and a knee head, neither of which were likely to have been features of the rapidly built lakes vessels. Her battery was twenty-eight 24pdrs, two of which were on pivots.[10]

General Pike was in service by 21 July 1813 and participated in squadron actions against the British in September. She also supported American troop movements and a blockade of Kingston harbour in 1814. She was laid up after the war and sold in 1825.

The schooner *Sylph* was designed by Eckford and laid down on 26 July. She was launched on 18 August–a building time of twenty-three days. Her dimensions are unknown but she was large enough to carry twelve 6pdrs and four 32s. She was later re-rigged as a brig and armed

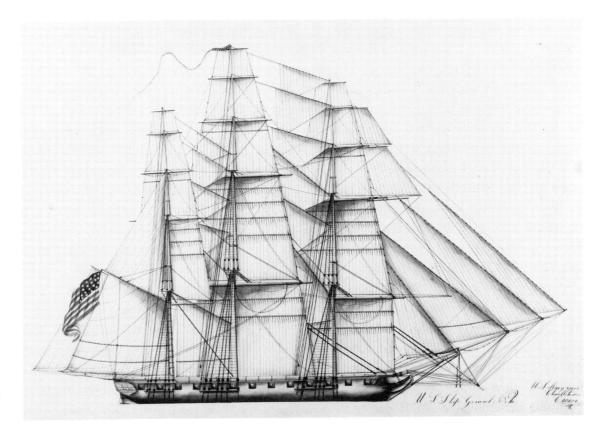

Sail plan of *General Pike* by Charles Ware. As with all of the lakes vessels, she was built quickly - 63 days from keel to launch - and probably did not have quarter galleries or knee head. [National Archives NH 57006]

with sixteen 24pdr carronades and two long 9pdrs.[11] Re-rigging schooners as brigs was common practice in the navy in this era. *Sylph* was in service by 21 August and participated in action against the British on 11 September. After useful service on Ontario throughout the war, she was laid up. It appears also that she, like many of the other small lakes vessels, was sunk for preservation after the war. She was sold in 1825.

The next building on Lake Ontario began in February 1814, consisting of two brigs and three frigates, all having been authorised in 1813. The two brigs were *Jones* and *Jefferson*; the frigates, *Plattsburg*, *Superior* and *Mohawk*.

The brigs appear to have been the result of an agreement with Adam and Noah Brown of New York City. The Secretary of the Navy convinced them to build three sloops of war on the lake, all based on the moulds of the *Peacock*, which was completing at the time. Though only two were built and they were brigs rather than sloops of war, the dimensions of the completed vessels tally fairly with those of *Peacock*. They were 121ft 6in between perpendiculars, 31ft 6in beam and 14ft 6in depth. The only discrepancy was that the brigs were 2ft 6in longer.[12] Both vessels were launched in April 1814, *Jefferson* on the 7th; *Jones* on the 10th. They also were laid up after the war and sold in 1825.

Of the three frigates, one, the *Plattsburg*, was not completed. She was designed by Adam and Noah Brown and was to have been the largest of the three. She was designed to carry 52 guns: thirty-two 24s and twenty 42pdr carronades. Her dimensions were supposedly 185ft on the keel, 46ft extreme beam and 1749 tons.[13] If these dimensions are accurate she would have been around 200ft between perpendiculars—the largest American frigate of the times. It is more likely that the length dimension was between perpendiculars rather than on the keel. In any event, she was incomplete at the end of the war and she was sold on the ways in 1825.

The frigate *Superior* was designed by Henry Eckford and was laid down on 11 February 1814. She was to carry 44 guns, but news of the supposed strength of the British squadron induced him to lengthen her by twenty feet and mount 62 guns on her. As completed she measured 180ft between perpendiculars, 43ft moulded beam and 1580 tons. These dimensions were comparable to the 1813 frigates such as *Guerriere*, which was 175ft by 45ft and 1500 tons. In the end she carried 58 guns: thirty 32s, twenty-six 42pdr carronades, and two 24s.

She was also built rapidly. She was launched on 1 May 1814. Chauncey wrote on her launch date that she was 'uncommon [*sic*] beautiful and well built ship, something larger than the *President* and could mount 64 guns', and built in less than eighty days.[14] She served through the summer and fall of 1814, but was in no significant engagements. Winter ended activity on the lakes and the conclusion of the war ended her usefulness. She was laid up and later sold.

Mohawk was also designed by Eckford, but was significantly smaller, measuring 155ft between perpendiculars, 37ft 6in beam and 15ft 6in in the hold. She was rated for 32 guns and was about 1350 tons, making the ship comparable in size to the 36-gun *Philadelphia* of 1799. She was laid down on 7 April and launched on 11 June 1814. *Mohawk* was commissioned shortly afterwards and in July sailed with Chauncey's fleet to confront the British at the head of the lake. The opposing fleet retired and was blockaded for forty-five days, bringing to an end naval activity for that year. The war ended on 28 December, and *Mohawk* was laid up. After amicable relations with Canada were established with the Rush Bagot agreement in 1817, the fleets on the lakes were no longer needed and the vessels were disposed of. Afterwards, the American naval presence on the lakes was confined to revenue vessels and a single naval ship with a battery limited by treaty.

The ultimate expression of the arms race on the lakes were the ships of the line. In response to the British construction of such ships, Noah and Adam Brown were called upon to provide designs for an American response. These were named *Chippewa* and *New Orleans*, and were 204ft between perpendiculars, and 56ft extreme beam. Though one source indicated they were to carry 87 guns, Chapelle called them 120-gun ships. Their dimensions place them between the 120-gun *Pennsylvania* and the typical American 74, so they would have been among the largest wooden warships built on the continent.

Both were laid down on 4 October 1814 and never

Ship of the line *New Orleans* on the stocks on Lake Ontario until 1883. At 204ft by 56ft, this ship would have been nearly as large as *Pennsylvania*. [US Naval Historical Center NH 9688]

launched. *Chippewa* was sold in 1823 but the frame of *New Orleans* remained on the stocks until sold in September 1883.

Lake Erie

Work on an American squadron on Lake Erie began after a suitable site was chosen at Presque Isle, now Erie, Pennsylvania. In January 1813 Chauncey requested that Captain Oliver Hazard Perry be sent to Erie to command that station; then, in February, directed Noah Brown to proceed to Erie and in the 'shortest time' build two brigs to carry eighteen 32pdrs and two long 9s, with draught about '6½ or 7 feet'.[15] These vessels were to become the *Lawrence* and *Niagara*.

Activity began in earnest in March 1813 with the arrival of Brown and carpenters from the east. He was the man 'to drive the business', and in a few days had built a house to lodge the carpenters, was getting 'clamps in for the beam & bottoms ready for caulking' of two small gunboats already begun, and had the keels laid or ready to lay of the two brigs, plus some frames cut for the latter.[16] Despite primi-

tive conditions, lack of supplies and iron for the fittings, most of the work on the two brigs was done by July, when Brown returned to the east coast. Since March, Brown had built the brigs, a 75-ton schooner, three gunboat schooners and rebuilt another. Incidental to the shipbuilding, Brown had constructed a blockhouse, guardhouse, barracks, blacksmith shop, mess building, an office, and boats and gun carriages. This had been done in a literal wilderness, with around 200 men.[17]

The two brigs were launched in May 1813, and commissioned on 4 August (*Niagara*) and 5 August (*Lawrence*). Their dimensions were 110ft between perpendiculars, 30ft extreme beam and 9ft depth of hold. Like the other vessels of these squadrons, they were of green wood. No plans of these vessels survive. After the war, *Niagara* was used as a station ship, then both vessels were sunk to preserve them. The *Lawrence* was raised in 1876 and disposed of. The *Niagara*'s hulk was raised in 1913. She was restored at that time, to mark the centenary of the Battle of Lake Erie, though the work was based on sparse information. Another restoration was needed in 1939, for which Howard I Chapelle prepared the plans. He wrote that his plans 'could not be accepted as wholly accurate', particularly as to the topsides and ends of the ship, which had rotted away through the years. He also indicated that the deck arrangements were conjectural, based on similar sized British naval brigs.[18]

The brig *Niagara* which exists today was built in 1988 under the direction of Melbourne Smith and incorporates some of the original timbers in non-structural areas. She is 110ft 8ft on the load waterline and 32ft moulded beam with a draught of 10ft 6in at the sternpost. It appears the new ship is somewhat deeper and wider than the original – and, of course, she has twin diesels in addition to her sails.[19] She is a sail training vessel and tourist attraction based in Erie, Pennsylvania.

The original *Niagara* and her sister ship each carried eighteen 32pdr carronades and two 12s. They were, of course, the mainstays of Perry's fleet on the lake, along with seven smaller vessels. They engaged and captured the six vessels of the British squadron on 10 September 1813 after a three-hour battle. It marked the first time in history that an entire British fleet had been captured. The crucial battle secured the American position on the lakes and ended the British attempts to invade via the Great Lakes and the Northwest Territory. And it gave America the famous phrase: 'We have met the enemy and they are ours . . .'

Lake Champlain

Two major warships were built on Lake Champlain under the leadership of Thomas MacDonough. They were in response to British expansion on that lake, which included the *Confiance*, a 36-gun frigate and the largest warship built on the lake. The first of the two American vessels laid down was *Saratoga*, a sloop of war designed by Noah Brown. She was a large ship – 143ft between perpendiculars, 36ft 6in moulded beam, and 12ft 6in in the hold, so comparable to *General Pike*. She carried 26 guns: twelve 32pdr carronades, six 42pdr carronades, and eight 24pdrs.[20]

She was built in about thirty days and launched on 11 April 1814. She was said to be a good sailer and was MacDonough's flagship in the battle at Plattsburgh Bay in September 1814. Her sailing qualities had little to do with the battle itself, of course, as she and the balance of the fleet were anchored during the engagement.

The brig *Eagle* was begun in July 1814, and launched on 11 August. Her design was similar to that of the *Niagara*: 128ft by 32ft, carrying twelve 32pdr carronades and eight

Brig *Niagara*, partly conjectural plan by H I Chapelle. [Smithsonian Institution]

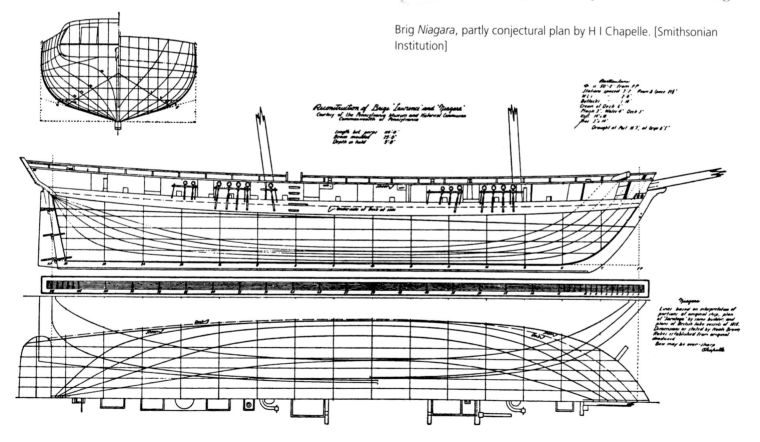

The modern 'replica' *Niagara*, a sail-training vessel and tourist attraction. [Courtesy U S Brig Niagara, Pennsylvania Historical and Museum Commission]

18s. She was built by Noah Brown in an astounding nineteen days and commissioned on 6 September. Five days later she played a major part in the battle at Plattsburg Bay.

Saratoga and *Eagle*, with two smaller ships and ten gunboats defeated the British fleet including *Confiance*, three

smaller ships and twelve gunboats on 11 September 1814. Both MacDonough's vessels were heavily damaged in the engagement, which lasted about two and a half hours. After the war they were laid up and both were sold in 1825. MacDonough's victory effectively ended the British invasion and forced the retreat of their forces to Canada. It also helped strengthen the position of the American peace negotiators at Ghent and contributed to the signing of the treaty ending the war on 28 December 1814.

* * * * *

The warships built on the lakes during the War of 1812 were, of course, a sidelight in the development of American naval vessels in general. The ships were serviceable, but hurriedly built in order to meet an immediate threat. As such they were of green timber and thus short-lived. They served their purpose quite well, as has been seen, and demonstrated both the skill of the American sailors in battle as well as the extraordinary capabilities of American shipbuilders and carpenters. Men such as Adam and Noah Brown and Henry Eckford, with the efforts of Isaac Chauncey, Oliver Hazard Perry and Thomas MacDonough carried out seemingly impossible tasks in creating whole squadrons – literally from the forests beside the lakes into the water – in a matter of months.

Plan of *Saratoga*, another swiftly built brig. Note her shallow draught and broad beam. [Howard I Chapelle, by courtesy of the Smithsonian Institution]

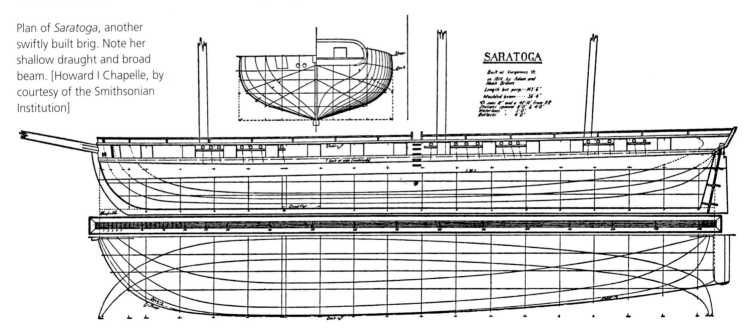

Galleys

During the Quasi-War with France Congress authorised not more than ten vessels to be built as galleys, on the southern coast as well as on the western rivers. The latter were built at Pittsburgh, Louisville and Marietta, Ohio Territory. Though built by the navy, it appears the funding for three of them may have come from the local populace. They were to be manned by the army, militia-fashion. Their complement was to be a lieutenant, a coxswain and twenty-five privates. Armament was to be one 24pdr and five or six brass howitzers. Dimensions: 52ft by 15ft by 5ft 8in depth. It appears that four designs were used, the first by Samuel Humphreys. All were sold or otherwise disposed of by February 1802. There were also four galley-gunboats built at Vergennes, Vermont on Lake Champlain in 1814, by A and N Brown, 75ft x 15ft; two were named *Allen* and *Centipede*. The former was still in service in May 1817 (RG 45, E209). The others were sunk for preservation (M125).

Beaufort: Beaufort, SC, sold 1 February 1802.
Charleston: Charleston, SC, sold 1 February 1802 (also referred to as *Mars*).
Governor Davie: Wilmington, NC, sold 1801.
Governor Williams: Wilmington, NC (turned over to Revenue Service, 1802).
South Carolina: Charleston, SC, sold 1 February 1802 (also called *Protector*).
St Mary's: St Mary's, GA (turned over to Revenue Service, 1801).
Savannah: Savannah, GA , sold 1 February 1802.
Senator Ross? (Built at Pittsburgh).
[Name unknown?] (Built at Louisville)
Marietta: Built at Marietta, Ohio Territory.

(Ref: *Naval Documents of the Quasi-War with France*, Vol VII; Chapelle, pp152-3.)

The Jefferson Gunboats

The first gunboats of this variety were acquired for work along the littorals of North Africa against the Barbary powers. Six were borrowed from Sicily by Edward Preble for this purpose. President Jefferson and others saw these vessels as a means of obtaining a coastal defence fleet for minimal investment in money and men. From 1803 to 1806, some 272 of these vessels were authorised by Congress. A total of 176 were completed, with fifteen of the total built on the Ohio River: Cincinnati and Marietta, Ohio, Eddyville and Louisville, Kentucky and Charleston, [West] Virginia. Six attempted the voyage to the Mediterranean; five arrived. Many were active during the War of 1812. Several were in Commodore Barney's flotilla, which in August 1814 was burned to prevent capture by the British invasion force which attacked Washington, DC.

They were built to several different designs, typically over 50ft in length and around 17ft broad, with 4-5ft in the hold. They were usually armed with two 24pdrs, on the centreline fore and aft. Some carried a pair of cannon mounted on a circular pivoting platform amidships, so that the recoil from one would swing the second gun into the firing position.

There was a major drawback to the entire concept of mounting large guns in a small vessel: firing the gun in broadside tended to capsize the boat or at least disrupt accurate aim. The result of this was that later designs incorporated guns mounted for forward or astern fire only. Most were out of service by 1815.

(Ref: Chapelle, pp190ff; Spencer Tucker, *The Jeffersonian Gunboat Navy*, University of South Carolina Press, 1996.)

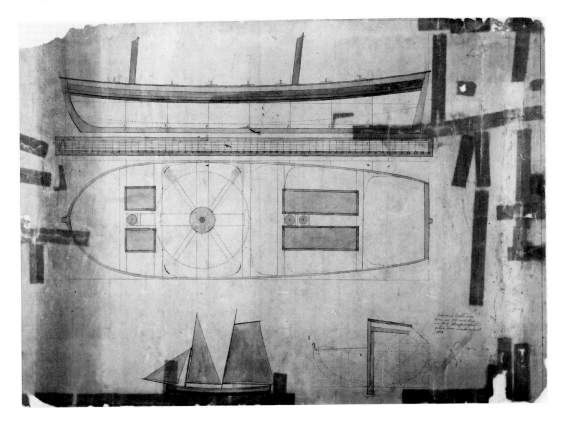

Draught of the Gunboats *Nos 29-37*, drawn at the request of Edward Preble about 1804. [National Archives NH 80-7-19A]

Revenue Cutters

War of 1812

As with the Quasi-War cutters, little concrete is known concerning design and construction of the War of 1812 vessels. The following amounts to most of the statistical information surviving for these ships.

Active, possibly chartered vessel, served 1812-1817.

Commodore Barry, 6 guns, 98 tons, served 1812, captured 3 August 1812.

Eagle, 130 tons?, 6 guns, served 1809-1814, captured August 1814.

Gallatin, served 1807-1813, destroyed by accident April 1813 at Charleston, SC.

James Madison, built at Baltimore 1807, captured British brig *Shamrock*; captured November 1812. (Plans thought to be of this vessel have proved to be otherwise.)

Jefferson, served 1802-1817, captured two British vessels.

Mercury, served 1807-1820, Ocracoke, North Carolina.

Surveyor, schooner, built at Baltimore 1807, 68ft x 19ft 6in, 75 tons, captured June 1813.

Vigilant, schooner, built at Newport, RI 1812, 60ft 7in x 18ft 9in, out of service 1842.

Mexican War, 1846-1848

The Revenue Service provided eleven vessels in co-operation with the navy and army, five of which were steamers. Of the six sailing vessels, four were topsail schooners of the *Morris* class, dimensions: 73ft 4in x 20ft 6in x 7ft 4in (design): these were *Morris*, *Oliver Wolcott* and possibly *Woodbury* and *Van Buren*.

Ewing, schooner, built Baltimore 1841, 91ft 6in x 22ft 9in, 170 tons, 8 guns.

Forward, schooner (brigantine?), built Washington, DC 1842, 89ft x 21ft 2in, 5 guns, sold 1865.

Levi Woodbury, schooner, built Baltimore 1837, *Morris* class?, 5 guns, sold 1847.

Morris, schooner, built New York Navy Yard 1830, *Morris* class, up to 6 guns, driven ashore 1846.

Oliver Wolcott, schooner, built New York Navy Yard 1831, *Morris* class, up to 6 guns, sold 1851.

Van Buren, schooner, built Baltimore 1839, possibly *Morris* class, up to 6 guns, sold June,1847.

Ref: US Coast Guard *Record of Movements* (CG Historian's Office), and Canney, *US Coast Guard and Revenue Cutters, 1790-1935*. National Archives RG 26 (Coast Guard and Revenue Service Records) and RG 36 (Customs Records).

Ship Construction, Dimensions and Service

Name	Builder Location	Laid down – Launched – Commissioned	Dimensions (feet-inches); Tonnage	Fate (day-month-year)
CONTINENTAL NAVY				
Randolph	Wharton/Humphreys Philadelphia	1775-10.7.76- 2.77	132-9pp x 34-6 x 18; ?t	Destroyed 17.3. 78
Hancock	Greenleaf/Cross Newburyport, MA	1776-10.7.76- 5.77	136-7 x 35-6 x 11-0½; 763t	Captured 8.7.77
Raleigh	Hackett/Hill/Paul Portsmouth, NH	21.3.76- 21.5.76-8.77	131-5 x 34 x 11; 697t	Captured 28.9.78
Warren	Talman Providence, RI	1776-15.5.76-12.76	132-1 x 34-5½ x 11; ?t	Burned 14.8.79
Washington	Eyre Philadelphia	1776-7.8.76-Never	?	Scuttled/ burned 1778
Virginia	Wells Baltimore	1776-12.8.76-1777	126-4 x 34-10 x 10-5½; 682t	Captured 31.3.78
Effingham	Grice Philadelphia	1776-10.31.76-Never	124-?	Scuttled/ burned 1778
Trumbull	Cotton Portland, CT	1776-5.9.76-5.80	?	Captured 9.8.81
Providence	Bowers Providence, RI	1776-18.5.76-12.76	126-7 x 33-10; 632t	Captured 12.5.80
Delaware	Coates Philadelphia	1776-12.7.76-3.77	119 x 32-11eb x 9-9; 563t	Captured 27.9.77
Boston	Cross Newburyport, MA	1776-3.6.76-1777	114-3 x 32 x 10-3; 514t	Captured 12.5.80
Montgomery	Burling Poughkeepsie, NY	7.3.76?-4.11.76-Never	?	Burned 7.10.77
Alliance	Hackett Portsmouth, NH	1777-28.4.78-1778	151pp x 36 x 12-6; 900t	Sold 3.6.85
Confederacy	Huntington Thames River, CT	1777-8.11.78-4.79	154-9pp x 37 x 12-3; 971t	Captured 15.4.81
Bourbon	Cotton Portland, CT	1779-31.7.83-Never	?	Sold 9.83
Ranger	Hackett Portsmouth, NH	1.77-10.5.77-11.77	116 x 34 x 13-6; 308t	Captured 12.5.80
Saratoga	Wharton & Humphreys Philadelphia	12.79-10.4.80-8.80	68 x 25-4 x 12; 150t	Lost 18.3.81

Name	Builder Location	Laid down – Launched – Commissioned	Dimensions (feet-inches); Tonnage	Fate (day-month-year)
America	Hackett Portsmouth, NH	5.77-5.11.82-Never	182-6ud x 59-6 x 23; 1982t	To France 3.9.82

FRIGATES 1794-1854

Name	Builder Location	Laid down – Launched – Commissioned	Dimensions (feet-inches); Tonnage	Fate (day-month-year)
Constitution	Hartt, Claghorn Boston	11.94-21.10.97-22.7.98	175 x 43-6 x 23-6; 1576t	In Comm, Boston
United States	Humphreys Philadelphia	12.94-10.5.97-11.7.98	175 x 43-6 x 23-6; 1576t	BU 1865
President	Cheeseman New York	?—10.4.00-5.9.00?	175 x 43-6 x 23-6; 1576t	Captured 15.1.15
Constellation	Stodder Baltimore	1795-7.9.97-26.6.98	163-3pp x 40 x 20; 1265t	BU 1854
Congress	Hackett Portsmouth, NH	1795-15.8.99-12.99	163-3pp x 40 x 20; 1265t	BU 1836
Chesapeake	Fox Norfolk, VA	10.12.98-2.12.99-22.5.00	152-6pp x 40 x 14; 1244t	Captured 1.6.13
Essex	E Briggs Salem, MA	13.4.99-30.9.99-12.99	140pp x 37 x 12-3; 850t	Captured 28.3.14
Philadelphia	Humphreys, Hutton, & Delavane Philadelphia	11.98-28.11.99-4.00	157pp x 39 x 13-6; 1240t	Captured 31.10.04
New York	Peck & Carpenter New York City	8.98-24.4.00-10.00	144-2pp x 37 x 11-9; 1130t	Laid up 1804
Boston	Hartt Boston	22.8.98-20.5.99-6.99	134pp x 34-6 x 11-6; 700t	Burned 24.8.14
John Adams	Pritchard Charleston, SC	?—5.6.99-25.8.99	127-9gd x 33-3eb x 16-10; 544t	BU 1829
Adams	Jackson & Sheffield Brooklyn, NY	30.7.98-8.6.99-9.99	113gd x 34 x 10-9; 530t	Burned 3.9.14
General Greene	Talman & DeWolf Warren, RI	8.98-21.1.99-6.99	124-3gd x 34-8 x 17-3; 655t	Burned 24.8.14
Insurgent	Lorient	11.91-27.4.93-6.93; USN:9.2.99	149gd x 37-5eb x 11-9; 950t	Lost 8.00
Macedonian	Woolwich DY	5.09-2.6.10; USN 25.10.12-Comm 4.13	156pp x 38-9 x 13-6; 1325t	BU 1829
Guerriere	Grice Philadelphia	1813-20.6.14-5.15	175pp x 44-6 x 13-8; 1511t	BU 1841
Columbia	Washington NYd	1813-not completed	175pp x 44-6 x 13-8; ?t	Burned 24.8.14
Java	Flannigan & Parsons Baltimore, MD	1813-4.1.14-8.15	175pp x 44-6 x 13-8; 1511t	BU 1842
Brandywine	Washington NYd	20.9.21-16.6.25-25.8.25	175pp x 45 x 14-4; 1708t	Burned 3.9.64
Potomac	Washington NYd	9.8.19-22.3.22-15.6.31	175pp x 45 x 13-4; 1708t	Sold 24.5.77

Name	Builder Location	Laid down–Launched –Commissioned	Dimensions (feet-inches); Tonnage	Fate (day-month-year)
Columbia	Washington NYd	11.25-9.3.36-5.38	175pp x 45 x 13-4; 1708t	Scuttled 20.4.61
Raritan	Philadelphia NYd	9.20-13.6.43-1.12.43	175pp x 45 x 13-4; 1708t	Scuttled 20.4.61
Savannah	Brooklyn NYd	7.20-24.5.42-15.10.43	175pp x 45 x 13-4; 1708t	Sold 9.27.83
Cumberland	Boston NYd	1825-24.5.42-11.43	175pp x 45 x 13-4; 1708t	Sunk 8.3.62
St Lawrence	Norfolk NYd	1826-25.3.47-17.8.48	175pp x 45 x 13-4; 1708t	Sold 31.12.75
Sabine	Brooklyn NYd	1823-2.12.55-23.8.58	190pp x 45 x 13-4; 1708t	Sold 23.9.83
Santee	Portsmouth NYd	8.21-16.2.55-8.6.61	190pp x 45 x 13-4: 1708t	Sold 29.7.1912
Hudson	Smith & Dimon New York	1825-18.11.25-27.9.28	177-10pp x 45 x 13-8; 1728t	Sold 4.6.44
Macedonian	Norfolk NYd	28.2.33-1.11.36-10.37	164pp x 41 x 18; 1341t	Sold 31.12.75
Congress	Portsmouth NYd	6.1.39-8.16.41-5.7.42	179pp x 46-6 x 15-5; 1867t	Sunk 8.3.62

SHIPS OF THE LINE

Name	Builder Location	Laid down–Launched –Commissioned	Dimensions (feet-inches); Tonnage	Fate (day-month-year)
Franklin	Humphreys, Penrose Philadelphia	1815-25.8.15-1815	187-11pp x 50 x 19-9; 2257t	BU 1853
Independence	Hartt & Barker Charlestown NYd	18.8.3-20.6.14-7.15	188pp x 50 x 20; 2259t	Sold 1914
Washington	Hartt & Badger Portsmouth NYd	3.14-1.10.14-28.8.15	188pp x 50 x 20; 2259t	BU 1843
Columbus	Washington NYd	6.16-1.3.19-7.9.19	191-10pp x 52 x 21-10; 2480t	Burned 20.4.61
Ohio	Eckford New York NYd	11.17-30.5.20-11.10.38	197-2pp x 53-10 x ?; 2757t	Sold 27.9.83
North Carolina	Philadelphia NYd	6.16-7.9.20-18.12.24	196-3pp x 53 x 21-8; 2633t	Sold 10.1.67
Delaware	Norfolk NYd	8.17-21.10.20-2.28	196-3pp x 53-10 x 21-8; 2633t	Burned 20.4.61
Vermont	Boston NYd	9.18-14.9.48-30.1.62	196-3pp x 53-10 x 21-8; 2633t	Sold 1902
New Hampshire (ex-*Alabama*)	Portsmouth NYd	1.6.19-23.1.64-11.5.64	196-3pp x 53-10 x 21-8; 2633t	Burned 23.5.1921
Pennsylvania	Philadelphia NYd	11.22-7.18.37-11.37	210pp x 56-9 x 23; 3100t	Burned 20.4.61

SLOOPS OF WAR

Name	Builder Location	Laid down–Launched –Commissioned	Dimensions (feet-inches); Tonnage	Fate (day-month-year)
Merrimack	Cross & Clark Newburyport, MA	9.7.98-12.10.98-1.99	467t	Sold 1801
Maryland	Wm Price Baltimore	7.98-3.6.99-9.99	114gd x 30-4eb x 12dr; 380t	Sold 1801
Patapsco	DeRochbrune Baltimore	1799-20.6.99-1799	?418 4/95t CH	Sold 1801
Portsmouth	Hackett Portsmouth, NH	?-11.10.98-1.99	593t	Sold 1801
Trumbull	Howland Norwich CT	?—?-3.00?	400t	Sold 1801
Connecticut	Overton Middletown, CT	1798-?-10.99	492t	Sold 1801

Name	Builder Location	Laid down – Launched – Commissioned	Dimensions (feet-inches); Tonnage	Fate (day-month-year)
Warren	Webster Salisbury, MA	?-26.9.99-10.99	385t	Sold 1801
Hornet	Price Baltimore	?-28.6.05-10.05	105pp x 29-7 x 14; 440^{64}/$_{94}$t CH	Lost 10.9.29
Wasp	Washington NYd	1805-4.21.06-5.07	105-7pp x 30-11 x ?; 450t	Captured 10.18.12
Ontario	Kemp Baltimore	1813-1813-10.25.13	117-11pp x 31-6 x 14-6; 509t	Sold 15.7.56
Erie	Kemp Baltimore	1813-3.11.13-3.14	117-11pp x 31-6 x 14-6; 509t	BU 1821
Argus	Washington NYd	1813-		Burned 24.8.14
Erie (2nd)	New York NYd	1821-?-1822-	121-11pp x 32-6 x 14-9; 559t	BU 1840?
Wasp	Cross & Merrill Newburyport, MA	1813-9.21.13-5.14	117-11pp x 31-6 x 14-2; 509t	Lost 10.14
Peacock	Brown New York	26.7.13-27.9.13-3.14	119pp x 31-6 x 14-2; 509t	BU 1828
Frolic	Barker Boston	1813-11.9.13-2.14	119-2½pp x 31-5½ x 14-6; 509t	Captured 20.4.14
Falmouth	Boston NYd	5.12.26-3.11.27-1.28	127-6pp x 33-9 x 15-3; 703t	Sold 7.11.63
Lexington	New York NYd	1825-9.3.26-12.6.26	127-pp x 33-6 x 15-3; 691t	Sold 1860
Warren	Boston NYd	1.6.25-29.11.26-14.1.27	127pp x 33-6 x 15-3; 691t	Sold 1.1.63
Natchez	Norfolk NYd	1827-8.3.27-7.27	127pp x 33-6 x 15-3; 691t	BU 1840
Boston	Boston NYd	13.5.25-15.10.26-1.26	127pp x 34 x 15-3; 700t	Lost 13.11.46
Vincennes	New York NYd	1825-27.4.26-27.8.26	127pp x 34 x 15-3; 700t	Sold 5.10.67
Fairfield	New York NYd	1828-28.6.28-8.28	127pp x 34 x 15-3; 700t	BU 1852
St Louis	Washington NYd	12.2.27-16.8.28-20.12.28	127pp x 34 x 15-3; 700t	Sold 5.6.1907
Vandalia	Philadelphia NYd	1828-26.8.28-6.11.28	127pp x 34 x 15-3; 700t	BU 1872
Concord	Portsmouth NYd	19.3.27-24.9.27-7.5.30	127pp x 34 x 15-3; 700t	Lost 2.10.43
John Adams (2nd)	Norfolk NYd	12.28-16.10.30-5.31	127pp x 34 x 15-3; 700t	Sold 5.10.67
Peacock (2nd)	New York NYd	1828-30.9.28-1.11.28	118pp x 31-6 x 14-10; 559t	Lost 18.7.41
Cyane	Boston NYd	1837-2.12.37-6.38	132-3pp x 35-3 x ?; 792t	Sold 30.7.87
Levant	New York NYd	1837-28.12.37-17.3.38	132-3pp x 35-3 x ?; 792t	Lost 9.60
Dale	Philadelphia NYd	1839-8.11.39-11.12.40	117-7pp x 32 x 15; 566t	Sold 1921
Decatur	New York NYd	1838-9.4.39-3.40	117-7pp x 32 x 15; 566t	Sold 17.8.65
Yorktown	Norfolk NYd	1838-17.6.39-12.40	117-7pp x 32 x 15; 566t	Wrecked 6.9.50
Preble	Portsmouth NYd	4.38-13.6.39-6.40	117-7pp x 32 x 15; 566t	Burned 27.4.63
Marion	Boston NYd	1838-24.4.39-4.10.39	117-7pp x 32 x 15; 566t	BU 1871
Saratoga	Portsmouth NYd	8.41-26.7.42-7.1.43	146-4pp x 35-3 x 16-3½; 882t	Sold 1907
Albany	New York NYd	1843-27.6.46-6.11.46	147-11pp x 38-6 x 17-9; 1042t	Lost 9.54
Portsmouth	Portsmouth NYd	15.6.43-23.10.43-10.11.44	151-10pp x 37-3 x 16-9; 1022t	Sold 12.7.1915

Name	Builder Location	Laid down – Launched – Commissioned	Dimensions (feet-inches); Tonnage	Fate (day-month-year)
Jamestown	Norfolk NYd	1843-16.9.44-25.1.45	163-5pp x 35 x 16-2; 988t	Sold 7.10.1915
Germantown	Philadelphia NYd	9.7.43-8.21.46-3.9.47	150pp x 36 x 16-8; 982t	Burned 20.4.61
Plymouth	Boston NYd	1843-11.10.43-4.44	147pp x 37-3 x 17-2; 974t	Captured 20.4.61
St Mary's	Washington NYd	1843-24.11.44-13.12.44	150pp x 36-6 x 16-6; 958t	Sold 8.08
Constellation	Norfolk NYd	25.6.53-26.8.54-28.7.55	176pp x 41 x 21; 1265t	At Baltimore

BRIGS AND SCHOONERS

Name	Builder Location	Laid down – Launched – Commissioned	Dimensions (feet-inches); Tonnage	Fate (day-month-year)
Pickering	Orlando, Merrill Newburyport, MA	1798-	58k x 20 x 9? 187t	Lost 8.00
Scammel	J K Hackett Portsmouth	1798-11.8.98-?	58k x 20 x 9-6 131t CH	Sold 12.01
Eagle	Brown Philadelphia	4.8.98-?-?	77gd x 23-8 x 9-2; 143t CH	Sold 17.6.01
Virginia	Hampton, VA	?	70k x 18-10 x 8-6; ?	Returned 1799
Pinckney	Pritchard Charleston, SC	1798	62k x 23 x 10-6; 195t	Sold 4.00
Enterprise	Spencer, MD	1799-?-12.99	60k x 22-6 x 9-6; 135t	Wrecked 9.77.9.23
Experiment	Price Baltimore	1799-?-11.99	60k x 22-6 x 9-6; 135t	Sold 1801
Argus	Hartt Boston	12.5.03-21.8.03-9.03	94-9pp x 27-4 x 12-8; 299t CH	Captured 14.8.13
Syren	Hutton Philadelphia	1803-6.8.03-27.8.03	93-3½pp x 27 x 12-6; 250t	Captured 12.7.14
Vixen	Price Baltimore	1803-25.6.03-3.8.03	84-7pp x 22-6 x 9-6; 170t	Captured 22.11.12
Nautilus	Spencer Baltimore	Purchase 5.03	87-6dk x 23-8 x 9-10; 105t	Captured 17.7.12
Ferret	Norfolk?	Comm 4.18.09	73dk x 23-8 x 7-8; 148t	Captured 17.7.13
Chippewa	Caleb Carr Warren, RI	1814-4.15-7.15	108 x 29-9 x 13-9?; 410t	Wrecked 12.12.16
Boxer	Churchill Middletown, CT	1814-5.15-?	115k x 29eb x 12-6; 370t	Lost 25.10.17
Saranac	Churchill Middletown, CT	1814-1815-12.15	115k x 29eb x 12-6; 360t	Sold 1818
Grampus	Washington	1820-21.8.21-1821	92-6pp x 24-6 x 9-6; 172t	Lost 3.43
Alligator	Boston	1820-2.11.20-4.21	86pp x 24-9 x 10-4; 198t	Wrecked 23.11.22
Dolphin	Philadelphia	1820-23.6.21-7.10.21	86pp x 24-9 x 10-4; 198t	Sold 2.12.35
Porpoise	Portsmouth	16.8.20-2.12.20-30.3.21	86pp x 24-9 x 10-4; 198t	Wrecked 2.11.33
Shark	Washington	1820-17.5.21-6.21	86pp x 24-9 x 10-4; 198t	Wrecked 10.9.46
Boxer	Boston	1831-22.11.31-1832	88pp x 23-6 x 10; 194t	Sold 7.8.48
Enterprise	New York	1831-26.10.31-15.12.31	88pp x 23-6 x 10; 194t	Sold 28.10.44
Experiment	(Annesley) Washington	1831-14.3.32-1832	88-6pp x 23-6 x 9; 176t	Sold 16.5.48

Name	Builder Location	Laid down–Launched –Commissioned	Dimensions (feet-inches); Tonnage	Fate (day-month-year)
Dolphin	New York	1836-17.6.36-6.9.36	88pp x 25 x 11; 224t	Burned 20.4.61
Porpoise	Boston	1836-31.5.36-25.8.36	88pp x 25 x 11; 224t	Lost 9.54
Truxtun	Norfolk	12.41-16.4.42-18.2.43	100pp x 27-4 x 13; 331t	Wrecked 14.8.46
Perry	Norfolk	18.2.43-9.5.43-13.10.43	105pp x 25 x 11-6; 280t	Sold 10.8.65
Bainbridge	Boston	1842-26.4.42-16.12.42	100pp x 25 x 11; 259t	Lost 21.8.63
Somers	New York	1842-4.16.42-5.12.42	100pp x 25 x 11; 259t	Lost 12.8.46
Lawrence	Culley Baltimore	1843-1.8.43-19.9.43	109pp x 26-2 x 13-3; 364t	Sold 1846

LAKES VESSELS

Name	Builder Location	Laid down–Launched –Commissioned	Dimensions (feet-inches); Tonnage	Fate (day-month-year)
Oneida	Eckford, Bergh Oswego, NY	1808-31.3.09-1809	85-6pp x 23eb x 8; 243t	Sold 5.25
Madison	Eckford Sacketts Harbor	?-26.11.12-4.13	112k x 32-6 x 11-6; 580t	Sold 30.4.25
General Pike	Eckford Sacketts Harbor	4.9.13-6.12.13-7.13	145pp x 37 x 15; 875t	Sold 30.4.25
Sylph	Eckford Sacketts Harbor	26.7.13-18.8.13-8.13	?	Sold 30.4.25
Jefferson	Eckford Sacketts Harbor	2.14-7.4.14-1814	121-6pp x 31-6 x 14-6; 500t	Sold 30.4.25
Jones	Eckford Sacketts Harbor	2.14-10.4.14-1814	121-6pp x 31-6 x 14-6; 500t	Sold 30.4.25
Plattsburgh	Brown Sacketts Harbor	1814-not completed	185k x 46-?; 1749t?	
Superior	Eckford Sacketts Harbor	11.2.14-1.5.14-1814	180pp x 43 x ?; 1580t	Sold 30.4.25
Mohawk	Eckford Sacketts Harbor	7.4.14-11.6.14-1814	155pp x 37-6 x 15-6; 1350t	Sold 30.4.25
Chippewa	Brown Storrs Harbor	5.10.14-not completed	204pp x 56; 2805t	Sold 1823
New Orleans	Brown Sacketts Harbor	5.10.14-not completed	204pp x 56; 2805t	Sold 1883\
Niagara	Brown Lake Erie	3.13-5.13-4.8.13	110pp x 30 x 9; 493t	Sold 12.7.25
Lawrence	Brown Lake Erie	3.13-24.5.13-5.8.13	110pp x 30 x 9; 493t	Sold 12.7.25
Saratoga	Brown Lake Champlain	7.3.14-11.4.14-1814	143pp x 36-6 x 12-6; 734t	Sold 1824
Eagle	Brown Lake Champlain	29.7.14-11.8.14-6.9.14	128 x 32; 500t	Sold 1825

NB. dk = length on deck; eb = extreme breadth; gd = length on gundeck; pp = between perpendiculars; CH = Custom House Measure; DY = Dockyard (British); NYd = Navy Yard (US).

Dimensions and Sizes of Materials for Building a Frigate of Forty-four Guns

	ft	ins
Length of the gun deck, from the rabbet of the stem to post	174	10½
Length of the keel for tonnage, allowing three-fifths of beam from twelve inches before the rabbet of the stem at the breadth line from the point where the three-fifths strike on the keel, to the rabbet of the post	145	
Moulded breadth of beam in the extreme part of the ship, which is at the upper edge of the second wale, and three and a half feet before the thirds of the keel, or one hundred feet two inches before the rabbet of the post	43	6
Height of the wing transom, above the rabbet of the keel	25	8½
Height of the lower deck transom, above the rabbet of the keel	20	9
Top side tumbles home amidships, at the under part of midship plank or covering board	3	
Height of the lower deck, in the side above the rabbet, at	16	11
Plank on lower deck beams		3½
Height between gun and lower deck	6	4
Gun deck plank		4
Height between decks, from gun to upper deck	7	
Upper deck plank		3
(?) amidship		3
Plank sheer or covering board		4½
To top of plank sheer	31	9
Height amidships of lower edge of the wale	17	11
(?) strakes of wales, ten inches wide are		5
Height from the top of the wale to port sill	3	3½
Height of the port	2	11
Height from the top of the port to the top of the plank sheer	2	7½
Height from top of rabbet to top of plank sheer	31	9
Depth in the hold taken from the strake next the limber strake	14	3
Height of the port sills on the quarter deck and forecastle	1	10
Height on the gun deck	2	4
Height fore and aft	3	5
Height up and down	2	11
Ports- Distance between ports	7	5
After port, aft side, before the rabbet of the post	6	4
Fifteen ports each side, besides the bridle or bow ports, if any		
Height of gun deck on the post, from a square line above the rabbet of the keel	27	
Height of the gun deck on the stem, from a square line above the rabbet of the keel	24	10
(?) -d raising at two-fifths of the beam, for the breadth of the floor	2	9
Room and space	2	2
Height of the breadth line		
- amid ships		-
- on the stem. This line is the upper edge of the second wale, from below all fore and aft		-
- on the transom		-

Drifts— Quarter deck and forecastle drifts, fourteen inches wide and three and a half inches thick

Flush drift, twelve inches wide and four inches thick

String, or first moulding strake above the ports, fourteen inches wide, and four and a half inches thick

*Keel—*Of good sound white oak, in three pieces; the middle piece to be not less than thirty feet, if to be had; scarfs not less than twelve feet, to be kept clear of the main and fore steps; sided in the midships eighteen inches; at the stem and post seventeen inches; and as deep as can be had; the scarfs all to be tabled and bolted with five bolts, one and one-eighth inches diameter; false keel six inches thick, but not to be put on until after the floor and keelson bolts are drove and riveted

*Keelson—*Sided eighteen inches amidships, and sixteen inches fore and aft end, and sixteen inches deep; scarfs not within fifteen feet of keel scarfs, or main or foremast steps; upper keelson eighteen by fifteen inches deep, to be hooped and joggled into the lower one, all fore and aft; scarfs clear of all other scarfs at least ten feet, to be bolted with one and three-eighths inch bolts through every timber and one in every cross-chock of one and one-eighth inches diameter

*Stem—*In two pieces, if to be had; the lower one of good white oak, sided seventeen inches, and moulded not less than twelve inches clear of the rabbet; scarfs not less than four feet, to be tabled and bolted with three bolts, one and one-eighth inches in diameter

*Apron—*Sided from twenty-eight to thirty inches at the upper end; and as the piece will work below, moulded at the upper end fourteen inches, and at the lower end seventeen inches

*Stern post—*Eighteen inches square at the head, sided seventeen inches below by three and a half feet fore and aft, including false post, and ten inches thick on the aft side, at the keel, to be fitted for a crooked headed rudder

*Inner Post—*To be twelve inches, fore and aft, to run from the transom to the keel; to be of live oak, sided at head from twenty to twenty-four inches, and at the heel, twelve inches

*Night Heads—*Sided from sixteen to eighteen inches; moulded twelve inches at head, and fourteen inches below

*Hawse-pieces—*To be four in number; sided eighteen inches, and to be bolted with one and one-eighth inch bolts into each other;

their heels, if possible, to run down below the lower deck breast hook

*Bow-timbers—*Sided twelve inches, and as long as possible; their heels well secured into the dead-wood; to be in number on each side as per draught

*Hawse-holes—*Two on each side; fifteen inches in diameter, and fourteen inches on a square between each other

*Wing Transom—*Twenty-nine feet long on the aft side; moulded and sided twenty-two inches to round up, and aft six inches; all the others sided fourteen inches ; the lower deck transom moulded as broad as can conveniently be had, for the better securing the ends of the deck plank; two bolts of one and one-eighth inches in diameter in the deck transom and all above it; all below, bolted with one bolt of one and one-quarter inches in diameter

*Fashion-pieces—*Two pair, sided twelve inches and moulded fifteen inches on the cant, as hereafter directed

*Deadwood, forward—*To secure the scarf of the stem and keel together, sided the same as the apron at the heel; at the after end twenty-four inches, and not less than twenty inches moulded over the scarf of the keel, and to run sufficiently aft; midship dead-wood fourteen inches broad and nine inches thick, to run from the deadwood forward to the stern-post knee; well fayed on the keel

*Rabbet of the main keel—*To be cut one inch below the upper edge; the garboard strakes to fay well to the deadwood all fore and aft; the deadwood to be tarred and papered with good, thick, substantial tarred sheathing paper, in order to prevent the ship from sinking if she should lose her keel

*Stern post knees—*Two good ones; the lower one to be as long as possible

*Floor and raising timbers—*Of good white oak, sided twelve and a half inches; moulded at the floor sirmark fifteen inches, and in the throat, from the top of the deadwood, twenty-one inches; to be bolted through the keel with one and three-eighths inch bolts; these bolts should be put as near the side of the keel as possible, in order to give room on the other side for the keelson bolts; one floor bolted near the larboard side of the keel, the other on the starboard side; the timber all to be double bolted from the foremast to within ten feet of the mizzenmast

Lower Futtocks—Of live oak, sided twelve inches in the midships, and something smaller at the fore and after ends of the ship, to butt against the side of the dead-wood amidships; to have cross-chocks fayed on the dead-wood, and their heels to be bolted through the keelson and keel with one and one-eighth inch bolts

Middle and upper futtocks and top timbers—Sided eleven and a half inches; top timbers moulded at the gunwale seven inches; at the port sill nine inches; all the other timber sized by a diminishing line from the port sill to the floor sirmark

Timbers, framed—Floor-timbers, lower futtocks, middle and upper, and top timbers, all to be framed in forms, and bolted with three bolts one and one-eighth inch square in each scarf, except the lower futtocks and floors, which should have one and one-fourth inch bolts. These timbers must be faced fair and true: for if they are not out of winding, it will be impossible to level the timbers with any truth

Main Wales—six strakes on each side, seven inches thick and ten inches wide

Black strakes—five in number. The first and second five and one-half inches thick; the third, five and one-fourth inches; the fourth, five inches; and the fifth, four and one-half inches thick, by ten inches wide; the upper edge of the black strake to be mitred down to a level, in order to carry the water out of the seam; plank between the black strake and the string, to be three and one-half inches thick

Thick work under the wales—first strake six inches thick; and second, five and one-half inches; third, of five inches; and fourth, of four and one-half inches; running plank, in the bottom, four inches thick; to be not less than six feet scarf, not less than four strakes between every two butts on the same timber; the seams to be made all a little out-gauged, and great care must be taken to bevel both edges of the plank that comes together alike; for, if one edge is hewn standing, the other must be under, which makes bad work, the plank with the under bevelling will caulk off

Bilge strakes outside—one, of six inches thick; two, of five and one-half ditto; two, of four and one half ditto, one each side, the middle strake to cover the butts of the timbers equally inside and out, to be reduced, fore and after ends, the same as the running plank

INSIDE WORK

Limber strakes—two on each side, six inches thick, and fourteen inches wide, bilge strakes three on each side, six inches thick, and fourteen inches wide, to be bolted through the outside bilge strake, in every third timber, with one inch bolts

Running Ceiling Plank—four inches thick

Lower deck clamps—two strakes on each side, five inches thick, and one strake four and a half inches, all hooked and joggled into each other, with hooks not less than two inches, reduced at fore and after ends

Steps of masts—the fore step to be placed between two breast hooks; the main step to be left so as to be set either forward or aft, as occasion may require; mizzen step to be two crochets; the arms of which ought to be run up as high as possible

Pillars or stanchions—three tiers under the gun deck, and one under the upper deck, made to shift

Breast hooks—of live oak, five in the hold, including the deck hooks, from eighteen to twenty feet long, if to be had, and bolted in every timber with bolts of one and one-fourth inch in diameter, as well as through the stem; and two between decks, secured as above , the deck breast hooks moulded as broad as possible, in order to give good hold for the deck plank

Transom riders—two on each side, under the lower deck, eighteen feet long; and sided twelve inches, bolted in every other timber with one and one-eighth inch bolts

Diagonal riders—six pair on each side, in the three principal pieces, with two shorter ones to complete the pair, tabled and bolted together with six iron bolts one and one-fourth inch square in each scarf, and three in the short pieces to bolted through the bottom plank, at every two feet, with one and one eighth inch copper bolts, the two midship ones to butt against each other; the foremost of the two midship riders to be cut with a bird's mouth, and to fit under the eighth beam from forward; the after one of the midship ones to be cut and fixed in the same manner under the eighth beam from aft the other riders, to be the distance of two beams apart, and fitted in the same manner, to be kept the same distance aft and forward at heel, as they are at the head, to be tenoned and bolted into the keelson

Lower deck beams—of the best heart pitch pine, sided sixteen inches, and moulded fourteen inches; the longest beam to spring six inches, and the rest by the same mould

Lodging knees – sided ten inches, body to reach the next beam and arm, six feet hooked into the beam; to lay two inches below the upper edge of the beam for the waterways, and thick stuff to joggle down, to be bolted with seven bolts one and one-fourth inch diameter

Dagger knees – sided eleven inches; body nine feet long; and arm seven feet, the arm hooked into the beam, and bolted with eight bolts one and one-fourth inch diameter

Lower deck transom knees – sided twelve inches, body ten and one-half feet long; arm seven feet, and bolted with thirteen bolts one and one-fourth inch diameter

Carlings – in three tier, six by nine inches, of white oak

Ledges – five by six inches, two between each beam

Mast carlings – for the main and foremast, ten by thirteen inches, to be kneed with four good knees; mizzen carling six by twelve inches, and kneed in the same manner; all of which pieces to be of live oak, and bolted with inch and seven-eighths bolts; gun deck carlings the same size, and secured in the same manner

Spar beams – one of live oak on each side of the main hatch, tabled, kneed and bolted, on the foreside of the beam, on the after part of the main hatch, twelve inches by fourteen; and for the gun deck the same

Solid waterways – of good long substantial white oak, worked with a feint hollow, rabbeted one and one-quarter inch above the deck, allowing two inches to be let down upon the beams; a good six inch oak strake joggled two inches into the edge of the waterway, and into and over the beams and ledges for the gun deck; a five and a half inch strake for the lower deck, and a five inch strake for the upper deck, all joggled in the same way, and bolted through the side every four feet, and through every beam, with one and one-eighth inch bolts, upper deck deck with inch bolts

Thick strakes on lower deck – two strakes of white oak plank five and one-half inches thick and not less than ten inches wide, bolted and joggled into each other; and over and into the beams and ledges two inches, running all fore and aft along side of the hatches; two other strakes on each side, fitted as above, midway between the waterways and hatch strakes, a long white oak knee to be fayed at the end of each pair, to be joggled over two beams, well bolted to the bow and stem with one and seven-eighth inch bolts; and two other white oak knees, to run from

the mizzenmast to the stern post, joggled over and into each beam, to be let down on the beams sufficient for the ledges to frame into them; one other to reach from the stem to the foremast, worked in the same manner; the arm part of each knee to be will bolted through the stern and post with one and one-fourth inch bolts

Lower deck plank – to be three and one half inches thick, of the best heart pitch pine, clear of all defects whatever

Orlop deck – to be laid six feet two inches below the upper part of the lower deck; beams of the best heart pitch pine, sided twelve inches, and moulded ten inches, laid with two inch common plank, kneed with one good live oak knee at each end, bolted with inch bolts; it will be best to put the clamps on the ceiling three inches thick

Spirketings – two strakes on each side on lower deck; five inches thick, hooked and joggled into each other, fitting in plank between the list and clamps four inches thick

Gun deck clamps – two strakes on each side, five inches thick, and one of four and one-half inches, joggled into each other two inches

Gundeck beams – one under each port and one between; of the best heart pitch pine, as near as the hatchways and masts will admit, as per draught, sided eighteen inches, and moulded fifteen inches; all other beams to be laid directly over and under the same

Standard knees – twelve on each side on the lower deck, one to be fayed over each beam, the diagonal riders come under, and the others placed amidships, sided thirteen inches, body to reach the upper edge of gun deck clamps, the arm six feet long; and bolted with eight bolts one and one-fourth inch diameter

Gun deck lodging knees – Sided ten inches, body to reach the next beam, arm six feet long, bolted with seven bolts of one inch and a quarter diameter

Hanging knees – Seven feet body and six feet arm, sided eleven inches, bolted with eight bolts one inch and a quarter diameter; the arms of all knees to be hooked and joggled into their respective beams

Gun deck transom knees – Sided twelve inches, body twelve feet long, arm seven feet, bolted with twelve bolts one inch and a quarter diameter

Carlings – In three tiers, six by nine inches, of white oak

Ledges – Five by six inches, of white oak, two between each beam

Plank – Four inches thick, six feet from the side, of the best white oak, clear of all sap and other defects whatever, the rest to be laid of the best heart pitch pine, clear of all sap and other defects whatever

Spriketing – To reach the port sill; and five inches thick; all scarfs should be kept clear of the ports; sill butts will shifted

Filling-in plank – Between the spirketing and clamps, three inches thick

Wing transom knees – Sided thirteen inches, body fourteen feet long and arm eight feet, bolted with fourteen bolts, one inch and a quarter diameter

Thick strakes – On the gun deck two strakes white oak plank six inches thick, and not less than ten inches wide, bolted and joggled into each other, and over and into the beams and ledges two inches, running all fore and aft along side the hatches. Two other strakes on each side, fitted as above, midway between the waterway and hatch strakes

UPPER DECK

Clamps – Two strakes on each side, four inches thick, hooked and joggled into each other

Beams – Placed over the gun deck beams, sided thirteen and fourteen inches, and moulded, of the best heart pitch pine

Quarter deck transom – Ten by ten, one knee at each end, sided eight inches, body and arm six feet, and bolted with eight bolts one inch diameter

Lodging knees – Sided seven inches and a half, body to reach the next beam, arm five to four feet and a half, hooked and joggled into every beam, and bolted with seven bolts one inch diameter

Hanging knees – sided eight inches, body six feet and a half long, and arm five feet, bolted with eight bolts one inch diameter

Carlings – Three tiers, except where the long coamings are five by eight inches, white oak

Ledges – Four and a half by six, white oak, two between each beam

Mast coamings – to be of good white oak as well as the hatch coamings; those for the main and foremast should be at least six inches clear of the mast all around, in order to give room for the mast to play, and more particularly for heaving down; the mizzen partners need not exceed three inches clear

Plank for deck – Three inches thick, five feet of which must be laid with oak from the side, the rest of the best heart pitch pine

Long Coamings – Of heart pitch pine, ten by seventeen inches, to be kept wide enough apart to take down the boat and room alongside for the men to pass from the gun to the upper deck

Stemson – Of live oak, sided seventeen inches, and moulded ten inches, to shift the scarfs of stem and apron to reach the upper deck breast hook

Leaden scuppers – On each side on the gun deck, cut elliptical, four by six

Seat transom – Across the stern, the height of the port sill to be joggled into the counter timbers, nine inches thick, and kneed at each end with one iron knee, to fay all along under the gallery door, and long enough to receive three bolts before it of one inch diameter, the thwartship arm four feet, to be bolted with three bolts, one inch diameter

Counter timbers – Of live oak, sided at the lower part of the windows and heel eleven inches, and the upper end six inches, to be filled in from the lower part of the window to the wing transom with red cedar, except in the wake of the gun room ports

Cable bitts – Two pairs, of good tough strong white oak, twenty two inches square, and to taper below the lower deck beams to sixteen inches, cross pieces to be twenty-two inches fore and aft, and twenty inches deep, to have a standard knee against each bitt, sided fourteen inches, to run forward over three beams, and scored down over each two inches, the arm to run to the opposite side of the cross piece

Catheads – Sided twenty inches and moulded eighteen inches

Treenails – For the bottom, of the best heart locust, to drive after a one inch and three-eighths auger; for the wales and upper works, to drive after a one inch and a quarter auger; to be all planed to a moot, and not suffered to be overhauled afterwards

Specification for *Constitution* and sisters, transcribed as printed from *American State Papers: Naval Affairs, Vol 1, 1794,* pp10-13.

Notes

Fuller details of works quoted in the Footnotes will be found in the Bibliography.

Abbreviations for works quoted frequently in the Footnotes are as follows:

ASP: American State Papers, Naval Affairs
Chapelle: Unless otherwise specified any reference is to *The History of the American Sailing Navy*
DANFS: Dictionary of American Naval Fighting Ships
DBW: Naval Documents Related to the United States Wars with the Barbary Powers
HSP: Historical Society of Pennsylvania
NARA: National Archives and Records Administration
NDAR: Naval Documents of the American Revolution
NMM: National Maritime Museum
ORN: Official Records of the Union and Confederate Navies in the War of the Rebellion
PEM: Peabody Essex Museum
QWD: Naval Documents related to the Quasi-War Between the United States and France
RG: Record Group
USNA: US Naval Academy

CHAPTER 1
Navy-built Ships of the American Revolution

1 William M Fowler, Jr, *Rebels under Sail*, pp212-5.

2 George F Emmons, *Statistical History of the Navy of the United States*, pp127-169.

3 Frank C Mevers, 'Congress and the Navy: The Establishment and Administration of the American Revolutionary Navy by the Continental Congress, 1775-1784', p49.

4 Fowler, p220.

5 Robert Gardiner (ed), *The Line of Battle*, p38.

6 Mevers, p117.

7 Dimensions of 36-gun frigates by Wharton & Humphreys and Ayers: Josiah Fox Papers, PEM.

8 Ibid; Howard I Chapelle, *History of the American Sailing Navy*, pp63-5; NARA RG 19 Plan, *Randolph*, 34-4-45.

9 Edward L Beach, *The United States Navy*, pp11-13; *NDAR*, Vol 9, p274 (G Collier to Howe, 12 July 1777).

10 *NDAR*, Vol 9, p9.

11 *NDAR*, Vol 9, p247 ('Description of Continental Frigates . . .' enclosure, 9 July 1777, J Brisbane to Howe).

12 Mevers, pp111-3; Chapelle, pp67-70.

13 *NDAR*, Vol 9, p828 (Whipple to Morris, 28 August 1777); Vol 10, p849 (T Thompson to Marine Committee, 28 September 1777).

14 Mevers, pp115-6; *NDAR*, Vol 4, pp8-9.

15 K Jack Bauer and Stephen S Roberts, *Register of Ships of the US Navy, 1775-1990*, p5.

16 Mevers, pp115-9.

17 NMM, Plan of *Virginia*, Neg 2351/39.

18 Bauer & Roberts, p5.

19 Mevers, p116; Bauer & Roberts, p6; Chapelle, p74.

20 Mevers, p115; Chapelle, p74.

21 *NDAR*, Vol 10, p587 (Howe to P Stevens, 23 November 1777); Bauer & Roberts, p6; Chapelle, p74.

22 Bauer & Roberts, p6.

23 *NDAR*, Vol 9, p247 (Brisbane to Howe, 9 July 1777).

24 Ibid.

25 Dept to J Hackett, 4 April 1794: NARA M729 War Department Naval Records.

26 Mevers, p123.

27 *NDAR*, Vol 7, pp1221-2 (Journal of Conn Council of Safety, 17 February 1777).

28 NMM Neg 6175/35; also found in Josiah Fox Papers, PEM: he adds length on upper deck 162ft, and length of keel for tonnage 135ft.

29 NMM Negs 8255 & 8257.

30 NMM Neg 6175/35; Chapelle, pp83-5.

31 Mevers, p124.

32 Bauer & Roberts, p8.

33 Mevers, p120.

34 *NDAR*, Vol 7, p957 (Langdon to W Whipple, 15 January 1777).

35 *NDAR*, Vol 7, p58 (Langdon to J Hancock, 6 November 1776).

36 Mevers, p121.

37 Bauer & Roberts, p16; Chapelle, p86.

38 *NDAR*, Vol 10, p1092 (Jones to W Whipple, 11 December 1777).

39 Bauer & Roberts, p16.

40 George H Preble, *History of the United States Navy Yard, Portsmouth, NH*, pp14-17.

CHAPTER 2
The Frigates Constitution, United States, President, Constellation, Congress, Chesapeake

1 Quoted in *The United States Navy*, by Edward L Beach, p33.

2 Coletta, Paolo (ed), *American Secretaries of the Navy*, Vol 1, pp38-9.

3 Ibid, p54, note 55.

4 F Williams, 30 October 1790; Pierce Butler, 15 November 1791; and Samuel Hodgson, 4 January 1794, letters to Henry Knox: War Department Naval Records, NARA M729.

5 Joshua Humphreys to Robert Morris, 6 January 1793: J Humphreys Letterbook, HSP.

6 H Knox to John Wharton, 12 May 1794 and to Secretary of the Treasury, 12 May 1794: NARA M729.

7 Josiah Fox Papers, PEM; Howard I Chapelle, *The History of the American Sailing Navy*, pp125-6.

8 Letter and transcription, Fox Papers, PEM.

9 Knox to John Wharton, 12 May 1794: War Dept Naval Records M729.

10 Ibid, Fox to Humphreys, no date; 1794 critique of Humphreys' 44-gun frigate model, in Fox Papers, PEM.

11 Ibid, Fox Papers, PEM; Chapelle, pp121-2.

12 Chapelle, pp120-3; Fox Papers, PEM.

13 Humphreys to Morris, 6 January 1793, Humphreys Letter Book, HSP.

14 See Fox Papers, PEM; War Dept Naval Records (M729); Humphreys Letter Book, HSP.

15 Chapelle, pp163 & 177.

16 Thomas Truxtun, *Remarks, Instruction and Examples Related to the Lattitude & Longitude, also The Variations of the Compass . . . etc.* Appendix.

17 Chapelle, p123.

18 *American State Papers, Naval Affairs* (hereafter cited as *ASP*), Vol 1, p8 (Report of Joshua Humphreys, 23 December 1794).

19 *ASP*, Vol 1, p6 (Report of Secretary of War, 19 December 1794).

20 Robert Gardiner (ed), *The Naval War of 1812*, pp160-1.

21 Robert Gardiner (ed), *The Line of Battle*, pp19-26.

22 Greer A Duncan, 'The Wood in Old Ironsides', *American Forests and Forest Life*, October 1925.

23 Thomas C Gillmer, *Old Ironsides: The Rise, Decline and Resurrection of the USS* Constitution, p136.

24 Charles Desmond, *Wooden Ship-Building*, p18.

25 *ASP*, Vol 1, pp8-10 & 17-18.

26 *ASP*, Vol 1, pp10-13.

27 Ibid.

28 *ASP*, Vol 1, p18.

29 Ibid, p28

30 Ibid (House Report #8, 17 June 1797: 'Progress in Building and Equipping Three Frigates').

31 Pickering to Stodder, 7 April 1796: M729 War Dept Naval Records.

32 Pickering to Truxtun, 2 November 1796 and 5 December 1796: M729 War Dept Naval Records.

33 F Alexander Magoun, *The Frigate Constitution and Other Historic Ships*, p67.

34 William P and Ethel L Bass, *Constitution Second Phase, 1802-1807*, pp13-18.

35 Tyrone Martin, *A Most Fortunate Ship*, pp24-5; Gillmer, p51.

36 Bruce Grant, *Captain of Old Ironsides*, pp29-30. As the 24s were ordered from and cast in England, and the 18s were said to have been from HMS *Somerset*, captured during the Revolution, *Constitution*'s entire battery was British-made.

37 Martin, pp4-17.

38 Ibid, pp16-20.

39 Ibid, pp44-7.

40 Ibid, pp60 & 77.

41 *Naval Documents Relating to the United States Wars with the Barbary Powers* (hereafter cited as *DBW*), Vol III, p451 (extract from log of N Haraden, Sailing Master, USS *Constitution*, 22 February 1804).

42 Bass, pp39-44.

43 Martin, pp88-90.

44 Ibid, pp91, 93, 101, 103, 120.

45 Ibid, pp129, 142; Grant, pp209, 213.

46 Bauer & Roberts, p8.

47 Martin, pp171, 180; painting by Cammillieri, Mariners' Museum, PN522-C102.

48 Painting 'Celebrating Washington's Birthday at Valetta, Malta in 1838', watercolour by James Evans; 'US Frigate *Constitution* off Scilly Light, 1835', Cammillieri painting, 1838, PEM; photographs of *Constitution* in refit, 1858, Portsmouth, NH.

49 Bauer & Roberts, p8.

50 Grant, pp385-6, n5.

51 George F Emmons, *Statistical History of the Navy of the United States*, pp88-90.

52 Ibid. Note that Emmons does not always identify sources of his quotations.

53 The author viewed the proceedings from USS *Halyburton*.

54 *ASP*, Vol 1, pp32, 39.

55 Chapelle, p131 and Plan 7 (the round house is mentioned again during her refit in 1806).

56 J Fox to T Tingey, 8 March 1806: Fox Papers, PEM.

57 *Naval Documents related to the Quasi-War Between the United States and France* (cited hereafter as *QWD*), Vol 1, p162 (this engraving is dated 24 July 1797, shortly after her launch and shows three rows of windows across her stern).

58 Chapelle, p130; Bauer & Roberts, p8.

59 *QWD*, Vol 1 (February 1797-October 1798), p232.

60 *QWD*, Vol 1, p424.

61 Ibid, p440.

62 Ibid, pp551-3.

63 Fox to Thomas Tingey, 15 September 1806: Fox Papers, PEM; Tingey to Secretary Smith, 16 September 1806: NARA RG 45 M125 (Captains' Letters).

64 Gardiner, *Naval War of 1812*, p49

65 Tingey to Fox, 7 and 15 May 1806: Fox Papers, PEM; Bauer & Roberts, p8; Benson Lossing, *Pictorial Field Book of the War of 1812*, p455.

66 John Shaw to B Crowninshield, 2 September 1815: NARA RG 45 M125.

67 Emmons, p93.

68 Martin, p198.

69 Bauer & Roberts, p8.

70 Chapelle, p134; *QWD*, Vol 5, p405.

71 *QWD*, Vol 5, p406.

72 *QWD*, Vol 6, pp418, 424, 445, 473, 522.; Vol 7, p79.

73 *DBW*, Vol 1, p473 (Truxtun to Dale).

74 Gardiner, *Naval War of 1812*, p32.

75 Bauer & Roberts, p8.

76 Fox to Tingey, 20 December 1808: Fox Papers, PEM.

77 Notebooks of James Fenimore Cooper, at Yale University Library (from letterbook of USS *President*); P Hamilton from J Rodgers, 23 September 1811.

78 Gardiner, *Naval War of 1812*, pp164-6.

79 Ibid.

80 Ibid.

81 Robert Gardiner, *The Heavy Frigate*.

82 Chapelle, p128; Bauer & Roberts, p9.

83 Sec of War to Stodder, 7 April 1796; Sec of War to Truxtun, 2 November 1796 and 5 December 1796: NARA M729, War Dept Naval Documents.

84 *QWD*, Vol 1, p212 (Truxtun to McHenry).

85 *QWD*, Vol 1, p301 (Truxtun to Stoddert).

86 *QWD*, Vol 2, p333.

87 *QWD*, Vol 5, p44.

88 *QWD*, Vol 5, pp162-9.

89 *QWD*, Vol 7, pp295, 298-9, 301-2, 304-5 (A Murray-R Smith correspondence).

90 *DBW*, Vol 2, p139 (Murray to Sec of Navy).

91 Dana M Wegner, *Fouled Anchors: The Constitution Question Answered*, p2.

92 Emmons, pp92-4.

93 Annual Report of the Secretary of the Navy, 1854, p475.

94 Wegner, pp3-4.

95 Ibid.

96 *ASP*, Vol 1, p19.

97 *QWD*, Vol 4, pp76-7.

98 *QWD*, Vol 5, p53.

99 *QWD*, Vol 5, p64.

100 Christopher McKee, *Edward Preble*, p79.

101 *QWD*, Vol 5, p454 (Court of Inquiry).

102 *QWD*, Vol 5, p70 (Preble's Journal).

103 *QWD*, Vol 4, pp140-1.

104 Bauer & Roberts, p9.

105 Charles Oscar Paullin, *Commodore John Rodgers*, pp251-5.

106 I Hull to Crowninshield, 20 and 26 August 1816: Benjamin J Crowninshield Papers, PEM.

107 Merle Westlake, 'The American Sailing Navy: Josiah Fox, Joshua Humphreys & Thomas Tingey', *American Neptune*, Vol 59, No 1, pp23-4.

108 Fox to Unidentified (naval agent in Norfolk?), 28 August 1798: Fox Papers, PEM.

109 Chapelle, p129.

110 Thomas Thompson to Fox, 27 October 1798: Fox Papers, PEM.

111 *QWD*, Vol 2, p472.

112 Fox to ?naval agent, 28 August 1798: Fox Papers, PEM.

113 Fox to Stoddert, nd; *QWD*, Vol 2, p526 (Stoddert to Fox): Fox Papers, PEM.

114 Charles W Goldsborough, *An Original and Correct List of the United States Navy, 1800*, p10; *DBW*, Vol 2, pp327 (Journal of Henry Wadsworth) & 332 (A Murray to Madrid Legation).

115 Bauer & Roberts, p9; Theodore Roosevelt, *The Naval War of 1812*, p101.

116 *DBW*, Vol 2, p162 (Morris to Sec of Navy).

117 James Fenimore Cooper Papers, Yale University (notebooks for Cooper's naval history); 'his dying words, a little changed by a poetical license . . .' (p106 of Cooper's *History of the Navy of the United States of America*).

118 Gardiner, *War of 1812*, pp160-6.

CHAPTER 3

Subscription, Navy-built and Captured Frigates, 1798–1815

1 Frederick C Leiner, *Millions for Defense: The Subscription Warships of 1798*, pp1-27.

2 Philip Chadwick Foster Smith, *The Frigate Essex Papers*, pp55-7.

3 Ibid, pp67, 127,148, 185.

4 *QWD*, Vol 4, p435 (Preble to Sec of Navy).

5 Ibid, pp188-9, *QWD*, Vol 5, pp498-9.

6 Fox to Tingey, 5 June 5 1809: Fox Papers, PEM.

7 Porter to Hamilton, 11 October 1811: NARA M147, Masters Commandant Letters.

8 Ibid, 25 October 1811.

9 Bauer & Roberts, p10; 'A Page from the Old Navy', *Naval Institute Proceedings*, October 1956, p1139; Takakjian, *The 32-gun Frigate Essex*, p15.

10 Gardiner, *Naval War of 1812*, pp82-3; Carpenter's Report of Damages (British), found in W H P Dunne Collection, Naval Historical Center, *Essex* File.

11 Leiner, pp59-62.

12 *Register of Officer Personnel . . . and Ships' Data* (*DBW*), pp70, 78; Martin, p24.

13 *ASP*, Vol 1, pp37-41 (Naval Expenditures, 22 March 1798).

14 Ibid, p76.

15 Leiner, pp60, 208 (note #28).

16 Ibid, pp64-5.

17 Chapelle, pp162-3, plan 9; S Humphreys to Board, 19 September 1819: NARA RG 45 E224, Letters Received by Board of Naval Commissioners. Samuel Humphreys was ordered to collect plans of the early vessels, and correspondence indicates there was a plan of *Philadelphia* and that no inboard plan was made of that ship.

18 *QWD*, Vol 4, p507 (Sec of Navy to Agents J & E Watson); Vol 5, p116 (Sec of Navy to Watsons), p202 (Sec of Navy to Sec of War), and p449 (Decatur to Sec of Navy).

19 Bauer & Roberts, p10.

20 *DBW*, Vol 3, p441 (Sec of Navy to Bainbridge).

21 Leiner, p69.

22 Ibid, pp140-1

23 *QWD*, Vol 1, pp146-7 (Stoddert to NY Committee).

24 Ibid, pp153-4 (Humphreys to Merchants Committee).

25 S Humphreys to Board, 20 January 1821: NARA RG 45 E224, Letters to Navy Commissioners. Humphreys indicated he supplied a 'copy' of the ship's plans for the Board, 'since he drew the original'.

26 Chapelle, pp161, 164, plan 10; *DBW*, Vol 7, plan of *New York*.

27 *DBW*, Vol 2, p403 (Wadsworth Journal); Gardner W Allen, *Our Navy and the Barbary Corsairs*, p125.

28 Leiner, pp146-7.

29 *QWD*, Vol 2, p97 (Sec of Navy to D Sears).

30 *QWD*, Vol 5, p327 (Sec of Navy to J & W Forbes).

31 Bauer & Roberts, p10; Chapelle, p166.

32 *QWD*, Vol 3, p224.

33 Leiner, p97.

34 *QWD*, Vol 4, p353 (*Constitution* Journal).

35 Leiner, p109.

36 *DBW*, Vol 7, p68; Chapelle, p66.

37 Fox to Sec of Navy, 18 June 1804 and 7 February 1806: Fox Papers, PEM.

38 P C Coker, III, *Charleston's Maritime Heritage 1670-1865*, pp139-40.

39 Fox to Samuel Evans, 17 May 1809: Fox Papers, PEM.

40 Coker, p140.

41 Paullin, *Rodgers*, p100-101; W H P Dunne, 'The South Carolina Frigate: A History of the US Ship *John Adams*', *American Neptune*, Winter 1987, p24.

42 Fox to Evans, 17 May 1809: Fox Papers, PEM.

43 Gardiner, *War of 1812*, pp32-3.

44 Allen, *Barbary Corsairs*, p129-30.

45 *DBW*, Vol 2, p432; Christopher McKee, *Edward Preble: A Naval Biography*, p119.

46 *DBW*, Vol 5, p529 (Shaw to Preble); Allen, *Barbary Corsairs*, p224.

47 Christopher McKee, *Edward Preble*, p280.

48 Fox to Tingey, 26 August (?) 1807: Fox Papers, PEM.

49 Leiner, p156.

50 Bauer & Roberts, p11.

51 J Barron to J Rodgers, 1 December 1827: Rodgers Collection, Historical Society of Pennsylvania.

52 Ibid, 'Exhibit', 1 June 1828.

53 J Rodgers to Sec of Navy John Branch, 2 August 1830: NARA RG 45 Subject File, Box 98.

54 Sec of Navy John Branch to John Rodgers: NARA RG 45 Subject File, Box 98.

55 Branch to Jackson, 14 August 1830, from John Spencer Bassett (ed), *Correspondence of Andrew Jackson*, Vol 4, p172 (quoted in 'Thorough and Efficient Repair: Rebuilding in the American Sailing Navy', MA Thesis by Brina Agranat, East Carolina University, 1993).

56 *DBW*, Vol 7, p67; Chapelle, p145; W H P Dunne Collection, Naval Historical Center, *Adams* File.

57 *DBW*, Vol 2, pp62-3 (Preble to Sec of Navy); p70 (Sec of Navy to Preble).

58 *QWD*, Vol 4, p577 (Captain Tryon, in New York *Daily Advertiser*).

59 *QWD*, Vol 5, p403.

60 Tingey to Jones, 7 September 7 1813: William Jones Papers, HSP.

61 Gardiner, *War of 1812*, p167.

62 Benson Lossing, *Pictorial Field Book of the War of 1812*, pp897-900.

63 *DBW*, Vol 7, p72-3; Chapelle, p145.

64 *QWD*, Vol 6, p308 (Gibbs & Channing to Sec of Navy).

65 Ibid, Vol 1, p536 (Gibbs & Channing to Messrs Joseph Anthony & Co).

66 *DANFS*, Vol 3, p44.; *An Encyclopedia of World History*, p862.

67 Paullin, *John Rodgers*, p41.

68 Ibid, pp47-50.

69 Ibid.

70 Leiner, pp83-5; Paullin, *Rodgers*, p62; *DQW*, Vol 4, pp229, 442, 577, Vol 5, p31.

71 *QWD*, Vol 4, pp30-1 (Murray to Sec of Navy).

72 James Tertius de Kay, *Chronicles of the Frigate Macedonian, 1810-1922*, p23.

73 Bauer & Roberts, p11.

74 Chapelle, p252.

75 Roosevelt, p63.

76 J Barker, E Hart to I Hull: 22 August 1816: NARA RG 45 M125.

77 S Humphreys to Board, 19 November 1829: NARA RG 45 E224; *ASP*, Vol 3, p769.

78 Barron to John Rodgers, 6 April 1831: copy found in Dunne Collection, Naval Historical Center, quoted in de Kay, p202.

79 de Kay, pp203-4.

80 de Kay, p205-6; Chapelle, p360-2.

81 J Rodgers to Smith Thompson, 15 April 1819: NARA RG 45, Entry 213, Letters from Board of Navy Commissioners to Sec of Navy; dimensions of *Cyane* supplied by R Gardiner.

82 Martin, pp161-2.

83 Bauer & Roberts, p12.

84 *ASP*, Vol 2, p458.

85 Humphreys to Board, 19 November 1829: NARA RG 45 E229.

86 Chapelle, p385.

87 Bauer & Roberts, p12.

88 Lossing, p456, note #3.

89 Doughty to Jones, 13 January 1813: Jones Papers, HSP.

90 See previous chapter on the earlier frigates and plans of both classes.

91 Rodgers to Sec of Navy Jones, 1 May 1814: NARA RG 45 M125.

92 Bainbridge to Crowninshield, 26 July 1815: NARA RG 45 M125.

93 A photo of the *Guerriere* Liverpool jug appeared in *Maine Antique Digest*, December 1999.

94 Allen, *Barbary Corsairs*, pp282-4; *DANFS*, Vol 3, pp181-2.

95 Bainbridge to Crowninshield, 26 July 1815: NARA RG 45 M125.

96 Warrington, H Page, F Grice to C H Morris, 9 September 1840 & Report, May 1841: NARA RG 45 Subject File, Box 122.

97 W H P Dunne Collection, Naval Historical Center, Date File on *Java*.

98 Journal of Navy Commissioners, Vol 1, p209, 5 August 1817: NARA RG 45 E209; Hull to Crowninshield, 24 July 1818: Crowninshield Papers, PEM; Hull to Sec of Navy, 25 February 1819: RG 45 M125.

99 J Rodgers to Sec of Navy L Woodbury, 30 June 1831: NARA RG 45, Entry 28, Letters from Board of Navy Commissioners, Vol 6.

100 K Jack Bauer, 'United States Naval Shipbuilding Programs, 1775-1860', MA Thesis, 1949, p55.

CHAPTER 4
The 'Gradual Increase' Frigates, 1816 –1861

1 K Jack Bauer, 'United States Naval Shipbuilding Programs, 1775-1860', pp48-51.

2 Paullin, *Naval Administration*, pp176-8.

3 Chapelle, p353 (Humphreys assumed the chief constructor's position in December 1826).

4 Andrew Lambert, *The Last Sailing Battlefleet*, pp61-4; W Roderick Stewart, 'Seppings Survivor', *Warship*, Vol VI, pp85-6.

5 Chapelle, pp364-5; Brian Lavery, *The Ship of the Line*, Vol 2, pp44-5.

6 NARA RG 19, Plan 40-9-5L, Elliptical Stern, April 1820.

7 NARA RG 19, Plans 134-2-10, 134-2-12, 134-2-14.

8 NARA RG 19, Plan 49-9-5.

9 NARA RG 19, Plan 40-9-5M.

10 Bauer & Roberts, p12.

11 Charles Lee Lewis, *David Glasgow Farragut*, pp172-3.

12 Ibid.

13 Ibid, pp174-7.

14 Samuel Eliot Morison, 'Old Bruin': Commodore *Matthew C Perry*, p117.

15 Emmons, p95.

16 Ibid, p96.

17 Doughty to J Rodgers/Board, 24 September 1821: RG 45 E224; NARA RG 19, Plans 134-2-10 & 134-2-14.

18 Downes to Board, 23 May 1834: NARA RG 45 E277, Reports on Sailing Qualities.

19 Emmons, pp94-5.

20 Bauer & Roberts, p12.

21 Morison, *Perry*, p222.

22 S Humphreys to W Bainbridge, 7 March 1827: NARA RG 45, Subject File, Box 13.

23 Emmons, p96.

24 Bauer & Roberts, p12.

25 S Humphreys to Board, 16 September 1839: NARA RG 45 E224.

26 Chapelle, Plan 29.

27 Morris to Paulding, 21 April 1840: NARA RG 45 E28; Canney, *The Old Steam Navy, Vol 1*, p22.

28 Bauer & Roberts, p12.

29 Emmons, p98; F H Gregory to Morris, 10 January 1845: NARA RG 45 E277, Reports on Sailing Qualities.

30 Emmons, p98.

31 NARA RG 19, Plan 109-3-8.

32 A Fitzhugh to A J Dallas, 8 February 1844 &

W Mervine to C W Skinner, 8 September 1847: NARA RG 45 E277, Reports on Sailing Qualities.

33 Spencer Tucker, *Arming the Fleet*, pp186-90.

34 Lenthall to Toucey, 15 August 1857: NARA RG 19 E49, Bureau of Construction and Repair to Sec of Navy.

35 Bauer & Roberts, p12

36 NARA RG 19 Plans 109-5-6 and 109-5-8, July, 1857.

37 Bauer & Roberts, p12.

38 *Official Records of the Union and Confederate Navies in the War of the Rebellion* (hereafter cited as *ORN*), Series I, Vol 5, pp734, 795.

39 *ORN*, Vol 6, pp226, 343.

40 *DANFS*, Vol 6, p366. Photo, Lightfoot collection.

41 Bauer & Roberts, p12.

42 Morison, *Perry*, pp181-2.

43 *Battles and Leaders of the Civil War*, Vol 1, p698.

44 Brina J Agranat, 'Thorough and Efficient Repair: Rebuilding in the American Sailing Navy', MA Thesis, 1993, pp351-2

45 Frank M Bennett, *Steam Navy of the United States*, Appendix B.

46 Agranat, pp352-4.

47 Coletta (ed), *American Secretaries of the Navy*, Vol 1, p237.

48 Emmons, p98.

49 Ibid.

50 Canney, *US Coast Guard and Revenue Cutters*, pp24-5.

51 Bauer & Roberts, p12.

52 Sec of Navy Report, 1854, p474.

53 Chapelle, Plan 32; NARA Plan 107-11-14E.

54 *ASP*, Vol 2, p746.

55 *ASP*, Vol 2, pp747-8 (the armament listed referred to '34-pound cannon', but the shot list therewith was 32-pound, indicating a misprint).

56 Cassin to Sec of Navy, 24 June and 7 September 1830: NARA RG 45 E28.

57 *DANFS*, Vol 3, p384.

58 de Kay, pp202-6. Mr de Kay, from whose book all the above facts are taken, places great store on nineteenth century sensibilities and romanticism in this regard, contending that the post-1835 *Macedonian* remained the 'very ship' captured from the British in 1812. It is noteworthy that, in this regard, I have even seen contemporary

correspondence referring to the 1813 American-built *Java* as a 'trophy ship'.

59 Emmons, p100-1.

60 Commandants of Navy Yards to Board of Navy Commissioners, Warrington to Board, 25 November 1835: NARA RG 45 E220.

61 J Rodgers to J Branch, Sec of Navy, 2 August 1830: NARA RG 45 Subject File, Box 98.

62 Chapelle, Plan 14, Prize Frigate *Macedonian*; NARA Plan 40-14-2E.

63 de Kay, p205.

64 Emmons, p101; Shubrick to C Morris, 30 June 1840: NARA RG 45 E28.

65 Grice to Stringham, 20 August 1845: NARA RG 45, Subject File, Box 42; Report, Humphreys, Rhodes, Lenthall, Hartt, 19 August 1845.

66 de Kay, pp238-41.

67 Bauer & Roberts, p14; Letter 1 May 1853: NARA RG 45 Subject File, Box 92.

68 de Kay, pp292-4

69 Bauer & Roberts, p9

70 S Humphreys to Board, 27 November 1835 and 23 April 1838: NARA RG 45 E224.

71 Chauncey to Dickerson, 28 March 1838: NARA RG 45 E28.

72 Report to Board, 6 July 1838; Humphreys & Lenthall to Board, 4 August 1838; Letter 2 January 1839; Humphreys to Board, 24 July 1838: NARA RG 45 E224.

73 Chauncey to Dickerson, 28 March 1838: NARA RG 45 E28.

74 Voorhees to Bureau of Construction & Repair, 18, March 1843 and 12 March 1845: NARA RG 45 E277, Reports on Sailing Qualities.

CHAPTER 5

The Ships of the Line

1 E H H Archibald, *The Fighting Ship of the Royal Navy 897-1984*, p65.

2 K Jack Bauer, 'Naval Shipbuilding Programs 1794-1860', *Military Affairs*, Spring 1965, p31.

3 Chapelle, p173.

4 Bauer, 'Naval Shipbuilding Programs', p33.

5 Lavery, Vol 2, pp42-3.

6 Gardiner, *Naval War of 1812*, pp184-9.

7 Lavery, *The Ship of the Line*, Vol 1, p146.

8 Ibid.

9 Emmons, pp86-7; Chapelle, p315.

10 NARA Plans, RG 19 and RG 74 (Bureau of Ordnance); Conversations with Colin Ratliff, David Taylor Naval Research Lab, January 2000.

11 Report, 4 February 1862: NARA RG 19 E49, Bureau of Construction and Repair Records.

12 Canney, *The Old Steam Navy*, Vol 1, p46.

13 Bainbridge to Jones, 31 March 1813: NARA RG 45, M125, Letters from Captains; Chapelle (p172) also noted the 'Independence' annotation but said it was on one of the other copies of the plan.

14 Jones to Bainbridge, 28 April 1813: NARA RG 45 M441.

15 Bainbridge to Sec of Navy, 19 November 1815: NARA RG 45 M125.

16 Bainbridge to Commissioners, 26 July 1815; Bainbridge to Crowninshield, 14 September 1815: NARA RG 45 M125.

17 14 September 1815: ibid.

18 Allen, *Our Navy and the Barbary Corsairs*, pp293-7.

19 S Humphreys to ?, 17 April 1817: NARA RG 45 Subject File, Box 42; J Rodgers to Crowninshield, 14 May 1817: NARA RG 45 E213.

20 Emmons, p86; Chapelle, p487.

21 *DANFS*, Vol 3, pp424-5.

22 George Henry Preble, *History of the United States Navy-Yard, Portsmouth, NH*, p30.

23 Hull to Jones, 17 October 1813: Secretary of the Navy William Jones Papers, HSP.

24 Grant, pp276-86; Preble, pp29-37.

25 Homans to Crowninshield, 31 July 1818: Crowninshield Papers, PEM.

26 Bauer, 'Naval Shipbuilding', pp33-4.

27 Bauer & Roberts, p4.

28 Emmons, p86.

29 C Morris to Paulding, 16 November 1840: NARA RG 45 E28.

30 Emmons, p86.

31 Chapelle, *The Search for Speed under Sail*, p256; Roosevelt, *Naval War*, pp195-6; Chapelle, *Sailing Navy*, p313; J Rodgers to Eckford, 5 December 1816: NARA RG 45 E217. (The changes amounted to slight alterations in the rake of rudder, stem, 'two fractions' fuller forward and a 'fraction leaner' aft.)

32 *ASP*, Vol 4, p753.

33 Ibid, p31.

34 *Naval Magazine*, Vol 2, November 1837, pp592-3.

35 J Smith to I Hull, 28 December 1838: NARA RG 45 E277.

36 Grant, p328-30.

37 Emmons, p88.

38 Bauer & Roberts, p4.

39 Lavery, *The Ship of the Line*, Vol 1, p147.

40 Quoted in Morison, *Perry*, p122.

41 Spencer Tucker, *Arming the Fleet*, p140.

42 Bauer & Roberts, p4.

43 Paullin, p330-3.

44 Emmons, p88.

45 Emmons, p88; *DANFS*, Vol 3, p255.

46 Bauer & Roberts, p4.

47 Emmons, p88.

48 Rodgers to Humphreys, 19 February 1820: NARA RG 45 E217.

49 Chapelle, *Sailing Navy*, p339.

50 NARA RG 19, Plan.

51 Lavery, *The Ship of the Line*, Vol 1, p178.

52 Humphreys to?, 27 June 1820: NARA RG 45 E224.

53 Quoted in Lavery, *The Ship of the Line*, Vol 1, Appendix XIII, p212.

54 Chapelle, pp371-2; *DANFS*, Vol 5, p250.

55 *DANFS*, Vol 5, p250.

56 Lavery, *The Ship of the Line*, Vol 1, p182.

57 Ibid, p190.

58 Ibid, p191.

59 'Ships *Neptune* and *Pennsylvania*', *The Military and Naval Magazine*, Vol I, March 1833, p58.

60 *ASP*, Vol 4, p30.

61 Ibid.

62 Figures from tables in Glete, *Navies and Nations*.

63 *DQW*, Vol 2, pp129-130 (Stodder to Rep Josiah Parker).

64 Dumas Malone, *Jefferson the President, First Term, 1801-1805*, p251.

65 Coletta (ed), *American Secretaries of the Navy*, Vol 1, p85 ('Robert Smith' by Frank L Owsley, Jr).

CHAPTER 6

The Sloops of War, 1798–1831

1 Allen, *Our Navy and the Barbary Corsairs*, p56; *QWD*, Vol 7, p371; Chapelle, p158.

2 *QWD*, Vol 3, pp1 & 19.

3 *QWD*, Vol 2, p288.

4 *QWD*, Vol 1, p525.

5 Chapelle, pp155-7.

6 Emmons, p6.

7 *QWD*, Vol 1, pp490-1.

8 *QWD*, Vol 4, p95.

9 *QWD*, Vol 3, p168 (S Higginson to Sec of Navy, 11 May 1799).

10 *DANFS*, Vol 4, p337.

11 Leiner, pp74-6.

12 *QWD*, Vol 1, pp170, 173.

13 *QWD*, Vol 1, p220 (Sec of Navy to A Campbell, 19 July 1798).

14 Geoffrey M Footner, *Tidewater Triumph*, pp70-3, 100-105; Leiner, p78.

15 Leiner, p78; Footner, p72.

16 Leiner, pp78-80.

17 *QWD*, Vol 3, pp296-7.

18 Paullin, *Rodgers*, p55 (this source puts the complement at 180, others make it 160 or 162; the latter is more likely, given *Patapsco*'s 140-man make-up).

19 Leiner, p79.

20 *QWD*, Vol 1, p533 (Truxtun to Yellot, 26 October 1798).

21 *QWD*, Vol 4, p159 (J Buchanan to Secretary of State).

22 Paullin, *Rodgers*, p62.

23 Ibid, pp60-71.

24 *QWD*, Vol 3, p377.

25 *QWD*, Vol 4, p357; Leiner, p79; Goldsborough, p6.

26 Leiner, pp84-5.

27 *QWD*, Vol 1, p130 (Sec of Navy to O Wolcott, 22 June 1798).

28 Copy of letter (from Fox Papers, PEM), Thomas Thompson to J Fox, 27 October 1798: Dunne Collection, Naval Historical Center; *QWD*, Vol 1, p356.

29 *QWD*, Vol 1, p491 (Sec of Navy to D MacNeill); Dunne Papers, Naval Historical

Center; *QWD*, Vol 4, p101 (Sec of Navy to G Cross, 20 August 1799).

30 T Thompson to J Fox, 24 June 1799: Dunne Papers, Naval Historical Center.

31 Paullin, *Rodgers*, p62.

32 Allen, *Our Naval War with France*, pp125-6.

33 *QWD*, Vol 2, p532 (Stoddert to J Howland, 30 March 1799); Vol 3, p1 (Stoddert to Jewett, 1 April 1799).

34 *QWD*, Vol 2, p532.

35 *QWD*, Vol 4, p406.

36 Emmons, p6.

37 *QWD*, Vol 1, pp185-6, (Stoddert to Hubbard, 10 July 1798).

38 *QWD*, Vol 1, pp218-9 (Stoddert to Hubbard, 18 July 1798).

39 *QWD*, Vol 1, p281 (Stoddert to Hubbard, 8 August 1798).

40 *QWD*, Vol 2, p134; Vol 3, p488 (Stoddert to Hubbard, 10 July 1799); Vol 4, p88 (Stoddert to Hubbard, 17 August 1799); Vol 4, p427 (Stoddert to Stephen Higginson, Co, 19 November 1799).

41 *QWD*, Vol 5, p403 (letter to *Salem Gazette*, 3 July 1800).

42 Leiner, p20; *QWD*, Vol 3, p14 (Stoddert to Johnson, 4 April 1799).

43 *QWD*, Vol 3, pp14-15 (Stoddert to Johnson, 4 April 1799).

44 *QWD*, Vol 3, p178 (Stoddert to Johnson, 13 May 1799) & p468 (Stoddert to T Newman, 6 July 1799); Chapelle, p145; Bauer & Roberts, p18.

45 *QWD*, Vol 4, p383 (Stoddert to Newman, 12 November 1799); p499 (Stoddert to S Higginson, & Co, 7 December 1799).

46 *QWD*, Vol 4, pp590-1 (Newman to Johnson, 31 December 1799); Log of *Warren*, 31 December 1799.

47 *DANFS*, Vol 8, p106; *QWD*, Vol 6, p255; Michael Palmer, *Stoddert's War*, p228.

48 Paullin, *Naval Administration*, pp132-3.

49 20 April 1807: Fox Papers, PEM.

50 Ibid.

51 Fox to C Goldsborough, 26 October 1805: Fox Papers, PEM (copy in Dunne Papers, Naval Historical Center).

52 I Chauncey to Sec of Navy, 18 July 1805, with drawing of head (transcribed from NARA M147

Letters from Commanders): Dunne Papers, Naval Historical Center; *DBW*, Vol 6, p515 (*Hornet* Log, 7 April 1807).

53 Bauer & Roberts, p25.

54 *DBW*, Vol 6, p374 (Chauncey to Preble, 21 February 1806).

55 *DBW*, Vol 6, p585 (Dent to Sec of Navy, 29 December 1807; Chapelle, p214.

56 Chapelle, p214.

57 Roosevelt, p94.

58 Ibid, pp237-8.

59 T Tingey to Fox, 20 January 1807: Fox Papers, PEM.

60 *DBW*, Vol 6, p545 (Smith to Sec of Navy, 9 July 1807).

61 Bauer & Roberts, p25.

62 Gardiner, *Naval War of 1812*, pp44-5; Roosevelt, pp59-60.

63 Footner, pp142-4, 194; Chapelle, *Search for Speed under Sail*, pp204-7.

64 Bauer & Roberts, pp17 & 25.

65 R Spence to Crowninshield, 20 March 1815: NARA M125.

66 J Rodgers to Smith Thompson, 17 July 1819: NARA RG 45 E213.

67 Report, W D Salter to Sec of Navy, 5 July 1836: NARA RG 45 E277.

68 Ridgely to Sec of Navy, 4 November 1813, 23 March 1814, 27 March 1814: C Ridgely Papers, Library of Congress.

69 J Rodgers to S Thompson, 18 & 27 July 1820: NARA RG 45 E213; J Rodgers to Chauncey, 23 April 1821: NARA RG 45 E217.

70 Doughty to Rodgers, 5 & 26 May 1821: NARA RG 45 E224; J Rodgers to James Tongue, 4 June 1821: NARA RG 45 E217.

71 Rodgers to Branch, 2 August 1830: NARA RG 45, Subject File; Rodgers to Branch, 2 August 1830: NARA RG 45 E28.

72 Doughty to Porter & Board, 9 September 1822: NARA RG 45 E224; Chapelle, p336 & 539 (Chapelle, the chief advocate of the 'administrative rebuilding' concept, terms the 1821 rebuilding a 'partial' rebuild apparently with the rationale that some parts of the old vessel were re-used).

73 S Humphreys to Board, 6 January 1841; Humphreys & Rhodes to Board, 20 April 1841: NARA RG 45 E224.

74 Chapelle, p258; Canney, *US Coast Guard and Revenue Cutters*, p5.

75 Roosevelt, pp178-80; *DANFS*, Vol 8, p140.

76 Roosevelt, pp182-4; *DANFS*, Vol 8, p140.

77 Footner, p103, 194.

78 Gardiner, *Naval War of 1812*, pp84-5.

79 Ibid.

80 Report, Thomas ap Catesby Jones, May 1826: NARA RG 45 E277.

81 Ibid.

82 Roosevelt, pp173-5.

83 Reports, T Jones, 1827: NARA RG 45 E277.

84 Ibid.

85 Report on repairs, June-November 1828: NARA RG 45 E5.

86 Chapelle, p263; Gardiner, *Naval War of 1812*, p85.

87 Canney, *Lincoln's Navy*, pp8-9.

88 Bauer, 'Naval Shipbuilding Programs', pp52-54.

89 Chapelle, p340-4; NARA Plans, 108-10-11 and 40-8-4A (annotations).

90 Tucker, *Arming the Fleet*, Table 19, p125.

91 Chapelle, p348 (plan of *Falmouth*).

92 Sloat to Board, 17 October 1840: NARA RG 45 E224; Bauer & Roberts, p18

93 S Humphreys & C Stewart to J Rodgers, 10 February 1831: NARA RG 45 E224.

94 Emmons, p107.

95 NARA Plans, 40-8-4A and 108-10-11.

96 S Humphreys to Board, 12 May 1840: NARA RG 45 E224; Perry, Stringham, Humphreys, Hartt, Lenthall, Benjamin Cooper, 28 May 1840: NARA RG 45 E28.

97 S Humphreys to Board, 19 November 1829: NARA RG 45 E224.

98 Emmons, pp110-11.

99 Ibid.

100 Report, J M McKeever to W M Crane, 3 May 1834: NARA RG 45 E277; Emmons, pp118-19.

101 *ASP*, Vol 3, p367 (Report of Navy Commissioners, 31 March 1829).

102 B Hoffman to Board, 26 January 1826: NARA RG 45 E277.

103 Humphreys, Lenthall and Hartt to Board, 31 May 1839: NARA RG 45 E224.

104 Bauer & Roberts, p18.

105 Reports, W B Finch to Board, 1827 and 1830: NARA RG 45 E277.

106 H Viola & C Margolis (eds), *Magnificent Voyagers*, pp152-3.

107 Ibid, end maps.

108 Report, E Valette to Board, 29 March 1836: NARA RG 45 E277.

109 Report, A S Mackensie to Board, 20 March 1839: NARA RG 45 E277.

110 J Sloat to Board, 10 December 1831: NARA RG 45 E277.

111 Bauer and Roberts, p18.

112 Morison, *Perry*, pp104-17.

113 J Rodgers to S Barron, 19 December 1828: Rodgers Family Collection, HSP; J Rodgers to Branch, 2 August 1830: NARA RG 45, Subject File, Box 98 (also in NARA RG 45 E28).

114 S Humphreys to Board, 12 January 1835: NARA RG 45 E224.

115 Warrington to Board, 20 January 1835: NARA RG 45 E220, Letters from Commandants of Navy Yards to Board of Navy Commissioners.

116 Bauer & Roberts, p18.

117 S Humphreys to J Rodgers, 24 April 1828: NARA RG 45 E224.

118 'Repairs to *Peacock*, June to Nov 1828 at NY': NARA RG 45 E5 Report, p40 (nd).

119 *ASP*, Vol 3, p273; Bauer & Roberts, p19.

CHAPTER 7
American Sloops of War, 1837–1855

1 Bauer, 'Naval Shipbuilding Programs', pp35-6.

2 NARA Plan 107-11-26 (*Cyane*, 1866).

3 Report, J Percival, 31 December 1838: NARA RG 45 E277; Emmons, p110.

4 Report, W K Latimer, 16 May 1841: NARA RG 45 E277.

5 Emmons, p108.

6 Bauer, 'Naval Shipbuilding Programs', p36.

7 Report, H W Ogden to Board, 1 June 1842: NARA RG 45 E277.

8 Report, J Aulick to Board, 29 January 1841: NARA RG 45 E277.

9 Ibid, 20 March 1841.

10 Emmons, p110-14.

11 Reports, H W Ogden, 5 May 1840 & 1 June

1842: NARA RG 45 E277.

12 Emmons, p112.

13 Bauer & Roberts, p20.

14 Emmons, p114; Report, Aulick to Board, 29 January 1841: NARA RG 45 E277.

15 Emmons, p114.

16 Canney, *US Revenue and Coast Guard Cutters*, p62.

17 Report, Aulick to Board, 29 January 1841: NARA RG 45 E277.

18 Emmons, p110-14.

19 Canney, *The Old Steam Navy, Vol I*, p151 (by this date, these 'rebuilds' were clearly illegal, as any repair over $3000 required a Board of Survey).

20 Coletta, Vol 1, pp186-7.

21 Tucker, *Arming the Fleet*, p151

22 Ibid, pp150-1, 186.

23 Bauer & Roberts, p20; NARA Plan 108-13-11B.

24 Emmons, p100; Report, Tatnall to Board, 9 January 1845: NARA RG 45 E277.

25 Reports, Tatnall to Board, 9 January 1845; Ogden to Board, 5 May 1840: NARA RG 45 E277.

26 Report, Tatnall to Board, 9 January 1845: NARA RG 45 E277.

27 Reports, 8 November 1902 and 7 March 1907: NARA RG 19 E88, Box 315.

28 F Grice to Shubrick, 29 April 1845: NARA RG 45 Subject File, AD Box 42.

29 Ibid, and W Shubrick to B Kennon, 5 May 1845.

30 S L Breese to Charles Morris, 23 December 1846 and to Charles Skinner, 8 September 1847: NARA RG 45 E277.

31 Emmons, pp102-3.

32 George Henry Preble, *History of the United States Navy Yard Portsmouth, NH*, p72.

33 S M Pook to J Nicholson, 11 May 1844: NARA RG 45 Subject File, Box 42.

34 Report, J Montgomery to W Bolton, nd (probably January 1845): NARA RG 45 E277; 'US Ships *Jamestown* and *Portsmouth*', *Nautical Magazine*, Vol 1, 1845, pp187-8.

35 Emmons, p100.

36 Emmons, p100; *Nautical Magazine*, Vol 1, 1845, pp184-6.

37 Emmons, p100; photos of ship.

38 de Kay, p232.

39 Report, G Blake to J Y Mason, 24 December 1846: NARA RG 45 E277 (this letter was mistakenly addressed to Mason, who had been succeeded as Secretary of the Navy by George Bancroft in March 1845).

40 Emmons, p102.

41 Report, H Henry to C Morris, 4 October 1846: NARA RG 45 E277.

42 Emmons, p102.

43 Tucker, pp206-7.

44 Emmons, p102.

45 Article from 'Sea Stories', March 1930: otherwise unidentified, found in NHC Ships History Branch, *St Mary's* File.

46 Agranat, p392.

47 Dana M Wegner, *Fouled Anchors: The Constellation* Question Answered, p4.

48 Ibid, pp4-5; Agranat, pp391-3.

49 Conversation with Glen Williams, Historian of *USS Constellation*, 7 July 2000.

50 Chapelle, p468; Bauer & Roberts, p23.

51 Letter, William P Schwartz [alias Samuel P Ramsey] Orderly Sergeant, USMC, to his family, 8 July 1856.

52 Bauer & Roberts, p23.

53 Conversations with Glen Williams, Historian of *USS Constellation*, 17 July 2000.

CHAPTER 8

Brigs and Schooners, 1798–1843

1 Canney, *US Coast Guard and Revenue Cutters*, pp1-4.

2 King, *George Washington's Coast Guard*, p145.

3 Listing found in M V Brewington's notes via I King, 1993; original at HSP.

4 *QWD*, Vol 3, p116 (Preble to Patten & Walker, 20 June 1799); McKee, *Preble*, pp58-9.

5 *QWD*, Vol 2, pp199 & 201 (Sec of Navy to Thomas Martin, 1 & 2 January 1799).

6 Ibid; Canney, *Revenue Cutters*, pp4-5.

7 Canney, *Revenue Cutters*, p5.

8 *QWD*, Vol 1, p503.

9 Emmons, p50; King, p165.

10 King, pp145-9; Bauer & Roberts, pp25-9.

11 Chapelle, pp146-8.

12 Ibid.

13 King, pp150-1; *QWD*, Vol 1, pp523-4 (Sec of Navy to H Desaussure, 12 October 1798).

14 *QWD*, Vol 2, pp87 & 290 (Sec of Navy to Heyward, 13 December 1798 and Sec of Navy to J Simons, 28 January 1799).

15 *QWD*, Vol 5, p426 (A Thomas to Comptroller of the Treasury, 18 April 1800).

16 *QWD*, Vol 2, p514 (Stoddert to Yellot, 25 March 1799).

17 *QWD*, Vol 3, p113 (Stoddert to Yellot, 30 April 1799).

18 Footner, p84.

19 *QWD*, Vol 5, p2, (Report, Edward Stevens to Silas Talbot, 2 January 1800).

20 Chapelle, pp145-7; Footner, pp88-91.

21 Footner, pp88-91.

22 *DBW*, Vol 1, p497 (Dale to Sec of Navy, 2 July 1801).

23 Footner, p93; *DBW*, Vol 2, p376 (Sec of Navy to Bainbridge, 21 March 1803).

24 Roosevelt, p119-21.

25 J Rodgers to Smith Thompson, 11 February 1819: NARA RG 45 E213.

26 *QWD*, Vol 5, pp1-5.

27 Footner, p93.

28 Chapelle, pp180-1; Coletta (ed), p81.

29 Bauer, 'Naval Shipbuilding Programs', p32.

30 *DBW*, Vol 2, p390 (Sec of Navy to Samuel Brown, Navy Agent, 13 April 1803).

31 Ibid; *DBW*, Vol 2, pp370-1 (Sec of Navy to Bainbridge, 7 March 1803).

32 *DBW*, Vol 2, p379 (Sec of Navy to Bainbridge, 29 March 1803).

33 Quoted in W H P Dunne, 'A Naval Architectural Study of the US Brig *Argus*', *Nautical Research Journal*, Vol 34, No 3 (September 1989), p129.

34 *DBW*, Vol 3, p66 (Decatur to Sec of Navy, 19 September 1803).

35 Dunne, '*Argus*', p130.

36 Gardiner, *Naval War of 1812*, pp62-3.

37 Dunne, '*Argus*', pp126-8.

38 *DBW*, Vol 2, p396 (Sec of Navy to Harrison, 30 April 1803)–'Name vessel Syren . . .' make 'appropriate figurehead'.

39 Bauer & Roberts, p25.

40 Chapelle, p186.

41 Footner, p96.

42 *DBW*, Vol 5, p101 (Haraden log, 26 October 1804).

43 *DBW*, Vol 2, p394, (Sec of Navy to Stricker, 28 April 1803); p404 (R Somers to his brother, 13 May 1803); p397 (Sec of Navy to Bainbridge, 5 May 1803).

44 *DBW*, Vol 2, p404 (Somers to brother, 13 May 1803); Bauer & Roberts, p35.

45 *DBW*, Vol 2, pp442 and 502 (Somers to Sec of Navy, 28 June 1803 & 31 July 1803).

46 *DBW*, Vol 4, p41 (Preble to Sec of Navy, 19 April 1804).

47 Roosevelt, p28; Emmons, p10 (Emmons also noted an 1812 *Ferret* purchased at Charleston).

48 Chapelle, p224; Westlake, 'American Sailing Navy', pp40-1.

49 Emmons, pp10-11.

50 Bauer, 'Naval Shipbuilding Programs', p33.

51 Morison, *Perry*, pp54-6.

52 Chapelle, pp286 & 289.

53 O H Perry to Crowninshield, 24 March 1815 and 8 May 1815: NARA M125.

54 Perry to Crowninshield, 10 May 1815: M125; Collection #24, Dimensions of *Congress* and other ships: Nimitz Library, USNA.

55 Chapelle, p324; Bauer, 'Naval Shipbuilding Programs', p34.

56 Rodgers to Eckford, 1 September 1819: NARA RG 45 E217.

57 Bauer & Roberts, p31.

58 Chapelle, p326-30; NARA Plans.

59 Ibid.

60 Bauer & Roberts, p31; Chapelle, p334.

61 J Collins Long to L Woodbury, 27 April 1832 & J Downes to Rodgers, 20 May 1832: NARA RG 45 E28.

62 Morison, pp69-70.

63 *ASP*, Vol 3, p754 (Report of Sec of Navy, 7 December 1830).

64 These vessels had been the schooners *Beagle, Fox, Greyhound, Ferrett, Jackell, Terrier, Weazel* and *Wildcat*; armed barges *Mosquito, Gallinipper, Gnat, Midge,* and *Sandfly*; plus the steam galliot *Sea Gull*. The latter was the first operational steamer in the navy.

65 Bauer, 'Naval Shipbuilding Programs', p35.

66 Linda McKee Maloney, 'A Naval Experiment', pp188-9.

67 Ibid, p190; Rodgers to Woodbury, June. 27, 1832. NARA RG 45 E28.

68 Ibid, pp190-1.

69 S Humphreys to Board, 13 January 1837: NARA RG 45 E224.

70 Maloney, p192.

71 Ibid, p194.

72 J Rodgers to J Branch, 6 April 1831: NARA RG 45 E28.

73 W Nichols to Board, 10 February 1840: NARA RG 45 E277.

74 A Mackenzie to Board, 21 November 1838: NARA RG 45 E277.

75 Ibid.

76 Ibid, 22 May 1839.

77 Bauer & Roberts, p26.

78 Journal of F A Roe, 5 December 1853: Library of Congress.

79 Bauer, 'Naval Shipbuilding Programs', p36.

80 Grice to Shubrick, 28 May 1842 (enclosure with letter from Shubrick to Warrington of same date): NARA RG 45 E28.

81 Warrington to Shubrick, 26 May 1842: NARA RG 45 E28.

82 'US Brig of War Truxtun', *US Nautical Magazine and Naval Journal*, Vol IV, No 6 (September 1856), p438; Chapelle, p435.

83 Ibid.

84 Emmons, p116.

85 Emmons, pp114 & 100.

86 Chapelle, p452; Bauer & Roberts, p27.

87 Chapelle, *Search for Speed*, p317.

CHAPTER 9
Vessels on the Northern Lakes

1 Coletta (ed), pp86-7.

2 Bauer & Roberts, p27.

3 Roosevelt, p85.

4 Chauncey to Jones, 13 August 1813: NARA M125, Roll 25.

5 Dudley (ed), *Naval War of 1812*, Vol 1, p297 (Sec of Navy Hamilton to Chauncey, 31 August 1812).

6 Ibid, p297, 316 (Journal of I Chauncey).

7 Ibid, p337 (Chauncey to Hamilton, 8 October 1812).

8 Ibid, p353, (Chauncey to Hamilton, 26 November 1812).

9 Chauncey to Jones, 24 April 1813: NARA M125, Roll 28.

10 Bauer & Roberts, p23; Ware Drawings (Sail plan of *General Pike*): NARA RG 45; Chapelle, p273.

11 Bauer & Roberts, p32.

12 Dudley (ed), Vol 2, p582 (Jones to Chauncey, 19 September 1813).

13 Bauer & Roberts, p15.

14 Chauncey to Jones, 14 May 1814: NARA M125, Roll 48,

15 Dudley (ed), Vol 2, p422 & 426 (Chauncey to Sec of Navy and Brown, 21 January 1813 & 18 February 1813).

16 Dudley, Vol 2, p440 (D Dobbins to Chauncey, 14 March 1813).

17 Lossing, pp511-12; Chapelle, p269.

18 Chapelle, pp270-1.

19 Press Kit and general information packet courtesy US Brig *Niagara*.

20 Roosevelt, p207.

Bibliography

Archival Sources

NATIONAL ARCHIVES, WASHINGTON DC

Record Group 19: Records of the Bureau of Construction and Repair
    E49: Letters from Bureau of Construction and Repair to Secretary of the Navy
    E88: Correspondence ('A' Documents), 1896-1925
    E1028: Ships' Plans (Cartographic & Architectural Branch)
Record Group 45: Records of the Secretary of the Navy
    Old Subject File
    E5: Letters to the Secretary of the Navy
    E28: Letters from the Board of Naval Commissioners
    E209: Journal of the Board of Naval Commissioners
    E213: Letters from Board of Naval Commissioners to Secretary of the Navy
    E220: Letters from Commandants of Navy Yards to Board of Naval Commissioners
    E224: Letters Received from Board of Naval Commissioners
    E229: Letters from the American Consul in London, 1831-1835
    E277: Reports of Sailing Qualities of Vessels
Microfilm:
    M125: Captains' Letters
    M147: Master Commandants' Letters
    M441: Letters from Secretary of the Navy to Commandants and Navy Agents, 1808-1865
    M729: War Department Naval Records

HISTORICAL SOCIETY OF PENNSYLVANIA

Joshua Humphreys' Letterbook
William Jones, Secretary of the Navy Papers
C Smith Papers
Rodgers Family Collection

LIBRARY OF CONGRESS

Charles Goodwin Ridgely Papers
F A Roe Journal

NIMITZ LIBRARY, US NAVAL ACADEMY

Special Collections #24, Dimensions of Frigate *Congress* and Other Naval Vessels

PEABODY ESSEX MUSEUM

Benjamin L Crowninshield Papers (Secretary of the Navy)
Josiah Fox Papers

YALE UNIVERSITY LIBRARY

James Fenimore Cooper Papers

NAVAL HISTORICAL CENTER, WASHINGTON NAVY YARD

Ships' History Files, Ships' History Branch
W H P Dunne Collection, Ships' History Branch

PUBLIC RECORD OFFICE, KEW, UK

Adm 106/1942: *Argus* Survey and Valuation, 16 September 1813

UNPUBLISHED MANUSCRIPTS AND PRIVATE SOURCES

Agranat, Brina, 'Thorough and Efficient Repair: Rebuilding in the Sailing Navy' (Master's Thesis, East Carolina University, 1993)
Bauer, K Jack, 'Naval Shipbuilding Programs, 1775-1880' (Master's Thesis, Indiana University, 1949)
Mevers, Frank Clem, 'Congress and the Navy: The Establishment and Administration of the American Revolutionary Navy by the Continental Congress, 1775-1784' (PhD Dissertation, University of North Carolina, 1972)
Brewington, M V, Notes on early US Revenue Service supplied to the author by Dr Irving H King, 1994
Schwartz, William P [alias Samuel P Ramsey], Orderly Sergeant, USMC, letters to his family, 1855-58, transcribed by Dr John F Schwartz, Gettysburg, PA (seen at USS *Constellation*, July 2000, courtesy Glen Williams, Historian, USS *Constellation*)

PUBLISHED GOVERNMENT SOURCES

American State Papers: Naval Affairs, 6 Volumes, Washington DC: Gales and Seaton, 1860-1861
Dictionary of American Naval Fighting Ships, 8 Volumes, Washington DC: Government Printing Office, 1959-1991
Dudley, William S (ed), *The Naval War of 1812: A Documentary History*, 2 Volumes, Washington: Naval Historical Center (Government Printing Office), 1985 & 1992
Naval Documents Related to the United States Wars with the Barbary Powers, 7 Volumes, Washington DC: Government Printing Office, 1934-1941

Naval Documents Related to the Quasi-War between the United States and France, 7 Volumes, Washington DC: Government Printing Office, 1934-1938

Naval Documents of the American Revolution, 10 Volumes, Department of the Navy, Naval History Division, GPO, 1964-

Annual Reports of the Secretary of the Navy, Washington DC: (various publishers)

Official Records of the Union and Confederate Navies in the War of the Rebellion, 30 Volumes, Washington DC: Government Printing Office, 1894-1921

Books and Articles

Allen, Gardner W, *Our Navy and the Barbary Corsairs*, New York: Houghton & Mifflin, 1905

Allen, Gardner W, *Our Naval War with France*, Boston: Houghton, Mifflin, 1909

Archibald, E H H, *The Fighting Ship of the Royal Navy, 897-1984*, New York: Military Press, 1987

Bass, William P & Ethel L, *Constitution Second Phase, 1802-1807*, published by authors, 1981

Bassett, John Spencer, *The Correspondence of Andrew Jackson*, 7 Volumes, Washington DC: Carnegie Institute of Washington, 1926-1935

Battles and Leaders of the Civil War, 4 Volumes, Secaucus, NJ: Castle, 1989 (reprint)

Bauer, K Jack, 'Naval Shipbuilding Programs, 1794-1860', *Military Affairs*, Spring 1965, pp29-40

Bauer, K Jack and Roberts, Stephen S, *Register of Ships of the US Navy, 1775-1990*, New York: Greenwood Press, 1991

Bayne, Julia, *History of Middlesex County*, New York: J B Beers & Co, 1884

Beach, Edward L, *The United States Navy: 200 Years*, New York: Henry Holt, c1986

Bennett, Frank M, *The Steam Navy of the United States*, Pittsburg: Warren & Co, 1896

Brady, William, *A Kedge-Anchor or Young Sailors' Assistant*, published by the author, New York, 1847

Brewington, M V, 'The Design of our First Frigates', *American Neptune*, VII, 1948, pp10-20

Canney, Donald L, *The Old Steam Navy, Volume 1: Frigates, Sloops, and Gunboats, 1815-1885*, Annapolis: Naval Institute Press, 1990

_____, *Lincoln's Navy*, London: Conway Maritime Press, 1998

_____, *US Coast Guard and Revenue Cutters, 1790-1935*, Annapolis: Naval Institute Press, 1995

Chapelle, Howard I, *The History of American Sailing Ships*, New York: W W Norton, 1935

_____, *The Baltimore Clipper: Its Origin and Development*, Salem, MA: Marine Research Society, 1930

_____, *The History of the American Sailing Navy*, New York: W W Norton, 1949

_____, *The Search for Speed Under Sail*, New York: Bonanza Press, 1967

_____, '*Wasp* and *Hornet*: U S N Sloops of War: 1805-1806', *The Mariner*, VI, No 2, April 1932, pp52-59

Chapelle, Howard I, and Leon J Polland, *The Constellation Question*, Washington DC: Smithsonian Press, 1970

Cheevers, James W, *The Figurehead of USS Delaware III*, US Naval Academy Museum, 1970

Coker, III, P C, *Charleston's Maritime Heritage, 1670-1865*, Charleston SC: Cokercraft Press, 1987

Coletta, Paolo (ed), *American Secretaries of the Navy*, 2 Volumes, Annapolis: Naval Institute Press, 1980

Cooper, James Fenimore, *History of the Navy of the United States of America*, 3 Volumes in 1, New York: Putnam & Co, 1856

de Kay, James Tertius, *Chronicles of the Frigate* Macedonian, *1809-1922*, New York: W W Norton, 1995

Desmond, Charles, *Wooden Ship-Building*, New York: Vestal Press, 1984 (reprint)

Duncan, Greer A, 'The Wood in Old Ironsides', *American Forest and Forest Life*, 2 October 1925

Dunne, William H P, 'The South Carolina Frigate', *The American Neptune*, Winter, 1987, pp22-32

_____, '"The Frigate *Constellation* was No More" Or was she?', *American Neptune*, 53, No 2, 1993, pp77-97.

_____, 'A Naval Architectural Study of the US Brig *Argus*', *Nautical Research Journal*, 34, No 3, September 1989, pp126-136

Emmons, George F, *Statistical History of the Navy of the United States*, Washington DC: Gideon & Co, 1853

Footner, Geoffrey M, *Tidewater Triumph: The Development and Worldwide Success of the Chesapeake Bay Pilot Schooner*, Centerville, MD: Tidewater Publishers, 1998

Fowler, William M, Jr, *Rebels under Sail: The American Navy during the Revolution*, New York: Charles Scribner's Sons, 1976

Gardiner, Robert, *The Heavy Frigate: Eighteen Pounder Frigates: Volume I, 1778-1800*, London: Conway Maritime Press, 1994

_____, *Frigates of the Napoleonic Wars*, London: Chatham Publishing, 2000

_____, (ed) *The Line of Battle: The Sailing Warship, 1650-1840*, London: Conway Maritime Press, 1992

_____, (ed), *The Naval War of 1812*, London: Chatham Publishing, 1998

Gilmer, Thomas C, *Old Ironsides: The Rise, Decline and Resurrection of the USS* Constitution, Camden ME: International Marine, 1993

Glete, Jan, *Navies and Nations: Warships, Navies and State Building in Europe and America 1500-1860*, 2 Volumes, Stockholm, 1995.

Goldsborough, Charles W, *An Original and Correct List of the United States Navy*, City of Washington: (no publisher), Nov 1800

Grant, Bruce, *Isaac Hull: Captain of Old Ironsides*, Chicago: Pellegrini and Cudahy, 1947

King, Irving H, *George Washington's Coast Guard*, Annapolis: Naval Institute Press, 1978

Lambert, Andrew, *The Last Sailing Battlefleet: Maintaining Naval Mastery 1815-1850*, London: Conway Maritime Press, 1991

Langer, William L, (ed), *An Encyclopedia of World History*, Boston: Houghton Mifflin Co, 1972

Lavery, Brian, *The Ship of the Line*, 2 Volumes, London: Conway Maritime Press, 1983-4

Leiner, Frederick C, 'The Subscription Warships of 1798', *American Neptune*, XLVI, No 3, Summer 1986, pp141-158

Leiner, Frederick C, *Millions for Defense: The Subscription Warships of 1798*, Annapolis: Naval Institute Press, 2000

Lewis, Charles Lee, *David Glasgow Farragut: Admiral in the Making*, Annapolis: Naval Institute Press, 1941

'Line of Battle Ship *Ohio*', *Naval Magazine*, 2, 1837, pp590-596

Lossing, Benson J, *The Pictorial Field-Book of the War of 1812*, New York: Benchmark Publishing Corporation, 1970 (reprint)

_____, *The Pictorial Field Book of the American Revolution*, 2 Volumes, Spartanburg SC: The Reprint Co, 1969 (originally published 1860)

Magoun, F Alexander, *The Frigate* Constitution *and other Historic Ships*, New York: Bonanza Books, 1978

Malone, Dumas, *Jefferson the President: First Term 1801-1805*, Boston: Little, Brown and Company, 1970

Maloney, Linda McKee, 'A Naval Experiment', *American Neptune*, XXXIV, No 3, July 1974, pp188-196

Martin, Tyron G, *A Most Fortunate Ship: A Narrative History of Old Ironsides*, Chester, CT: The Globe Pequot Press, 1980

McKee, Christopher, *Edward Preble: A Naval Biography, 1761-1807*, Annapolis: Naval Institute Press, 1972

Millar, John Fitzhugh, *Early American Ships*, Williamsburg, VA: Thirteen Colonies Press, 1986

Miller, Nathan, *Sea of Glory*, New York: David McKay, 1974

Morison, Samuel Eliot, *'Old Bruin' Commodore Matthew Calbraith Perry*, Boston: Little, Brown and Company, 1967

Palmer, Michael A, *Stoddert's War: Naval Operations During the Quasi-War with France, 1798-1801*, Columbia, SC: University of South Carolina Press, 1987

Patterson, Howard, *Patterson's Illustrated Nautical Dictionary*, New York: self-published, 1891

Paullin, Charles Oscar, *Paullin's History of Naval Administration, 1775-1911*, Annapolis: Naval Institute Press, 1968

_____, *Commodore John Rodgers: Captain, Commodore, and Senior Officer of the American Navy, 1773-1838*, Cleveland: The Arthur H Clark Company, 1910

Preble, George Henry, *History of the United States Navy-Yard at Portsmouth, NH*, Washington DC: Government Printing Office, 1892

Roosevelt, Theodore, *The Naval War of 1812*, New York: The Modern Library, 1999 (reprint)

Roscoe, Theodore, and Fred Freeman, *Picture History of the US Navy*, New York: Bonanza Books, 1956

'Ships *Neptune* and *Pennsylvania*', *The Military and Naval Magazine*, 1, No 1, March 1833, p58

Smith, Philip Chadwick Foster, *The Frigate Essex Papers: Building the Salem Frigate, 1798-99*, Salem: The Peabody Museum, 1974

Stewart, W Roderick, 'Seppings Survivor', *Warship*, VI, 1982 pp81-87

Takakjian, Portia, *The 32-gun Frigate Essex*, London: Conway Maritime Press, 1990

'Thoughts on the Navy', by 'AS', *Naval Magazine*, 2, Jan 1837, pp32-37

Truxtun, Thomas, *Remarks, Instruction, & Examples Related to the Latitude and Longitude*, Philadelphia: T Dobson, 1794

Tucker, Spencer, *Arming the Fleet: US Navy Ordnance in the Muzzle-loading Era*, Annapolis: Naval Institute Press, 1989

_____, *The Jeffersonian Gunboat Navy*, University of South Carolina Press, 1993

'US Brig of War *Truxtun*', *US Nautical Magazine and Naval Journal*, 4, No 6, Sept 1856, pp437-439 and plans

'US Ships *Jamestown* and *Portsmouth*', *Nautical Magazine*, 1, 1845, pp184-188

Viola, Herman J, and Margolis, Carolyn, (eds), *Magnificent Voyagers: The US Exploring Expedition, 1838-1842*, Washington, DC: Smithsonian Institution Press, 1985

von Pivka, Otto, *Navies of the Napoleonic Era*, New York: Hippocrene Books, 1980

Wegner, Dana M, *Fouled Anchors: The* Constellation *Question Answered*, Bethesda, MD: US Navy David Taylor Research Center, 1991

Westlake, Merle, 'The American Sailing Navy, Josiah Fox, Joshua Humphreys, and Thomas Tingey', *American Neptune*, 59, No 1, 1999, pp21-41

Index